SOCIAL DECISION MAKING

Social Dilemmas, Social Values,
and Ethical Judgments

T0330864

Organization and Management Series

Series Editors

Arthur P. Brief
University of Utah

James P. Walsh
University of Michigan

Lampel/Shamsie/Lant (Eds.): *The Business of Culture: Strategic Perspectives on Entertainment and Media*

Lant/Shapira (Eds.): *Organizational Cognition: Computation and Interpretation*

Lord/Brown (Aus.): *Leadership Processes and Follower Self-Identity*

Margolis/Walsh (Aus.): *People and Profits? The Search Between a Company's Social and Financial Performance*

Messick/Kramer (Eds.): *The Psychology of Leadership: Some New Approaches*

Miceli/Dworkin/Near (Aus.): *Whistle-Blowing in Organizations*

Pearce (Au.): *Organization and Management in the Embrace of the Government*

Peterson/Mannix (Eds.): *Leading and Managing People in the Dynamic Organization*

Rafaeli/Pratt (Eds.): *Artifacts and Organizations: Beyond Mere Symbolism*

Riggio/Murphy/Pirozzolo (Eds.): *Multiple Intelligences and Leadership*

Roberts/Dutton (Eds.): *Exploring Positive Identities and Organizations: Building a Theoretical and Research Foundation*

Schneider/Smith (Eds.): *Personality and Organizations*

Smith (Ed.): *The People Make the Place: Dynamic Linkages Between Individuals and Organizations*

Thompson/Choi (Eds.): *Creativity and Innovation in Organizational Teams*

Thompson/Levine/Messick (Eds.): *Shared Cognition in Organizations: The Management of Knowledge*

SOCIAL DECISION MAKING

Social Dilemmas, Social Values, and Ethical Judgments

Edited by

Roderick M. Kramer, Ann E. Tenbrunsel, and Max H. Bazerman

Routledge
Taylor & Francis Group
New York   London

Psychology Press
Taylor & Francis Group
711 Third Avenue
New York
NY 10017

Psychology Press
Taylor & Francis Group
2 Park Square, Milton Park,
Abingdon, Oxfordshire
OX14 4RN

10 9 8 7 6 5 4 3 2 1

International Standard Book Number: 978-1-84169-899-1 (Hardback)
International Standard Book Number: 978-0-41565-422-7 (Paperback)
Routledge is an imprint of the Taylor & Francis Group, an informa business
First issued in paperback 2013

Library of Congress Cataloging-in-Publication Data

Kramer, Roderick Moreland, 1950-
    Social decision making : social dilemmas, social values, and ethical judgments / Roderick M. Kramer, Ann E. Tenbrunsel, Max H. Bazerman.
      p. cm.
    ISBN 978-1-84169-899-1 (hardback)
    1. Decision making--Social aspects. 2. Judgment. 3. Social skills. 4. Social values. 5. Problem solving. I. Tenbrunsel, Ann E. II. Bazerman, Max H. III. Title.

BF448.K73 2009
302.3--dc22   2008050792

Visit the Taylor & Francis Web site at
http://www.taylorandfrancis.com

and the Psychology Press Web site at
http://www.psypress.com

Contents

SECTION II   Social Values, Social
Control, and Cooperation

SECTION III Ethical Judgments, Fairness, and Equality

Francesca Gino, Don A. Moore, and Max H. Bazerman

SECTION IV   Commentary and Reflections

Series Foreword

Simply put, this is an important book. Not only does it honor a distinguished social scientist, Dave Messick, its contributors offer an array of innovative or fresh perspectives on an array of topics located on the moral side of the study of organizational behavior. Examples of these include external validity and ecological relevance in trust dilemma research, detection of social value orientation at zero acquaintance, why we fail to notice unethical behavior, and fairness and preference for underdogs. We are exceedingly pleased that Rod Kramer, Ann Tenbrunsel, and Max Bazerman chose our series for their provocative collection.

Arthur P. Brief
James P. Walsh

Acknowledgments

This is a book about social decisions and the role that cooperation plays in social life. Fittingly, the process of putting this volume together has been wonderfully social and cooperative from the outset. There are many individuals whom we would like to thank. We wish to thank Arthur Brief and Jim Walsh for their enthusiastic endorsement of this project. We also thank Anne Duffy for her skillful editorial acumen and consistent support of this project. This book benefited enormously from her guidance at every step of the way, from conference to completed manuscript. Christopher Myron was a tremendous resource and we are grateful for his meticulous attention to the finer details of pulling this volume together. Our production editor, Robert Sims, guided the final pages with precision and graciousness. We thank Catherine Haga of the Stanford Business School for her tremendous work on the manuscript. Dave Messick would like to express special thanks to Morris Kaplan for his enduring support of Dave's scholarly research and for his friendship.

Editors

Roderick M. Kramer is the William R. Kimball Professor of Organizational Behavior at the Stanford Business School. Kramer is the author or coauthor of more than 100 scholarly articles. His work has appeared in leading academic journals, such as *Journal of Personality and Social Psychology, Administrative Science Quarterly,* and the *Academy of Management Journal,* as well as popular magazines such as the *Harvard Business Review.* He is the author or coauthor of numerous books, including *Negotiation in Social Contexts, The Psychology of the Social Self, Trust in Organizations: Frontiers of Theory and Research, Power and Influence in Organizations, Psychology of Leadership, Trust and Distrust Within Organizations,* and *Trust and Distrust: Progress and Promise in Theory and Research.*

Ann E. Tenbrunsel (Ph.D., Northwestern University; M.B.A. Northwestern University; B.S.I.O.E. University of Michigan) is a professor in the College of Business Administration at the University of Notre Dame and the Arthur F. and Mary J. O'Neil Codirector of the Institute for Ethical Business Worldwide. Her research interests focus on decision-making and negotiations, with a specific emphasis on ethics. Ann has published in these areas in refereed journals such as *Administrative Science Quarterly, Academy of Management Review, Academy of Management Journal, Journal of Personality and Social Psychology,* and *Organization Behavior and Human Decision Processes.* She is also the author or coauthor of several books on these topics including *Codes of Conduct: Behavioral Research Into Business Ethics, Environment, Ethics, and Behavior* and *Research on Managing Groups and Teams: Ethics.* Prior to entering academics, Ann worked as a sales force and marketing consultant for ZS Associates and as a sales support analyst and engineer for S. C. Johnson and Son.

Max H. Bazerman is the Jesse Isidor Straus Professor at the Harvard Business School and is affiliated formally with the Harvard Kennedy School, the Psychology Department, and the Program on Negotiation at

Harvard. He is the coauthor of *Negotiation Genius* (2007, with Deepak Malhotra) and *Judgment in Managerial Decision Making* (7th edition, 2008, with Don A. Moore). From 2002 to 2008, he was consistently named one of the top 40 authors, speakers, and teachers of management by Executive Excellence. In 2003, he received the Everett Mendelsohn Excellence in Mentoring Award from Harvard University's Graduate School of Arts and Sciences. In 2006, he received an honorary doctorate from the University of London (London Business School), the Kulp-Wright Book Award from the American Risk and Insurance Association for *Predictable Surprises* (with Michael Watkins), and the Life Achievement Award from the Aspen Institute's Business and Society Program. In 2008, he was the Distinguished Educator Award from the Academy of Management.

Contributors

Scott T. Allison
Department of Psychology
University of Richmond
Richmond, VA

Terry L. Boles
Tippie College of Business
University of Iowa
Iowa City, IA

Arthur P. Brief
David Eccles School of Business
University of Utah
Salt Lake City, UT

Jenni L. Burnette
Department of Psychology
University of Richmond
Richmond, VA

Robyn M. Dawes
Department of Social & Decision
  Sciences
Carnegie Mellon University
Pittsburgh, PA

Sreedhari D. Desai
David Eccles School of Business
University of Utah
Salt Lake City, UT

Jennifer M. George
Jones Graduate School of
  Management
Rice University
Houston, TX

Kevin W. Gibson
Department of Philosophy
  and School of Business
  Administration
Marquette University
Milwaukee, IL

Francesca Gino
Kenan-Flaguer Business School
University of North Carolina
Chapel Hill, NC

Janusz L. Grzelak
Department of Psychology
University of Warsaw
Poland

D. Michael Kuhlman
Department of Psychology
University of Delaware
Newark, DE

Erik W. de Kwaadsteniet
Department of Social and
  Organizational Psychology
Leiden University
The Netherlands

Jeff A. Joireman
Department of Marketing
Washington State University
Pullman, WA

Huy Le
Department of Psychology
University of Central Florida
Orlando, FL

David M. Messick
Santa Barbara, CA

Don A. Moore
Tepper School of Business
Carnegie Mellon University
Pittsburgh, PA

J. Keith Murnighan
Kellogg School of Management
Northwestern University
Evanston, IL

Gregory Northcraft
Department of Business
    Administration
University of Illinois at
    Urbana–Champaign
Champaign, IL

Hannah-Hanh D. Nguyen
Department of Psychology
California State University, Long
    Beach
Long Beach, CA

Madeleine Page
Department of Psychology
University of Delaware
Newark, DE

Peter Rives
Center Point Human Services
Winston-Salem, NC

Charles D. Samuelson
Department of Psychology
Texas A&M University
College Station, TX

Gregory P. Shelley
Department of Psychology
Kutztown University
Kutztown, PA

Eric Van Dijk
Department of Social and
    Organizational Psychology
Leiden University
The Netherlands

Paul A. M. Van Lange
Department of Social Psychology
VU University, Amsterdam
The Netherlands

Kristen M. Watrous-Rodriguez
St. Mary's University
San Antonio, TX

Henk A. M. Wilke
Department of Social and
    Organizational Psychology
Leiden University
The Netherlands

Arjaan P. Wit
Department of Social and
    Organizational Psychology
Leiden University
The Netherlands

Erin Yeagley
Department of Psychology
University of Delaware
Newark, DE

1

Social Dilemmas, Social Values, and Ethical Judgments: Touchpoints and Touchdowns in a Distinguished Scholarly Career

Roderick M. Kramer
Stanford Business School

Ann E. Tenbrunsel
University of Notre Dame

Max H. Bazerman
Harvard University

This *festschrift* honors David M. Messick's distinguished career as a social scientist. More precisely, we honor Dave's *two* scholarly careers — the first as a preeminent experimental social psychologist and the second as a distinguished organizational behavior theorist. Given Dave's dual personality (professionally speaking), we faced something of a daunting challenge in putting together this volume. Dave's theoretical papers and empirical research have engaged so many important questions, cross so many disciplinary boundaries, and reflect such wide-ranging collaborations that a neat, tidy, or comprehensive compendium was difficult to compose.

In our role as editors, we were acutely aware that sins of omission would be inevitable when trying to do justice to Dave's notable and varied scholarly career. We are biased by our associations with Dave. Rod has known Dave the longest, meeting him in 1980 when Rod joined the doctoral program at UC–Santa Barbara. Dave introduced Rod to the study of social dilemmas, resulting in a fruitful and enduring collaboration and friendship. Max got to know Dave in the 1990s as he joined the faculty at

Northwestern and shifted his research agenda toward the psychology of ethics. Ann's research interest in ethics began when Dave joined the faculty in her first year of her doctoral program and the first study of her dissertation was drafted in Dave's experimental methods class. All of us have written multiple papers with Dave, see ourselves as students of Dave's, are friends with him, and have consumed too many bottles of wine with him (he has a habit of ordering one more bottle than others might in similar situations). And all of us have experienced moving in a new research direction, only to find that Dave was covering similar turf a decade or more earlier.

Ultimately, in organizing this volume, we settled on trying to touch primarily on three streams of research in social psychology and organizational theory to which Dave made major and enduring contributions, and that engaged the bulk of his time and attention: social dilemmas, social values, and ethics. We also endeavored, however, to capture the broad social impact of that research on multiple generations of social scientists. In that spirit, we have assembled original contributions from many of Dave's former students and collaborators. The contributors come from many parts of the world, which is not surprising given the expansive reach of Dave's research.

By way of preface, we should note that Dave began his academic career as an experimental psychologist, earning his B.A. in psychology from the University of Delaware in 1961. He then went on to earn his Ph.D. in social psychology from the University of North Carolina 4 years later. Dave has always had a strong love of — and facility with — mathematics and its application to psychological problems. Not surprisingly, therefore, many of his earliest academic contributions, such as those that examined multiple-choice decision behavior, reflect his strong mathematical bent and insights (e.g., Messick & Rapoport, 1965).

After earning his doctorate, Dave accepted a position as an assistant professor of social psychology at the University of California at Santa Barbara. He, Judy, and his sons made the long trek across the country in an overloaded Nash Rambler. He was one of the first social psychologists to recognize the importance of game theory to social psychology and to explore game theoretic behavior within experimental settings (e.g., Messick & McClintock, 1968; Messick & Rapoport, 1965). Further, and no less importantly, Dave helped pioneer the use of computer-controlled experimentation so that he and his collaborators could rigorously and systematically study the psychological determinants and consequences of judgment and decision-making within laboratory settings (e.g., Messick & Rapoport, 1964; Messick & McClintock, 1967).

One early and influential stream of research, begun in the 1970s, examined judgment and choice behavior in mixed-motive games such as the two-person and *n*-person Prisoner's Dilemma. A particularly fruitful line of inquiry — much of it done with his Santa Barbara colleague Charles ("Chuck") McClintock — explored the nature of social values and how they affect judgment and choice (e.g., Messick & McClintock, 1968). Social values reflect individuals' preferences for various self-outcome distribution patterns. As Dave and Chuck demonstrated, individuals differ in the extent to which they prefer, for instance, outcomes that maximize their own individual gain, their joint gain, or their relative gain over other social actors with whom they are interdependent. In a series of influential papers, Dave not only elaborated the theoretical underpinnings of such preferences (McCrimmon & Messick, 1976; Messick & McClintock, 1968), he developed a rigorous method for measuring them and tracing their consequences (Kramer, McClintock, & Messick, 1986; McClintock, Messick, Campos, & Kuhlman, 1973).

It was also in the 1970s that Dave's interest in group decision-making began to take shape. His initial papers on individual judgment and collective behavior were anchored around the basic question of whether one should or should not join a union (Messick, 1973), a deceptively simple-seeming decision that is prototypic of many more complex, real-world mixed-motive conflicts. In such situations, individuals have incentives to cooperate in order to create public goods from which all, including self, benefit. However, they also realize they can free ride on the productive efforts of others, thereby avoiding the costs of contribution. Hence, the dilemma. Dave's interest in the social psychology of fairness also developed rapidly during this period, leading to a body of highly regarded work on equity and fairness (e.g., Messick & Cook, 1983; Messick & Sentis, 1979, 1983).

The 1980s ushered in yet another productive research period, as Dave turned to a problem that was just beginning to capture scholarly attention — viz., the problem of cooperation and competition among groups of individuals sharing scarce resource pools. At the time, interest in this topic was anything but academic. Resource scarcities were front-page news at the time — including even a serious local water shortage in the Santa Barbara area, followed also by national fuel shortages and other environmental scarcities. Dave approached this important problem with his characteristic creative energy and intelligence. He and his collaborators at Santa Barbara developed a new laboratory paradigm for systematically studying resource consumption behavior in such situations (Parker et al., 1983). They demonstrated the usefulness of the paradigm in a series of empirical studies investigating psychological and structural determinants of choice behavior (e.g., Messick et al., 1983; Samuelson, Messick, Rutte, & Wilke, 1984). Their computer-based model of a replenishing resource pool became a widely used experimental analogue for studying social dilemma behavior throughout the 1980s and is still in use today by social psychologists and behavioral economists studying social dilemmas.

During this same period, in a fruitful collaboration with his Santa Barbara colleague Marilynn Brewer, Dave produced a conceptual overview of social dilemmas theory and research that became one of the most cited pieces in this rapidly growing literature (Messick & Brewer, 1983). Their paper helped orient not only their own students but a long line of empirical investigators around the world as to how to productively think about and study social dilemma behavior. This was followed by subsequent reviews that updated researchers on "state-of-the-art" theory and research in this area (e.g., Liebrand, Messick, & Wilke, 1992; Messick, 1991).

Dave's own work in this area, conducted with a number of his students, contributed the useful notion that decisions in mixed-motive situations often reflect the operation of various social decision heuristics — judgmental rules of thumb (Allison & Messick, 1990). These heuristics could help decision-makers navigate even the thorniest of dilemmas. Dave's work on the use of the equality heuristic constitutes just one example of such a heuristic (Messick & Schell, 1992). As Dave wisely notes, 50/50 is typically not fair but is a useful and expedient social heuristic to avoid discussing what is fair (think of the last time you split a bill in a restaurant when the other couple consumed more than twice as much wine and food as you did).

As perusal of his vita reveals, Dave's contributions to these major streams of contemporary social psychological theory are truly impressive. Equally revealing and impressive, however, are his numerous contributions to small but rich research tributaries. These contributions reflect Dave's broad curiosity about the world, as well as his willingness to be pulled in interesting directions by his students and collaborators. In this vein, his papers have examined, for instance, heuristics for determining the optimal interval between medical checkups (Klatzky, Messick, & Loftus, 1992); the role of the "Will Rogers illusion" in social judgments (Messick & Asuncion, 1993); the social facilitation of running (Worringham & Messick, 1983); the reverse outcome bias (Boles & Messick, 1995); the uniqueness bias (Goethals, Messick, & Allison, 1991); ethical fading (Tenbrunsel & Messick, 2004); and the Muhammad Ali Effect (Allison, Messick & Goethals, 1989) — to name just a few. Long before it was fashionable, Dave manifested an enthusiasm for cross-cultural research (e.g., Messick, 1988).

Such a steady accumulation of contributions to his chosen discipline of social psychology would seem to be more than enough for one career. And Dave could have been forgiven had he decided to simply kick up his heels and sit back on the veranda of his villa in the hills overlooking Santa Barbara. Yet, in 1992, he did just the opposite and took on the challenge of a second career. It came by way of the opportunity to join the organizational behavior faculty at Northwestern University's Kellogg Graduate School of Management. Dave accepted and equally happily accepted the prestigious Morris and Alice Kaplan Professorship of Ethics and Decision in Management. Max played a role in hiring Dave (proving wrong the social psychologists around the country who asserted that "Messick will never leave Santa Barbara") and sees this hire as one of the few most important things he did in his 15 years at Northwestern.

For Kellogg, some saw hiring Dave as a stretch for distinguished professorship in ethics, but Dave made the transition from lab-coated experimenter to real-world organizational ethics scholar with his amazing grace, flair, enthusiasm, and success. He proved an adept and original thinker when it came to the application of social psychological research to problems of fairness and ethics in organizational settings (Darley, Messick, & Tyler, 2001; Messick & Tenbrunsel, 1996; Tenbrunsel & Messick, 1996), and in his discussion of the logic of appropriateness framework (Messick, 1999), he set the stage for the importance of understanding the construal of an ethical dilemma and its contribution to ethical fading (Tenbrunsel & Messick, 1999). He also ventured into new areas, such as leadership (Messick & Bazerman, 1996; Messick & Kramer, 2004; Wilke, Rutte, Wit, Messick, & Samuelson, 1986) and the emerging area of environmental organizational psychology (e.g., Bazerman, Messick, Tenbrunsel, & Wade-Benzoni, 1997).

It is characteristic of Dave that he not only became a major researcher but an effective thought leader. In consensus with all those who know him or his work, we see Dave as the key intellectual figure in bringing psychology to the topic of ethics and permanently transforming how professional schools think about ethics. Dave made it clear that the decisions of organizational actors are at the core of organizational ethics and encouraged all of us to think about the malleability of the mind as a key component for improving ethics in organizations. He also created models and mechanisms that have profoundly influenced thousands of his own MBA students and executives and tens of thousands of the students of other scholars through his mentoring and writing. As business schools realized the need to transform their educational processes in the field of ethics, Dave has become the most influential intellectual on the topic. He also mentored a series of excellent doctoral students, including Terry Boles, Don Moore, Ann Tenbrunsel, Kim Wade-Benzoni, and Mark Weber, who are continuing to develop Dave's perspective on ethics.

As one might infer from the number of successful collaborations he has had, Dave has always been a true social psychologist — and we emphasize the word *social* here. He not only crosses intellectual borders easily, he travels easily across geographic and cultural ones as well. One of the most enduring and significant impacts has been his sustained collaboration with his University of Groningen colleagues. Some of the early — and best — studies on social dilemmas and fairness came out of that fruitful collaboration (e.g., Messick, Wilke, & Liebrand, 1992). And, he builds institutions along the way. The Kellogg School now has an endowed Ethics Center (The Ford Center), in large part due to Dave's efforts. Though one could say that this book is a tribute to the end of a career, it is evident from the chapters in this book that his contribution is only just beginning.

OVERVIEW OF THE PRESENT VOLUME

As noted earlier, it is probably impossible (and certainly not easy) to give a full and faithful reflection of Dave's exceptionally productive and creative scholarly career in a conventionally sized edited volume. Nonetheless, we have tried to bring together in this one book leading social psychologists and organizational theorists whose work provides a representative sample — if not always adequately capturing the full flower and flavor — of Dave's multifaceted intellectual legacy. The contributors to this volume have in common the fact that they have all worked closely with and have been strongly influenced by Dave. The theoretical diversity and conceptual depth of the contributions in this volume, of course, are no accident. They are simply and appropriately reflective of the diverse and profound impact Messick has had on several generations of social scientists.

The present volume is organized into four sections. The first three sections are organized around the central themes and foci of Dave's own theorizing and empirical work. Section I addresses the topic of social dilemmas. Section II of the volume explores issues of social values, social control, and cooperation. In Section III, we turn attention to questions about ethics and fairness in judgment and choice. Appropriately, we think, the volume concludes with a fourth section containing two more personal and reflective essays on Dave's career. The first is by Robyn M. Dawes, Dave's long-time friend and collaborator. Few scientists have observed Dave so closely and for so long — or have engaged in so closely similar research interests and approaches. Robyn's comments are appropriately provocative and playful. The second and concluding essay of this volume goes straight to the horse's mouth (well, that may not be the best metaphor, but it's the best we could think of — we are, after all, social scientists and not poets). Dave offers us his own view of the intellectual paths he has chosen and the meaning of the cumulative journey to which they led. His students and collaborators will treasure it, and we hope that readers of this book will find it inspiring.

REFERENCES

Allison, S. T., & Messick, D. M. (1990). Social decision heuristics in the use of shared resources. *Journal of Behavioral Decision Making, 3*, 195–204.

Allison, S. T., Messick, D. M., & Goethals, G. R. (1989). On being better but not smarter than others: The Muhammad Ali effect. *Social Cognition, 7*, 275–295.

Bazerman, M. H., Messick, D. M., Tenbrunsel, A. E., & Wade-Benzoni, K. A. (Eds.). (1997). *Environment, ethics, and behavior: The psychology of environmental valuation and degradation.* San Francisco: The New Lexington Press.

Boles, T. L., & Messick, D. M. (1995). A reverse outcome bias: The influence of multiple reference points on the evaluation of outcomes and decisions. *Organizational Behavior and Human Decision Processes, 61*, 262–275.

Darley, J. M., Messick, D. M., & Tyler, T. R. (Eds.). (2001). *Social influences on ethical behavior in organizations.* Mahwah, NJ: Lawrence Erlbaum.

Dawes, R. M., & Messick, D. M. (2000). Social dilemmas. *International Journal of Psychology, 35*(2), 111–116.

Goethals, G. R., Messick, D. M., & Allison, S. T. (1991). The uniqueness bias: Studies of constructive social comparison. In J. Suls & T. A. Wills (Eds.), *Social comparison: Contemporary theory and research* (pp. 149–176). New York: Erlbaum.

Klatzky, R. L., Messick, D. M., & Loftus, J. (1992). Heuristics for determining the optimal interval between checkups. *Psychological Science, 3,* 279–284.

Kramer, R. M., McClintock, C. G., & Messick, D. M. (1986). Social values and cooperative response to a simulated resource conservation crisis. *Journal of Personality, 54,* 596–577.

Liebrand, W. B. G., Messick, D. M., & Wilke, H. A. M. (1992). Social dilemmas: The state of the art. In W. B. G. Liebrand, D. M. Messick, & H. A. M. Wilke (Eds.), *Social dilemmas: Theoretical issues and research findings* (pp. 3–40). London: Pergamon.

McCrimmon, K. R., & Messick, D. M. (1976). A framework for social motives. *Behavioral Science, 21,* 86–100.

Messick, D. M. (1968). Choice behavior as a function of expected payoff. *Journal of Experimental Psychology, 76,* 544–549.

Messick, D. M. (1973). To join or not to join: An approach to the unionization decision. *Organizational Behavior and Human Performance, 10,* 145–156.

Messick, D. M. (1988). Coda. In M. Bond (Ed.), *The cross-cultural challenge to social psychology* (pp. 286–289). Newbury Park, CA: Sage.

Messick, D. M. (1999). Alternative logics for decision making in social settings. *Journal of Economic Behavior and Organization, 39,* 11–28.

Messick, D. M., & Asuncion, A. (1993). The Will Rogers illusion in judgments about social groups. *Psychological Science, 4,* 46–48.

Messick, D. M., & Bazerman, M. (1996). Ethical leadership and the psychology of decision making. *Sloan Management Review, 37,* 9–22.

Messick, D. M., & Brewer, M. B. (1983). Solving social dilemmas: A review. In L. Wheeler & P. Shaver (Eds.), *Review of personality and social psychology* (Vol. 4, pp. 11–44). Beverly Hills: Sage.

Messick, D. M., & Cook, K. S. (Eds.). (1983). *Equity theory: Psychological and sociological perspectives.* New York: Praeger.

Messick, D. M., & Kramer, R. (Eds.). (2004). *The psychology of leadership: New perspectives and research.* Mahwah, NJ: Lawrence Erlbaum.

Messick, D. M., & McClintock, C. G. (1968). Motivational bases of choice in experimental games. *Journal of Experimental Social Psychology, 4,* 1–25.

Messick, D. M., & Rapoport, A. (1964). Computer controlled experiments in psychology. *Behavioral Science, 9,* 378–382.

Messick, D. M., & Rapoport, A. (1965). A comparison of two payoff functions on multiple-choice decision behavior. *Journal of Experimental Psychology, 69,* 75–83.

Messick, D. M., & Rutte, C. G. (1992). The provision of public goods by experts: The Groningen study. In W. B. G. Liebrand, D. M. Messick, & H. A. M. Wilke (Eds.), *Social dilemmas: Theoretical issues and research findings* (pp. 101–109). London: Pergamon.

Messick, D. M., & Sentis, K. P. (1979). Fairness and preference. *Journal of Experimental Social Psychology, 15,* 418–434.

Messick, D. M., & Sentis, K. P. (1983). Fairness, preference, and fairness biases. In D. M. Messick & K. S. Cook (Eds.), *Equity theory: Psychological and sociological perspectives* (pp. 61–94). New York: Praeger.

Messick, D. M., & Tenbrunsel, A. E. (1996). Behavioral research into business ethics. In D. M. Messick & A. E. Tenbrunsel (Eds.), *Codes of conduct* (pp. 1–10). New York: Russell Sage.

Messick, D. M., Wilke, H. A. M., Brewer, M. B., Kramer, R., Zemke, P. E., & Lui, L. (1983). Individual adaptations and structural changes as solutions to social dilemmas. *Journal of Personality and Social Psychology, 44,* 294–309.

Parker, R., Lui, L., Messick, C., Messick, D. M., Brewer, M., Kramer, R., et al. (1983). A computer laboratory for studying social dilemmas. *Behavioral Science, 28,* 298–304.

Samuelson, C., Messick, D. M., Rutte, C., & Wilke, H. A. M. (1984). Individual and structural solutions to resource dilemmas in two cultures. *Journal of Personality and Social Psychology, 47,* 94–104.

Tenbrunsel, A. E., & Messick, D. M. (1996). Behavioral research, business ethics, and social justice. *Social Justice Research, 9*(1), 1–6.

Tenbrunsel, A. E., & Messick, D. M. (1999). Sanctioning systems, decision frames, and cooperation. *Administrative Science Quarterly, 44,* 684–707.

Tenbrunsel, A. E., & Messick, D. M. (2001). Power asymmetries and the ethical atmosphere in negotiations. In J. M. Darley, D. M. Messick, & T. R. Tyler (Eds.), *Social influences on ethical behavior in organizations.* (201-216) Mahwah, NJ: Lawrence Erlbaum.

Tenbrunsel, A. E., & Messick, D. M. (2004). Ethical fading: The role of self-deception in unethical behaviour. *Social Justice Research, 17,* 223–236.

Wilke, H. A. M., Rutte, C. G., Wit, A. P., Messick, D. M., & Samuelson, C. D. (1986). Leadership in social dilemmas: Efficiency and equity. In H. A. M. Wilke, D. M. Messick, & C. G. Rutte (Eds.), *Experimental social dilemmas* (pp. 55–76). Frankfurt: Peter Lang.

Worringham, C., & Messick, D. M. (1983). Social facilitation of running: An unobtrusive study. *Journal of Social Psychology, 121,* 23–29.

Section I

Social Dilemmas

2

Group Discussion and Cooperation in Social Dilemmas: Does the Medium Matter?

Charles D. Samuelson
Texas A&M University

Kristen M. Watrous-Rodriguez
St. Mary's University

Considerable research has focused on understanding why group discussion promotes cooperation in social dilemmas (e.g., Chen & Komorita, 1994; Dawes, McTavish, & Shaklee, 1977; Kerr & Kaufman-Gilliland, 1994; Orbell, van de Kragt, & Dawes, 1988; Sally, 1995). Several causal explanations (i.e., group identity, commitment-making, norms) have been proposed and tested experimentally. This chapter reviews the literature on group discussion and cooperation to further explore *why* and *how* face-to-face discussion exerts this robust effect. We also extend the current conversation by considering whether various forms of electronic technology (e.g., e-mail, Internet conferencing) allow small groups to capture the proven benefits of discussion without the limiting requirement of collocation. We report preliminary findings from three experimental studies in our lab that investigate some unanswered questions. Our literature review and conceptual analysis suggest some important theoretical implications for understanding discussion's effect in social dilemmas and a promising agenda for future research.

It is beyond empirical doubt that face-to-face (FTF) group discussion increases cooperation in social dilemmas relative to no-communication conditions (e.g., Bornstein, 1992; Bornstein, Rapoport, Kerpel, & Katz, 1989; Bouas & Komorita, 1996; Braver, 1995; Dawes et al., 1977; Isaac & Walker, 1988; Jerdee & Rosen, 1974; Jorgenson & Papciak, 1981; Kerr, Garst,

Lewandowski, & Harris, 1997; Kerr & Kaufman-Gilliland, 1994; Messick, Allison, & Samuelson, 1988; Orbell et al., 1988; Ostrom & Walker, 1991; Ostrom, Walker, & Gardner, 1992; van de Kragt, Orbell, & Dawes, 1983). A comprehensive meta-analysis by Sally (1995), reviewing 35 years of experimental social dilemma studies, concluded that communication was the strongest and most reliable predictor of cooperation. These findings are robust in both public goods and resource dilemma paradigms (Bicchieri, 2002; Dawes, 1980; Kerr & Park, 2001; Komorita & Parks, 1995; Kopelman, Weber, & Messick, 2002; Messick & Brewer, 1983; Ostrom, 1998).

This chapter will focus on the questions of why and how group discussion produces this beneficial effect. One goal is to provide a critical review of the literature that examines the proposed causal explanations for the communication effect. We also discuss more recent experimental work on computer-mediated communication (CMC) that may have important theoretical implications for understanding discussion's effect. The chapter is organized as follows. First, we begin with a review of the literature on group discussion in social dilemmas. Second, we discuss CMC research that has investigated group processes and performance on mixed-motive tasks. Third, we summarize the findings of several experimental studies in our lab that address gaps in the existing literature. Finally, we draw conclusions from our review and analysis of this body of research and suggest new research directions.

REVIEW OF EXISTING SOCIAL DILEMMA LITERATURE

Over the years, several alternative explanations have been advanced to explain discussion's effect (Bicchieri, 2002; Dawes, 1980; Kerr, 1995; Messick & Brewer, 1983; Orbell et al., 1988). One account is that communication invokes normative pressures toward cooperation because group discussion is likely to be biased toward the more socially desirable cooperative norm (Messick & Brewer, 1983). This would lead participants to believe that cooperation is expected and induce members to make prosocial choices. Thus, the process of group discussion may activate a generic norm of cooperation within the group; members are assumed to share this norm prior to discussion, and then discussion triggers it (Bicchieri, 2002; Kerr, 1995). However, Orbell et al. (1988) and Kerr and Kaufman-Gilliland

(1994) both presented empirical results that rejected this hypothesis of a generalized norm of benevolence toward group members.

A second explanation is that group discussion creates a spontaneous common bond among members, reflected in enhanced group identity (Dawes, Orbell, & van de Kragt, 1988; Dawes, van de Kragt, & Orbell, 1990; Orbell et al., 1988). The resulting in-group bias (Brewer, 1979; Tajfel & Turner, 1979) motivates group members to create positive social identity and solidarity through cooperative behavior. This enhanced sense of group identity may increase interpersonal attraction and "we" feelings among group members, which in turn should increase the likelihood of cooperative choices (Brewer, 1979; Messick & Brewer, 1983). Numerous studies have shown that minimal information and interaction are necessary to create ingroup identification through manipulations of "common fate" (Brewer & Kramer, 1986; Kramer & Brewer, 1984; Tajfel, 1970). The extensive research program of Dawes, Orbell, and van de Kragt has presented persuasive theoretical argument and empirical support in favor of this group identity hypothesis (Dawes et al., 1977, 1990; Orbell et al., 1988; Orbell, van de Kragt, & Dawes, 1991; van de Kragt et al., 1983).

However, other researchers have reported experimental results that question the central role of group identity in explaining discussion's effect (Bouas & Komorita, 1996; Henry, 2000; Kerr et al., 1997; Kerr & Kaufman-Gilliland, 1994). Consequently, a third causal explanation was proposed that group discussion offers an opportunity for group members to make commitments or promises to cooperate (Kerr & Kaufman-Gilliland, 1994; Orbell et al., 1988). Two psychological mechanisms could produce increased cooperation from public commitments during discussion. First, cognitive dissonance (Festinger, 1957) might motivate participants to uphold a previous public commitment (Cialdini, 2001; Janis & Mann, 1977; Kiesler, 1971). Second, as Orbell et al. (1988) explain:

> If the utility of marginal gains is decreasing (cf. Kahneman & Tversky, 1982), it will become progressively easier for people to keep their own commitments as they expect more and more others to keep their commitments. By this *linear expectations* model of promise making, therefore, discussion works because it provides the opportunity for subjects to make believable commitments to each other that they will cooperate. It does depend on the existence of a norm, but only one for keeping promises, not one that involves cooperation per se. (p. 812)

According to this commitment hypothesis, the number of cooperative choices should be a linear function of the number of group members making a credible promise to cooperate. Orbell et al. (1988) found that only consensual promising by all group members will guarantee a high level of cooperation.

Kerr and Kaufman-Gilliland (1994) reported strong support for the effects of promises on cooperation but found relatively weak evidence regarding the consensual promising version of the commitment hypothesis. They also conducted analyses of covariance (ANCOVAs) suggesting that though group identity did account for some variance in cooperation, it was not the primary cause of the communication effect. Kerr and Kaufman-Gilliland (1994) interpreted their results as compelling empirical support for commitment/promise-keeping as the dominant causal explanation. We note here that their theoretical analysis rested on the assumption that group members who experienced high levels of group identity would only choose to cooperate if they believed that their choice would make a difference (i.e., be efficacious) for improving the group's outcomes. Though based on a logical assumption, this inference excludes the alternative possibility that participants might have attached symbolic value to their cooperative choices as a means to maintain group solidarity (Bicchieri, 2002).

In a subsequent study, Bouas and Komorita (1996) hypothesized that less than universal promising might be sufficient to produce discussion's effect. Their experimental results showed that perceived consensus among group members was the most important condition for explaining the high level of cooperation following group discussion. Bouas and Komorita (1996) also evaluated the group identity hypothesis and concluded from their mediation analyses, like Kerr and Kaufman-Gilliland (1994), that this account was not a viable explanation for their empirical results. Additionally, Bouas and Komorita (1996) replicated Dawes et al.'s (1977) earlier finding that discussion about a topic irrelevant to the social dilemma problem (yet relevant to college students; i.e., tuition increases) does not increase cooperation above the no-communication baseline; this result provided yet another strong rejection of the simple "humanization" hypothesis (Bicchieri, 2002; Dawes, 1980).

If only perceived consensus (Bouas & Komorita, 1996) is required to sustain the discussion effect, then is communication among all members required? And if not, what kind of restricted communication will be effective? There is solid evidence that limited communication in the form of written "pledges" can increase cooperation. For example, Chen and Komorita (1994), using a public goods paradigm, manipulated the degree of "bindingness" of preplay individual pledges to cooperate and found that cooperation was maximized under conditions in which members' commitments to contribute were guaranteed at either the minimum or mean level of all members' pledges. Chen (1996) further showed that group-based pledges (i.e., mean-binding pledge) were more effective than individual-based pledges at eliciting cooperation. In fact, the levels of cooperation in this study's group-based pledge conditions were not different from the face-to-face discussion control condition. Chen (1996) concluded that group identity and perceptions of criticality were both plausible explanations for their results. Other experiments have investigated whether communication between subgroups (e.g., dyads) within the larger group can also boost cooperation; the general findings confirm the efficacy of partial FTF communication strategies (Braver & Wilson, 1986; Kinukawa, Saiijo, & Une, 2000). However, the specific content of messages sent to others is critical. Sending brief, preplay numerical messages about intended choices does not increase cooperation rates (Bochet, Page, & Putterman, 2006; Palfrey & Rosenthal, 1991; Wilson & Sell, 1997).

Another relevant question is whether commitments by group members during discussion are followed because members fear sanctions from others or themselves, if promises are broken. In short, is the commitment explanation driven by conformity to a social norm or a personal norm (Kerr, 1995)? In a follow-up study, Kerr et al. (1997) manipulated anonymity directly such that no participants, including the experimenter, knew what choices each participant made during the experiment. With complete anonymity, they still found that group members carried through on their public promises to cooperate at a high rate. Kerr et al. (1997) concluded that the commitment effect observed in the earlier study by Kerr and Kaufman-Gilliland (1994) was not caused by conformity to a social norm but rather by adherence to an internalized personal norm to keep one's promises.

Bicchieri (2002) has proposed that the Kerr et al. (1997) results may also be consistent with an alternative normative explanation. She suggests that certain experimental conditions may trigger behavioral scripts that embed specific norms prescribing appropriate behavior in particular situations (Hertel & Kerr, 2001). This argument contends that the critical psychological mechanism implicated by the commitment hypothesis is the activation of a contingent social norm for keeping one's promises, when one expects that others will and when one believes that others expect you to abide by the promise–keeping norm (Bicchieri, 2002, 2006). Her normative account is more similar to Orbell et al.'s (1988) linear expectations hypothesis, which predicts that commitments are more likely to be made (and kept) because one expects other group members to do likewise. We will return to Bicchieri's (2006) theory of social norms later in our conclusions.

Currently, the consensus among social dilemma researchers leans toward the commitment/promise-keeping hypothesis as the prevailing causal explanation (Kerr & Park, 2001; Kopelman et al. 2002). However, our reading of this literature suggests that definitive conclusions about the necessary and sufficient conditions for the discussion effect may be premature. We agree with Bicchieri (2002) that the available empirical evidence from a relatively small number of experimental studies is not sufficient to rule out group identity or a number of alternative, norm-based explanations. Moreover, it has been suggested previously that more than one causal mechanism may operate concurrently or in recursive relationships (Chen, 1996; Orbell et al., 1988). For example, perceived consensus (or unanimity) in commitment-making may activate a sense of group identity, which in turn results in more cooperative choices. Or, alternatively, group discussion about the dilemma may engender feelings of group identity, which then motivates members to make promises to cooperate.

Within the past 20 years, the rapid growth of Internet-based information technologies has increased research interest in how people interact and make decisions in CMC environments. Much of this work has been done by researchers outside mainstream social psychology in disciplines such as communication, information systems, organizational behavior, and experimental economics. We turn now to a review of this interdisciplinary literature with the focus on studies exploring the impacts of CMC in experimental tasks involving conflicts of interest among group members.

COMPUTER-MEDIATED COMMUNICATION IN MIXED-MOTIVE TASKS

One commonality among past laboratory studies of communication in social dilemmas is that they have employed FTF, non-mediated modes of communication. We believe that it is important to consider the role of CMC in social dilemmas. Mediated communication has been used in actual common resource allocation situations. For example, the Federal Communications Commission (FCC) now conducts auctions for spectrum allocations electronically. Online conflict mediation services (e.g., SquareTrade) are becoming commonplace when buyers and sellers on eBay experience disputes (Friedman et al., 2004; Katsch & Rifkin, 2001). Computer-supported modeling played a major role in successful multiparty negotiations over the Law of the Sea Treaty (Nyhart & Samarasan, 1989) and has been applied to other stakeholder conflicts over water resources management (Zigurs, Reitsma, Lewis, Hubscher, & Hayes, 1999). Online Internet-based technologies in the future could be used by multiple parties to improve current regional, state, or federal management of renewable natural resources. For example, fishing boats could be required to communicate with regulatory agencies via wireless Internet technology to report current catch data to coordinate collective use of fishery resources in real time (cf. Dietz, Ostrom, & Stern, 2003). Thus, the practical significance of research on CMC for application in real-life social dilemmas is clear.

Another reason for studying computer-mediated communication in social dilemmas is that it could refine our theoretical understanding of how the three causal explanations operate. The action of the three mechanisms depends on communication, and variation in relevant communication processes could mediate how these mechanisms work. For example, though group identity effects may be triggered simply by cognitive categorization processes (Kramer & Brewer, 1984), the nature and degree of communication within the group that enhances ingroup–outgroup differences is positively related to strength of ingroup identification (Brewer, 1979; Tajfel & Turner, 1979). Different modalities of communication — including face-to-face, audio, video, and text-mediated — have been shown to substantially alter the process and outcomes of communication (Poole, Shannon, & DeSanctis, 1992; Williams, 1977). This suggests a method for assessing whether group identity is a plausible explanation of cooperation in social dilemmas. If communication factors that create group identity can be manipulated experimentally, then systematic variations in group identity can be related to cooperation in social dilemmas (Bouas & Arrow, 1996). Thus, this approach has potential to provide researchers with information on the extent to which group identity affects cooperation and the processes by which group identity is created (or eroded) in social dilemma situations.

An extensive experimental literature exists on the effects of CMC on group decision-making processes and outcomes (Baltes, Dickson, Sherman, Bauer, & LaGanke, 2002; Bordia, 1997; Fjermestad & Hiltz, 1999; McGrath & Hollingshead, 1994; Scott, 1999). Baltes et al. (2002) have reported a comprehensive meta-analysis that concluded that use of CMC, compared to FTF, often results in inferior group performance (and lower member satisfaction). However, this empirical generalization depends on the type and complexity of the group task (DeSanctis & Gallupe, 1987; Straus & McGrath, 1994; Zigurs & Buckland, 1998). The exception to this general pattern occurs for creativity tasks (McGrath, 1984) involving idea generation (Dennis & Valacich, 1993; Gallupe, Bastianutti, & Cooper, 1991). Relative to creativity, intellective, and decision tasks, considerably less attention has focused on how group performance in mixed-motive conflict tasks (Komorita & Parks, 1995; McGrath, 1984) is affected by communication medium.

There is, however, an emerging body of research on the use of CMC in two-party negotiation tasks (Moore, Kurtzberg, Thompson, & Morris, 1999; Morris, Nadler, Kurtzberg, & Thompson, 2002; Naquin & Paulsen, 2003; Thompson & Nadler, 2002). These negotiation studies have used text-based CMC such as e-mail or instant messaging. Thompson and Nadler's (2002) review concludes that negotiation behavior and performance are influenced by communication medium, but results are mixed. For example, CMC negotiators make more multi-issue offers, achieve more equal distributive outcomes, and earn joint economic profits equal to (or higher than) FTF negotiators (Croson, 1999). However, FTF negotiators have lower impasse rates, settle within the positive bargaining zone, and experience greater rapport more often than e-mail negotiators (Thompson & Nadler, 2002). Further experimental research is needed to clarify this picture.

Within the past decade, there has also been growing interest in various forms of CMC in two-person Prisoner's Dilemma and multiperson public goods games (Adriansen & Hjelmquist, 1999; Bochet et al., 2006; Bos, Olson, Gergle, Olson, & Wright, 2002; Brosig, Ockenfels, & Weimann, 2003; Frohlich & Oppenheimer, 1998; Jensen, Farnham, Drucker, & Kollock, 2000; Kiesler, Sproull, & Waters, 1996; Wilson, Straus, & McEvily, 2006; Wilson & Sell, 1997; Zheng, Veinott, Bos, Olson, & Olson, 2002). Bicchieri and Lev-On (2007) reviewed this literature and concluded that there is some evidence that text-based CMC like e-mail

(Frohlich & Oppenheimer, 1998) can increase cooperation (relative to no-discussion baseline). However, the consistent finding is that FTF discussion yields higher levels of cooperation than text-based CMC. There is also some preliminary evidence that videoconferencing technology produces comparable levels of cooperation in social dilemmas to FTF communication (Bos et al., 2002; Brosig et al., 2003). Bicchieri and Lev-On (2007) note that causal mechanisms for these empirical results have yet to be investigated.

Research on information richness reveals how the structures provided by CMC technology might influence group communication processes. Information richness theory (Daft & Lengel, 1984, 1986) posits that CMC is a less rich communication medium than FTF communication. CMC lacks many of the nonverbal cues available to FTF communicators (Kiesler & Sproull, 1992). Hence, coordination is often more difficult in CMC than in FTF communication because a major portion of feedback is transmitted nonverbally (Burgoon & Hoobler, 2002). Moreover, because fewer types of cues are transmitted in CMC than FTF communication, less information is exchanged per unit time. For ambiguous group tasks like social dilemmas, media that carry more information may be advantageous. These characteristics of CMC would appear to make it less effective than FTF communication as a medium for facilitating cooperation in social dilemmas. This conclusion is supported by studies in which people report their media preferences. FTF communication is preferred by more participants than CMC or other communication modes such as telephone (Poole et al., 1992).

A more recent conceptual framework, Media Synchronicity Theory (MST; Dennis & Valacich, 1999), proposes that media should be matched not to specific group tasks but rather with two fundamental group communication processes: conveyance and convergence. According to Media Synchronicity Theory, media can be classified according to five primary characteristics: (a) immediacy of feedback, (b) symbol variety, (c) parallelism, (d) rehearsability, and (e) reprocessability. Dennis and Valacich (1999) hypothesized that conveyance processes (e.g., information exchange and deliberation) will require media with low synchronicity (low feedback immediacy and high parallelism) to achieve high group performance. In contrast, MST predicts that convergence processes (reaching group consensus on information meaning) will need media with high synchronicity (high feedback immediacy and low parallelism) for high group performance. Group discussion in a social dilemma situation would involve both conveyance and convergence processes. However, the group identity and commitment/promise-keeping explanations would implicate the importance of convergence processes in eliciting high levels of cooperation from group members following discussion. Thus, our general expectation that text-based CMC (low synchronicity) would be a less effective communication mode than FTF (high synchronicity) in a social dilemma context is consistent with MST.

Another negative effect stems from the relative slowness of text-based CMC compared to FTF modalities (Walther, 2002). This effect is related to limitations of the channel itself; also, participants may be less familiar with CMC and thus may experience both technical and interpretive difficulties. The technical difficulties stem from lack of familiarity with the particular features of the group communication support software. Interpretive difficulties occur because subjects have relatively less experience with CMC compared to FTF modalities. Hence, they might be expected to take longer to interpret CMC than FTF messages and be less certain of their interpretations (Cramton, 2002). The increased time necessary to form stable interpretations in CMC will slow down the communication process overall and, in most cases, the time to reach group decisions (Baltes et al., 2002). Several studies have found that impression and attitude formation are slower and less positive in initial interactions in CMC than in FTF communication (Walther, 1994, 1996). These studies also report that, over time, impressions and attitudes formed through CMC can become similar in valence to those formed through FTF communication, sometimes even exceeding them (Walther, 2002).

However, CMC also enjoys some potential advantages over FTF communication. First, lack of nonverbal cues may prevent the exchange of information that could escalate conflicts (Poole, Holmes, & DeSanctis, 1991). For example, a hostile glance in response to a comment can be observed in FTF communication but not in CMC mode. Second, CMC allows more deliberation and editing of comments prior to transmission (rehearsability) relative to FTF communication (Dennis & Valacich, 1999). This "editing" capability may enable participants to present themselves and their arguments in a more reasoned manner than in FTF communication (Hiltz & Turoff, 1978; Rice, 1984). Third, messages in CMC are text-based and external to the sender and receiver because they are displayed on the material medium of a computer screen. Messages in FTF communication are transmitted directly from sender to receiver; hence, the impersonal nature of CMC messages may lead group members to view them as more objective. Objective messages may be considered common property of the group, thereby depersonalizing the conflict compared to the FTF modality (Poole et al., 1992). Finally, the slower pace and reduced social cues in CMC may mitigate negative spirals of competitiveness in conflicts. This positive effect occurs because parties have more opportunity to reflect on their own and others' actions and cue restriction eliminates less controllable nonverbal cues that may transmit negative reactions.

On balance, this cost–benefit analysis (Poole et al., 1991) suggests that the negative effects of text-based CMC outweigh its benefits in a mixed-motive group task. Furthermore, several previous experimental studies comparing FTF with text-based CMC in social dilemma situations (Bochet et al., 2006; Brosig et al., 2003; Frohlich & Oppenheimer, 1998; Kiesler et al., 1996) support this general prediction.

COMPUTER-MEDIATED COMMUNICATION IN THE COMMONS: STUDY 1

In collaboration with colleagues from communication and information systems, we have conducted several experimental studies to further investigate the causal mechanisms underlying the FTF communication effect by manipulating the medium of communication (Poole, Samuelson, El-Shinnawy, Vinze, & Lane, 2008; Samuelson et al., 2008; Watrous, 2004), which has demonstrable effects on communication processes within small groups (Poole et al., 1992; Williams, 1977). Our literature review underscores the need for studies that help clarify the relationships among or integrate these causal factors (group identity, commitment/promise-keeping). We now present an overview of the initial study (Samuelson et al., 2008) to illustrate our research approach.

We used computer software (FISH; Gifford & Wells, 1991) to simulate a commons dilemma (Dawes, 1980; Hardin, 1968). The primary goal in FISH is to maximize profit for each fishing boat. The game is played over multiple "seasons" and fishers must decide how many fish to catch in each season independently. Fishers earn money for each fish caught; costs are incurred for fishing time as well as fixed costs for leaving port each season. Individual profit is calculated simply by total income minus total costs. This group task falls within the mixed-motive conflict classification using

McGrath's (1984) task circumplex. Group members are confronted with the challenging problem of determining the sustainable yield that can be extracted from the fishery without depleting the fish stocks for future use. Thus, there is a problem-solving aspect to this group task in terms of deciding the optimal fishing strategy.

However, there is also a major coordination problem in this group task, which can only be managed through cooperation of all group members on a consensual group fishing strategy. In general, the optimal strategy is to catch only as many fish each season as can be replaced through the reproductive process that occurs at the end of each season.[1] Optimal group performance (i.e., economic profit) requires accurate information exchange, problem analysis and deliberation, and firm commitments of cooperation from members to execute the group's strategy. Deviations from this optimal group strategy result in lower group profit scores due to premature depletion of fish stocks.

A familiar axiom in CMC research is that making predictions about group performance for any particular group task depends, in large part, on the nature of the technology itself (Dennis & Valacich, 1999; DeSanctis & Gallupe, 1987; Maruping & Agarwal, 2004; Zigurs & Buckland, 1998). The type of group support system employed in the present study, a group communication support system (GCSS, Hollingshead & McGrath, 1995; Level 1, DeSanctis & Gallupe, 1987), gives rise to a specific set of predictions based on the particular structures it provides. GCSSs typically provide members with the ability to enter messages into a shared space that displays the group discussion. GCSSs may also incorporate other features to facilitate communication, such as topic headings or discussion threads to organize comments, electronic brainstorming or idea generation, and routines for evaluating ideas through voting, rating, or other means.

The GCSS employed in this study, FACILITATE.COM, was a Web-based conferencing system that displays comments organized by topic. Participants were given the basic communication features to create a CMC condition that differed from FTF discussion only in terms of communication modality. Our immediate goal in the present study was not to design the optimal group decision support system (GDSS) that would outperform FTF communication; rather, it was to manipulate only the mode group members used to communicate to determine how the processes of communication change group performance. A Level 1 GDSS (DeSanctis & Gallupe, 1987) was deemed appropriate for this purpose.

We should note that our use of synchronous communication technology in a commons dilemma paradigm is novel. The present experiments extend the CMC literature by studying the impact of communication medium in a replenishable resource dilemma, a type of social dilemma paradigm used extensively in previous experimental research (e.g., Gardner, Ostrom, & Walker, 1994; Hine & Gifford, 1996b; Kramer & Brewer, 1984; Messick et al., 1983; Roch & Samuelson, 1997; Samuelson, 1993). We also use larger groups (7–9 persons) in this mixed-motive conflict task than have been employed in previous CMC research (Scott, 1999). The larger group size, coupled with a group task of higher complexity (DeSanctis & Gallupe, 1987; Zigurs & Buckland, 1998), creates a unique research context to study the effects of CMC on cooperation.

Based on our conceptual analysis, we advanced six hypotheses about the impacts of CMC on group processes and outcomes in a resource dilemma conflict. Because CMC groups were expected to underperform FTF groups on most processes that mediate outcomes of resource conflict (e.g., commitment-making), we expected that they would achieve lower group performance levels than FTF groups. In this study, several types of group performance outcomes were assessed. Effective management of the common resource was measured by the following dependent variables: (a) group performance and (b) member satisfaction with group outcomes. Specifically, group performance was indexed by: (a) total group economic profit, (b) total fish caught by group, (c) number of seasons until total depletion of fish stocks, and (d) number of fish remaining in common pool after final season. The first two measures assess the group's economic profitability (efficiency) of resource use, whereas the latter two focus on the sustainability of group resource management. The first hypothesis is that FTF groups will earn higher economic profit (i.e., catch more total fish) than CMC groups (H1). Our second hypothesis is that FTF groups will achieve more sustainable resource management outcomes than CMC groups (H2).

Because previous research (Baltes et al., 2002) has typically found lower satisfaction in CMC groups (relative to FTF), we expected a similar pattern. Moreover, past research on resource dilemmas has documented that group members are less satisfied with group outcomes when the resource pool is depleted compared to conditions in which it is managed effectively (Samuelson & Messick, 1986; Samuelson, Messick, Rutte, & Wilke, 1984).

Thus, we expected that FTF groups would experience higher satisfaction with group performance than CMC groups (H3).

We advanced three additional hypotheses related to the processes that may produce these group outcomes. First, we expected CMC groups (relative to FTF) to report lower levels of group identity because of their slower rate of communication and information poor channels. Communication is essential to identity formation and any medium that slows it down will impede processes that build the group's sense of itself (Fiol & O'Connor, 2005). Furthermore, empirical studies have reported lower group identity in CMC groups, compared to groups using FTF communication (Bouas & Arrow, 1996; Scott & Fontenot, 1999). Hence, our fourth hypothesis is that CMC groups will report lower group identity than FTF groups (H4).

Second, we predicted that CMC would have a negative impact on commitments by group members to cooperate in resource dilemma conflicts. Previous research suggests that the greater the number of members who make explicit commitments to cooperate, the more constructive will be the group's management of the social dilemma. One effective and common way of making a commitment to cooperate occurs when one member asks others to commit and they do so almost simultaneously, by acclamation. This process functions to elicit the type of universal commitment that Orbell et al. (1988) argue will promote a high level of subsequent cooperation. It is also a very public way of committing. However, CMC in general, and the FACILITATE.COM system in particular, makes it more difficult to extract commitments from members. The parallel processing that commonly occurs in CMC imposes coordination difficulties that make commitment by acclamation more difficult than in FTF communication. In addition, the interaction-based "bandwagon effect" that often promotes mutual commitment-making is more difficult to sustain in CMC. Thus, our fifth hypothesis is that CMC groups will make fewer commitments to cooperate than FTF groups (H5).

Third, we expected that members of CMC groups would make more negative attributions to other members than would members of FTF groups.[2] An important attribution in conflict situations concerns the degree to which others are cooperative or competitive. Thomas and Pondy (1977) observed that competitive attributions may set up a self-reinforcing cycle in which members assume that others are competitive and, in "self-defense," act competitively themselves, which causes others to react competitively, and so on, escalating the conflict. Though interacting with others may change these attributions, changes in attributions based on interaction with others will occur more slowly in CMC because of its lower rate of message exchange (Straus & McGrath, 1994). Cramton (2001), in a study of virtual distributed teams, found that members of CMC groups made more negative, personal attributions regarding others' behaviors. For example, a group member who did not answer e-mails promptly was assumed to be uncommitted to the team; the possibility that there was a technical problem or the member was out of town was not considered. Cramton (2002) suggests that the fundamental attribution error (Ross, 1977) is more likely to occur in CMC than in FTF communication. Similarly, Thompson and Nadler (2002) reported that e-mail negotiators demonstrate the sinister attribution error (Kramer, 1994), where malevolent intentions are attributed to the other party, more often than FTF negotiators. Hence, our sixth hypothesis is that members of CMC groups will make more negative, competitive attributions toward others than members of FTF groups (H6).

Overview of Procedures

Participants were 320 undergraduate students in introductory psychology and speech communication classes at Texas A&M University, assigned to 41 groups (7 to 9 persons). Participants received credit toward course requirements or extra credit. The number of groups randomly assigned to each experimental condition was 20 (FTF) or 21 (CMC).[3]

We used two communication modes: groups discussed decision strategies in either an FTF discussion or a CMC mode. Each group was given 10 minutes to discuss fishing strategies in the first FISH session and their plans for a second FISH session following the discussion period. In the FTF mode, we seated participants around a rectangular table in a small private room. We videotaped each FTF group discussion using a small ceiling-mounted camera. In the CMC sessions, our groups used FACILITATE.COM, a commercially available Web-based software system that enables synchronous (or asynchronous) computer conferencing. Participants could freely enter comments on an electronic "white board" and build on others' ideas. The group discussion was displayed on a Web page that organized comments and "builds" (comments on comments) in hierarchical fashion. Statements were displayed under the topic heading to which they were associated. FACILITATE.COM enables group members to enter ideas under various topics as they wish. Although FACILITATE.

COM provides the capability to meet in different place/time, our participants were present in the same computer lab and took part in the computer conference simultaneously. We seated individuals at separate workstations spaced apart such that though participants could see some other group members, nonverbal communication (e.g., facial cues, gestures) was difficult.

We used a common dilemma simulation based on a fishing metaphor as our experimental task. The program (FISH 2.11; Gifford & Wells, 1991) simulates the process of harvesting from a common ocean fishery by multiple fishers and renewal of fish stock through natural reproductive processes. Graphically, FISH displays on the computer screen the exact number of fish available for harvesting. As the available stock declines, the number of fish on the screen decreases accordingly. FISH provides regular feedback to fishers on their own catches, other fishers' catches, current fish stock available, income, costs, and profits on each season. Group members interact in real time over a series of fishing seasons. We regard FISH as a realistic experimental resource dilemma task well suited for our study.

There are 24 parameters in the FISH program. We used an initial and maximum fish stock of 100 fish. In the first FISH session, the task was limited to a maximum of five seasons, although we did not inform participants about this value to discourage end game strategies. We set the maximum number of seasons to 10 in the second FISH session. The spawning (replenishment) rate was 1.50, but participants were not given the exact spawning rate. We set the costs of fishing activities as follows: (a) leave port to begin fishing ($15.00 per season) and (b) time spent fishing ($1.00 per minute). Fishers received $10.00 income per fish caught. Total career profit per fisher was simply the total career income minus total career costs.

The experimental procedure was divided into four phases: (a) FISH task (Session 1), (b) 10-minute group discussion period, (c) FISH task (Session 2), and (d) postexperimental questionnaire. We escorted participants into the computer lab and seated them at workstations. Participants were informed that they would be taking part in a group decision-making task in which they would interact with other group members via the computer system. We also told them that a period of communication would be allowed at a predetermined point during the session. No communication of any kind with other group members was allowed until the experimenter told them to begin group discussion.

Depending on experimental condition, the procedure diverged at this point. CMC groups received instructions on how to access and use FACILITATE.COM. The communication program was described as an "electronic bulletin board" in which all group members could post their own ideas and respond to others' ideas sequentially. After explaining the basic mechanics of how to add ideas and build on existing ideas, we instructed participants to log in to a computer conference and type a brief practice message. We assigned each group member a different letter (A, B, etc.) to identify them in the computer conference. We reminded participants that talking aloud during the computer conference was prohibited and that all communication would be accomplished through the computer conference later in the session.

Both FTF and CMC groups received a brief verbal introduction to the FISH experimental task. Participants then read more detailed instructions to FISH on their computer screens. A sample demonstration screen for FISH was displayed on an overhead projector. Specific points highlighted were maximum size of common fish stock, consequences of catching all available fish, and the concept of "spawning" (replenishment process). Participants were reminded that spawning could only occur when all fishers returned to port during an active season and there were fish remaining in the stock pool. Participants received no information about the exact replenishment rate. Participants were instructed that the FISH task would end in one of two ways: either when the fish stocks were depleted to zero or when the computer automatically terminated the FISH session. The objective of FISH was explained by the experimenter as maximizing individual profit, but that there were several different ways to accomplish this goal and participants would have the opportunity to find the most effective fishing strategy during the FISH session.

We established a reward structure to provide financial consequences for both individual and group decisions during the FISH task. We told participants that there was a chance that they would be paid in cash for their decisions. A lottery drawing would be held at the end of the entire experiment and each group would be issued one lottery ticket for every $100 of profit earned in FISH. One group would be selected at random as the lottery winner. We told participants that cash payments to members of the winning group would be based on total individual profits in both FISH sessions using a conversion rate of $1.00 for every $20.00 of individual profit.

Following these lottery instructions, participants started the FISH task. This initial FISH session continued for up to five seasons. If the group ended the fifth season with fish remaining in the ocean stocks, then the FISH program terminated. At this point, the FISH software displayed feedback on the computer screen, including cumulative catch totals, income, expenses, and profits. We then tallied individual and group profit totals and recorded them on a feedback sheet that was provided to the group during the discussion period. We conducted the first FISH session to provide baseline group performance data.

Group members were then allowed to communicate for 10 minutes. We escorted the FTF groups to a separate room and seated members around a rectangular table. We then read aloud the rules for group discussion, which allowed participants to discuss the FISH task and harvest strategies in the second session. Physical threats and side payments outside the experiment were prohibited. The experimenter then left the room and monitored the group discussion via the video camera system. For CMC groups, participants remained seated at their workstations. We read the same discussion instructions used in the FTF condition with the following changes. The instructions stated that all communication between members was to be conducted via the computer conferencing system, FACILITATE.COM. During the CMC discussion period, the computer displayed the identifying letter of each participant next to each comment on the screen. This letter designation was unrelated to the participant's FISH identification number. The experimenter returned briefly to tell FTF participants when they had 5 minutes left and suggested that the group move the discussion toward a common solution. In the CMC condition, we gave the same time reminder and created a new topic heading in FACILITATE.COM labeled "Common Solution."

Upon completion of the group discussion, all participants returned to the FISH program. We gave them final instructions about the second session of the FISH task, noting that the maximum number of seasons would be randomly determined by the computer. Participants then commenced fishing. The program continued until either the fishery stock was depleted to zero or until the 10th season was completed. Immediately following the second FISH session, we administered the postexperimental questionnaire. We recorded the individual and group profit totals for Session 2 and displayed this feedback on an overhead projector.

We used the group-level variable of total economic profit as the primary measure of group performance. The total number of fish caught (per group) was also included as a measure of cooperative restraint, as well as two indices of sustainability in resource management (number of seasons until depletion, final fish stock size).[4] Additional dependent measures were collected in the postexperimental questionnaire. The questionnaire included items about satisfaction with the group discussion process and outcomes, perceptions of inclusion in group discussion, and feelings of group identity (measured by Hinkle, Taylor, Fox-Cardamone, & Crook's [1989] 9-item Group Identification Scale, e.g., "I identify with this group," "I think this group worked well together," "I feel strong ties to this group"). A final section assessed perceptions of the FISH task, satisfaction with group performance, individual motivations for catching fish, and causal attributions for group performance and others' behaviors.

The group discussion videotapes (FTF condition) and computer conference transcripts (CMC condition) were coded by two independent raters for the number of commitments to cooperate made by group members. A coding system was created that identified each time a member made an explicit commitment to the group's final course of action. Commitments to courses of action other than the group's final decision were not considered in the coding process because they had no connection to subsequent group activity. Coders also identified whether an explicit "pledge of commitment" was made by each group. A pledge of commitment occurred when one member explicitly asked others to commit and they did so.

Group Performance Results

Table 2.1 presents the group means for the analyses of H1 and H2. Our first hypothesis was confirmed: FTF groups earned significantly more economic profit and caught more fish than CMC groups. We also found support for H2: FTF groups demonstrated more sustainable resource management of the fishery stock than CMC groups, in terms of both the number of seasons until depletion and final stock size. In short, the results for all four FISH dependent measures told the same story: FTF groups performed significantly better than CMC groups.[5] In support of H3, Table 2.1 shows that FTF groups reported being more satisfied with their group's performance (using fishery stock) than CMC groups. Given the group performance differences induced by communication mode, this

TABLE 2.1

Means for Dependent Variables (Second Session) by Condition

	Condition	
DV	**FTF**	**CMC**
Total profit ($)	1153	842
Fish caught	185	130
Seasons	9.31	6.13
Final stock pool size	21.44	5.07
Satisfaction with group	4.18	3.23
Group identity	34.54	40.54
Commitments (%)	0.67	0.20
Attributions to Others		
Others sustain fishery stock	5.36	4.39
Others concerned for group well-being	4.73	3.75
Others harvest more fish for self	3.88	4.58
Others harvest more fish than you	3.49	4.28

result was expected based on previous research on CMC and resource dilemmas (Baltes et al., 2002; Samuelson & Messick, 1986).

Group Identity

The Group Identification Scale (Hinkle et al., 1989) is scored such that lower scores reflect higher group identity. Table 2.1 reveals that CMC groups experienced lower group identity than FTF groups. Though there was a significant group effect (i.e., group-to-group variation within conditions), our prediction (H4) that the CMC medium would produce less group identification among members than FTF groups was supported. Moreover, this group identity effect validates our assumption that the manipulation of communication medium has direct observable effects on group processes occurring during group discussion (Poole et al., 1992). This result provides further empirical support for theoretical arguments asserting the central role of group identity in explaining the beneficial effect of FTF discussion on cooperation (Dawes et al., 1990; Orbell et al., 1988). Group communication via a CMC mode fails to produce the same level of group identity observed in FTF discussion groups.

Commitments to Group Harvest Strategies

H5 was evaluated by analyzing the frequency of pledges of commitment by members to cooperate with a group harvest strategy during group discussion. Consistent with predictions, Table 2.1 reveals that FTF groups made commitments to cooperate on a group strategy roughly three times more often than did CMC groups.[6] This finding demonstrates clearly how changes in communication mode can impact convergence processes (Dennis & Valacich, 1999) in groups facing a complex, mixed-motive conflict task. Moreover, this result is consistent with the commitment/promise-keeping explanation for the FTF discussion effect (Bouas & Komorita, 1996; Kerr & Kaufman-Gilliland, 1994).

Attributions to Other Group Members

Table 2.1 shows that members of CMC groups made more negative attributions to others, compared to FTF group members. Specifically, CMC group members attributed significantly less intent to others to sustain the fishery stock pool and be concerned with the group's well-being, relative to FTF group members. In addition, CMC group members made more competitive attributions by inferring more intent to others to harvest more fish for themselves and catch more fish than other participants, compared to FTF group members. Thus, H6 received clear support and provides additional evidence that manipulation of communication medium affects important group process variables.

REPLICATION: STUDY 2

We performed a second experiment (Poole et al., 2008) to (a) replicate the results from Study 1 and (b) test whether providing groups with a simple discussion agenda would improve group performance in the FISH task and possibly reduce (or eliminate) the FTF advantage. A between-subjects 2×2 factorial design was used crossing two levels of Communication Mode (FTF vs. CMC) with two levels of Agenda (Agenda, No Agenda). All other methods were identical to Study 1. The results of this second study replicated the findings for the dependent measures described in Study 1.[7]

We conclude from this study that our empirical results from Study 1 are robust, at least for the specific text-based CMC system (FACILITATE. COM) used in these experiments.

REPLICATION AND EXTENSION: STUDY 3

Watrous (2004) conducted a subsequent experiment that differed from the previous two studies by including a formal polling mechanism during group discussion and replacing FACILITATE.COM with Microsoft NetMeeting software (chat-based CMC system). Two additional conditions were included: (a) group members were required to conduct one public "straw" poll of members' intended choices (number of fish caught per season) at the end of the 10-minute discussion period, and (b) groups were required to conduct two public polls (after 5 minutes and at discussion's end). In contrast to our previous findings, Watrous (2004) found no statistical differences (based on a sample of 67 six-person groups) in group performance between the three CMC conditions (no poll, one poll, two poll) and the FTF condition. However, there were significant differences in the number of groups reaching consensus as a function of communication mode and polling condition. Specifically, CMC one-poll groups (83%) reached consensus on a collective fishing strategy most often, relative to FTF groups (77%), CMC two-poll groups (56%), and CMC no-poll groups (32%). These findings of Study 3 (Watrous, 2004), juxtaposed with our results from Studies 1 and 2, suggest the possibility of significant interactions between group communication technology features, communication processes, and group outcome variables.

CONCLUSIONS

Our review has focused on the current state of the literature on why and how group discussion enhances cooperation in social dilemmas. Two contrasting explanations have survived the initial rounds of experimental testing: group identity vs. commitment-making. Some recent reviewers (Kerr & Park, 2001; Kopelman et al., 2002) have suggested that the weight of the empirical evidence favors the commitment/promise-keeping account. Moreover, Kerr et al. (1997) have presented persuasive data in support of a version of the commitment hypothesis in which group members conform to a personal norm to keep their promises once made. This interpretation implies that the commitment explanation involves not just the act of making promises per se but a normative component. Specifically, when people discuss the social dilemma, the situation appears to activate a personal norm that says to our conscience, "personal commitments must be honored" (Kerr et al., 1997).

This version of the commitment explanation is generally consistent with the theory of social norms proposed by Bicchieri (2006; see also Bicchieri, 2002; Bicchieri & Lev-On, 2007). She advances a norm-based explanation for the FTF communication effect grounded in social cognition theory and research (Fiske & Taylor, 1991; Hamilton, 2005) that is similar conceptually to Cialdini, Kallgren, and Reno's (1991) focus theory of normative conduct. According to this theory, a social norm of promise-keeping refers to a "behavioral rule that is followed only if certain conditions are met, but otherwise may be disregarded" (Bicchieri & Lev-On, 2007, p. 143). More formally, Bicchieri (2006) specifies these conditions as:

(a) the individual knows that a *behavioral rule* (**R**) exists and applies to *situations* of type **S,** and (b) the individual prefers to conform to **R** in situations of type **S** on the condition that the individual believes that a sufficiently large subset of the *population* (**P**) conforms to **R** in situations of type **S** (*empirical expectations*), and either (1) the individual believes that a sufficiently large subset of **P** expects the individual to conform to **R** in situations of type **S** (*normative expectations*), *or* (2) the individual believes a sufficiently large subset of **P** expects the individual to conform to **R** in situations of type **S**, prefers the individual to conform, and may sanction behavior (*normative expectations with sanctions*). (p. 11)

Bicchieri's (2006) emphasis on contingent application of social norms appears generally compatible with the appropriateness framework proposed by Messick (1999). Building on March's (1994) "logic of appropriateness" (p. 58); Messick (1999) suggests that we can better understand decision-making in social situations by analyzing how people make judgments on three aspects: (a) appropriateness, (b) identity, and (c) rule-based choice. March (1994) has summarized the basic logic behind this choice model with the following question: "What *decision rule* is *appropriate* for a *person* like me to use in a *situation* like this?" (p. 58). Weber, Kopelman, and Messick (2004) have applied this appropriateness framework to assess its heuristic value in integrating research findings in the experimental social dilemma literature. In particular, we concur with their conclusion about the impact of group discussion: "Communication studies, by their nature, are highly social. They are … precisely the kinds of situations in which we would expect the appropriateness framework to offer a more compelling account of observed behavior than an EU [Expected Utility] or rational choice model" (Weber et al., 2004, p. 297).

The appropriateness framework forces us to focus on subtle features of our experimental situations that may (inadvertently) affect the conclusions we reach. For example, influential studies that have found support for group identity (e.g., Orbell et al., 1988) used a procedure in which a large group of participants ($N = 14$) is subdivided into two smaller groups, thus creating an ingroup and outgroup. These experiments also typically employ a one-shot public goods dilemma game in which group members make anonymous choices and do not expect future interaction in subsequent games. Could these methodological features "prime" participants to think about group identity either before or during discussion? Similarly, in a prominent study confirming the commitment/promise-keeping account (Kerr & Kaufman-Gilliland, 1994), all female participants in a single group are given 5 minutes for group discussion, expect repeated decisions (eight rounds), and are told that they will be making repeated judgments about their expectations about others' choices and perceptions of efficacy. Should we be surprised when we learn that commitment/promise-keeping was a stronger mediating variable than group identity in this experimental setting? Situational cues in this study that might increase the salience of group identity appear to be absent.[8] This is not to say that these studies are flawed methodologically; rather, they differ in ways that may be more significant theoretically than we think. Messick's (1999) appropriateness framework and Bicchieri's (2006) theory lead us to ask specific questions about the impact of these (seemingly) mundane details of our experimental situations. The answers to these questions may help explain why researchers draw divergent conclusions about why discussion works.

We have also extended the conversation about the communication effect in this chapter by reviewing more recent literature on group discussion in CMC contexts. How does research on CMC in social dilemmas shed light on the proposed causal explanations? In a recent review, Bicchieri and Lev-On (2007) concluded that the effectiveness of CMC depends on the way in which the communication medium handles three critical factors: (a) coordination, (b) credibility, and (c) dissemination. They argue that though some forms of CMC (videoconferencing) show comparable levels of cooperation to FTF modes (Bos et al., 2002; Brosig et al., 2003), text-based CMC does considerably less well because the medium fails to provide the support required to coordinate promises among group members, make them credible, and distribute information with speed and clarity to all members about such promises. The implication is that forms of CMC like videoconferencing that more closely mimic the conditions of FTF communication may succeed because they rectify these problems of coordination, credibility, and dissemination. This would appear to be an eminently testable proposition.

Our own experimental work (Poole et al., 2008; Samuelson et al., 2008; Watrous, 2004) provides an initial demonstration of the utility of experimental manipulations of communication mode that directly affect communication processes. We found reliable differences between FTF and text-based CMC groups in terms of group identity, the frequency of commitments to a group harvest strategy, and attributions toward other group members. Moreover, these effects on process variables were associated with the predicted effects on group resource management (economic profit and resource sustainability) of the commons. In turn, these group outcomes produced higher levels of group satisfaction in the FTF condition (relative to CMC). These results are consistent generally with the group identity and commitment/promise-keeping explanations. The differences in group identity as a function of communication medium suggest that FTF communication creates stronger feelings of group identity and promotes more commitments to cooperate, which together result in more cooperative behavior and positive group outcomes.

These research findings underscore the importance of communication processes in the constructive management of resource dilemmas. The finding that CMC groups performed worse than FTF groups makes it clear that not just any communication will suffice to induce cooperation. This outcome, of course, was expected and hardly surprising given the previous CMC research literature (Baltes et al., 2002; Bicchieri & Lev-On, 2007). Communication through the GCSS was more difficult and ambiguous than through the FTF mode and less effective in creating feelings of group identity and positive attributions toward others. Inspection of the CMC transcripts suggests that participants had trouble establishing and following the threads of their discussions. Perhaps the impersonal or awkward nature of the CMC conferencing technology prevented participants from making connections with others and inhibited the formation of "common ground." Alternatively, the text-based CMC technology may have been deficient because it failed to facilitate the coordination of credible promises of cooperation and slowed down the flow of such information to group members (Bicchieri & Lev-On, 2007). Research using more "user-friendly" software to support CMC that addresses these problems directly may produce more favorable group outcomes (Watrous, 2004).

FINAL THOUGHTS

Given the small number of experimental studies reporting competitive tests and their unique methodological features, we conclude there is insufficient empirical basis for rejecting group identity in favor of the commitment/promise-keeping explanation for group discussion's effect. It appears that the scientific debate over which explanation is "correct" has obscured the alternative reality that the communication effect may be driven by multiple causal factors operating independently or in concert. It is ironic that we reach this conclusion now given that Orbell et al. (1988) made precisely the same point nearly 20 years ago. We suggest that testing alternative, integrated theoretical approaches may be more productive to the research enterprise than premature closure. With apologies to our great American humorist, Mark Twain, rumors of the "death" of the group identity hypothesis may be greatly exaggerated.

In conclusion, our review suggests that understanding the communication effect could be guided profitably by Bicchieri's (2006) theory of social norms and Messick's (1999) appropriateness framework. New research questions are derivable from this general mode of thinking. For example, under what conditions will group identity (induced by discussion) result in high levels of cooperation? Both theoretical frameworks dictate that we must identify cues in the group's discussion (or experimental setting) that trigger activation of specific behavioral rules (e.g., scripts, norms) that apply in that particular social situation. This approach suggests new research strategies to delineate further the reasons for discussion's effect. For example, cues consistent with one local norm ("promises should be kept") or another ("strangers can't be trusted") could be manipulated to assess their effects on cooperation. Hertel and Kerr (2001) provided a compelling demonstration of this research approach in the minimal group paradigm. Researchers seeking to explain the success of FTF communication in social dilemmas may want to follow their promising lead. Exploring the nuances of the communication process in a computer-mediated environment is a complementary research direction we find especially promising.

NOTES

1. In our group task, the sustainable yield requires each group member to catch approximately 4–5 fish per season, depending on group size. Groups could catch no more than 33 fish total per season without decreasing the stock size from its maximum value of 100 (using 1.5 replenishment rate).

2. Because we predicted that CMC groups would perform more poorly on the FISH task than FTF groups, we assumed that this lower group performance would result in overconsumption of fish. Previous research by Hine and Gifford (1996a) found that under these conditions (overuse), group members typically made more negative attributions (e.g., greed, ignorance) to others than when the resource pool was managed sustainably.

3. Due to various computer network or software malfunctions, data from 12 groups were unusable. An equal number of groups ($N = 6$) was dropped from each experimental condition. The final sample used for data analysis included 29 groups (FTF condition, $N = 14$; CMC condition, $N = 15$).

4. The most commonly used measure of cooperation in resource dilemma studies is the number of resource units consumed (e.g., Brewer & Kramer, 1986; Hine & Gifford, 1996b; Messick et al., 1983). In these studies, it is assumed that more resource units taken by group members indicates less cooperation. In the FISH task, group performance outcomes are influenced directly by the level of individual cooperative restraint displayed by group members.

5. We performed univariate nested analyses of variance (ANOVAs) on all FISH dependent measures in the first session and found no significant differences (using $p = .20$) for communication mode. These results reduce the plausibility of selection as a threat to explaining the observed differences between conditions in Session 2.

6. The sample size was 22 groups for this analysis because of missing or inaudible videotape recordings for 7 groups. However, the number of omitted groups was approximately equal (FTF, $N = 4$; CMC, $N = 3$) across conditions.

7. The only exception to this summary statement is the content coding of the commitment data from the FTF videotapes and CMC transcripts. This coding work is currently in progress.

8. Generally, gender differences in social dilemma experiments have been mixed. However, in one of Kramer and Brewer's (1984) studies (Experiment 1), the group identity manipulation had no effect on the cooperation rate of female participants, whereas it was influential for males. The authors concluded that gender may have interacted with specific features of the group identity operationalization (e.g., perceived competitiveness between groups). They did not find the same gender interaction effect in subsequent studies when the group identity manipulation was changed to eliminate this feature. The sensitivity of this interaction effect to subtle situational cues makes sense from an appropriateness perspective (Messick, 1999).

ACKNOWLEDGMENTS

We would like to acknowledge the support of a grant from the Interdisciplinary Research Initiatives program of the Office of the Vice President and Associate Provost for Research at Texas A&M University. We also thank the following undergraduates who served as experimenters and assisted with the literature review for this chapter: Greg Trippe, Robin Penick, Doug French, Rachel Harper-Tarantolo, Malika Mitchell, Katie Vidrine, Kristin Wolf, Daniel Nicely, and Eric Strongin.

REFERENCES

Adriansen, L., & Hjelmquist, E. (1999). Group processes in solving two problems: Face-to-face and computer-mediated communication. *Behaviour and Information Technology, 18,* 179–198.

Baltes, B. B., Dickson, M. W., Sherman, M. P., Bauer, C. C., & LaGanke, J. S. (2002). Computer-mediated communication and group decision making: A meta-analysis. *Organizational Behavior and Human Decision Processes, 87,* 156–179.

Bicchieri, C. (2002). Covenants without swords: Group identity, norms, and communication in social dilemmas. *Rationality and Society, 14,* 192–228.

Bicchieri, C. (2006). *The grammar of society: The nature and dynamics of social norms.* New York: Cambridge University Press.

Bicchieri, C., & Lev-On, A. (2007). Computer-mediated communication and cooperation in social dilemmas: An experimental analysis. *Politics, Philosophy, Economics, 6,* 139–168.

Bochet, O., Page, T., & Putterman, L. (2006). Communication and punishment in voluntary contribution experiments. *Journal of Economic Behavior and Organization, 60,* 11–26.

Bordia, P. (1997). Face-to-face versus computer-mediated communication: A synthesis of the experimental literature. *The Journal of Business Communication, 34,* 99–120.

Bornstein, G. (1992). The free rider problem in intergroup conflicts over step-level and continuous public goods. *Journal of Personality and Social Psychology, 62,* 597–602.

Bornstein, G., Rapoport, A., Kerpel, L., & Katz, T. (1989). Within and between group communication in intergroup competition for public goods. *Journal of Experimental Social Psychology, 25,* 422–436.

Bos, N., Olson, J., Gergle, D., Olson, G., & Wright, Z. (2002). Effects of four computer-mediated communications channels on trust development. *Proceedings of the ACM Conference on Human Factors in Computing Systems, 4,* 135–140.

Bouas, K. S., & Arrow, H. (1996). The development of group identity in computer and face-to-face groups with membership change. *Computer Supported Cooperative Work, 4,* 153–178.

Bouas, K. S., & Komorita, S. S. (1996). Group discussion and cooperation in social dilemmas. *Personality and Social Psychology Bulletin, 22,* 1144–1150.

Braver, S. L. (1995). Social contracts and the provision of public goods. In D. A. Schroeder (Ed.), *Social dilemmas: Perspectives on individuals and groups* (pp. 69–86). Westport, CT: Praeger.

Braver, S. L., & Wilson, L. A., III. (1986). Choices in social dilemmas: Effects of communication within subgroups. *Journal of Conflict Resolution, 30,* 51–61.

Brewer, M. B. (1979). Ingroup bias in the minimal intergroup situation: A cognitive-motivational analysis. *Psychological Bulletin, 86,* 307–324.

Brewer, M. B., & Kramer, R. M. (1986). Choice behavior in social dilemmas: Effects of social identity, group size, and decision framing. *Journal of Personality and Social Psychology, 50,* 543–549.

Brosig, J., Ockenfels, A., & Weimann, J. (2003). The effect of communication media on cooperation. *German Economic Review, 4,* 217–241.

Burgoon, J. K., & Hoobler, G. D. (2002). Nonverbal signals. In M. L. Knapp & J. A. Daly (Eds.), *Handbook of interpersonal communication* (3rd ed., pp. 240–299). Thousand Oaks, CA: Sage.

Chen, X. P. (1996). The group-based binding pledge as a solution to public good problems. *Organizational Behavior and Human Decision Processes, 66,* 192–202.

Chen, X. P., & Komorita, S. S. (1994). The effects of communication and commitment in a public goods social dilemma. *Organizational Behavior and Human Decision Processes, 60*, 367–386.

Cialdini, R. B. (2001). *Influence: Science and practice* (4th ed.). Boston: Allyn & Bacon.

Cialdini, R. B., Kallgren, C. A., & Reno, R. R. (1991). A focus theory of normative conduct: A theoretical refinement and reevaluation of the role of norms in human behavior. *Advances in Experimental Social Psychology, 24*, 201–234.

Cramton, C. D. (2001). The mutual knowledge problem and its consequences for dispersed collaboration. *Organization Science, 12*, 346–371.

Cramton, C. D. (2002). Attribution in distributed work groups. In P. J. Hinds & S. Kiesler (Eds.), *Distributed work* (pp. 191–212). Cambridge, MA: MIT Press.

Croson, R. (1999). Look at me when you say that: An electronic negotiation simulation. *Simulation and Gaming, 30*, 23–37.

Daft, R. L., & Lengel, R. H. (1984). Information richness: A new approach to managerial behavior and organizational design. *Research in Organizational Behavior, 6*, 191–233.

Daft, R. L., & Lengel, R. H. (1986). Organizational information requirements, media richness, and structural design. *Management Science, 32*, 554–571.

Dawes, R. M. (1980). Social dilemmas. *Annual Review of Psychology, 31*, 169–193.

Dawes, R. M., McTavish, J., & Shaklee, H. (1977). Behavior, communication, and assumptions about other people's behavior in a commons dilemma situation. *Journal of Personality and Social Psychology, 35*, 1–11.

Dawes, R. M., Orbell, J. M., & van de Kragt, A. J. C. (1988). Not me or thee but we: The importance of group identity in eliciting cooperation in dilemma situations. *Acta Psychologica, 68*, 83–97.

Dawes, R. M., van de Kragt, A. J. C., & Orbell, J. M. (1990). Cooperation for the benefit of us, not me, or my conscience. In J. J. Mansbridge (Ed.), *Beyond self-interest* (pp. 97–110). Chicago: University of Chicago Press.

Dennis, A. R., & Valacich, J. S. (1993). Computer brainstorms: More heads are better than one. *Journal of Applied Psychology, 78*, 531–537.

Dennis, A. R., & Valacich, J. S. (1999). Rethinking media richness: Towards a theory of media synchronicity. *Proceedings of the 32nd Hawaii International Conference on Systems Sciences, 1*, 1–10.

DeSanctis, G., & Gallupe, R. B. (1987). A foundation for the study of group decision support systems. *Management Science, 33*, 589–609.

Dietz, T., Ostrom, E., & Stern, P. C. (2003). The struggle to govern the commons. *Science, 302*, 1907–1912.

Festinger, L. (1957). *A theory of cognitive dissonance.* Evanston, IL: Row, Peterson.

Fiol, C. M., & O'Connor, E. J. (2005). Identification in face-to-face, hybrid, and pure virtual teams: Untangling the contradictions. *Organization Science, 16*, 19–32.

Fiske, S. T., & Taylor, S. E. (1991). *Social cognition* (2nd ed.). New York: McGraw-Hill.

Fjermestad, J., & Hiltz, S. R. (1999). An assessment of group support systems experimental research: Methodology and results. *Journal of Management Information Systems, 15*, 7–149.

Friedman, R., Anderson, C., Brett, J., Olekalns, M., Goates, N., & Lisco, C. C. (2004). Positive and negative effects of anger on dispute resolution: Evidence from electronically mediated disputes. *Journal of Applied Psychology, 89*, 369–376.

Frohlich, N., & Oppenheimer, J. (1998). Some consequences of email vs. face-to-face communication in experiment. *Journal of Economic Behavior and Organization, 35,* 389–403.

Gallupe, R. B., Bastianutti, L. M., & Cooper, W. H. (1991). Unblocking brainstorms. *Journal of Applied Psychology, 76,* 137–142.

Gardner, R., Ostrom, E., & Walker, J. (1994). Social capital and cooperation: Communication, bounded rationality, and behavioral heuristics. In U. Schulz, W. Albers, & U. Mueller (Eds.), *Social dilemmas and cooperation* (pp. 375–412). Heidelberg: Springer.

Gifford, R., & Wells, J. (1991). FISH: A commons dilemma simulation. *Behavior Research Methods, Instruments, and Computers, 23,* 437–441.

Hamilton, D. L. (Ed.). (2005). *Social cognition: Key readings.* New York: Psychology Press.

Hardin, G. (1968). The tragedy of the commons. *Science, 162,* 1243–1248.

Henry, K. B. (2000). Perceptions of cooperation in a longitudinal social dilemma. *Small Group Research, 31,* 507–527.

Hertel, G., & Kerr, N. L. (2001). Priming ingroup favoritism: The impact of normative scripts in the minimal group paradigm. *Journal of Experimental Social Psychology, 37,* 316–324.

Hiltz, S. R., & Turoff, M. (1978). *The network nation: Human communication via computer.* Reading, MA: Addison-Wesley.

Hine, D. W., & Gifford, R. (1996a). Attributions about self and others in commons dilemmas. *European Journal of Social Psychology, 26,* 429–445.

Hine, D. W., & Gifford, R. (1996b). Individual restraint and group efficiency in commons dilemmas: The effects of two types of environmental uncertainty. *Journal of Applied Social Psychology, 26,* 993–1009.

Hinkle, S., Taylor, L. A., Fox-Cardamone, D. L., & Crook, K. F. (1989). Intragroup identification and intergroup differentiation: A multi-component approach. *British Journal of Social Psychology, 28,* 305–317.

Hollingshead, A. B., & McGrath, J. E. (1995). Computer-assisted groups: A critical review of the empirical research. In R. A. Guzzo, E. Salas, & Associates (Eds.), *Team effectiveness and decision making in organizations* (pp. 46–78). San Francisco: Jossey-Bass.

Isaac, R. M., & Walker, J. (1988). Communication and free-riding behavior: The voluntary contribution mechanism. *Economic Inquiry, 26,* 585–608.

Janis, I. L., & Mann, L. (1977). *Decision-making.* New York: Free Press.

Jensen, C., Farnham, S. D., Drucker, S. M., & Kollock, P. (2000). The effect of communication modality on cooperation in online environments. *CHI Letters, 2,* 470–477.

Jerdee, T. H., & Rosen, B. (1974). Effects of opportunity to communicate and visibility of individual decisions on behavior in the common interest. *Journal of Applied Psychology, 59,* 712–716.

Jorgenson, D., & Papciak, A. (1981). The effects of communication, resource feedback, and identifiability on behavior in a simulated commons. *Journal of Experimental Social Psychology, 17,* 373–385.

Kahneman, D., & Tversky, A. (1982). The psychology of preferences. *Scientific American, 246,* 160–173.

Katsch, E., & Rifkin, J. (2001). *Online dispute resolution: Resolving conflicts in cyberspace.* San Francisco: Jossey-Bass.

Kerr, N. L. (1995). Norms in social dilemmas. In D. A. Schroeder (Ed.), *Social dilemmas: Perspectives on individuals and groups* (pp. 31–47). Westport, CT: Praeger.

Kerr, N. L., Garst, J., Lewandowski, D. A., & Harris, S. E. (1997). That still, small voice: Commitment to cooperate as an internalized versus a social norm. *Personality and Social Psychology Bulletin, 23,* 1300–1311.

Kerr, N. L., & Kaufman-Gilliland, C. M. (1994). Communication, commitment, and cooperation in social dilemmas. *Journal of Personality and Social Psychology, 66,* 513–529.

Kerr, N. L., & Park, E. S. (2001). Group performance in collaborative and social dilemma tasks. In M. A. Hogg & R. S. Tindale (Eds.), *Blackwell handbook of social psychology: Group processes* (pp. 107–138). Malden, MA: Blackwell.

Kiesler, C. (1971). *Conformity.* Reading, MA: Addison-Wesley.

Kiesler, S., & Sproull, L. (1992). Group decision making and communication technology. *Organizational Behavior and Human Decision Processes, 52,* 96–123.

Kiesler, S., Sproull, L., & Waters, K. (1996). A prisoner's dilemma experiment on cooperation with people and human-like computers. *Journal of Personality and Social Psychology, 70,* 47–65.

Kinukawa, S., Saiijo, T., & Une, M. (2000). Partial communication in a voluntary-contribution-mechanism experiment. *Pacific Economic Review, 5,* 411–428.

Komorita, S. S., & Parks, C. D. (1995). Interpersonal relations: Mixed-motive interaction. *Annual Review of Psychology, 46,* 183–207.

Kopelman, S., Weber, J. M., & Messick, D. M. (2002). Factors influencing cooperation in commons dilemmas: A review of experimental psychological research. In E. Ostrom, T. Dietz, N. Dolšak, P. C. Stern, S. Stonich, & E. U. Weber (Eds.), *The drama of the commons* (pp. 113–156). Washington, DC: National Academy Press.

Kramer, R. M. (1994). The sinister attribution error: Paranoid cognition and collective distrust in organizations. *Motivation and Emotion, 18,* 199–230.

Kramer, R. M., & Brewer, M. B. (1984). Effects of group identity on resource use in a simulated commons dilemma. *Journal of Personality and Social Psychology, 46,* 1044–1057.

March, J. G. (1994). *A primer on decision making.* New York: Free Press.

Maruping, L. M., & Agarwal, R. (2004). Managing team interpersonal processes through technology: A task-technology fit perspective. *Journal of Applied Psychology, 89,* 975–990.

McGrath, J. E. (1984). *Groups: Interaction and performance.* Englewood Cliffs, NJ: Prentice-Hall.

McGrath, J. E., & Hollingshead, A. B. (1994). *Groups working with technology.* Newbury Park, CA: Sage.

Messick, D. M. (1999). Alternative logics for decision making in social settings. *Journal of Economic Behavior and Organization, 39,* 11–28.

Messick, D. M., Allison, S. T., & Samuelson, C. D. (1988). Framing and communication effects on group members' responses to environmental and social uncertainty. In S. Maital (Ed.), *Applied behavioural economics* (Vol. 2, pp. 677–700). New York: New York University Press.

Messick, D. M., & Brewer, M. B. (1983). Solving social dilemmas: A review. *Review of Personality and Social Psychology, 4,* 11–44.

Messick, D. M., Wilke, H., Brewer, M. B., Kramer, R. M., Zemke, P., & Lui, L. (1983). Individual adaptations and structural change as solutions to social dilemmas. *Journal of Personality and Social Psychology, 44,* 294–309.

Moore, D. A., Kurtzberg, T. R., Thompson, L., & Morris, M. W. (1999). Long and short routes to success in electronically mediated negotiations: Group affiliations and good vibrations. *Organizational Behavior and Human Decision Processes, 77,* 22–43.

Morris, M. W., Nadler, J., Kurtzberg, T. R., & Thompson, L. (2002). Schmooze or lose: Social friction and lubrication in e-mail negotiations. *Group Dynamics: Theory, Research, and Practice, 6*, 89–100.

Naquin, C. E., & Paulsen, G. D. (2003). Online bargaining and interpersonal trust. *Journal of Applied Psychology, 88*, 113–120.

Nyhart, J. D., & Samarasan, D. K. (1989). The elements of negotiation management: Using computers to help resolve conflict. *Negotiation Journal, 5*, 42–62.

Orbell, J. M., van de Kragt, A. J. C., & Dawes, R. M. (1988). Explaining discussion-induced cooperation. *Journal of Personality and Social Psychology, 54*, 811–819.

Orbell, J. M., van de Kragt, A. J. C., & Dawes, R. M. (1991). Covenants without the sword: The role of promises in social dilemma circumstances. In K. J. Koford & J. B. Miller (Eds.), *Social norms and economic institutions* (pp. 117–133). Ann Arbor: University of Michigan Press.

Ostrom, E. (1998). A behavioral approach to the rational choice theory of collective action. *American Political Science Review, 92*, 1–22.

Ostrom, E., & Walker, J. (1991). Cooperation in a commons: Cooperation without external enforcement. In T. R. Palfrey (Ed.), *Laboratory research in political economy* (pp. 287–322). Ann Arbor: University of Michigan Press.

Ostrom, E., Walker, J. M., & Gardner, R. (1992). Covenants with and without a sword: Self-governance is possible. *American Political Science Review, 86*, 404–417.

Palfrey, T. R., & Rosenthal, H. (1991). Testing for the effects of cheap talk. *Games and Economic Behavior, 3*, 183–220.

Poole, M. S., Holmes, M., & DeSanctis, G. (1991). Conflict management in a computer-supported meeting environment. *Management Science, 37*, 926–953.

Poole, M. S., Samuelson, C. D., El-Shinnawy, M., Vinze, A., & Lane, J. A. S. (2008). [Communication medium and agenda effects on cooperation in the commons]. Unpublished raw data.

Poole, M. S., Shannon, D. L., & DeSanctis, G. (1992). Communication media and negotiation processes. In L. L. Putnam & M. E. Roloff (Eds.), *Communication and negotiation* (pp. 46–66). Newbury Park, CA: Sage.

Rice, R. (1984). *The new media: Communication, research, and technology.* Beverly Hills: Sage.

Roch, S. G., & Samuelson, C. D. (1997). Effects of environmental uncertainty and social value orientation in resource dilemmas. *Organizational Behavior and Human Decision Processes, 70*, 221–235.

Ross, L. (1977). The intuitive psychologist and his shortcomings: Distortions in the attribution process. *Advances in Experimental Social Psychology, 10*, 173–220.

Sally, D. (1995). Conversation and cooperation in social dilemmas. *Rationality and Society, 7*, 58–92.

Samuelson, C. D. (1993). A multiattribute evaluation approach to structural change in resource dilemmas. *Organizational Behavior and Human Decision Processes, 55*, 298–324.

Samuelson, C. D., & Messick, D. M. (1986). Alternative structural solutions to resource dilemmas. *Organizational Behavior and Human Decision Processes, 37*, 139–155.

Samuelson, C. D., Messick, D. M., Rutte, C. G., & Wilke, H. A. M. (1984). Individual and structural solutions to resource dilemmas in two cultures. *Journal of Personality and Social Psychology, 47*, 94–104.

Samuelson, C. D., Poole, M. S., El-Shinnawy, M., Vinze, A., Baker, G. A., & Lane, J. A. S. (2008). *Electronic group discussion and cooperation in the commons.* Unpublished manuscript, Department of Psychology, Texas A&M University, College Station, TX.

Scott, C. R. (1999). Communication technology and group communication. In L. R. Frey, D. S. Gouran, & M. S. Poole (Eds.), *The handbook of group communication theory and research* (pp. 432–472). Thousand Oaks, CA: Sage.

Scott, C. R., & Fontenot, J. C. (1999). Multiple identifications during team meetings: A comparison of conventional and computer-supported interactions. *Communication Reports, 12*, 91–99.

Straus, S. G., & McGrath, J. E. (1994). Does the medium matter? The interaction of task type and technology on group performance and member reactions. *Journal of Applied Psychology, 79*, 87–97.

Tajfel, H. (1970). Experiments in intergroup discrimination. *Scientific American, 223*, 96–102.

Tajfel, H., & Turner, J. C. (1979). An integrative theory of intergroup conflict. In W. G. Austin & S. Worchel (Eds.), *The social psychology of intergroup relations* (pp. 33–47). Monterey, CA: Brooks/Cole.

Thomas, K. W., & Pondy, L. R. (1977). Toward an "intent" management model of conflict management among principal parties. *Human Relations, 30*, 1089–1102.

Thompson, L., & Nadler, J. (2002). Negotiating via information technology: Theory and application. *Journal of Social Issues, 58*, 109–124.

van de Kragt, A. J. C., Orbell, J. M., & Dawes, R. M. (1983). The minimal contributing set as a solution to public goods problems. *American Political Science Review, 77*, 112–122.

Walther, J. B. (1994). Anticipated ongoing interaction versus channel effects on relational communication in computer-mediated interaction. *Human Communication Research, 20*, 473–501.

Walther, J. B. (1996). Computer-mediated communication: Impersonal, interpersonal, and hyperpersonal interaction. *Communication Research, 23*, 3–43.

Walther, J. B. (2002). Time effects in computer-mediated groups: Past, present, and future. In P. J. Hinds & S. Kiesler (Eds.), *Distributed work* (pp. 235–257). Cambridge, MA: MIT Press.

Watrous, K. M. (2004). *Effects of communication mode and polling on communication in a commons dilemma.* Unpublished master's thesis, Texas A&M University.

Weber, J. M., Kopelman, S., & Messick, D. M. (2004). A conceptual review of decision making in social dilemmas: Applying a logic of appropriateness. *Personality and Social Psychology Review, 8*, 281–307.

Williams, E. (1977). Experimental comparisons of face-to-face and mediated communication: A review. *Psychological Bulletin, 84*, 963–976.

Wilson, J. M., Straus, S. G., & McEvily, B. (2006). All in good time: The development of trust in computer-mediated and face-to-face teams. *Organizational Behavior and Human Decision Processes, 99*, 16–33.

Wilson, R. K., & Sell, J. (1997). Liar, liar …: Cheap talk and reputation in repeated public goods settings. *Journal of Conflict Resolution, 41*, 695–717.

Zheng, J., Veinott, E., Bos, N., Olson, J. S., & Olson, G. W. (2002). Trust without touch: Jumpstarting long-distance trust with initial social activities. *Proceedings of the ACM Conference on Human Factors in Computing Systems, 4*, 141–146.

Zigurs, I., & Buckland, B. K. (1998). A theory of task/technology fit and group support systems. *MIS Quarterly, 22*, 313–334.

Zigurs, I., Reitsma, R., Lewis, C., Hubscher, R., & Hayes, C. (1999). Accessibility of computer-based simulation models in inherently conflict-laden negotiations. *Group Decision and Negotiation, 8*, 511–533.

3

On the Importance of Equality in Social Dilemmas

Eric Van Dijk, Arjaan P. Wit,
Henk A. M. Wilke, and Erik W. de Kwaadsteniet
Leiden University, The Netherlands

> I propose that the idea of equality has properties that make it a useful
> guideline or benchmark in making decisions. (Messick, 1993, p. 11)

In social dilemmas, people face a mixed-motive situation in which they
may be motivated to further their own interests but also to further the
collective interest, knowing that both interests collide (for overviews
on social dilemmas, see, e.g., Dawes, 1980; Komorita & Parks, 1995;
Kopelman, Weber, & Messick, 2002; Messick & Brewer, 1983). Many different types of social dilemmas can be distinguished (see, e.g., Messick &
Brewer, 1983). Consider, for example, the problem of maintaining collective resources. Resources such as energy, oil, and water can be regarded as
collective resources that should be consumed wisely. In such situations,
group members may face the dilemma that, despite the collective interest
to restrict consumption, it may be in their personal interest to consume
excessively. This dilemma of whether or not to restrict consumption of
scarce resources is referred to as the *resource dilemma*. Another example
refers to the provision of public goods when individuals can contribute
to provide a public good, knowing that they can benefit from the provision even if they have not contributed to its provision. This dilemma of
whether or not to contribute to the public good is referred to as the *public
good dilemma*.

THE COMPLEXITY OF SOCIAL DILEMMAS

Social dilemmas are complex. In such dilemmas like the resource or public good dilemma, group members face the complex task of deciding on how to deal with the mixed-motive context that they face. The individual group members face the dilemma of putting their own interests first or putting the collective interest first. The complexity of this decision problem is often exacerbated because opportunities for communication with other group members are limited. In small group settings, communication may to some extent be feasible and allow people to discuss the complexities of the situation at hand and to engage in the making of commitments to cooperate and mutual promise-making (see, e.g., Braver & Wilson, 1986; Caldwell, 1976; Kerr & Kaufman-Gilliland, 1994; Orbell, van de Kragt, & Dawes, 1988; van De Kragt, Orbell, & Dawes, 1983). Such within-group communication is not possible in larger scale dilemmas. To incorporate this added complexity, most experimental studies on social dilemmas investigate how people decide when they have no possibility for communication; that is, when group members decide privately and anonymously. Thus, in a typical social dilemma experiment, participants learn that their decisions will never be made public to their fellow group members. This characteristic is generally referred to as *social uncertainty*; people often have to decide in situations in which they are uncertain about what others will decide (Messick, Allison, & Samuelson, 1988).

The situation becomes even more complicated if one realizes that social dilemmas are often also characterized by environmental uncertainty (Messick et al., 1988; for an overview, see Van Dijk, Wit, Wilke, & Budescu, 2004). That is, people may often be uncertain about the characteristics of the task environment of the dilemma. For example, in resource dilemmas, group members may be uncertain as to how large the resource is from which they can harvest (e.g., Budescu, Rapoport, & Suleiman, 1990; De Kwaadsteniet, Van Dijk, Wit, & De Cremer, 2006; Gustafsson, Biel, & Gärling, 1999, 2000; Suleiman & Budescu, 1999). One may also be uncertain about the number of group members (Takigawa & Messick, 1993) or in public good dilemmas about the threshold for providing a public good (Suleiman, Budescu, & Rapoport, 2001; Wit & Wilke, 1998).

From the above it is clear that it is not an overstatement to say that social dilemmas present people with a complex decision problem. So how do people decide in these complex situations? Well, one way to approach complexity is by going for simplicity. This was, for example, acknowledged by Tversky and Kahneman (1974), who noted that in the estimation of probabilities, people use simple heuristics like availability, representativeness, and anchoring.

Related to this, Messick (1993, 1995) has pointed to the fact that in situations of interdependence, people often base their decisions on what he referred to as the *equality heuristic*.

THE SIMPLICITY OF EQUALITY

In his article "Equality as a Decision Heuristic," Messick (1993) argued that many decisions are made on the basis of simple heuristics. That is, people often use simple rules to decide, and these decisions are often highly effective. Messick argued that equality can be viewed as a decision heuristic because it satisfies (at least) three characteristics:

- Equality is simple
- Equality is effective
- Equality is fair and justifiable

Equality is simple because you often do not need much information for its application. For example, if group members need to decide how to collectively divide $100, they only need to know how many group members there are. For alternative rules, additional information is required. For instance, to allocate on the basis of need (see, e.g., Deutsch, 1975), one requires information of the individual needs of all persons involved. Thus, equality is effective because it usually generates a solution on who should do or receive what, whereas other rules may not generate such an unequivocal solution. A final advantage of equality that Messick (1993) discussed is that the use of equality is easily justifiable because it is often perceived as being in line with a general norm of fairness. Thus, when asked why they did what they did, people may find it easier to justify a decision that is based on equality. As Messick (1993) stated, "it is hard to imagine a more pervasive principle of making allocation decisions that the principle of equality" (p. 29).

Based on these considerations, Messick (1993) proposed that in decision-making on the allocation of "goods and bads," people often anchor their decisions on the equality rule, the simple, efficient, and justifiable rule. This introduction and characterization of equality as a decision heuristic has been very important for the advancement of social dilemma research. The notion that people anchor their decisions on equality and that this anchoring process may be highly effective implies that equality may be used as a basis for tacit coordination. If all members apply the same rule, they may effectively solve the social dilemma they face. This has led researchers to suggest that decision-making in social dilemmas may be understood by considering the relation between equality and tacit coordination. In this chapter, we will discuss how the insights shaped our thinking and inspired us to investigate how equality affects decision-making in social dilemmas.

EQUALITY AND TACIT COORDINATION

Although the characterization of equality as a basis for decision-making in situations of interdependence extends beyond the social dilemma, the insight is of special relevance to this domain. In particular, the notion of the effectiveness of equal division suggests that adherence to equality may be an effective means to secure the collective interest. In other words, it can be viewed as a means to solve the social dilemma. In this respect, the notion of people anchoring their decisions on the basis of an equality heuristic relates to Schelling's (1960) theorizing on tacit coordination (see also Allison, McQueen, & Schaerfl, 1992).

In his book *The Strategy of Conflict*, Thomas Schelling (1960) introduced the notion of tacit coordination by stating that many complex decisions are often tacitly solved. To illustrate this, he gave the example of two people who try to meet each other on a particular day in New York City. The two do not have a prior understanding of where and when the meeting should take place, and they cannot contact each other to solve the problem. Schelling asked his participants where they would then go to try meet the other. The findings showed that the majority of the participants stated that they would go to New York's Grand Central Station. Moreover, when asked at what time they would try to be there, the majority responded that they would go there at 12:00 noon. What this illustration shows, is that even complex problems — like trying to meet someone else in a city of millions without having an understanding on where and when to meet the other — can be solved by tacit coordination. In this process, people base their decisions on "focal points," which are choice options that are salient to all people involved. In the New York City problem, Grand Central Station and 12:00 noon apparently provided the participants with such focal points.

Although Messick's (1993) insights on the use of equality are more specific than the general insights of Schelling (1960) on tacit coordination, the connection is clear. Like Schelling, Messick suggested that complex allocation situations such as social dilemmas can be tacitly solved if people anchor their decisions on clear and unambiguous rules. And in this respect, he particularly drew attention to the use of equality. In the context of interdependence and social dilemmas, he thus identified equal division as a salient cue that could serve as a focal point for coordination. Schelling (1960) also hinted on the use of equality as a basis for tacit coordination. In this respect, he made a connection to fairness as a basis for tacit coordination when he remarked that "The moral force of fairness is greatly reinforced by the power of a 'fair' result to focus attention, if it fills the vacuum of indeterminacy that would otherwise exist" (p. 73). It is interesting to see that Schelling even illustrated his ideas with an example that closely fits with Messick's ideas on the importance of equality when he asked participants to divide $100 into two piles. Almost without exception, the participants created two piles of $50 each. Whereas in this context fairness was not an issue, as participants only had to divide the money in two piles, equality clearly served as a focal point. Both Messick and Schelling thus agree on saying that simple rules, like equality, may be instrumental in helping people solve complex decision problems.

EQUAL TO WHAT?

People may differ on many dimensions; for example, in terms of needs, inputs, or wealth. One could, of course, take all of these differences into account when deciding on what to do in a social dilemma. As Messick (1993) noted, however, information on some dimensions may be more available than information on others. People may, for example, realize that some members may have higher needs than others but simply lack the information to distinguish between members on the basis of need. In the absence of such information, the most prominent solution may be to simplify matters and adhere to the rule of equality. For a social dilemma this could mean that all members should display similar behavior: In resource dilemmas, harvests should be equal for all group members, and in public good dilemmas, contributions should be equal for all group members. Earlier studies by Allison and Messick (1990) clearly provided supportive evidence for this idea in resource dilemmas, and subsequent studies by, for example, Rutte, Wilke, and Messick (1987), provided similar support in public good dilemmas.

On some occasions, however, people may have information at their disposal that provides them with multiple possible dimensions of equality. In such situations, the question becomes to what does equality refer. Consider, for example, the dilemma of public good provision in which group members know that some of them possess more endowments than others (e.g., Rapoport, 1988; Van Dijk & Wilke, 1995, 2000). Does equality mean that all group members should contribute an equal amount? Or, if people differ in the wealth, should they all contribute an equal proportion of their endowments? Or should they perhaps contribute in such a way that they all eventually end up with equal outcomes? These questions refer to the issue of what dimension is used for equality and thus basically raise the question of "equality to what?" (Messick, 1993).

The study of such asymmetric dilemmas (i.e., dilemmas where people may differ in the endowments they possess and/or the interest they may have in maintaining or providing public goods) is not only important because such situations are more in accordance with reality, where symmetry may be more of an exception than the rule. On a more theoretical level, the study of asymmetric dilemmas raises new questions, including the question of what is equal and what is fair. On some occasions, people may have different ideas on what is fair. That is, people may have egocentric perceptions of fairness (e.g., Babcock, Loewenstein, Issacharoff, & Camerer, 1995; Messick & Sentis, 1983). To investigate this possibility, Wade-Benzoni, Tenbrunsel, and Bazerman (1996) compared behavior in a symmetric resource dilemma to behavior in an asymmetric resource dilemma. In the asymmetric dilemma, members faced multiple types of asymmetry, making it difficult (ambiguous) to determine what would be fair. For example, some members could harvest more than others but also learned that they had a low interest in the future of the resource. Others learned that they could harvest less but also that they had a high interest in the future of the resource. In agreement with the proposition that asymmetry can induce ambiguity and egocentric perceptions, the findings indicated that especially in the asymmetric dilemma, perceptions of fairness were shaped by self-interest.

Note, however, that by itself asymmetry does not necessarily have to lead to ambiguity. In the Wade-Benzoni et al. (1996) study, participants faced a situation where several asymmetries were compounded. This combination apparently led to a situation where participants disagreed on what would be fair. On other occasions — for example, when they only face one type of asymmetry — people may agree on what should be the basis of fairness. In several studies (Van Dijk & Wilke, 1995, 2000; Wit, Wilke, & Oppewal, 1992) we presented participants with asymmetric public good dilemmas, in which some members possessed more endowments than others (i.e., asymmetry of endowments). In such dilemmas, group members strive to contribute an equal share of their endowments. That is, group members tend to anchor their contributions to the public good on the rule that prescribes that group members should contribute an equal proportion of their endowments to the public good. To further illustrate this, consider the situation in which members of a four-person group (a) know that two of the members each possess $100 and that the two other members each possess $50, and (b) know that they can provide an attractive public good if the group succeeds in contributing $120. In such a situation, the typical finding is not that group members decide to each contribute $30 (which would be an equal share of the provision point). Rather, they contribute equal proportions so that the "rich" members each contribute $40, and the "poor" members each contribute $20 (i.e., all members contribute 40% of their endowments)

We also investigated how such asymmetries work out in resource dilemmas. For example, in our studies (Van Dijk & Wilke, 1995, 2000) we investigated how people decide when facing a resource dilemma in which group members have unequal access to a common resource (cf. Samuelson & Messick, 1986). Note that asymmetry of access may be considered as the resource dilemma counterpart of asymmetry of endowments in the public good dilemma. Whereas asymmetric endowments in a public good dilemma means that some members can contribute more to the public good than others, asymmetric access in a resource dilemma means that some members can harvest more than others. This conceptual resemblance, however, did not lead to similar findings. That is, in contrast to the results we obtained in asymmetric public good dilemmas, we did not find that people harvested equal proportions. Rather, members harvested equally in absolute terms from the common resource.

Taken together, these findings indicate that different dimensions may be more important in public good dilemmas than in resource dilemmas. In subsequent studies (Van Dijk & Wilke, 2000) we shed light on the underlying process that explains this difference. Group members were more concerned with how the final outcomes would eventually be distributed over all group members in resource dilemmas than in public good dilemmas. The most comprehensive account that we provided for this focus on the final outcomes dimension was that public good dilemmas and resource dilemmas differ with regard to the relation between the final outcomes of group members and the decision that group members have to make. This relation is more direct in the resource dilemma than in the public good dilemma. In the resource dilemma, people decide how much they harvest and these harvests directly determine their final outcomes. Such a direct relation is not present in the public good dilemma. In such dilemmas, people typically decide how much to contribute, but the final outcomes they eventually obtain consist of the number of endowments they keep to themselves (i.e., do not contribute) plus their share of the public good. What this means is that in the public good dilemma the decision people make (i.e., how much endowments they contribute) is only indirectly related to the distribution of final outcomes. We realize that with some additional arithmetic, people facing a public good dilemma can calculate the number of endowments they keep to themselves by subtracting their contribution from the initial endowments they possessed. The point to acknowledge, however, is that this calculation does require an additional step and that the situation does not stimulate people to make this additional calculation. As a result, the final outcomes may not surface as a salient dimension to which people apply equality.

Several conclusions can be drawn on the basis of the above findings. The first is that they underscore Messick's argument that group members anchor their decisions on equality. The second conclusion is that different dilemmas may evoke different notions as to what constitutes equality. Moreover, these differences are the result of a differential salience of the dimensions that are used for equality. As such, the findings underscore the importance of posing the "equality to what" question. Applying equality does not necessarily mean that people simply allocate equally whatever you ask them to allocate (but see Harris & Joyce, 1980; Messick & Schell, 1992) or that they do not consider the consequences of their decisions. In this respect, equality may be more than a simple heuristic (see also Van Dijk & Wilke, 1996). Nevertheless, the basic premise stands: people anchor their decisions on equality.

EQUALITY AND UNCERTAINTY

We started out by stressing the complexities of social dilemmas and by pointing out that social and environmental uncertainty contribute to this complexity. So how does equality relate to social and environmental uncertainty? Again, posing the question may be simpler than answering it. On the one hand, one could argue that social uncertainty may enhance the attractiveness of equality. In situations where people cannot communicate to each other and decisions are made privately, people may realize that tacit coordination can only be achieved by applying an unambiguous rule. Environmental information (e.g., on the size of the group and the resource) may be used as focal points to provide such an unambiguous rule. Environmental uncertainty may therefore also affect how people deal with social uncertainty (see also Van Dijk et al., 2004, on the interplay between social and environmental uncertainty).

A first thing that environmental uncertainty may do is that it may affect the answer to the "equality to what" question. That is, environmental uncertainty may affect which dimension people take as a basis for tacit coordination. We demonstrated this in a study in which we introduced asymmetries that we also used in Van Dijk and Wilke (1995) and we investigated how people tacitly coordinated their decisions in public good dilemmas and resource dilemmas. As we noted above, the findings of Van Dijk and Wilke (1995) indicated that when in a public good dilemma, endowments are distributed asymmetrically, such that some members possess more endowments than others, people contribute equal proportions. Thus, people with twice as many endowments as others also contribute twice as much. With asymmetry of access in the resource dilemma, people tend to discard the fact that some members can harvest more than others. Regardless of access, people harvest equally from the common resource. In Van Dijk, Wilke, Wilke, and Metman (1999), we took these observations as the starting point of our research.

We first of all concluded from the findings of Van Dijk and Wilke (1995) that participants apparently use different information for tacit coordination in the public good dilemma than in the resource dilemma. For example, the dimension of (asymmetric) endowments was used for tacit coordination in the public good dilemma, but the dimension of (asymmetric) access was apparently not used as a dimension in the resource dilemma. Based on this analysis, we expected that uncertainty about the access of each group member would not affect tacit coordination in the resource dilemma. In the public good dilemma, we did expect that uncertainty about the endowments positions of other group members would affect tacit coordination.

Our results corroborated these hypotheses. In the resource dilemma, participants harvested equally, regardless of whether they were uncertain about the access that their fellow group members had. In the public good dilemma, participants harvested equal proportions when they were certain about each other's endowments position (cf. Van Dijk & Wilke, 1995). But this changed when participants were uncertain about the endowments that their fellow group members possessed. In this case, we did not observe that participants contributed in proportion to the endowments they possessed (such that members with more endowments contributed more than members with few endowments). Rather, group members contributed equally, regardless of the endowments they possessed, such that each group member contributed one fourth of the threshold for provision. Environmental uncertainty about the endowments that each group member possessed thus led to a shift in the equality dimension. In the case of certainty about the endowments positions, participants applied equality to the endowments dimension by adhering to the rule that each member should contribute an equal proportion of the endowments that he or she possessed. In the case of uncertainty about the endowment positions, people appeared to strive for "absolute equality," prescribing that — irrespective of endowments one possessed — each member should make an equal contribution.

In more general terms, the studies by Van Dijk et al. (1999) indicated that people are more likely to tacitly coordinate their choice behavior on the basis of certain information than on uncertain information. As a result of this, environmental uncertainty may lead to a shift in dimensions to which equality is applied. And when information about, for example, endowment positions becomes uncertain, people may rely on a more basic rule that does not require this uncertain information. As Messick already argued, equal division when defined in absolute terms may be considered as the most basic rule that only requires minimal information. For example, to distribute money over group members, you only need to know (a) how much money there is and (b) how many group members there are. You do not need additional information about their individual needs, their inputs, or anything else. But what if even the most basic application of the equality rule becomes difficult or impossible to implement?

WHAT IF EQUALITY CANNOT BE APPLIED?

In some circumstances, even the most basic and simple version of the equality rule may not apply. Consider, for example, a public good dilemma with an uncertain number of group members. Or a resource dilemma in which the size of the resource is uncertain. How should one in such situations apply even the most basic version of the equal division rule? In the case of resource size uncertainty in a resource dilemma, one could, of course, first make a personal estimate of how large the resource might be and then use this estimate to calculate what would be an equal share. Note, however, that even if one were to do this, it remains unclear what the result of the calculation would be. Would one expect others to come up with the same estimate and thus with a similar idea on what an equal share would be? In terms of Messick, one could argue that such an application of equality may not be effective in solving the social dilemma at hand. The concept of tacit coordination — that underlies the importance of equality as an effective decision heuristic — is based on the assumption that people will expect that others in their group will make the same inferences and calculations as they do. Environmental uncertainty, however, may undermine this process if it undermines people's expectations that others will come up with the same inferences that they do.

If so, one could expect that environmental uncertainty may lower the effectiveness of decision-making in social dilemmas. Indeed, previous research in resource dilemmas has shown that resource size uncertainty may lead to overharvesting (e.g., Budescu et al., 1990; Gustafsson et al., 1999). In subsequent studies, however, we took a slightly different approach. In De Kwaadsteniet, Van Dijk, Wit, and De Cremer (2006), we did reason that environmental uncertainty may disturb the tacit coordination process, but we did not predict that it would inevitably lead to an increase of self-interested behavior. Rather, we predicted that people would be more likely to rely on their personal dispositions to cooperate or not.

Our reasoning was based on the theoretical insights of Snyder and Ickes (1985; see also Van Lange, De Cremer, Van Dijk, & Van Vugt, 2007). When discussing the relation between personality and social behavior, Snyder and Ickes argued that situations may differ in the extent to which they provide salient cues for people to base their decisions on. In this context, they differentiated between "weak" and "strong" situations and stated that "'strong' situations tend to be those that provide salient cues to guide behavior ... 'weak' situations tend to be those that do not offer salient cues to guide behavior" (p. 901). Based on these insights, one could characterize a situation of environmental uncertainty in which even the most basic rule of equality cannot be applied as a weak situation. So how do people decide when facing such a weak situation? Snyder and Ickes (1985) answered this question by suggesting that "measures of traits and dispositions should typically predict behavior better in weak situations than in strong situations" (p. 904).

In De Kwaadsteniet et al. (2006), we tested these ideas by turning to what may be considered as the most basic and important personality characteristic in social dilemma research: social value orientation. With this approach, our studies were once again connected to Messick's work, most notable to the work of Messick and McClintock (1968), who showed that people can be differentiated on the basis of their social motivations, also referred to as *social value orientations* (see also Van Lange et al., 2007). The most common social value orientations are individualists, competitors, and prosocials. Individualists primarily want to increase their own outcomes. Competitors strive to increase the difference between their own and others' outcomes. Prosocials strive for equality of their own and others' outcomes and aim to maximize the collective outcomes.

In De Kwaadsteniet et al. (2006), we assessed the participants' social value orientations and distinguished between proselfs (i.e., participants who were either individualists or competitors) and prosocials. After this, we presented our participants with a one-trial resource dilemma in which participants were either certain or uncertain how much they could harvest without jeopardizing the collective interest. The results showed that when participants were facing environmental certainty, they strongly anchored their decisions on the equal division rule, irrespective of their social value orientations. With this finding we thus replicated earlier findings on the use of the equal division rule in resource dilemmas. When the participants faced environmental uncertainty, however, we observed a different pattern. Under these circumstances we indeed found that participants did not use equality as a basis for their decisions. Instead, they relied on their social value orientations: Only those individuals who were disposed to put their own interests first (i.e., proselfs) tended to harvest excessively in a situation of environmental uncertainty. Prosocials responded with restricting their harvests (for related findings, see also S. G. Roch & Samuelson, 1997).

It thus seems that environmental uncertainty may indeed undermine tacit coordination but this does not necessarily mean that it results in general overharvesting. It seems more accurate to say that if environmental characteristics (such as environmental uncertainty) preclude efficient tacit coordination on the basis of equal division, people base their decisions on their personal dispositions. When we relate these statements to the notions of tacit coordination (Schelling, 1960) and the importance of equality (Messick, 1995), one could argue that to use equality as a basis for tacit coordination, one needs a strong situation.

SO WHY DO PEOPLE USE EQUALITY?

Even though environmental characteristics may reduce the use of equality, the conclusion remains that in many (strong) situations people do use equality as a basis for tacit coordination. This raises the question of what we should conclude if we see people adhering to equality. Traditionally, the main response in social dilemma research has been that if people adhere to equality, they do this because they value equality and fairness (for reviews on the importance of fairness and norms in social dilemmas, see, e.g., Kerr, 1995; Schroeder, Steel, Woodell, & Bembeneck, 2003). Messick's insights on equality as a decision heuristic and Schelling's theorizing on tacit coordination are in this respect important because they offer another explanation for the use of equality: People may rely on norms of fairness for instrumental reasons and because it helps them to tacitly coordinate.

Combined with Messick's insights on social value orientations (e.g., Messick & McClintock, 1968), this raises the question of whether different people may adhere to equality for the same or for different reasons. Whereas prosocials are known to value equality as a goal, proselfs are not characterized by such a preference for equality. So what does it mean if proselfs and prosocials (tacitly) agree on using equality as a basis for their decisions? It seems likely that whereas equality may be a goal in itself for prosocials, this is probably not the main reason for proselfs to adhere to equality. For proselfs, equality may be a means to coordinate rather than a goal in itself. Thus, proselfs may anchor their decisions on equality merely because it helps them to solve the dilemma they face and because it helps them to secure their own interests.

It is difficult to disentangle these motives and thus to differentiate between what one could call *true fairness* and *instrumental fairness* (see also Van Dijk & De Cremer, 2006). Of course, one could ask people why they adhere to equality, but such an approach may not do the job, especially in situations in which both motives align. Stouten, De Cremer, and Van Dijk (2005) took a different approach to this issue. Rather than asking participants for possible reasons underlying the use of equality, they studied how people react when they find out that others did not adhere to the equality rule. For this purpose, Stouten et al. (2005) presented their participants with a public good dilemma in which all members possessed an equal number of endowments. As in the previous dilemmas we discussed, the total contributions should surpass a certain threshold for the public good to become available. Not surprisingly, the majority of the group members adhered to the equal division rule. The interesting part was that after this dilemma, participants were informed that their group had not contributed enough. They learned that the total contributions fell short to reach the threshold needed for provision because one member had contributed less than an equal share. Of course, irrespective of what one's own main motive would have been to adhere to equality — true fairness or instrumental fairness — people may be expected to react negatively to such feedback and to become angry. If one values equality as a goal in itself, one may be angry because a norm has been violated. If one values equality for instrumental reasons, one may be angry because the own outcomes have been reduced. To distinguish between these two motives, Stouten et al. (2005) then provided half of their participants with additional feedback. These participants were informed that even though the contributions fell short, the public good would be provided after all. Thus, for these participants the initial failure in providing the public good turned out to be a success after all. For the other half of the participants the feedback that the public good was not provided remained unchanged.

Stouten et al. (2005) investigated the subsequent emotional reactions of proselfs and prosocials. Their findings fit with the view that proselfs may value equality for different (i.e., more instrumental) reasons than prosocials. More specifically, the results showed that prosocials were not affected by whether or not the public good was provided after all. Irrespective of this subsequent feedback, they were angry and unhappy. This fits with the notion that for them equality is a norm that one should adhere to. The fact that afterwards the public good may be provided after all does not turn something that is "wrong" into a good thing. The emotional reactions of proselfs, however, were affected by the subsequent feedback. They were only angry and unhappy when the initial feedback was unchanged and thus when the public good was not provided. When learning that the public good would be provided after all, they were happy and not angry anymore. This fits with the notion that proselfs primarily rely on equality for instrumental reasons; i.e., to provide the public good. For them, a violation of equality is not necessarily wrong in a moral sense, and if the public good can be provided after all, this allows them to reason that "all is well that ends well."

Whereas social dilemma research has not paid much attention to emotional reactions, the findings of Stouten et al. (2005) showed how a study of emotional reactions may provide new insights regarding the importance of equality. More recently, De Kwaadsteniet, Van Dijk, Wit, and De Cremer (2008) also showed the benefits of studying emotions in their study on environmental uncertainty. As we noted earlier, environmental uncertainty may reduce adherence to equality if the environmental uncertainty makes it difficult to determine what would be an equal share. De Kwaadsteniet et al. (2008) used this idea to study emotional and retributive reactions after collective overuse in a resource dilemma. In one of their experiments, they presented participants with bogus feedback that the collective resource had supposedly been overused and that one of their fellow group members had supposedly taken more from the collective resource than the others had. This either happened in a situation of environmental certainty or uncertainty. In the case of environmental certainty, the size of the common resource had been known to the five group members (i.e., 500 units). In the case of environmental uncertainty, the exact size of the resource had been unknown to the five group members (i.e., they only knew the upper and lower limits of the resource; i.e., the size would be somewhere between 100 and 900 units). The findings indicated that the emotional reactions toward the member who harvested more than the others were strongly affected by the context in which this behavior occurred. Participants were angrier at this member when the group had faced environmental certainty than when they had faced environmental uncertainty. Moreover, participants were more willing to punish this group member under environmental certainty than under environmental uncertainty. Subsequent mediation analyses revealed that these differences resulted from a difference in causal attributions. That is, the overuse was attributed more strongly to the situation (external attribution) in the case of environmental uncertainty than in the case of environmental certainty. Put differently, whereas the individual group member was strongly blamed for harming the collective by violating equality in a situation of certainty, the group member was judged less harshly in a situation of environmental uncertainty (see also Rutte, Wilke, & Messick, 1987).

EQUALITY AND JUSTIFIABILITY

Messick (1995) suggested that the prevalence of equality may be due to its simplicity, effectiveness, and justifiability. As our selective overview has indicated, the notions of simplicity and effectiveness have — directly or indirectly — been addressed in several social dilemma studies. Little attention has been paid to the justifiability of equality. Recently, however, we investigated what happens when people think they have to justify their decision to their fellow group members. In De Kwaadsteniet, Van Dijk, Wit, De Cremer, and De Rooij (2007), we assessed the effect in a five-person resource dilemma situation with either environmental certainty (i.e., certainty about the resource size, 500 units) or environmental uncertainty (i.e., uncertainty about the resource size, 100–900 units). If equality can indeed be used to justify one's decisions, one would expect that the use of equality would be increased in situations in which one would be held accountable for one's decisions (Lerner & Tetlock, 1999; Tetlock, 1992). This is indeed what we observed when participants faced environmental certainty: Participants who thought that they would be held accountable more strongly adhered to equality and the variance in the participants' decisions was reduced such that more participants harvested exactly one fifth of the common resource (i.e., 500 units). We did not observe such a general convergence toward a specific level of harvests in the case of environmental uncertainty. There we saw a more complex picture emerging. When asked how large they thought the resource was, we did observe that participants who thought that they would be held accountable were more likely to report a resource size that was about five times as high as their own harvest (implying that they tried to harvest an equal share of their own estimate of the uncertain resource size). However, this did not result in a lower variance or a general convergence to a specific level of harvests such as we observed in the case of environmental certainty. Apparently, when the resource size is uncertain, equality may be used to justify one's decision, without resulting in (efficient) tacit coordination. This study not only illustrates the advantage of Messick's theorizing to treat justifiability as a separate reason for using equality and distinctively different from effectiveness. It also shows that the use of equality should not be narrowed down to considering only its potential to ensure or facilitate tacit coordination. In situations that do allow for communication and in which decisions do not remain anonymous, justification may contribute to the popularity of using equality.

THE PREREQUISITES FOR TACIT COORDINATION ON EQUALITY: HAVING A COMMON UNDERSTANDING

So far, our overview has shown that in situations that do not allow for communication with others, the potential for tacit coordination may be one of the main reasons for using equality. In this respect, it is worth taking a closer look at what it takes to tacitly coordinate on the basis of equality. The main prerequisite for tacit coordination appears to be that people should have the feeling that they and the other persons involved have a common understanding of the situation they are facing. For tacit coordination, people need to "read the same message in the common situation, to identify the one course of action" (Schelling, 1960, p. 54). The importance of a common understanding is central in research on socially shared cognition (e.g., Thompson & Fine, 1999; Tindale, Meisenhelder, Dykema-Engblade, & Hogg, 2004). Socially shared cognition incorporates many related concepts like shared mental models (Cannon-Bowers, Salas, & Converse, 1993), team mental models (Klimoski & Mohammed, 1994), and transactive memory systems (Wegner, 1987). These concepts all tend to ascribe a positive value to shared cognition. The sharing of knowledge or perceptions may, for example, enhance group productivity and increase the quality of group decisions (see Cannon-Bowers & Salas, 2001). Research on shared cognition has mainly investigated social interaction and task and teamwork and as such has paid little attention to tacit coordination. So how would a common understanding operate in social dilemma situations that do not allow for communication?

Whereas the studies on environmental uncertainty shed some light on this issue, the picture they provide is far from complete. For example, on the basis of these studies one might be tempted to conclude that if an individual faces environmental certainty (e.g., if he or she knows how large the resource is and how many group members there are), equality will do the job. However, because tacit coordination hinges on the feeling of a common understanding, certainty may not be enough to ensure tacit coordination. If you do not expect the group members to share a common understanding, you may refrain from basing your decisions on equality, even if you have all the information you need to determine what would be an equal share. We demonstrated this in a series of studies in which we investigated several factors that may affect the feeling of a common understanding (Van Dijk, De Kwaadsteniet, & De Cremer, 2009).

In a first experiment, we presented participants with a resource dilemma in which the group could obtain a bonus if they succeeded in restricting their harvests (cf. Van Dijk & Wilke, 1995). Participants faced a resource dilemma in which four group members could harvest from a common resource of 400 units. If the group would succeed in restricting their collective harvests to 220 units, the group members would obtain a bonus of 300 units that would be divided equally among the four members. Participants thus faced a situation of environmental certainty. In agreement with the notion that people anchor their decisions on equality, participants predominantly harvested an equal share (i.e., 55 units). Subsequently, however, we provided them with feedback about the alleged outcome. We either informed them that the group had harvested too much (failure feedback) or that the group had succeeded in sufficiently restricting their harvests (success feedback). After this, participants were presented with a second trial in which they faced the same dilemma. We used this manipulation to investigate whether the tacit coordination process would be affected by such feedback. Would participants again base their decisions on equality in the second trial? We expected this to be the case when they received success feedback. After all, success feedback would signal that coordination was successful and that the group members shared a common understanding of the dilemma situation. However, after failure feedback we did not expect such anchoring on equality because we reasoned that failure feedback would essentially signal that apparently the group lacked a common understanding of the situation (otherwise they would have succeeded). In terms of Snyder and Ickes (1985), we thus expected that failure feedback would turn a strong situation into a weak situation. In agreement with their notion that people are then more likely to base their decisions on personal characteristics, we indeed observed that social value orientations did affect decisions after failure feedback but not after success feedback. After failure feedback, prosocials harvested less than proselfs.

Whereas this first experiment supported our idea that failure feedback may undermine the feeling of a common understanding, even in situations of environmental certainty, we provided a more direct test of the importance of a common understanding in a second experiment (Van Dijk et al., 2009, Experiment 2). In a similar resource dilemma, we now manipulated the information participants thought to be available to their fellow group members. Whereas all participants learned that the group would obtain the bonus if the group succeeded in harvesting 220 units, we told half of the participants that their fellow group members were not informed about the exact threshold. Note that this would not affect the possibility for the participants themselves to determine what would be an equal share of the threshold (i.e., 55 chips). However, even though it would be possible to determine this, we did not expect them to use this as a benchmark for their decision. Because in this situation participants would have no reason to expect a common understanding on what to decide, we instead expected them to base their harvesting decisions on their social value orientations. Our results confirmed our predictions, thereby suggesting that when people do not feel that their group has a common understanding of the situation, the social dilemma turns into a weak situation.

CONCLUDING REMARKS

In this chapter, we discussed the importance of equality and focused on how Messick's ideas on equality contributed to our thinking on tacit coordination social dilemmas. Our initial studies on this topic were focused on identifying which dimensions people use as a basis for tacit coordination. These studies showed that people indeed often base their decisions on equality (whether on different dimensions in the resource dilemma than in the public good dilemma). In our subsequent studies, we also investigated when people deviate from equality. In this line of research we showed that when equality loses it coordinating potential — e.g., due to environmental uncertainty or lack of a common understanding — people are more likely to base their decisions on their own social value orientations. These studies thus show the boundary conditions of both equality and social value orientations. When tacit coordination on equality is out, social value orientations are in. And when tacit coordination on equality is in, social values are out. All these elements are in fact part of Messick's theorizing, which brought equality (Messick, 1993, 1995), environmental uncertainty (Messick et al., 1988), and social value orientations (Messick & McClintock, 1968) to the attention of social dilemma researchers. In a way, one could thus even argue that the question of when people use equality as a benchmark for their decisions and when they use their social value orientations boils down to the question of "when which idea of Messick applies."

REFERENCES

Allison, S. T., McQueen, L. R., & Schaerfl, L. M. (1992). Social decision making processes and the equal partitionment of shared resources. *Journal of Experimental Social Psychology, 28*, 23–42.

Allison, S. T., & Messick, D. M. (1990). Social decision heuristics in the use of shared resources. *Journal of Behavioral Decision Making, 3*, 195–204.

Babcock, L., Loewenstein, G., Issacharoff, S., & Camerer, C. (1995). Biased judgments of fairness in bargaining. *American Economic Review, 85*, 1337–1343.

Braver, S. L., & Wilson, L. A. (1986). Effects of communication within subgroups. *Journal of Conflict Resolution, 30*, 51–62.

Budescu, D. V., Rapoport, A., & Suleiman, R. (1990). Resource dilemmas with environmental uncertainty and asymmetric players. *European Journal of Social Psychology, 20*, 475–487.

Caldwell, M. (1976). Communication and sex effects in a five-person prisoner's dilemma game. *Journal of Personality and Social Psychology, 33*, 273–280.

Cannon-Bowers, J. A., & Salas, E. (2001). Reflections on shared cognition. *Journal of Organizational Behavior, 22*, 195–202.

Cannon-Bowers, J. A., Salas, E., & Converse, S. (1993). Shared mental models in expert team decision making. In N. J. Castellan (Ed.), *Individual and group decision making* (pp. 221–246). Hillsdale, NJ: Lawrence Erlbaum.

Dawes, R. M. (1980). Social dilemmas. *Annual Review of Psychology, 31*, 169–193.

De Kwaadsteniet, E. W., Van Dijk, E., Wit, A., & De Cremer, D. (2006). Social dilemmas as strong versus weak situations: Social value orientations and tacit coordination under resource uncertainty. *Journal of Experimental Social Psychology, 42*, 509–516.

De Kwaadsteniet, E. W., Van Dijk, E., Wit, A. P., & De Cremer, D. (2008). Emotional and retributive reactions after overuse in social dilemmas: The role of causal attributions under resource size uncertainty. Unpublished manuscript.

De Kwaadsteniet, E. W., Van Dijk, E., Wit, A., De Cremer, D., & De Rooij, M. (2007). Justifying decisions in social dilemmas: Justification pressures and tacit coordination under environmental uncertainty. *Personality and Social Psychology Bulletin, 33*, 1648–1660.

Deutsch, M. (1975). Equity, equality, and need: What determines which value will be used as the basis for distributive justice? *Journal of Social Issues, 31*, 137–150.

Gustafsson, M., Biel, A., & Gärling, T. (1999). Over-harvesting of resources of unknown size. *Acta Psychologica, 103*, 47–64.

Gustafsson, M., Biel, A., & Gärling, T. (2000). Egoism bias in social dilemmas with resource size uncertainty. *Group Processes and Intergroup Relations, 4*, 351–365.

Harris, R. J., & Joyce, M. A. (1980). What's fair? It depends on how you phrase the question. *Journal of Personality and Social Psychology, 38*, 165–179.

Kerr, N. L. (1995). Norms in social dilemmas. In D. Schroeder (Ed.), *Social dilemmas: Social psychological perspectives* (pp. 31–47). New York: Pergamon.

Kerr, N. L., & Kaufman-Gilliland, C. M. (1994). Communication, commitments, and cooperation in social dilemmas. *Journal of Personality and Social Psychology, 66*, 513–529.

Klimoski, R., & Mohammed, S. (1994). Team mental model: Construct or metaphor? *Journal of Management, 20*, 403–437.

Komorita, S. S., & Parks, C. D. (1995). Interpersonal relations: Mixed-motive interaction. *Annual Review of Psychology, 46*, 183–207.

Kopelman, S., Weber, J. M., & Messick, D. M. (2002). Factors influencing cooperation in commons dilemmas: A review of experimental psychological research. In E. Ostrom, T. Dietz, N. Dolšak, P. Stern, S. Stonich, & E. U. Weber (Eds.), *The drama of the commons* (pp. 113–156). Washington, DC: National Academy Press.

Lerner, J. S., & Tetlock, P. E. (1999). Accounting for the effects of accountability. *Psychological Bulletin, 125*, 255–275.

Messick, D. M. (1993). Equality as a decision heuristic. In B. A. Mellers & J. Baron (Eds.), *Psychological perspectives on justice* (pp. 11–31). New York: Cambridge University Press.

Messick, D. M. (1995). Equality, fairness, and social conflict. *Social Justice Research, 8*, 153–173.

Messick, D. M., Allison, S. T., & Samuelson, C. D. (1988). Framing and communication effects on group members' responses to environmental and social uncertainty. In S. Maital (Ed.), *Applied behavioral economics 2* (pp. 677–700). Brighton, UK: Wheatsheaf.

Messick, D. M., & Brewer, M. B. (1983). Solving social dilemmas. In L. Wheeler & P. R. Shaver (Eds.), *Review of personality and social psychology* (Vol. 4, pp. 11–44). Beverly Hills, CA: Sage.

Messick, D. M., & McClintock, C. G. (1968). Motivational basis of choice in experimental games. *Journal of Experimental Social Psychology, 4,* 1–25.

Messick, D. M., & Schell, T. C. (1992). Evidence for an equality heuristic in social decision making. *Acta Psychologica, 80,* 311–323.

Messick, D. M., & Sentis, K. P. (1983). Fairness, preference, and fairness biases. In D. M. Messick & K. S. Cook (Eds.), *Equity theory: Psychological and sociological perspectives* (pp. 61–94). New York: Praeger.

Orbell, J. M., van de Kragt, A. J. C., & Dawes, R. M. (1988). Explaining discussion-induced cooperation. *Journal of Personality and Social Psychology, 54,* 811–819.

Rapoport, A. (1988). Provision of step-level goods: Effects of inequality in resources. *Journal of Personality and Social Psychology, 54,* 432–440.

Roch, S. G., & Samuelson, C. D. (1997). Effects of environmental uncertainty and social value orientations in resource dilemmas. *Organizational Behavior and Human Decision Processes, 70,* 221–235.

Rutte, C. G., Wilke, H. A. M., & Messick, D. M. (1987). Scarcity or abundance caused by people or the environment as determinants of behavior in a resource dilemma. *Journal of Experimental Social Psychology, 23,* 209–216.

Samuelson, C. D., & Messick, D. M. (1986). Inequities in access to and use of shared resources in social dilemmas. *Journal of Personality and Social Psychology, 51,* 960–967.

Schelling, T. C. (1960). *The strategy of conflict.* Oxford, UK: Harvard University Press.

Schroeder, D. A., Steel, J. E., Woodell, A. J., & Bembeneck, A. F. (2003). Justice within social dilemmas. *Personality and Social Psychology Review, 7,* 374–387.

Snyder, M., & Ickes, W. (1985). Personality and social behavior. In G. Lindzey & E. Aronson (Eds.), *Handbook of social psychology: Vol. 2. Special fields and applications* (pp. 883–947). New York: Lawrence Erlbaum.

Stouten, J., De Cremer, D., & Van Dijk, E. (2005). All is well that ends well, at least for pro-selfs: Emotional reactions to equality violation as a function of social value orientation. *European Journal and Social Psychology, 35,* 767–783.

Suleiman, R., & Budescu, D. V. (1999). Common pool resource dilemmas with incomplete information. In D. V. Budescu, I. Erev, & R. Zwick (Eds.), *Games and human behavior* (pp. 387–410). Hillsdale, NJ: Erlbaum.

Suleiman, R., Budescu, D. V., & Rapoport, A. (2001). Provision of step-level public goods with uncertain provision threshold and continuous contribution. *Group Decision and Negotiations, 10,* 253–274.

Takigawa, T., & Messick, D. M. (1993). Group size uncertainty in shared resource use. *Japanese Psychological Research, 35,* 193–203.

Tetlock, P. E. (1992). The impact of accountability on judgment and choice: Toward a social contingency model. In M. O. Zanna (Ed.), *Advances in experimental social psychology* (Vol. 25, pp. 331–376). San Diego, CA: Academic Press.

Thompson, L., & Fine, G. A. (1999). Socially shared cognition, affect, and behavior: A review and integration. *Personality and Social Psychology Review, 3,* 278–302.

Tindale, R. S., Meisenhelder, H. M., Dykema-Englblade, A. A., & Hogg, M. A. (2004). Shared cognition in small groups. In M. B. Brewer & M. Hewstone (Eds.), *Social cognition* (pp. 268–297). Malden, MA: Blackwell.

Tversky, A., & Kahneman, D. (1974). Judgement under uncertainty: Heuristics and biases. *Science, 185*, 1124–1130.

van de Kragt, A. J. C., Orbell, J. M., & Dawes, R. M. (1983). The minimal contributing set as a solution to public goods problems. *American Political Science Review, 77*, 112–122.

Van Dijk, E., & De Cremer, D. (2006). Tacit coordination and social dilemmas: On the importance of self-interest and fairness. In D. De Cremer, M. Zeelenberg, & J. K. Murnighan (Eds.), *Social psychology and economics* (pp. 141–154). Mahwah, NJ: Lawrence Erlbaum.

Van Dijk, E., De Kwaadsteniet, E. W., & De Cremer, D. (2009). Tacit coordination in social dilemmas: The importance of having a common understanding. *Journal of Personality and Social Psychology, 96*, 665–678.

Van Dijk, E., & Wilke, H. (1993). Differential interests, equity, and public good provision. *Journal of Experimental Social Psychology, 29*, 1–16.

Van Dijk, E., & Wilke, H. (1995). Coordination rules in asymmetric social dilemmas: A comparison between public good dilemmas and resource dilemmas. *Journal of Experimental Social Psychology, 31*, 1–27.

Van Dijk, E., & Wilke, H. (1996). Tacit coordination and fairness judgments in social dilemmas. In W. B. G. Liebrand & D. M. Messick (Eds.), *Frontiers in social dilemmas research* (pp. 117–134). Berlin: Springer Verlag.

Van Dijk, E., & Wilke, H. (2000). Decision-induced focusing in social dilemmas: Give-some, keep-some, take-some and leave-some dilemmas. *Journal of Personality and Social Psychology, 78*, 92–104.

Van Dijk, E., Wilke, H., Wilke, M., & Metman, L. (1999). What information do we use in social dilemmas? Uncertainty and the employment of coordination rules. *Journal of Experimental Social Psychology, 35*, 109–135.

Van Dijk, E., Wit, A., Wilke, H., & Budescu, D. V. (2004). What we know (and do not know) about the effects of uncertainty on behavior in social dilemmas. In R. Suleiman, D. V. Budescu, I. Fischer, & D. M. Messick (Eds.), *Contemporary psychological research on social dilemmas* (pp. 315–331). New York: Cambridge University Press.

Van Lange, P. A. M., De Cremer, D., Van Dijk, E., & Van Vugt, M. (2007). Self-interest and beyond: Basic principles of social interaction. In A. W. Kruglanski & E. T. Higgins (Eds.), *Social psychology: Handbook of basic principles* (2nd ed., pp. 540–561). New York: Guilford.

Wade-Benzoni, K. A., Tenbrunsel, A. E., & Bazerman, M. H. (1996). Egocentric perceptions of fairness in asymmetric, environmental social dilemmas: Explaining harvesting behavior and the role of communication. *Organizational Behavior and Human Decision Processes, 67*, 111–126.

Wegner, D. M. (1987). Transactive memory: A contemporary analysis of the group mind. In B. Mullen & G. R. Goethals (Eds.), *Theories of group behavior* (pp. 185–208). New York: Springer Verlag.

Wit, A. P., & Wilke, H. A. M. (1998). Public good provision under environmental and social uncertainty. *European Journal of Social Psychology, 28*, 249–256.

Wit, A. P., Wilke, H. A. M., & Oppewal, H. (1992). Fairness in asymmetric social dilemmas. In W. Liebrand, D. Messick, & H. Wilke (Eds.), *Social dilemmas: Theoretical issues and research findings* (pp. 183–197). New York: Pergamon.

4

Social and Temporal Orientations in Social Dilemmas

Paul A. M. Van Lange
Vrije Universiteit, Amsterdam, The Netherlands

Jeff A. Joireman
Washington State University

The health and vitality of relationships, groups, and society at large are strongly challenged by social dilemmas, or conflicts between short-term self-interest and long-term collective interest. Pollution, depletion of natural resources, and intergroup conflict can be characterized as examples of urgent social dilemmas. This chapter advances a conceptual framework in which we analyze social dilemmas in terms of social and temporal concerns relevant to the social (individual vs. collective) and temporal (short-term vs. long-term) conflicts underlying social dilemmas. We discuss the plasticity of social orientations (altruism, cooperation, egalitarianism, individualism, competition, aggression) and temporal orientations (short-term orientation, future orientation) within the context of Messick and colleagues' recent appropriateness framework (Weber, Kopelman, & Messick, 2004).

Conflicts between immediate self-interest and longer term collective interests are so pervasive in everyday life that one can go so far as to claim that the most challenging task that governments, organizations, and even partners in a relationship face is to successfully manage conflicts between self-interest and collective interest. In the social and behavioral sciences, these "challenging tasks" are often studied within the rich literature of *social dilemmas*, broadly defined as situations in which short-term individual and long-term collective interests are at odds (Dawes & Messick, 2000; Komorita & Parks, 1995; Messick & Brewer, 1983). Given their pervasive nature, it is important to understand factors that influence cooperation in social dilemmas. To that end, we advance a conceptual framework in which we analyze social dilemmas in terms of several social and temporal orientations relevant to decision-making in social dilemmas, including altruism, cooperation, egalitarianism, individualism, competition, and aggression, as well as present and future time orientations.

Readers familiar with his work will no doubt recognize that interest in these orientations can largely be traced back to several of David Messick's early, and now classic, publications in the field. Messick and Thorngate (1967), for example, drew attention to the importance of a competitive (relative gain) orientation within experimental games, and Messick and McClintock (1968) outlined the decomposed game method for assessing a broader array of orientations within mixed motive situations. And, in a later paper, Messick and McClelland (1983) highlighted the importance of temporal concerns in social dilemmas.

In the present chapter, we pay tribute to David Messick's work by revisiting the notion of social and temporal orientations within social dilemmas. Our analysis recognizes both the stability and plasticity of people's social and temporal orientations across time and situations. To account the plasticity of these orientations, we offer a slot machine metaphor[1] that emphasizes that while certain individuals may be generally predisposed toward one of these orientations, most or all people also have "slots" for each of these orientations, and people and situations differ in the probability with which each of these orientations may be activated.

In our mind, the notion that people may flexibly adopt any number of social or temporal orientations based on the situation dovetails nicely with Messick's recent appropriateness framework in social dilemmas (Weber et al., 2004). According to their appropriateness framework, when deciding how to act in a social dilemma, people try to answer the question, "What does a person like me do in a situation like this?" (p. 281). The appropriateness framework suggests that people base their decisions on their definition of the situation, their identity at the time, and decision rules or heuristics. Depending on one's answers to these questions, one might adopt any number of social or temporal orientations. If the situation is defined as an economic transaction, for example, an individualistic orientation may appear reasonable, whereas a cooperative orientation may be more reasonable when the situation is defined as an ethical dilemma (Tenbrunsel & Messick, 1999). Similarly, if identification with a group is high, those who typically adopt an individualistic orientation may come to view a cooperative orientation as a more appropriate choice (De Cremer & Van Vugt, 1999). Finally, if features of the situation, such as the ease of equal division, make an equality rule salient, egalitarianism is more likely to be followed (Allison & Messick, 1990). In sum, both the slot machine metaphor and the appropriateness framework advanced by Messick and his colleagues suggest that the probability of adopting one of the eight orientations outlined in this chapter will vary both within and across individuals; moreover, they will be susceptible to situational manipulations.

SOCIAL DILEMMAS

The majority of societal problems involve multiple actors whose choices impact both their own and others' well-being (i.e., most involve a certain degree of social interdependence). Many of the most challenging interdependence problems can further be viewed as *social dilemmas*, or situations in which short-term individual and long-term collective interests are at odds (Messick & Brewer, 1983). Framed as such, social dilemmas can be seen to involve two conflicts of interest, including a social conflict between individual and collective interests and a temporal conflict between short-term and long-term interests. These conflicts of interest, in turn, afford a range of possible social and temporal orientations that people bring to bear on their decisions in social dilemmas (for an overview of eight orientations, see Table 4.1). The six social orientations each deal with the extent to which an individual is concerned with his own and another's well being and are commonly referred to as *social value orientations* (McClintock, 1972; Messick & McClintock, 1968; Van Lange, 1999). These orientations include altruism (maximizing others' well-being), cooperation (maximizing joint outcomes), egalitarianism (minimizing the difference between own and others' outcomes), individualism (maximizing own outcomes), competition (maximizing the difference between own and others' outcomes), and aggression (minimizing others' outcomes). Also relevant are two temporal orientations, namely, a present time orientation and a future time orientation (e.g., Strathman, Gleicher, Boninger, & Edwards, 1994; Zimbardo & Boyd, 1999).

TABLE 4.1

Logical and Paradoxical Effects of Six Social and Two Temporal Orientations

Orientation	Outcome Maximized	Logical Effect	Paradoxical Effect
Altruism	MaxOther	Promotes cooperation	Helps an individual at expense of group
Cooperation	MaxJoint	Promotes cooperation	Helps ingroup at expense of outgroup and overall collective
Egalitarianism	MinDiff	Promotes cooperation	Encourages (negative) reciprocity
Individualism	MaxOwn	Undermines cooperation	Cooperation as a means to achieving long-term self-interest (reciprocity)
Competition	MaxRel	Undermines cooperation	Encourages cooperation in groups
Aggression	MinOther	Undermines cooperation	Restores fairness by punishing noncooperation
Present	MaxPresent	Undermines cooperation	Motivates cooperation if consequences are immediate
Future	MaxFuture	Promotes cooperation	Reduces cooperation if consequences are only immediate

Note: MaxOther = maximization of others' outcomes; MaxJoint = maximization of joint outcomes; MinDiff = minimization of absolute differences in own and others' outcomes; MaxOwn = maximization of own outcomes; MaxRel = maximization of own outcomes relative to others' outcomes); MinOther = minimization of others' outcomes; MaxPresent = maximization of present outcomes; MaxFuture = maximization of future outcomes.

BASIC PRINCIPLES OF SOCIAL AND TEMPORAL ORIENTATIONS

The theoretical basis for the eight orientations we discuss is largely derived from empirical and conceptual work by Messick and McClintock (1968) that later strongly influenced key assumptions of interdependence theory (Kelley et al., 2003; Kelley & Thibaut, 1978). The key idea is that in settings of social interdependence, people "transform" what is commonly referred to as the *given decision matrix* into an *effective decision matrix* that is more closely linked with behavior. To illustrate, people playing a social dilemma are given a payoff matrix by an experimenter. The payoffs in this matrix correspond to the standard payoffs in a prisoner's dilemma, where (a) a noncooperative, self-regarding choice yields greater outcomes for self than a cooperative, other-regarding choice, yet (b) both individuals' outcomes are greater when they both make a cooperative choice than when they both make a noncooperative choice. To account for the fact that some people cooperate in situations like the Prisoner's Dilemma, interdependence theory assumes that people utilize broader considerations to transform the objective payoffs in the given matrix into a set of more subjective payoffs in the effective matrix that make cooperation a reasonable choice (e.g., Joireman, Kuhlman, Van Lange, Doi, & Shelley, 2003; Van Lange, De Cremer, Van Dijk, & Van Vugt, 2007).

Our goal in the present chapter is to consider how a set of these broader considerations — the six social orientations and two temporal orientations — can shape decision-making in social dilemmas. Much like Messick and McClintock (1968), we assume that the different orientations are susceptible to both individual variation and situational variation based on a slot machine metaphor of these social and temporal orientations.

SLOT MACHINE METAPHOR OF SOCIAL AND TEMPORAL ORIENTATIONS

It is not uncommon for scientists and laypeople alike to assume (often implicitly, we believe) that an orientation must translate directly into behavior. Perhaps due to the human need for predictability and control, we tend to believe that "prosocial people behave (almost) always prosocially" just as "competitive people behave (almost) always competitively" (Ross, 1977). Rather than taking a deterministic perspective, a more accurate characterization of the dispositional view is probabilistic, based on the assumption that people differ in the probability with which one or more of the interpersonal orientations will be activated. As a metaphor, we prefer to frame this process in terms of the slot machine model of social and temporal orientations. We suggest that for relatively stable orientations (as dispositions or as partner-specific orientations), people differ in terms of the percentages of slots that represent the various social and temporal orientations — just as slot machines represent different frequencies of bananas, lemons, and oranges (so we assume). For example, a cooperative person is a person with a relatively high percentage of cooperative slots (let's say, 70%), and relatively low percentages of individualistic and competitive slots (let's say, 20% and 10%). The reverse pattern is likely to hold for a competitive person, whereas an individualistic person may take an intermediate position (with 60% individualistic slots, 20% cooperative slots, and 20% competitive slots).

The slot machine metaphor of interpersonal orientations is reasonable because people behave in a variety of different interaction situations, even with the same partner. Experience accumulates across interaction situations, which is likely to shape a "probability distribution of interpersonal orientations" (Van Lange & Joireman, 2008). Indeed, it would appear maladaptive if people relied on only a single orientation in their interactions with others, even if the situational features are the same. The slot machine model of interpersonal orientation is also plausible because (a) there is variation in the external (and impersonal) circumstances to which individuals may respond in some way (e.g., the weather, noise) and (b) there is a fair amount of variation within an individual even on a day-to-day basis that may also exert influences on the activation of a particular orientation (e.g., differences in mood states or differences in energy levels on a particular day).[2]

One reason we introduce the slot machine metaphor is that it holds potentially important implications. One implication is that the metaphor assumes flexibility and adaptation. Much past theorizing implicitly assumes that individuals with prosocial orientation would virtually be alien to a competitive motivation, just as individuals with competitive orientations would virtually be alien to any of the prosocial motivations. As an "antidote" to thinking in terms of such one-to-one links between individual differences in orientations and the activation of such orientations, the slot machine suggests that the opposing orientations can in fact be activated in people — albeit with a smaller probability than the orientation that is more typical of that individual. Further, if a person were to repeatedly (and rigidly) adopt the same orientation across multiple partners, or even the same partner, the person would be unlikely to adapt to small-but-important changes in the situation or the partner's behavior. Indeed, rigidity would probably imply that one does not even notice certain changes in the situations (e.g., new possibilities for effective communication) or changes in the partner's behavior (e.g., increased tendency toward cooperation, increased tendency toward "cheating"). Hence, social and temporal orientations require flexibility to be adaptive — and indeed, if we were to be the slave of a particular orientation, our adaptive quality, and hence survival opportunities, would be very slim. (As a side note, the slot machine model is also relevant to other constructs [including dispositions]; the model is perhaps even more relevant to interaction-relevant constructs, because they should especially benefit from flexibility in "coping" with the dynamics of social interaction situations.)

A second implication of the slot machine metaphor is that people will have experience with different motivational states corresponding to the eight orientations we discuss. This is important, because it suggests that people should be able to change perspectives when called for. For example, prosocials (altruists, cooperators, and egalitarians combined) are more likely than individualists and competitors to evaluate others' cooperative and noncooperative actions in terms of good versus bad, associating cooperation with goodness and noncooperation with badness (a "morality" perspective). Conversely, individualists and competitors are more likely than prosocials to evaluate other's actions in terms of strength and weakness, associating cooperation with weakness and noncooperation with strength (a "might" perspective; Liebrand, Jansen, Rijken, & Suhre, 1986; Van Lange & Kuhlman, 1994). According to the slot machine metaphor, people should not find it hard to change perspectives: Prosocials should be able to adopt a perspective whereby competing is seen as a sign of strength, whereas competitors should be able to see that cooperation is often the right (or good) thing to do. People should also adapt by changing perspectives when dealing with different partners (e.g., their close partner vs. a second-hand car salesman [or at least the stereotype thereof]).

Taken together, there is growing evidence in support of the slot machine model of social and temporal orientations (for a fuller discussion, see Van Lange & Joireman, 2008). That is, the most accurate characterization of consistent differences in social and temporal orientations is by conceptualizing these differences in terms of the probability with which a particular orientation may be activated. In doing so, the model also emphasizes flexibility and "adaptive value" in responding to different partners, and different situations. We now consider the logical and paradoxical effects of the six social orientations and two temporal orientations.[3]

SOCIAL ORIENTATIONS (LOGICAL EFFECTS)

Altruism

The claim that altruism should be considered an interpersonal orientation is rather controversial. However, when focusing on studies in which feelings of interpersonal attachment, empathy (or sympathy), or relational commitment are studied, altruism may very well exist. As a case in point, Batson and Ahmad (2001) had participants play a single-trial Prisoner's Dilemma in which the other made the first choice. Before the social dilemma task, the other shared some personal information that her romantic partner had ended the relationship with her and that she found it hard to think about anything else. Batson and Ahmad compared three conditions, one of which was a high-empathy condition in which participants were asked to imagine and adopt the other person's perspective. The other conditions were either a low-empathy condition, in which participants were instructed to take an objective perspective on the information shared by the other, or a condition in which no personal information was shared. After these instructions, participants were informed that the other makes a noncooperative choice. Batson and Ahmad found that nearly half of the participants (45%) in the high-empathy condition made a cooperative choice, whereas the percentages in the low-empathy and control conditions were very low, as shown in earlier research (less than 5%, as in Van Lange, 1999). Hence, this study provides an interesting demonstration of the power of empathy in activating choices that can be understood in terms of altruism, in that high-empathy participants presumably assigned substantial weight to the outcomes for the other at the expense of their own outcomes. In fact, there is recent evidence indicating that the induction of empathy (through a story about another participant's father diagnosed with a brain tumor) activates an orientation to enhance other's outcomes (MaxOther) but not other prosocial orientations (such the minimization of absolute differences in outcomes for self and other, or MinDiff; see Van Lange, 2008).

Cooperation

A second social orientation relevant within social dilemma settings is a desire to maximize joint outcomes, typically referred to as *cooperative orientation*. A desire to maximize joint outcomes can arise from several sources. To begin, there is a fair amount of research showing that a notable percentage of people (46%) adopt a cooperative orientation in dilemma-type settings even when there is no strategic reason to do so (e.g., no anticipated future interaction; Au & Kwong, 2004). The enhancement of joint outcomes may also arise out of strategic self-interest, as when individualists cooperate with a partner pursuing a tit-for-tat strategy (Kuhlman & Marshello,

1975). People may also seek to enhance joint outcomes out of a desire to enhance the well-being of their group as a whole (a tendency sometimes referred to as *collectivism*; Batson, 1994) and/or because they strongly identify with their group (e.g., Brewer & Kramer, 1986; Van Vugt & Hart, 2004). A classic case in point is research by Brewer and Kramer (1986), in which participants were categorized as psychology students (i.e., the actual participants, hence strong group identity) or economics students (i.e., weak group identity). Using a resource dilemma, Brewer and Kramer showed that under conditions of strong identity, individuals were more likely to behave cooperatively when it was essential to the group (i.e., when the resources were near depletion). Such cooperative efforts were not observed when group identity was low. It has been suggested that under conditions of strong identity, there may be a blurring of the distinction between personal outcomes and collective outcomes — that is, me and mine becomes we and ours (e.g., Van Vugt & Hart, 2004). In sum, a desire to enhance joint outcomes can arise out of several different processes, and this desire typically enhances people's willingness to cooperate in social dilemmas.

Egalitarianism

The existence of egalitarianism or equality may be derived from various lines of research. To begin with, several experiments have been conducted within the realm of resource-sharing tasks to examine the factors that may determine different "rules of fairness." In these tasks, a group of people shares a resource and the problem that these decision-makers are confronted with is how to optimally use the resource without overusing it. Research by Allison and Messick (1990) provided a powerful demonstration of what happens in such situations. That is, their results showed that when participants (in a group of six people) are asked to harvest first from the common resource, people almost without exception use the equal division rule. Allison and Messick (1990) suggested that equality represents a decision heuristic that has the advantages of being simple, efficient, and fair. As such, equality has great potential to promote the quality and effectiveness of interpersonal relationships and therefore can be considered as a "decision rule" that is deeply rooted in people's orientations toward others. Since then, several experimental studies have revealed that egalitarianism is a powerful consideration in a wide variety of interdependence situations.

Individualism

Though we suggest that self-interest alone is too limited to fully understand social interaction, individualism, or concern with own outcomes, it is likely to be a prominent orientation in a variety of contexts. In fact, individualism may well be one of the primary anchors that people use to interpret interpersonal situations. In many ways, people may approach an interpersonal problem as if it were an impersonal problem and then "add" interpersonal preferences to it. For example, in deciding whether to go to a movie with a friend, people may first consider the movie that they wish to see and later think (or inquire) about the preferences of the friend and then whether, how, or even why they should take account of the friend's preferences. A concern with one's own outcomes is an important orientation, and the literature documents numerous phenomena that align with an individualistic orientation, such as the effects of payoff structure, the success of tit-for-tat for eliciting cooperation, and effects of various forms of reward and punishment (see Komorita & Parks, 1995).

Competition

There is also strong evidence in support of competition as an orientation quite distinct from self-interest. As noted earlier, the work by Messick and McClintock (1968) has inspired considerable research that reveals that not only cooperative orientations but competitive orientations may underlie social interactions. The importance of competition is even more directly shown in research on a decision-making task that represents a conflict between, on the one hand, cooperation and individualism (Option A) and, on the other hand, competition (Option B). Hence, the only consideration to choose Option B is to receive better outcomes (or less worse outcomes) than the other, even though one could do better for oneself by choosing Option A. Research using this so-called Maximizing Difference Game has revealed that quite a few people choose the competitive alternative; it is also of some interest to note that among some (young) age groups, competitive tendencies tend to be even more pronounced (McClintock & Moskowitz, 1976). Specifically, among very young children (3 years old), individualistic orientation dominates, after which competition becomes more pronounced (4–5 years), which is then followed by cooperative orientation (6–7 years). Further, one might wonder whether it is the aversion of "getting behind" or the temptation of "getting ahead" that underlies such competition. In a very nice study by Messick and Thorngate (1967), it was shown that the former tendency (aversive competition) is much more pronounced than the latter tendency (appetitive competition; i.e., not losing seems a stronger motive than winning). Thus, there is little doubt that competition is an important orientation that needs to be carefully distinguished from self-interest.

Aggression

The orientation of aggression has received very little attention in research on social dilemmas. It is interesting to note that, especially in comparison to the orientation of altruism, much research on aggression focuses on genetic and biological factors. Examples are not only twin studies but studies focusing on associations of aggression with hormonal activity, such as variations in levels of testosterone. Importantly, the correlation between aggressiveness and testosterone is especially pronounced for scale items assessing aggressiveness in response to provocation (Olweus, 1979), suggesting that aggression needs to be considered in terms of anger that is interpersonally activated. For example, it may well be that tendencies toward aggression are most pronounced among those who do not expect others to behave selfishly. As a case in point, Kelley and Stahelski (1970) provide some evidence for what they referred to as *overassimilation*, the tendency for cooperative individuals (at least, some cooperative individuals) to behave even more noncooperatively than the fairly noncooperative partner with whom one interacts (see also Liebrand et al., 1986).

TEMPORAL ORIENTATIONS (LOGICAL EFFECTS)

Also relevant to decision-making in social dilemmas are temporal orientations (for a review, see Joireman, 2005). One relevant construct that has received a fair amount of attention in the dilemmas literature is individual differences in the consideration of future consequences (CFC; Strathman et al., 1994), defined as "the extent to which people consider the potential distant outcomes of their current behaviors and the extent to which they are influenced by these potential outcomes" (p. 743). Those low in CFC (present oriented) are concerned with the immediate but not the delayed consequences of their actions, whereas those high in CFC (future oriented) are concerned with the delayed but not the immediate consequences of their actions.[4]

An increasing number of studies indicate that CFC predicts decision-making across a range of applied social dilemma settings (for a review, see Joireman, Strathman, & Balliet, 2006). As an example, in their original study, Strathman et al. (1994) showed that individuals high in CFC were less likely than those low in CFC to support off-shore drilling for oil when it would yield long-term negative consequences, despite the fact that drilling would also yield short-term benefits. More recent studies have shown that individuals high in CFC are more likely to engage in a number of environmentally frendly behaviors, support structural solutions to commuting dilemmas (Joireman et al., 2001), and resist the urge to respond aggressively when insulted (e.g., Joireman, Anderson, & Strathman, 2003; Joireman, Van Lange, & Van Vugt, 2004; Kortenkamp & Moore, 2006). Frequently, these differences are magnified when the long-term consequences of a behavioral option are more salient; for example, when people believe that commuting by car leads to long-term environmental problems (Joireman et al., 2004) or when aggression is likely to carry future negative consequences (Joireman, Anderson et al., 2003). In sum, present and future orientations are important predictors of behavior in interdependent settings including social dilemmas.

SOCIAL ORIENTATIONS (PARADOXICAL EFFECTS)

Presumably, most scientists (and policy-makers) expect more desirable outcomes from prosocial orientations (altruism, cooperation, and, perhaps, equality) and future orientations than from individualism, competition, or aggression, or a present orientation. Indeed, these effects are "logical" because social dilemmas are defined in terms of the conflict between short-term self-interest and long-term collective interest. However, as we will discuss below, there may also be paradoxical effects, such that altruism, cooperation, equality, and future orientation can pose a threat to desirable collective outcomes, while individualism, competition, aggression, and short-term orientation may actually promote desirable collective

outcomes. Awareness of such paradoxical effects can be crucially important to designing policy for promoting desirable behavior and discourag-
ing undesirable behavior.

Altruism

As noted earlier, altruism may come into being when people empathize
with another person. It should be clear that several media campaigns use
empathy to promote donations to poor countries, to various health organizations, and to charity (e.g., helping the homeless after a natural disas-
ter). These forms of public education may be especially effective when they
include a "story" about a victim who is in serious need. Often the victim is
"individualized" by informing the public about some personal qualities.
Such information may be especially likely to activate empathy and helping
in turn. Activating empathy may thus be an important solution to various
forms of helping, including donations, volunteering, and participation in
some collective action (e.g., protesting against war).

It is interesting, however, that empathy may not always yield benefits at the
collective level. In fact, there is research indicating that feelings of empathy
could promote choices that benefit one particular individual in a group — at
the expense of outcomes for the entire group (Batson et al., 1995). As such,
empathy can sometimes form a threat to cooperative interaction, just as selfishness can. That is, feelings of empathy may lead one to provide tremendous support to one particular person, thereby neglecting the well-being
of the collective. For example, as noted by Batson et al. (1995), an executive
may retain an ineffective employee for whom he or she feels compassion
to the detriment of the organization. Another example is that parents may
sometimes be so supporting of their children that it harms collective interest in a serious manner (e.g., not making an attempt to stop their making
noise in public situations; see Batson and Moran [1999]).

Cooperation

A strong concern with collective well-being — cooperation — almost
always supports actions that are collectively desirable. There is, however,
one very important exception to this rule, namely, when social dilemmas
take the form of multilayered social dilemmas, in which "cooperation" is
good for one's own group but bad for another group — and bad for the

entire collectivity (see Bornstein, 1992). Consider, for example, the soldier fighting for his (or her) own country but killing soldiers from the other country, thereby causing bad effects for the entire collective. It is this type of "cooperation action" that often is supported and respected by ingroup members that threatens collective well-being (for evidence, see Insko & Schopler, 1998). In that sense, cooperation can be a risky orientation, especially because intergroup conflicts, once started, are often very hard to resolve.

Egalitarianism

Often equality supports collectively desirable actions. In fact, sometimes donations, volunteering, and related forms of helping may be rooted in "a sense of fairness": to enhance the situation of those who are worse off than oneself. Indeed, campaigns aimed at fostering helping behavior could sometimes emphasize not only empathy but also feelings of justice — does it feel right when we do not stop the suffering? Also, when a majority of people make a cooperative choice (e.g., not overusing water), policy-makers could indeed make salient that important fact — because getting more than others for the wrong reasons simply does not feel good, and it is very difficult to justify to oneself or to others.

Despite its benefits, equality can also entail risks to collective outcomes. First, if individuals are primarily concerned with equality, then they may show an aversion to being taken advantage of and end up following "bad apples" in the group who choose not to cooperate (e.g., Rutte & Wilke, 1992). Indeed, violations of equality will be especially salient in others' actions, and such actions are likely to occur in large groups. As such, small violations of equality (e.g., a self-regarding choice) may set off noncooperative responses by the many members of the group, thereby running the risk of creating an atmosphere of distrust and concern with self.

Second, on a related note, a strong concern with equality may harm collective outcomes because people do not want to unilaterally invest in situations where such investing cannot occur simultaneously. For example, building exchange systems often takes time and unilateral actions — an example is the exchange of expertise among colleagues. If one, a statistics expert, is very seriously concerned about equality, then he or she may not want to invest too much time into conducting complex, time-consuming analyses, if there is a bit of uncertainty that the other (an expert in writing) is not going to reciprocate. Thus, the collectively desirable outcomes (a joint high-quality product) are less likely to be obtained if it takes unilateral investment that challenges equality. And indeed, most situations of mutual helping are characterized by the very fact that one has to make a start in dyads (e.g., mutual babysitting among young parents) and groups (e.g., somebody has to initiate costly action to get organized for a joint activity); and so, a strong concern with equality (along with uncertainty) may undermine beneficial exchange.

Third, sometimes it may not be wise to emphasize equality in relationships, groups, and organizations. For example, in marital relationships, a discussion about equality may well be an indicator that a couple is on its way to divorce, perhaps because such discussions can undermine propartner motivation (e.g., responding to the partner's needs; Clark & Mills, 1993). Similarly, in groups and organizations, communicating equality may lead to social bookkeeping that may undermine organizational citizenship behavior, the more spontaneous forms of helping colleagues that are not really part of one's job but are nonetheless essential to the group or organization.

Individualism

The paradoxical effects of individualism are a little more subtle — but quite common, we suggest. Individualism is often a powerful motivation to engage in cooperative behavior — and one that works through the reciprocity mechanism. The best illustration of this phenomenon is the classic work on the so-called tit-for-tat strategy (i.e., responding in kind, thus reciprocating cooperation and noncooperation in the next interaction) that has been shown to be so effective in eliciting cooperation from people in situations in which partners respond to one another's actions for some time (Axelrod, 1984; for an empirical review, see Komorita & Parks, 1995). Indeed, it has been shown that tit-for-tat in many environments is even more effective than unconditional forms of cooperation in eliciting cooperation. Important research by Kuhlman and Marshello (1975) has subsequently shown that tit-for-tat primarily helps motivate people with an individualistic orientation to cooperate. This finding, replicated and extended in a variety of ways (e.g., across interdependent situations, McClintock & Liebrand, 1988; in situations in which people could choose to become more or less interdependent,

Van Lange & Visser, 1999), is very important because it demonstrates that individualism could be a powerful motivation underlying cooperative behavior.

Similarly, in the context of ongoing relationships, it appears that prosocials are willing to engage in sacrifices for their partner irrespective of their level of commitment to the partner. In contrast, individualists are willing to sacrifice primarily or only if they are strongly committed to their partner (see Van Lange, Agnew, Harinck, & Steemers, 1997). This finding, too, suggests that individualistic motivation may "translate" into cooperative behavior, in order to benefit from reciprocity in the near or more distal future.

Competition

A strong concern with receiving better outcomes — and not getting worse outcomes — than others is often conflicting with good outcomes for the collective. In fact, there is some evidence indicating that it is exceptionally hard to seduce individuals with competitive orientations to behave cooperatively. As noted earlier, they do not cooperate, even if the partner pursues tit-for-tat in an iterated social dilemma. At the same time, competition can sometimes be a powerful means to cooperation. Competition can have beneficial effects in multilayered social dilemmas that we discussed above for cooperation. When there are two (or more) well-defined groups who comprise the entire collective, sometimes competition between the groups helps the entire collective. The competition should then deal with something desirable. For example, in the Netherlands, there is a contest between cities aiming for the award "Cleanest City." As another example, two departments at a university may do better (yielding greater research output and enhanced teaching) if the university provides extra resources for only excellent departments. In fact, organizations often use competition as a means to promote functioning. Sometimes such practices take explicit forms, when, for example, competitive reward structures are being implemented: your evaluations and salary depend on your performance relative to others' performances. But even when not done explicitly, the performances of others typically matter in most organizations, because many jobs lack objective criteria, and so managers will often rely on social standards for evaluating individual performance.

Aggression

Just as a competitive orientation can sometimes yield positive outcomes, aggression may also serve a useful function in groups. As noted earlier, individuals are likely to act aggressively to another person in a dyad or other people in the group who fail to cooperate. As such, aggression, at least genuine forms, may often serve to regulate fairness and promote cooperation. For example, people may use aggression as an instrument for encouraging cooperation by exhibiting instrumental cooperation or altruistic punishment. Instrumental cooperation refers to all behaviors by which individuals contribute to the quality of a system that rewards cooperators or punishes noncooperators (Yamagishi, 1986). An example is a contribution to the maintenance of sanctioning systems such as monitoring devices needed for "publicizing" or punishing noncooperators. Altruistic punishment refers to all behaviors by which individuals are willing to engage in costly acts by which noncooperators are directly punished (Fehr & Gächter, 2002).

TEMPORAL ORIENTATIONS (PARADOXICAL EFFECTS)

Though it seems intuitively obvious that a future orientation is always beneficial, a close inspection of the literature reveals several apparently paradoxical effects. For example, as noted earlier, Strathman and colleagues (1994) found that people high in CFC were less likely to support off-shore oil drilling when it carried short-term benefits and long-term costs. However, when the temporal ordering of the costs and benefits was reversed (i.e., drilling produced short-term costs and long-term benefits), individuals high in CFC were more likely than those low in CFC to support off-shore drilling. In a similar fashion, those high in CFC were more likely than those low in CFC to respond to an insult in an aggressive manner when they believed that aggression would carry immediate negative consequences but no long-term negative consequences (Joireman, Anderson et al., 2003). Finally, recent work has shown that individuals high in CFC are less likely than those low in CFC to engage in organizational citizenship behaviors when they believe they would soon be leaving an organization (Joireman, Kamdar, Daniels, & Duell, 2006). Taken together, these studies indicate that though a future orientation may often encourage cooperation in social dilemma settings, a future orientation can also have paradoxical effects under certain conditions.

CONCLUDING COMMENTS

The present analysis emphasizes the importance of social orientations and temporal orientations as two relatively distinct underpinnings of behavior in social dilemmas. Both sets of orientations can be traced back to classic work by Messick and his colleagues (Messick & McClelland, 1983; Messick & McClintock, 1968). Our slot machine metaphor, furthermore, suggests considerable flexibility in the activation and use of these orientations in line with Messick and colleagues' more recent appropriateness framework (Weber et al., 2004). Our focus on paradoxical effects can also be embedded within the appropriateness framework, because an altruistic orientation may be appropriate (i.e., helpful to the group) under certain circumstances but inappropriate (i.e., not helpful to the group) under other circumstances.

Though we have couched our discussion of these orientations within classic definitions of social dilemmas, we believe that it is important to recognize that social dilemmas may not always be what they appear to be at first glance. Moreover, the way decision-makers define the situation is likely to have important implications for which of the various orientations they judge to be the most appropriate. As a case in point, we argue that many social dilemmas in everyday life are in fact multiply structured in terms of social orientations, because these social dilemmas represent different layers. For example, in multilayered social dilemmas (Wit & Kerr, 2002; see also team games, Bornstein, 1992), one may distinguish among at least three layers or entities, including the individual, the ingroup (and outgroup), and the entire collective. What do these entities mean for the social orientations that may (or may not) be activated? The soldier deciding whether to fight for "his country" is faced with this layered social dilemma, as are many employees who sometimes must decide among pursuing his or her self-interest, the interests of the unit or team in which he or she is working, and the interests of the entire organization. For example, to ask for greater resources than one actually needs (e.g., very advanced computers) may at times help management appreciate the performance of one's own unit a bit more, but an organization is obviously not served by units that are always asking for greater resources than they actually need. Thus, layered social dilemmas may bring about problems in that a prosocial orientation may well translate into cooperation with ingroup members, which may exert detrimental effects for the larger collective.

However, layered social dilemmas also bring about opportunities for promoting collectively desired behaviors. Sometimes, it is even possible to make salient a layer to the social dilemma that would otherwise remain subtle or even unnoticed. For example, the installation of an award for a group category makes that subgroup salient (e.g., the clean city award), which may eventually help the entire country. A large organization can award working units for hiring categories of people that are underrepresented, such as ethnic minorities. Thus, it is of great importance for policy-makers to analyze the situation carefully in terms of differing layers and the ways in which the interests correspond versus conflict for each pair of the layer (individual vs. ingroup, individual vs. collective, and ingroup vs. collective). Creative and powerful solutions to social dilemmas may be generated if one is able to induce or make salient a new layer in the social dilemma that in many ways serves as a psychological tool for promoting desirable outcomes for the entire collective. Given the strong effects of empathy that we discussed earlier, one promising tool may be to induce empathy with members of the "other group" (Penner, Dovidio, Piliavin, & Schroeder, 2005).

In conclusion, the health and vitality of relationships, groups, and society at large are strongly challenged by social dilemmas. Informed by various lines of research, particularly on social value orientation and the consideration of future consequences, we argue that social and temporal orientations are essential to understanding larger societal problems. Society as a whole has been seriously threatened by environmental problems, such as pollution or massive overuse of natural resources, and intergroup conflict. Both problems are challenging because a short-term individualistic orientation seems so prevalent in such large-scale contexts. Creative solutions may be sought by, perhaps, emphasizing what small (and psychologically close) communities can do to trigger the kind of motivation that helps us promote greater outcomes for all of us, now and in the future. Often these are the logical effects of the other-regarding and long-term orientations, but sometimes one needs to creatively think about the paradoxical effects of self-regarding and short-term orientations. The latter effects may not always be salient, but they may sometimes be powerfully used to the benefit of all of us.

NOTES

1. We are indebted to Dave Messick and Chuck McClintock, who emphasized in their stochastic model of social orientations differences in probability in the activation of orientations (Messick & McClintock, 1968), and to Mike Kuhlman, who adopted this reasoning and then informally made reference to "slot machines" in describing social orientations. He used this concept during informal discussions at the Third International Conference on Social Dilemmas (Groningen, The Netherlands).

2. We realize that the concept of "slot machine" may carry the connotation of randomness and that the reader might think that a shift from one slot to another is a strictly random process (as it seems to be in a real slot machine — from lemons to cherries). The slot machine as used metaphorically here is a model that states that people differ in the relative availability (or percentages) of the social and temporal orientations that we highlight in this chapter. Specifically, people differ in the probability distributions with which the various social and temporal orientations might be activated. The activation of a particular orientation (e.g., prosocial orientation) itself is often not a random process — rather, it is more likely that this is a functional "response" (conscious or not) to aspects of the other person (e.g., is the other a person I like or trust?) or aspects of the situation (e.g., this is a situation in which I do not have complete information; let's give the other the benefit of the doubt by making an other-regarding choice). Further, it is also likely that "neighboring orientations" (such as cooperation and egalitarianism) are more likely to be activated in concert (as we discuss later) and may be more likely to be the two social orientations between which people shift. The latter issue would represent an intriguing topic for future research but is at present a matter of speculation.

3. We adopted a parsimonious approach to six social orientations and two temporal orientations by not considering their combined or interactive effects (even though such effects are plausible; see Van Lange et al., 1997) or by examining each of these orientations as a continuum ranging from low to high. The primary reason for this approach is that it allows us to discuss more clearly the logical and paradoxical effects they may exert in the context of social dilemmas and related situation.

4. In keeping with our focus on distinct social orientations (altruism, cooperation, etc.), we have framed the two temporal orientations as categories. However, CFC can also be viewed as a more continuous construct, with people scoring relatively high or relatively low, just as people can vary on a continuum from low temporal discounters to high temporal discounters. From a similar standpoint, the same "non-categorical" argument can be advanced for social orientations, even though their relatively distinct decision rules might suggest otherwise. It is these decision rules that we assume are captured with decomposed games and related measurement techniques (see Van Lange, 1999; Van Lange, Bekkers, Schuyt, & Van Vugt, 2007).

REFERENCES

Allison, S. T., & Messick, D. M. (1990). Social decision heuristics in the use of shared resources. *Journal of Behavioral Decision Making, 3*, 23–42.

Au, W. T., & Kwong, J. Y. Y. (2004). Measurements and effects of social-value orientation in social dilemmas: A review. In R. Suleiman, D. V. Budescu, I. Fischer, & D. M. Messick (Eds.), *Contemporary psychological research on social dilemmas* (pp. 71–98). New York: Cambridge University Press.

Axelrod, R. (1984). *The evolution of cooperation.* New York: Basic Books.

Batson, C. D. (1994). Why act for the public good. *Personality and Social Psychology Bulletin, 20*, 603–610.

Batson, C. D., & Ahmad, N. (2001). Empathy-induced altruism in a Prisoner's Dilemma II: What if the target of empathy has defected? *European Journal of Social Psychology, 31*, 25–36.

Batson, C. D., Batson, J. G., Todd, R. M., Brummett, B. H., Shaw, L. L., & Aldeguer, C. M. R. (1995). Empathy and collective good: Caring for one of the others in a social dilemma. *Journal of Personality and Social Psychology, 68*, 619–631.

Batson, C. D., & Moran, T. (1999). Empathy-induced altruism in a prisoner's dilemma. *European Journal of Social Psychology, 29*, 909–924.

Bornstein, G. (1992). The free-rider problem in intergroup conflicts over step-level and continuous public goods. *Journal of Personality and Social Psychology, 62,* 597–606.

Brewer, M. B., & Kramer, R. M. (1986). Choice behavior in social dilemmas: Effects of social identity, group size, and decision framing. *Journal of Personality and Social Psychology, 50,* 543–549.

Clark, M. S., & Mills, J. (1993). The difference between communal and exchange relationships: What it is and is not. *Personality and Social Psychology Bulletin, 19,* 684–691.

Dawes, R. M., & Messick, D. M. (2000). Social dilemmas. *International Journal of Psychology, 35,* 111–116.

De Cremer, D., & Van Vugt, M. (1999). Social identification effects in social dilemmas: A transformation of motives. *European Journal of Social Psychology, 29,* 871–893.

Fehr, E., & Gächter, S. (2002). Altruistic punishment in humans. *Nature, 415,* 137–140.

Insko, C. A., & Schopler, J. (1998). Differential distrust of groups and individuals. In C. Sedikides, J. Schopler, & C. A. Insko (Eds.), *Intergroup cognition and intergroup behavior: Toward a closer union* (pp. 75–107). Hillsdale, NJ: Erlbaum.

Joireman, J. (2005). Environmental problems as social dilemmas: The temporal dimension. In A. Strathman & J. Joireman (Eds.), *Understanding behavior in the context of time: Theory, research, and application* (pp. 289–304). Mahwah, NJ: Lawrence Erlbaum.

Joireman, J. A., Anderson, J., & Strathman, A. (2003). The aggression paradox: Understanding links among aggression, sensation seeking, and the consideration of future consequences. *Journal of Personality and Social Psychology, 84,* 1287–1302.

Joireman, J. A., Kamdar, D., Daniels, D., & Duell, B. (2006). Good citizens to the end? It depends: Empathy and concern with future consequences moderate the impact of a short-term time horizon on OCBs. *Journal of Applied Psychology, 91,* 1307–1320.

Joireman, J. A., Kuhlman, D. M., Van Lange, P. A. M., Doi, T., & Shelley, G. P. (2003). Perceived rationality, morality, and power of social choice as a function of interdependence structure and social value orientation. *European Journal of Social Psychology, 33,* 413–437.

Joireman, J., Strathman, A., & Balliet, D. (2006). Considering future consequences: An integrative model. In L. Sanna & E. Chang (Eds.), *Judgments over time: The interplay of thoughts, feelings, and behaviors* (pp. 82–99). Oxford, UK: Oxford University Press.

Joireman, J., Van Lange, P. A. M., & Van Vugt, M. (2004). Who cares about the environmental impact of cars? Those with an eye toward the future. *Environment and Behavior, 36,* 187–206.

Joireman, J. A., Van Lange, P. A. M., Van Vugt, M., Wood, A., Vander Leest, T., & Lambert, C. (2001). Structural solutions to social dilemmas: A field study on commuters' willingness to fund improvements in public transit. *Journal of Applied Social Psychology, 31,* 504–526.

Kelley, H. H., Holmes, J. W., Kerr, N. L., Reis, H. T., Rusbult, C. E., & Van Lange, P. A. M. (2003). *An atlas of interpersonal situations.* New York: Cambridge.

Kelley, H. H., & Stahelski, A. J. (1970). Social interaction basis of cooperators' and competitors' beliefs about others. *Journal of Personality and Social Psychology, 16,* 66–91.

Kelley, H. H., & Thibaut, J. W. (1978). *Interpersonal relations: A theory of interdependence.* New York: Wiley.

Komorita, S. S., & Parks, C. D. (1995). Interpersonal relations: Mixed-motive interaction. *Annual Review of Psychology, 46,* 183–207.

Kortenkamp, K. V., & Moore, C. F. (2006). Time, uncertainty, and individual differences in decisions to cooperate in resource dilemmas. *Personality and Social Psychology Bulletin, 32,* 603–615.

Kuhlman, D. M., & Marshello, A. (1975). Individual differences in game motivation as moderators of preprogrammed strategic effects in prisoner's dilemma. *Journal of Personality and Social Psychology, 32,* 922–931.

Liebrand, W. B. G., Jansen, R. W. T. L., Rijken, V. M., & Suhre, C. J. M. (1986). Might over morality: Social values and the perception of other players in experimental games. *Journal of Experimental Social Psychology, 22,* 203–215.

McClintock, C. G. (1972). Social motivation: A set of propositions. *Behavioral Science, 17,* 438–454.

McClintock, C. G., & Liebrand, W. B. G. (1988). Role of interdependence structure, individual value orientation, and another's strategy in social decision making: A transformational analysis. *Journal of Personality and Social Psychology, 55,* 396–409.

McClintock, C. G., & Moskowitz, J. M. (1976). Children's preference for individualistic, cooperative, and competitive outcomes. *Journal of Personality and Social Psychology, 34,* 543–555.

Messick, D. M., & Brewer, M. B. (1983). Solving social dilemmas: A review. In L. Wheeler & P. Shaver (Eds), *Review of personality and social psychology* (Vol. 4, pp. 11–44). Beverly Hills, CA: Sage.

Messick, D. M., & McClelland, C. L. (1983). Social traps and temporal traps. *Personality and Social Psychology Bulletin, 9,* 105–110.

Messick, D. M., & McClintock, C. G. (1968). Motivational bases of choice in experimental games. *Journal of Experimental Social Psychology, 4,* 1–25.

Messick, D. M., & Thorngate, W. B. (1967). Relative gain maximization in experimental games. *Journal of Experimental Social Psychology, 3,* 85–101.

Olweus, D. (1979). Stability of aggression patterns in males: A review. *Psychological Bulletin, 86,* 852–875.

Penner, L. A., Dovidio, J. F., Piliavin, J. A., & Schroeder, D. A. (2005). Prosocial behavior: Multilevel perspectives. *Annual Review of Psychology, 56,* 365–392.

Ross, L. (1977). The intuitive psychologist and his shortcomings: Distortions in the attribution process. In L. Berkowitz (Ed.), *Advances in experimental social psychology* (vol. 10, pp. 173–220). New York: Academic Press.

Rutte, C. G., & Wilke, H. A. M. (1992). Goals, expectations and behavior in a social dilemma situation. In W. B. G. Liebrand, D. M. Messick, & H. A. M. Wilke (Eds.), *Social dilemmas* (pp. 289–305). Elmsford, NY: Pergamon.

Strathman, A., Gleicher, F., Boninger, D. S., & Edwards, C. S. (1994). The consideration of future consequences: Weighing immediate and distant outcomes of behavior. *Journal of Personality and Social Psychology, 66,* 742–752.

Tenbrunsel, A. E., & Messick, D. M. (1999). Sanctioning systems, decision frames, and cooperation. *Administrative Science Quarterly, 44,* 647–707.

Van Lange, P. A. M. (1999). The pursuit of joint outcomes and equality in outcomes: An integrative model of social value orientation. *Journal of Personality and Social Psychology, 77,* 337–349.

Van Lange, P. A. M. (2008). Does empathy trigger only altruistic motivation? How about selflessness or justice? *Emotion, 8,* 766–774.

Van Lange, P. A. M., Agnew, C. R., Harinck, F., & Steemers, G. (1997). From game theory to real life: How social value orientation affects willingness to sacrifice in ongoing close relationships? *Journal of Personality and Social Psychology, 73*, 1330–1344.

Van Lange, P. A. M., Bekkers, R., Schuyt, Th., & Van Vugt, M. (2007). From gaming to giving: Social value orientation predicts donating to noble causes. *Basic and Applied Social Psychology, 29*, 375–384.

Van Lange, P. A. M., De Cremer, D., & Van Dijk, E., & Van Vugt, M. (2007). Self-interest and beyond: Basic principles of social interaction. In A. W. Kruglanski & E. T. Higgings (Eds.), *Social psychology: Handbook of basic principles* (2nd ed., pp. 540–561). New York: Guilford.

Van Lange, P. A. M., & Joireman, J. (2008). How we can promote behavior that serves all of us in the future. *Social Issues and Policy Review, 2*, 127–157.

Van Lange, P. A. M., & Kuhlman, D. M. (1994). Social value orientations and impressions of a partner's honesty and intelligence: A test of the might versus morality effect. *Journal of Personality and Social Psychology, 67*, 126–141.

Van Lange, P. A. M., & Visser, K. (1999). Locomotion in social dilemmas: How we adapt to cooperative, tit-for-tat, and noncooperative partners. *Journal of Personality and Social Psychology, 77*, 762–773.

Van Vugt, M., & Hart, C. M. (2004). Social identity as social glue: The origins of group loyalty. *Journal of Personality and Social Psychology, 86*, 585–598.

Weber, J. M., Kopelman, S., & Messick, D. M. (2004). A conceptual review of decision making in social dilemmas: Applying a logic of appropriateness. *Personality and Social Psychology Review, 8*, 281–307.

Wit, A. P., & Kerr, N. L. (2002). "Me versus just us versus us all" categorization and cooperation in nested social dilemmas. *Journal of Personality and Social Psychology, 83*, 616–637.

Yamagishi, T. (1986). The provision of a sanctioning system as a public good. *Journal of Personality and Social Psychology, 51*, 110–116.

Zimbardo, P., & Boyd, J. (1999). Putting time in perspective: A valid, reliable individual differences metric. *Journal of Personality and Social Psychology, 77*, 1271–1288.

5

In the Eye of the Beholder: Payoff Structures and Decision Frames in Social Dilemmas

Ann E. Tenbrunsel
University of Notre Dame

Gregory Northcraft
University of Illinois

Although original conceptualizations of social dilemmas did not assume that outcome matrixes — payoff structures detailing the costs and benefits of cooperation — were objective and fixed (Kelley & Thibaut, 1978), most empirical research on social dilemmas has implicitly made such an assumption. Drawing on the "logic of appropriateness" framework (March, 1995; Messick, 1999), which argues that to understand behavior we need to first understand the decision-maker's construal of the situation, we explore the implications of a subjective and fluid outcome matrix, one that exists only within the eye of the beholder. We argue that, depending on the frame with which a decision-maker perceives the social dilemma, there can be a different effective outcome matrix for every decision-maker and a differential importance of any given outcome matrix in predicting behavior. With an interest toward more successfully managing social dilemmas, we identify the characteristics of frames that may lead to effective matrices that, unbeknownst to the decision-maker, encourage defection and reduce the probability of successful cooperation.

Hillary Clinton (1996) popularized the phrase, "It takes a village ..." to capture the sentiment that many of the most important accomplishments in life cannot be the product of one individual's efforts but instead must reflect the effective joint action of many. Organizations exist, for example, because people can accomplish things working together that are well beyond the reach of any individual (Northcraft & Neale, 1990) — but only if the members of those organizations can figure out how to work together effectively.

Research on social dilemmas (e.g., Hardin, 1968; Liebrand, Messick, & Wilke, 1992; Messick & Brewer, 1983; Messick et al., 1983) has done a lot to illuminate the factors that determine whether individuals will work together effectively. A social dilemma exists when the dominant group solution is to cooperate (e.g., work together, conserve natural resources) but the dominant individual solution is to defect (e.g., slack, consume natural solutions). The social dilemma paradigm has been used to study a variety of situations in which outcomes are interdependent, including situations involving friends, business partners, and nations (Kelley & Thibaut, 1978; Liebrand et al., 1992; Messick & Brewer, 1983; Messick et al., 1983; Pruitt & Carnavale, 1993).

Though work on social dilemmas has been fruitful, yielding significant insights, the conclusions that can be drawn from this research have been unnecessarily constrained by a fundamental assumption made in the empirical investigations of these situations. Though earlier conceptualizations of such dilemmas noted the importance of understanding the payoff structure (i.e., the costs and benefits of cooperating and defecting) as perceived by the decision-maker (Kelly & Thibaut, 1978), most empirical tests have assumed that the payoff structure is fixed and objective, perceived identically by all decision-makers. This assumption limits the generalizability of these findings, constraining the applicability of findings to situations in which the objective, given payoff structure cannot be influenced by subjective interpretation.

Though this assumption poses a problem to social dilemma research, it is not one that is insurmountable. The "logic of appropriateness" framework (March, 1995; Messick, 1999) suggests that we can best understand behavior, expectations, and norms by understanding the way in which a decision situation is framed by decision-makers. In doing so, this conceptualization offers a theoretical lens by which we can incorporate the decision-maker's perception of the situation into social dilemma research and to better understand the perceived matrix upon which the decision-makers in social dilemmas are operating.

The goal of this chapter is to bring perception of the payoff structure, or the effective matrix, back to the forefront. This goal is made possible through the integration of two important streams of Dave Messick's work — social dilemma research and the logic of appropriateness framework.

His contribution to these areas has been immensely valuable in shedding insight into how and why people behave the way that they do, and this chapter suggests that the proposed integration of these two areas can provide even further insight. It is important to note that though our theoretical focus is derived from the area of social dilemmas (because this is where the concept of effective versus given matrices originated), our arguments are also applicable to other mixed-motive interdependent situations, such as negotiations and group processes, and we make those connections where appropriate.

To bring payoff structure perceptions back to the forefront, we first review the fundamental tenets of social dilemmas, noting that subjective perceptions were originally identified as such but subsequently forgotten. We then review the "logic of appropriateness" framework, including empirical research that supports it, as a theoretical lens on which such subjective perceptions can be studied. The discussion then identifies characteristics of frames that may lead to effective matrices that encourage unintentional defection. Our work is intended to encourage additional research in this area that can increase understanding of how to effectively manage social dilemmas.

SOCIAL DILEMMAS

In the original articulation of interdependence theory, Kelley and Thibaut (1978) suggested that the resolution of the tension between choices which are favorable to an individual and those which are favorable to the group can be portrayed as a function of participants' beliefs about the outcomes (or payoffs) of their actions: "If a person knows (or thinks he knows) the contingent relations between his own and his partner's actions, on the one hand, and his own outcomes, on the other, he has a basis for deciding what to do …" (p. 4). Thus, for Kelley and Thibaut (1978), the outcome matrix — a table that reflects the anticipated individual and joint payoff structure for participants — represents a key unit of analysis in understanding the determinants of effective joint action.

In their original formulation of the problems with social interdependence, Kelley and Thibaut (1978) differentiated between two different outcome matrixes: the given outcome matrix, and the effective outcome matrix. The *given* matrix refers to some form of objective outcome matrix — possibly a set of outcomes an individual is told ("given") to expect from a choice between two actions. The *effective* matrix is instead the outcome matrix that an individual has in mind when making the choice between dedicating personal resources to the pursuit of individual or group goals. The importance of this distinction between given and effective outcomes lies in the fact that the given (objective) outcome matrix is not what determines behavior. What instead determines behavior is the effective matrix — the result of an individual (subjectively) transforming the given matrix into the set of outcomes that are effectively considered by that decision-maker in making the focal choice.

The effective matrix is central in understanding behavior in interdependent situations and (of special interest to this chapter) to research on social dilemmas. In the real world, outcome matrixes are rarely given to decision-makers in any meaningful sense of the word. Instead, for any individual there is a myriad (infinite number?) of possible implications (in terms of outcomes) for any particular choice. For reasons of bounded rationality (Simon, 1957), no decision-maker can possibly attend to (or process and integrate into a single decision) all of them. However, even if a decision-maker could, differences in individuals' attentions and experiences should lead to different perceptions of the outcomes. So, as shown in Figure 5.1, decision-makers transform the reality around them by selecting a manageable subset of all possible outcome options on which to focus — the effective matrix. Because of the subjectivity involved in the transformation process, this effective matrix may look nothing like what

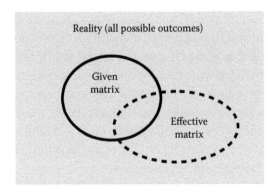

FIGURE 5.1
The given and the effective matrices.

others looking at the same situation think that decision-maker's outcome choices look like — including not looking like any outcome matrix that decision-maker has been given! In fact, any given matrix provided to a decision-maker may simply represent the effective matrix of the individual giving (providing) that matrix.

The notion that individuals act more on the effective matrix — one in which the value of an outcome is dependent on the subjective weight given to one's own outcome and the subjective weight given to others' outcomes — than on the given matrix is at the core of independence theory (Kelley & Thibaut, 1978). However, despite Kelley and Thibaut's expressed concerns about "... our dissatisfaction with simplistic experimentation in which the matrix defined by the experimenter was naively assumed to be the effective one" (p. 15), most empirical research on social dilemmas has failed to embrace or explore the importance of the given/effective matrix distinction. The legitimacy of the conclusions and practical suggestions from social dilemma research, which are based on the assumption that behavior was driven by the given matrix, are thus called into question.

In this chapter, we hope to address this concern by illuminating how the transformation of given matrices (or infinite reality more generally) into a manageable (but understandably limited or "bounded") effective matrix — which then is the ultimate determinant of choice behavior — can be systematically predicted. In particular, we draw on the logic of appropriateness framework (March, 1995; Messick, 1999) to suggest that decision-makers faced with a social dilemma first determine the type of situation with which they are faced — known as their *decision frame*. That assessment in turn determines the decision-maker's expectations of other actors, the decision-maker's beliefs about the appropriate norms in the situation, and the decision-maker's actions. Furthering our understanding of this process is thus the first step in gaining a better understanding of the effective matrix and, ultimately, behavior in social dilemmas.

LOGIC OF APPROPRIATENESS FRAMEWORK AND DECISION FRAMES

At the heart of the logic of appropriateness framework is the central tenet that individuals' behaviors are best understood by first understanding the type of decision with which decision-makers perceive that they are faced (March, 1995; Messick, 1999). Drawing from March's (1995) theory of decision-making and from some of the basic tenets in naturalistic decision-making theories (Connolly & Koput, 1997), image theory (Beach, 1993), explanation-based theories (Pennington & Hastie, 1988), situation-matching theories (Klein, 1989; Noble, 1989), adaptive decision-making theory (Payne, Bettman, & Johnson, 1993), and interdependence theory (Kelley & Thibaut, 1978), Messick (1999) proposed that decision-makers first determine the type of situation that they feel they are in and that this determination dictates behaviors, norms, and expectations.

Using a personal example of a Ping-Pong competition at a vacation resort (see also Dawes' discussion of this example elsewhere in this volume), Messick argues that his initial perception of the situation was a competitive one, a perception that in turn drove his behavior (to compete), his expectations of others (that everyone else would compete), and his norms of the situation (that competition was the governing rule). After making it to one of the final rounds, Messick notes his surprise when he realized that the only people remaining were children. At that point, he realized that his perception of the situation had been quite different from that of other adults in the situation: whereas he had perceived the situation as one of competition with the corresponding goal of winning, other adults had perceived it as one of cooperation with a goal of letting one of the children win. The perception of the situation by the other adults led to differences in behaviors, expectations, and norms — they played to lose, not to win; they expected other adults to lose and not win; and they believed the norm to be one of letting children win the competition. As Messick argues, the extreme embarrassment he felt at the time was driven by recognition of these very different perceptions of the situation, perceptions that in turn drove the differences in behavior, expectations, and norms.

Messick has suggested that understanding the decision-maker's assessment of the situation is central, not only in gaining insight into the example described above but for a significant portion of the empirical findings from social science. For example, he argues that procedure effects in experimental research are driven by differences in situation construals, such that varying the procedure changes the assessment of the situation, which in turn changes behavior. Boles and Messick's (1990) work on ultimatum games provides support for this assertion. In their experiment, an "allocator" was given a certain amount of money to divide between himself and a "recipient." If the recipient accepted the allocation, the recipient received the amount proposed to them and the allocator received the rest; if the recipient rejected the allocation, the recipient and the allocator both received nothing. Boles and Messick (1990) found that the decision to accept the offer depended on whether recipients received the money or the instructions for the game (described above) first: if recipients first had the money in hand and then received the instructions, they were more likely to accept an unfair offer that benefited the allocator than if they were first given the instructions and then received the money. These results were explained by suggesting that the order in which the recipient received the money versus instructions influenced perceptions of the situation — perceptions which in turn drove behavior. When the money was received before the instructions, the situation was coded as "good," but when the instructions were given first and the money after that, the situation was coded as "bad." These perceptions in turn determined whether an unfair allocation was accepted or rejected.

There is some evidence to suggest that such situation construals may be instrumental in affecting behavior within social dilemma settings, independent of the given payoff matrix. In an insightful investigation of the public goods problem (in which individuals must decide how much, if any, to contribute to a common resource) versus the commons dilemma (in which individuals must decide how much, if any, of a common resource to take), Brewer and Kramer (1986) demonstrated that despite being "outcome equivalent," the two were not "psychologically equivalent," with individuals keeping more resources for themselves in the public goods dilemma than in the common resource dilemma. Pillutla and Chen (1999) also found that the type of dilemma affected cooperation rates, such that describing the resources in a social dilemma as social goods versus monetary goods significantly increased cooperation though the given payoff matrix remained the same; similarly, Liberman, Samuels, and Ross (2004) demonstrated that the name of the game — Wall Street versus Community Game — substantially affected cooperation rates, even more so than individuals predicted that it would. Labeling the first person in a social dilemma as a leader versus a supervisor versus a guide was also found to significantly influence cooperation, despite given payoff structures that were equivalent (Samuelson & Allison, 1994).

De Dreu and McCusker (1997) provide evidence of the impact that characterizing outcomes as losses versus gains had on behavior in a social dilemma, with that effect determining the prosocial behavior of the decision-maker. Arguing that cooperation has a higher value than defection for individuals with a cooperative motive but that the reverse is true for those with individualistic and competitive motives, they found that cooperators cooperated more when outcomes were characterized in terms of losses than in terms of gains, though such characterization had no effect for competitors. Most important to our arguments is that their results suggest that the impact of a payoff structure depends on the lens through which participants perceive that payoff structure, with different lenses yielding different valuations of outcomes and, subsequently, different behaviors.

Tenbrunsel and Messick (1999) provided a direct examination of situation construals, in the form of decision frames, on behavior in a dilemma situation. Individuals were placed in the role of a manufacturer in a toxic gas–emitting industry and had to make a decision about whether to cooperate and adhere to an industry agreement to voluntarily reduce emissions or to defect by not adhering to the agreement. Individuals' decisions to reduce emissions depended on whether they perceived the situation through an ethics frame or a business frame: Individuals who perceived the decision through a business frame were more likely to defect than those who perceived the decision through an ethics frame. Thus, though the given matrix was consistent in the experimental materials, behavior was influenced by the frame that was adopted. Thus, as illustrated in Figure 5.1, contextual frames can determine which elements of the environment are attended to (what is salient in the situation) and what value is attached to those elements that are salient.

Tenbrunsel and Messick (1999) proposed a "signaling-processing model" to describe the relationships between decision frames and behavior. More specifically, they argued that different situational cues — presence of a sanctioning system, language euphemisms, etc. — signaled a particular frame through which the decision-maker perceived the decision. The decision processing that occurred within each frame was then unique to the frame that was adopted. For example, when the participants described above saw the decision through a business frame, the strength of the sanction (i.e., How much is the fine? What is the probability that I will get caught?) influenced behavior; however, when the participants saw the decision through an ethical frame, the strength of the sanction had no effect on behavior. The decision processing, and the factors that influence it, are thus specific to the frame through which the decision-maker perceives the decision.

Combined, the findings of these studies highlight the potential offered by an integration of the logic of appropriateness framework (March, 1995; Messick, 1999) with social dilemma research. Understanding the way in which situations are construed by the individual — i.e., the decision frame — may help to identify which factors (i.e., costs and benefits) influence a decision-maker involved in a social dilemma and what he might do. Weber, Kopelman, and Messick (2004) made a similar observation in their review of existing social dilemma findings within the logic of appropriateness framework. We extend their observation by connecting this framework to that of the effective matrix, arguing that this integration will provide insight into the perceived payout structure, a crucial but neglected concept in social dilemma research. Further, as described below, this integration between the original conceptualization of payoff structures (Thibaut & Kelley, 1978) and decision frames reveals an important but neglected topic in social dilemma research — namely, that of unintended defection.

UNINTENDED DEFECTION

We argue that decision frames — and the consequent idiosyncratic transformation of given matrices into effective matrices — are particularly important to understand because certain types of decision frames are more likely to lead to cooperation failures in social dilemmas, but not necessarily because decision-makers are not trying to cooperate. Rather, despite the best of intentions of decision-makers, differences in decision frames can promote effective matrices that lead actors to unknowingly defect. The danger for social dilemmas raised is this: A decision-maker's idiosyncratic transformation of given matrices into effective matrices may lead that decision-maker to believe that he or she is selecting a mutually beneficial (cooperative) course of action — or at worst a personally beneficial course of action to which interdependent others are indifferent. Yet, when viewed by other interdependent parties, such behavior may be perceived as defection.

Critical to understand, then, is the characteristics of frames that lead to effective matrices that promote defection, especially when defection was not the intended goal. In the Ping-Pong example, perceiving the situation as a competition led to different behaviors than perceiving it as a "let the kids win" situation, suggesting that goals or motivations may be one characteristic of frames that influence whether defection is encouraged. In the following section, we discuss three additional characteristics of frames that may also lead to unintended defection: (mis)perception of actor independence, limited consequence scope, and asymmetries in outcome valuation.

(Mis)perception of Actor Independence

Frames can differ in the degree to which actors are seen as independent, a perception that in turn drives differences in the resulting effective matrices. At the extreme, a perception of complete independence in a social dilemma transforms the social dilemma into a decision dilemma (e.g., Behn & Vaupel, 1982) that entails no considerations of others' actions or their outcomes. Without a consideration of others, cooperation does not enter into the actor's choice set and defection ensues.

Price wars provide a good illustration of the impact that perceived independence can have on subsequent behavior (e.g., Rockmann & Northcraft, 2008). In such price wars, firms typically lower prices for their products in order to capture greater market share. Behind this price-reduction behavior lies the belief that the firm faces a simple choice between (a) maintaining prices and thus maintaining current market share versus (b) lowering prices and thus increasing market share. A recent example of price war behavior is reflected in the competition for doctoral students in business schools, where some schools are dramatically increasing stipends offered to admitted students — in one case, by 45% over the previous year (Rust, 2008) — in order to capture a greater share of the Ph.D. student market.

The problem with these behaviors is their necessary but unacknowledged interdependence, reminiscent of the decision failures that occur in the "dollar auction" exercise (Shubik, 1971) because players fail to appreciate (at their considerable peril) the motivations of other interdependent players. In any social context, competitive actions do not occur in a vacuum and likely will elicit interdependent reactions by others that can "undo" the intended value of the initial action. In the examples noted above, price reductions by one firm intended to capture additional market share often elicit similar price reductions by other players in the market, which in the end make price no more a purchase consideration than it was initially. Everyone retains their same initial market share but at a lower revenue-per-customer price point. In the Ph.D. student recruitment example, increases in stipends offered by one school to admitted students are matched by other schools. In the end, all schools may attract the same students they would have attracted but at a higher cost to all schools. From the initiator's perspective, the decision may have been framed as simply a smart strategic strategy; however, the lack of consideration of interdependence resulted in this strategic move being perceived by other firms or other universities as defection, a perception that in turn encouraged others to defect.

Frames that vary in the degree of perceived independence will in turn produce variance in the resulting effective matrices. The more a decision-maker, in comparison to others, perceives the decision as one involving independence, the less the decision-maker will appreciate the potential backlash from a competitive choice and, consequently, the more "defection" behaviors will be valued in the effective matrix. The decision-maker is thus more likely to defect in the eyes of others, even though the decision-maker may not be aware that he or she is doing so.

Limited Consequence Scope

Another important characteristic of frames that may promote unintentional defection is limited consideration of the scope of the consequences. In other words, the consequences that are considered depend on the frame through which the decision is perceived, and a limiting frame can yield limited appreciation of all possible ramifications of defection. For example, conflict frames are argued to be metaschematic, guiding which information is perceived and interpreted (Pinkley, 1990; Pinkley & Northcraft, 1994). Examining the consequences through a particular frame may lead the decision-maker to perceive that he has cooperated but lead others, who are looking through a different frame that considers a different set of consequences, to perceive non-cooperation.

This non-cooperation stemming from appreciation of only a limited scope of consequences is well captured by a scene from the movie, *Class Action* (Shelby, Ames, Shed, & Apted, 1991), in which an automobile manufacturing executive (George Getchell) explains to his lawyers (Maggie Ward and Michael Grazier) why a faulty blinker circuit that caused fatal car crashes was not replaced:

Ward: May I ask a question please?

Getchell: Sure.

Ward: Why didn't you just change the blinker circuit? (pause) It's just a question.

Getchell: I told Flannery about the problem a month or so before he died. He called in his head bean counter.

Ward: What's a bean counter?

Grazier: Risk Management expert, right, George?

Getchell: So Flannery shows him the data and asks him how much it would cost to retrofit ...

Ward: You mean recall?

Getchell: Yeah, you got it — to retrofit 175,000 units. You multiply that by 300 bucks per car, give or take. You're looking at right around $50 million. So the Risk Management guy, he crunches the numbers some more. He figures out you'd have one of those fireball collisions about every 3000 cars. That's 158 explosions.

Ward: Which is almost exactly as many plaintiffs as there are.

Getchell: These guys know their numbers! So you multiply that by $200,000 per lawsuit. That's assuming everyone sues and wins. $30 million max. See, it's cheaper to deal with the lawsuits than it is to fix the blinker. It's what the bean counters call a simple actuarial analysis.

The problem here is not that the automobile executive has failed to appreciate the interdependence of his actions. On the contrary, he appears to have carefully calculated the cost of that interdependence: on the average, a check for $200,000 for every one of his customers who sues after being involved in a "fireball collision" in one of his cars. The problem here is that the automobile executive appears to be assuming that his effective matrix has incorporated all of the relevant consequences (and valued them appropriately) for all involved parties. He believes that his actions have saved his company millions, at no cost to his customers or even possibly a slightly lower price for customers on the car, by assuming customer indifference between $200,000 versus avoiding a fireball collision. What he does not consider is the valuation that those involved in a collision would put on avoiding a collision, resulting in the perception that the executive has defected, delaying the expense of human suffering and loss of life in order to save the company millions.

A combination of these first two problems — (mis)perception of actor independence and limited consequence scope — occurs when a decision-maker's frame results in a consideration of only some but not all interdependent parties that are considered part of the dilemma and hence not all consequences are represented in the effective matrix. Take, for example, discussion concerning teaching loads and student enrollments that often occurs between the faculty and administration of a college. The administration wants higher enrollments to increase revenue, and the faculty wants lower enrollments to reduce teaching load. They reach a mutually beneficial agreement by enlarging average class sizes, thereby providing the opportunity to increase enrollments while reducing teaching loads — which unfortunately fails to consider the consequences of that decision for the quality and intimacy of instruction for the college's students. The decision-makers' effective matrix encourages cooperation but it overlooks the outcomes for involved parties they did not consider, thereby leading to the perception by those students and their (paying) parents that the faculty and administrators have acted non-cooperatively.

A real example of the above occurred in the case of the pregnancy hormone, diethylstilbestrol (DES), taken by pregnant mothers who were at risk for a problem pregnancy (Messick & Bazerman, 1996). The risks of taking the hormone were greatest for the yet-to-be-born daughters to these mothers, yet these actors were not considered. Manufacturers of the hormone may have intended to cooperate, but their frame only included an assessment of risks to mothers and failed to consider the consequences to the more affected party, producing a disastrous defection.

Parasitic integration, which involves negotiated agreements that are Pareto superior to some negotiators but suboptimal to others, provide another illustration of the problem of limited consequence scope (Gillespie & Bazerman, 1997). In these types of agreements, the size of the pie does not change but, rather, some negotiators increase their "pie slice" by taking it from others. The agreement between Schering-Plough and Upsher-Smith provides a classic example of parasitic integration (Bazerman, 2007). This agreement involved Schering-Plough's offering Upsher-Smith $60 million for five pharmaceutical products, while at the same time Upsher-Smith agreed to delay its introduction of a generic drug, a drug that would pose a significant threat to the near monopoly that Schering-Plough had for that product. Though advantageous to both companies, the cost was born by society. As Gillespie and Bazerman (1997) note, the consequences of such types of agreements are anything but desirable: "Far from enhancing the welfare of the broader organization or community, some agreements … actually withdraw resources from a subset of negotiators or from the broader community" (p. 274).

We argue that underlying these situations is the selection of decision frames that considers some but not all of the consequences, in turn leading actors to select what they believe to be a cooperative choice. However, those interdependent actors not included (along with neutral observers such as juries) have an effective matrix that looks quite different, one that includes the costs and benefits to additional participants. According to their effective matrices, the actor's decision may appear as clear defection.

Valuation Asymmetry

The valuation of outcomes and benefits and, more particularly, the value asymmetry that exists across frames of involved actors is a third characteristic to consider in the case of unintended defection. The problem this raises for cooperation in social dilemmas stems from the idea that the transformation of a given matrix into an effective matrix actually requires two steps. First, the decision-maker must decide what consequences are relevant to the decision for all parties involved. And second, the decision-maker must assign value to those relevant consequences. As noted by the examples provided above, the idiosyncratic transformation process may result in interdependence being ignored, or it may result in some consequences being overlooked. However, even when interdependence is acknowledged and even when the consequences of interest to all parties are factored into the decision, a decision-maker's projection of his or her own values on the consequences of interest (e.g., Dawes & Mulford, 1966) may still lead that decision-maker to select a course of action that looks to him or her like cooperation (possibility of mutual benefit to all interdependent parties) but that looks a lot like defection from the perspective of interdependent others. This is because it is not just the consequences that determine whether or which joint courses of action are mutually beneficial — it is the value that the interdependent parties each personally attach to those consequences along with the assumption that others have the same frame. When a decision-maker attaches value to the consequences in the effective matrix he or she bases a choice on, that decision-maker may not realize that the valuations of others are unlikely to be the same. Natural asymmetry in the personal valuing of consequences may mean that a consequence the decision-maker thought interdependent others would view as a benefit may instead be viewed by them as nothing short of a betrayal.

Prospect theory (Kahneman & Tversky, 1979) provides a classic example of how the "framing"[1] of outcomes in terms of losses or gains might affect the asymmetric valuation of identical outcomes, in this case by affecting risk references. Decision-makers evaluate the prospects of gains differently than the prospect of losses — in particular, losses loom larger (have more impact or import) than gains of identical magnitude in a subjective valuing sense. Critically, however, whether particular outcomes are framed as gains or losses is highly dependent upon what reference point the decision-maker evaluates those outcomes against. Two different decision-makers evaluating the same outcome against different reference points could potentially assign totally different subjective values to the same outcome prospect, leading to different effective matrices.

An example of this problem is provided by the subprime mortgage lending crisis, which significantly lowered housing prices (e.g., Ruben, 2008). Housing sales have also experienced significant drops — in part because sellers seem to be psychologically incapable of accepting the fact that their houses are suddenly worth less. The result is that buyers (anchored by current lower valuations) are making what they feel are "good faith" offers, whereas sellers (anchored by previous higher valuations) are making what they feel are good faith demands — and yet there remains an unbridgeable gap between the offers and the demands. Working from the same reference points, the possibility of mutual gain probably exists. Working from different reference points, however, each side views the other side's actions as irrationally non-cooperative.

Extending this example to a dilemma situation, unintended defection can occur, not because decision-makers choose to defect, but rather because the frame through which they perceive the dilemma dictates the valuation of the relevant outcomes, hence affecting the effective matrix. Individuals who are considering the same level of interdependence and the same consequences may have very different effective matrices because the frames through which they view the social dilemmas are different. Though each cooperates in terms of his own effective matrix, the behavior looks like defection for those who view the dilemma with a different effective matrix.

IMPLICATIONS FOR SOCIAL DILEMMA RESEARCH

We have argued in this chapter that social dilemma research has over-looked the important role played by the effective matrix (Kelley & Thibaut, 1978), instead focusing on the given matrix. This is problematic, produc-ing possibly questionable conclusions about how differences in the given matrix lead to varying degrees of defection and cooperation when such matrices may have had very little impact on behavior. In fact, our argu-ments suggest that real-world social dilemmas — where individuals must extract their effective matrix from an infinite range of possibilities — should be harder for participants to understand and manage than those in admittedly limited experimental settings where the given matrix may be all that decision-makers have to consider. Even in such limited settings, however, value intrusions might occur that would create a divergent effec-tive matrix, such as valuing the opportunity to create new friendships with fellow experiment participants more than the "given" outcomes of the experiment.

We have offered the logic of appropriateness framework (March, 1995; Messick, 1999) and the corresponding notion of decision frames as a means by which to bring back the effective matrix and hence enhance our under-standing of social dilemmas. In doing so, we add a theoretical perspec-tive to the work on biases and their contribution to undesirable outcomes (Messick & Bazerman, 1996), suggesting that the decision frame that one adopts may unknowingly encourage faulty decision-making.

At the root of the problem we identify are differences in effective matri-ces across participants in social dilemmas and between participants and non-participants (such as legislators and their constituents or litigants and their jurors). If everyone examines a dilemma with the same effective matrix — i.e., with the same sense of interdependence, the same set of consequences, and the same valuations across outcomes — then unin-tended defection should not be an issue. Defection might still result, but it would be intended. Contributing to the problem is the lack of realization by decision-makers that their effective matrices are not "the" given matrix upon which others are operating but rather that each participant (and non-participant) may be basing their actions and judgments off of their own effective matrices. Research on the "false consensus" effect (Marks & Miller, 1987) suggests that individuals often project their own preferences onto others and thereby assume that others prefer and value what they do; similarly, we argue that individuals project their own effective matrices onto others. This can result in individuals being blindsided, falsely believing that they are cooperating and perceiving that everyone else believes that, too.

Important for social dilemma research then is to understand the factors that drive particular decision frames and, at the same time, lead decision-makers to perceive that others are viewing the situation through the same frame. As Neale, Huber, and Northcraft (1987) state, "... there exist in many decision settings both task-responsive and contextual influences which frame individual judgments in systematic, predictable ways" (p. 229). Different frames can be produced, for example, by differences in the euphemisms describing the dilemma (Tenbrunsel & Messick, 2004). Indeed, Pillutla and Chen (1999) found that labeling the dilemma as one involving social versus monetary goods increased cooperation, a characterization that we argue affected the degree of perceived independence, the relevant consequences, the valuation of outcomes and, ultimately, behavior.

Work on strategic decision-making provides another example of how language contributes to how a decision is perceived. A central view in the strategy field is that the labeling and categorizing of decision problems by managers significantly shapes organizational responses to those problems (Mintzberg, Raisinghani, & Theoret, 1976; Papadakis, Lioukas, & Chambers, 1998). Problems coded as threats or crises, for example, have been argued to engage different reactions than those coded as opportunities (Fredrickson, 1985; Jackson & Dutton, 1988). More specifically, coding the situation as a threat versus a challenge is asserted to change whether outcomes are viewed as losses versus gains: "Threat appraisals are those in which the perception of danger exceeds the perception of abilities or resources to cope with the stressor. Challenge appraisals, in contrast, are those in which the perception of danger does not exceed the perception of resources or ability to cope. Presumably, threatened individuals perceive the potential for loss, with little if anything to be gained in the situation. Challenged individuals, however, perceive the possibility of gain ... as well as loss in the situation" (Tomaka, Blascovich, Kelsey, & Leitten, 1993; p. 248). Thus, differences in which an identical situation is labeled or framed can impact whether the outcomes are coded as losses or gains, which, in turn (we argue), elicits asymmetries in the effective matrices for the participations.

Frames may also be dictated by what is perceived to be the desired decision process, such as whether rationality is valued (Zhong, 2007). Zhong discusses the ethical dangers of rational decision-making, demonstrating that priming rational decision leads to increased cheating and reduced charitable donations. In this sense, rational decision-making is argued to "license" unethical behavior, focusing attention exclusively on tangible monetary outcomes. Along these same lines, Dane and Pratt (2007) note that systematic rational decision processes are quite different from more holistic, intuitive ones. The difference between intuition and rationality again could determine what elements and whose elements are relevant for valuing in order to decide what course of action to take in a social dilemma. For example, systematic rational processes may be more exhaustive in whose preferences and issues are considered, but intuitive processes (as noted by Zhong) may be more inclusive in the valuing process (i.e., take less concrete feelings into account).

Frames may also be driven by the culture within which the decision takes place. Corporate culture is argued to impact the causal background against which events are retrospectively interpreted (McGill, 1996). Similarly, culture may dictate the frame through which prospective decisions are made. A corporate culture that emphasizes profit, for example, may lead to effective matrices that are characterized by higher valuations of monetary outcomes than those cultures that emphasize more social, intangible outcomes. National cultures also may vary in the extent to which they emphasize or "prime" individual versus collective concerns (Oyserman & Lee, 2008). The real danger here is that cross-cultural social dilemmas will involve cultural frames that dictate what elements should be considered and how those elements should be valued — but differently for different cultures. For example, collectivists are likely to incorporate into their thinking the preferences and values of a broader array of stakeholders than their individualistic counterparts.

A critical conclusion of this discussion is that the effective management of social dilemmas may depend on factors that lead individuals to understand what frame others have selected and, in turn, the effective matrix from which they are operating. Research on perspective taking (e.g., Epley, Caruso, & Bazerman, 2006; Galinsky, Maddux, Gilin, & White, 2008; Neale & Bazerman, 1983) has validated its importance to negotiation success — knowing what others value makes it easier to identify positions that will satisfy everyone. Similarly in social dilemmas, knowing what others value — and what effective matrix they may be perceiving — seems an essential prerequisite to differentiating between cooperative and competitive responses.

CONCLUSIONS

The oil crisis. Global warming. Food shortages. Nuclear arms. Resolving social dilemmas has never been more important. To do so requires that we get "inside" the minds of those who make the decisions and understand the basis by which they make them, including the participants they are involving and those they are not, the outcomes they perceive as the consequences of their choices, and the value they attach to those consequences. We have argued that such an understanding necessitates the resurrection of the effective matrix, an important but unfortunately neglected topic in the social dilemma arena, and, further, that the logic of appropriateness framework can be useful in that endeavor. These two research streams were fundamental in the research career of Dave Messick and his work offered illuminating insights to each. As suggested in this chapter, however, it is the integration of the two that may make the greatest contribution yet.

NOTE

1. It is important to note that this definition of *frame* is a more narrow definition of frame than that which is discussed in this chapter. The notion of framing in Kahneman and Tversky's (1979) prospect theory refers to how outcomes are characterized; the notion advanced in this chapter is much more general, referring to the way in which the entire decision (social actors involved, inputs, outputs, goals, etc.) is depicted. Thus, the framing found in prospect theory is a partial subset of the more general notion of framing discussed in this chapter.

REFERENCES

Bazerman, M. H. (2007). Behavioral decision research, legislation, and society: Three cases. *Capitalism and Society, 2*(1), Article 2.

Beach, L. R. (1993). *Image theory: Decision making in personal and organizational contexts.* Chichester, UK: Wiley.

Behn, R. D., & Vaupel, J. W. (1982). *Quick analysis for busy decision makers.* New York: Basic Books.

Boles, T. L., & Messick, D. M. (1990). Accepting unfairness: Temporal influence on choice. In K. Borcherding, O. I. Larichev, & D. M. Messick (Eds.), *Contemporary issues in decision making* (pp. 375–390). Amsterdam: North Holland.

Brewer, M. B., & Kramer, R. M. (1986). Choice behavior in social dilemmas: Effects of social identity, group size and decision framing. *Journal of Personality and Social Psychology, 50*(3), 543–549.

Clinton, H. R. (1996). *It takes a village.* New York: Simon & Schuster.

Connolly, T., & Koput, K. (1997). Naturalistic decision making and the new organizational context. In Z. Shapiro (Ed.), *Organizational decision making* (pp. 282–303). Cambridge, UK: Cambridge University Press.

Dane, E., & Pratt, M. G. (2007). Exploring intuition and its role in managerial decision making. *Academy of Management Review, 32*, 33–54.

Dawes, R., & Mulford, M. (1966). The false consensus effect and overconfidence: Flaws in judgment or flaws in how we study judgment. *Organizational Behavior and Human Decision Processes, 65*, 201–211.

De Dreu, C. K. W., & McCusker, C. (1997). Gain-loss frames and cooperation in two-person social dilemmas: A transformational analysis. *Journal of Personality and Social Psychology, 72*, 1093–1106.

Epley, N., Caruso, E. M., & Bazerman, M. H. (2006). When perspective taking increases taking: Reactive egoism in social interaction. *Journal of Personality and Social Psychology, 91*, 872–889.

Fredrickson, J. W. (1985). Effects of decision motive and organizational performance level on strategic decision processes. *Academy of Management Journal, 28*(3), 821–843.

Galinsky, A. D., Maddux, W. W., Gilin, D., & White, J. B. (2008). Why it pays to get inside the head of your opponent: The differential effects of perspective taking and empathy in negotiations. *Psychological Science, 19*(4), 378–384.

Gillespie, J., & Bazerman, M. H. (1997). Parasitic integration. *Negotiation Journal, 13*, 271–282.

Hardin, G. (1968). Tragedy of the commons. *Science, 162*, 1243–1248.

Jackson, S. E., & Dutton, J. E. (1988). Discerning threats and opportunities. *Administrative Science Quarterly, 33*(3), 370–387.

Kahneman, D., & Tversky, A. (1979). Prospect theory: An analysis of decision making under risk. *Econometrica, 73*, 263–291.

Kelley, H. H., & Thibaut, J. W. (1978). *Interpersonal relations: A theory of interdependence.* New York: Wiley-Interscience.

Klein, G. A. (1989). Recognition-primed decisions. In W. B. Rouse (Ed.), *Advances in man-machine system research* (Vol. 5, pp. 47–92). Greenwich, CT: JAI Press.

Liberman, V., Samuels, S. M., & Ross, L. (2004). The name of the game: Predictive powers of reputations versus situational labels in determining prisoner's dilemma game moves. *Personality and Social Psychology Bulletin, 30*(9), 1175–1185.

Liebrand, W. B. G., Messick, D. M., & Wilke, H. A. M. (Eds.). (1992). *Social dilemmas: Theoretical issues and research findings.* Oxford, UK: Pergamon.

March, J. G. (1995). *A primer on decision making.* New York: Free Press.

Marks, G., & Miller, N. (1987). Ten years of research on the false-consensus effect: An empirical and theoretical review. *Psychological Bulletin, 102,* 728–735.

McGill, A. L. (1996). Responsibility judgments and the causal background. In D. M. Messick & A. E. Tenbrunsel (Eds.), *Codes of conduct: Behavioral research into business ethics.* New York: Russell Sage.

Messick, D. M. (1999). Alternative logics for decision making in social settings. *Journal of Economic Behavior & Organization, 39*(1), 11–28.

Messick, D. M., & Bazerman, M. H. (1996). Ethical leadership and the psychology of decision making. *Sloan Management Review,* 9–22.

Messick, D. M., & Brewer, R. M. (1983). Solving social dilemmas: A review. In W. L. Whealer & P. Shaver (Eds.), *Review of personality and social psychology* (Vol. 4, pp. 11–44). Beverly Hills, CA: Sage.

Messick, D. M., Wilke, H., Brewer, M. B., Kramer, R. M., Zemke, P. E., & Lui, L. (1983). Individual adaptations and structural change as solutions to social dilemmas. *Journal of Personality and Social Psychology, 44,* 294–309.

Mintzberg, H., Raisinghani, D., & Theoret, A. (1976). The structure of unstructured decision processes. *Administrative Science Quarterly, 21,* 246–275.

Neale, M. A., & Bazerman, M. H. (1983). The role of perspective-taking ability in negotiating under different forms of arbitration. *Industrial and Labor Relations Review, 36,* 378–388.

Neale, M. A., Huber, V. L., & Northcraft, G. B. (1987). The framing of negotiations: Contextual vs. task frames. *Organizational Behavior and Human Decision Processes, 39,* 228–241.

Noble, D. (1989). *Application of a theory of cognition to situation assessment.* Vienna, VA: Engineering Research Associates.

Northcraft, G. B., & Neale, M. A. (1990). *Organizational behavior: A management challenge.* Chicago: Dryden Press.

Oyserman, D., & Lee, S. W. S. (2008). Does culture influence what and how we think? Effects of priming individualism and collectivism. *Psychological Bulletin. 134*(2), 311–342.

Papadakis, V. M., Lioukas, S., & Chambers, D. (1998). Strategic decision making processes: The role of management and context. *Strategic Management Journal, 19*(2), 115–147.

Payne, J. W., Bettman, J. R., & Johnson, E. J. (1993). *The adaptive decision maker.* Cambridge, UK: Cambridge University Press.

Pennington, N., & Hastie, R. (1988). Explanation-based decision making: Effects of memory structure on judgment. *Journal of Experimental Psychology: Learning, Memory and Cognition, 14,* 521–553.

Pillutla, M. M., & Chen, X. P. (1999). Social norms and cooperation in social dilemmas: The effect of feedback and norms. *Organizational Behavior and Human Decision Processes, 78*(2), 81–103.

Pinkley, R. L. (1990). Dimensions of conflict frame: Disputant interpretations of conflict. *Journal of Applied Psychology, 75,* 117–126.

Pinkley, R. L., & Northcraft, G. B. (1994). Conflict frames of reference: Implications for dispute processes and outcomes. *Academy of Management Journal, 37,* 193–205.

Pruitt, D. G., & Carnevale, P. J. (1993). *Negotiation in social conflict. Mapping social psychology series.* Belmont, CA: Thomson Brooks/Cole Publishing Co.

Rockmann, K. W., & Northcraft, G. B. (2008). To be or not to be trusted: The influence of media richness on deception and defection. *Organizational Behavior and Human Decision Processes, 107,* 106–122.

Ruben, B. (2008, April 24). Falling house prices take toll in Va. suburbs. *Washington Post,* p. VA21.

Rust, R. (2008). The marketing professor shortage. ELMAR. Retrieved February 25, 2008, from http://ama-academics.communityzero.com/elmar?go+174986z

Samuelson, C. D., & Allison, S. T. (1994). Cognitive factors affecting the use of social decision heuistics in resource sharing tasks. *Organizational Behavior and Human Decision Processes, 58*(1), 1–27.

Shelby, C., Ames, C., & Shad, S. (Writers), & Apted, M. (Director). (1991). Class Action [Motion picture]. United States: 20th Century Fox Films.

Shubik, M. (1971). The dollar auction game: A paradox in non-cooperative behavior and escalation. *Journal of Conflict Resolution, 15,* 545–547.

Simon, H. A. (1957). *Administrative behavior.* New York: MacMillan.

Tenbrunsel, A. E., & Messick, D. M. (1999). Sanctioning systems, cooperation and decision construals. *Administrative Science Quarterly, 44,* 684–707.

Tenbrunsel, A. E., & Messick, D. M. (2004). Ethical fading: The role of self-deception in unethical behavior. *Social Justice Research, 17,* 223–236.

Tomaka, J., Blascovich, J., Kelsey, R. M., & Leitten, C. L. (1993). Subjective, physiological, and behavioral effects of threat and challenge appraisal. *Journal of Personality and Social Psychology, 65*(2), 248–260.

Tversky, A., & Kahneman, D. (1981). The framing of decisions and the psychology of choice. *Science, 211,* 453–463.

Weber, J. M., Kopelman, S., & Messick, D. M. (2004). A conceptual review of decision making in social dilemmas: Applying a logic of appropriateness. *Personality and Social Psychology Review, 8*(3), 281–307.

Zhong, C.-B. (2007). *The ethical dangers of rational decision making.* Anaheim, CA: Academy of Management.

6

Dilemmas and Doubts: How Decision-Makers Cope With Interdependence and Uncertainty

Roderick M. Kramer
Stanford Business School

> Dilemmas are characterized by more or less equal motivational tugs from opposite directions, so that whichever way one succumbs, one pays an equal cost for the abandonment of the other. (Lim, 2008, p. 7)

> Who said a dilemma had only two horns? He must have been fooling around with little dilemmas. ... A real dilemma has between eight and ten horns and can kill you. (Ernest Hemingway, quoted in Hotchner, 2008, p. 109)

At a February 12, 2002, Defense Department briefing, reporters confronted Secretary of Defense Donald Rumsfeld with a series of probing questions regarding what significance, if any, should be attached to the Bush administration's failure to find evidence of weapons of mass destruction (WMD) in Iraq. "Reports that say something hasn't happened are always interesting to me," Rumsfeld responded, with an air of almost bemused resignation. "As we know," he went on to explain, "there are 'known knowns.' There are the things we know we know. We also know there are 'known unknowns.' That is to say, we know there are some things we don't know. But there are also 'unknown unknowns,' the ones we don't know we don't know (Ezard, 2003, p.1)."

The lexicographic oddness of his statement notwithstanding, I suspect that most of us have some sense for what Rumsfeld was trying to say (although even one White House aide, when asked to explain the remarks, responded, "We *think* we know what he is saying — but we're not sure."). One reasonable parsing of the statement might go something like this: "The world is a dangerous place. Moreover, it may be dangerous in different and more deadly ways than you imagine." In short, there may be more threats in heaven and earth than are dreamt of in your philosophy — or reported by the *New York Times*. When in doubt, Rumsfeld implies, it's better to be safe than sorry.

Whether or not we agree with Rumsfeld's worldview, his remarks remind us that the world in which we live is full of uncertainties. Most of these uncertainties are benign. Some are not. And if these dangerous uncertainties are not anticipated and properly addressed by responsible decision-makers, the most severe consequences can follow. In the case of national security, for example, ignorance pertaining to an adversary's malignant intentions and the concomitant failure to take protective actions against them may prove fatal — as the events of September 11, 2001, made all too clear. Thus, Rumsfeld's assertion stands as a reminder also that — like it or not — we seldom exercise full control over our own fates. Instead, our fortunes are more often interdependent with those of others.

Situations where decision-makers exert such mutual "fate control" over each other are known formally as *interdependence dilemmas*. The study of decision-making in interdependence dilemmas has a long and venerable history in the social sciences, fueled in large measure by Kelley and Thibaut's seminal treatment (Kelley & Thibaut, 1978). In the decades since that influential analysis, our appreciation of the myriad forms that interdependence dilemmas assume — and the decisional complexities they create — have received extensive attention from social psychologists (see Kelley et al., 2003, for a comprehensive review). My own research in this area, spanning nearly three decades, has focused on identifying the psychological and structural determinants of decision-making in a variety of interdependence dilemmas. These include the commons dilemma (Kramer & Brewer, 1984; Kramer, McClintock & Messick, 1986; Messick, Brewer, Wilke, Kramer, Zemke-English, 1983), public goods dilemma (Brewer & Kramer, 1986), security dilemma (Kramer, 1987; Kramer, 1989; Kramer, Meyerson, & Davis, 1990), negotiation dilemmas (Kramer & Messick, 1995; Kramer, Newton, & Pommerenke, 1993; Kramer, Pommerenke, & Newton, 1993; Kramer, Pradhan-Shah, & Woerner, 1995), intra- and interorganizational resource dilemmas (Kramer, 1991; Kramer & Messick, 1996), and trust dilemmas (Cook et al., 2004; Kramer, 1994; Kramer & Messick, 1998; Messick & Kramer, 2001).

Each of these dilemmas possesses distinctive features and manifest intriguing properties. They present, in short, decision theorists with precisely the sort of engaging puzzles and paradoxes that Dave admits to relishing in his biographical essay presented later in this volume.

In this chapter, I aim to provide an overview of some of my research on decision-making under uncertainty in interdependence dilemmas. This research program has deliberately taken a multimethod approach, aiming to get us at least halfway around the track, if not yet quite "full circle" in our understanding of how decision-makers think about — and respond to — social interdependence (cf. Cialdini, 1980). As social scientists, I believe we learn best when we move systematically back and forth between laboratory and field — fine-tuning our intuitions and insights about the decision-making process as it unfolds, not only in the cloistered confines of the psychological laboratory but also in the "booming, buzzing confusion" of real-world settings involving real decision-makers confronting dilemmas of real consequence.

In that spirit, I begin with a brief description of exploratory work undertaken in experimental settings with undergraduate students as study participants. I then move into the field, examining how experienced and expert decision-makers deal with interdependence. I should note for clarity's sake that this chapter is not intended as a comprehensive or integrative review of the extant literature. Instead, I have endeavored to make this a more personal, somewhat autobiographical chapter. I adopted this approach because this is a volume in honor of Dave's contributions to the scholarly development of his students and collaborators. In my case, Dave's intellectual fingerprints can be found everywhere throughout my writing. And it is worth noting in this regard that seven of my scholarly papers, as well as two of the edited volumes with which I been involved, are coauthored with Dave. Dave's intellectual insight and infectious enthusiasm for research has kept the game afoot and the chase exciting all these years. I feel fortunate to have had not only his formative mentorship but also his enduring friendship. Interdependence is always pretty — but with Dave, it has been a source of both enduring pleasure and ongoing inspiration.

SETTING THE STAGE: THE "SIMPLE" ANATOMY OF INTERDEPENDENCE DILEMMAS

In their comprehensive atlas of interdependence dilemmas, Kelley et al. (2003) provide a systematic catalog of the logically possible forms such dilemmas take. To set the stage for a discussion of the individual studies to be discussed below, a brief overview of the general anatomy of an interdependence dilemma, and the role uncertainty plays in it, may be useful. Trust dilemmas constitute a prototypic and illustrative example of decision-making involving both interdependence and social uncertainty. Formally, trust dilemmas possess a deceptively simple decision structure. A social actor S, hoping to realize some perceived benefit, is tempted to engage in trusting behavior with one or more other social actors. Engaging in such behavior, however, exposes S to the prospect that his or her trust might be exploited or betrayed by the other party or parties. Hence, the choice dilemma for S, most starkly stated, is whether to trust or not to trust.

Although the logical structure of choice in trust dilemmas can be expressed simply, such decisions are psychologically quite complex. They resemble other forms of approach-avoidance conflict, in that a decision-maker is simultaneously attracted to the prospect of obtaining some desired benefit while hoping also to avoid disappointment or loss. The psychological complexity of trust dilemmas is further animated, of course, by the inherent and inescapable uncertainties we face whenever we find ourselves trying to assess the trustworthiness of other people on whom we must rely or depend. We can never know with complete certainty, for example, another person's true character or underlying motivation. Nor can we ever fully comprehend their intentions toward us. And we can never completely monitor all of their relevant actions, especially those behaviors they might engage in behind our backs. As trust theorist Diego Gambetta (1988) once noted in this regard, "The condition of ignorance or uncertainty about other people's behavior is central to the notion of trust. It is related to the limits of our capacity ever to achieve a full knowledge of others, their motives, and their responses" (p. 218). However much we might desire transparency and clarity in our relations with others, there will always be a curtain of doubt interposed between our self and other people.

From the standpoint of contemporary theory and research on decision-making, Gambetta's observation raises a variety of cogent but analytically rather vexing questions. First and foremost, perhaps, is how people decide to cope with or respond to such uncertainty. On what basis, for example, do they assess another person's trustworthiness or lack of trustworthiness? Under what circumstances are we likely to decide to give someone the benefit of the doubt when entering into a potentially profitable trust relationship? In short, on what psychological grounds do we predicate trust in another or risk cooperating with them? These are some of the central questions this chapter examines.

STUDYING INTERDEPENDENCE AND UNCERTAINTY IN EXPERIMENTAL SETTINGS

My initial interest in the problem of how decision-makers respond to interdependence and social uncertainty was stimulated by research that Dave Messick and Marilynn Brewer were doing at Santa Barbara when I began my graduate work there in 1980. They were investigating psychological and structural factors that influence trust and cooperation in various kinds of social dilemmas. I was fortunate enough to be included in their small, tight-knit research group.

In one of our first studies (Messick et al., 1983), we investigated how decision-makers' expectations of reciprocity influence their willingness to exercise personal self-restraint in a commons dilemma. Such expectations represent one important cognitive measure of social trust. Similarly, people's willingness to exercise personal restraint when sharing a common resource pool can be viewed as a behavioral indicator of social trust (although it can obviously reflect other motives as well; see, e.g., Kramer et al., 1986). Consistent with our theoretical expectations, we found that individuals who expected reciprocal restraint from other group members were more likely to exercise personal self-restraint themselves. This restraint was especially evident, moreover, under conditions of increasing resource scarcity.

In subsequent experiments, Marilynn Brewer and I (Brewer & Kramer, 1986; Kramer & Brewer, 1984) extended this line of investigation by examining the effects of group-based trust on personal restraint in social dilemmas. Drawing on Brewer's previous work on ingroup bias, we reasoned that individuals within a small, cohesive social group might possess a generalized or "depersonalized" form of trust in other ingroup members. Within the context of our minimal laboratory groups, our data provided some support for this notion, although the data revealed a complex picture. In particular, we found that a variety of factors influenced people's trust-related expectations and choice behavior. These factors included such things as (a) the decision structure of the dilemma, (b) the size of the group confronting the dilemma, and (c) the level of salient social categorization. In terms of their relevance to the present chapter, the results served to indicate just how psychologically complex individuals' responses to social uncertainty can be: When doubt exists regarding others' trustworthiness, decision-makers tend to try to "fill in the holes" in their understanding, using whatever social information or cues are available.

The next experiments we conducted explored in more detail the effects of various psychological variables — including decision framing, level of salient social categorization, and mental simulation on judgment and choice (Kramer, 1989; Kramer et al., 1990). Specifically, we explored how the framing of a risky decision (i.e., whether resource allocation decisions were framed in terms of prospective gains versus losses) influenced decision-makers' preferences for different outcome distributions. We also investigated how engaging in "best-case" versus "worst-case" mental simulations about an opponent's actions affected judgment and choice. Interestingly, we found that simply having people think about worst-case possibilities regarding their opponents' intentions and behaviors increased their willingness to allocate resources to protect against those imagined threats.

Using a different laboratory paradigm — this one designed to simulate an *n*-person trust dilemma — an additional study explored the effects of uncertainty on a variety of social cognitive processes that contribute to distrust and suspicion of other social actors (Kramer, 1994). The results of this experiment demonstrated that situationally induced self-consciousness — which can be construed as a psychological proxy for perception of social threat — led decision-makers to overestimate others' lack of trustworthiness. Similarly, the results showed that providing study participants an opportunity to ruminate about others' motives and intentions also increased suspicion and distrust of other individuals. Construed broadly, these results suggested how normatively "irrational" psychological factors can nonetheless influence judgment and choice in such situations.

To summarize, the results of these laboratory studies identified a wide range of social psychological variables that influence trust-related judgment and choice in situations involving social uncertainty. Although interesting and informative, there was one important way in which these findings were limited. All of these experiments involved undergraduate students with little prior formal training or experience with trust dilemmas. It is reasonable to presume, therefore, that on average these study participants did not possess much strategic sophistication or expertise regarding how to think about social uncertainty. In this respect, the external validity of these findings is somewhat suspect. Specifically, they raise the obvious question: How might more expert or experienced decision-makers think about and respond to social uncertainty? Accordingly, I decided to explore how sophisticated and experienced decision theorists might deal with the problem of social uncertainty. I was also interested in exploring methodologies that would enable a researcher to engage in richer and more inductive exploration of experienced decision-makers' adaptive strategies. Accordingly, my colleagues and I decided to conduct a computer tournament using such expert decision-makers. The results of that study are described next.

GETTING INSIDE THE HEADS OF THE EXPERTS: INSIGHTS FROM A COMPUTER-BASED TOURNAMENT

Another approach to studying how decision-makers think about, and respond to, social uncertainty is to use computer-based tournaments in which researchers "pit" different experts and their adaptive strategies against each other. By so doing, an investigator can systematically assess the comparative efficacy of their strategies under a wide array of conditions. As Axelrod (1980a, 1980b, 1984) brilliantly demonstrated, this tournament approach enables researchers to inductively evaluate which decision rules or strategies are particularly good at generating mutually productive and sustainable relationships of mutual trust or cooperation. A computer tournament in which participants have to explicitly design their strategies for playing against other strategies also provides a way for researchers to systematically study decision-makers' a priori beliefs and expectations regarding others' motives, intentions, and actions. In designing a strategy, after all, designers have to decide not only how they will respond to the social uncertainty inherent in the task but how they think others will respond to it. In other words, they not only have to decide how they will cope with the "unknown unknowns" in the situation, they have to try to project how others will cope as well.

The methodology we used was modeled after Axelrod's (1984) original computer tournaments on the evolution of cooperation (see Bendor, Kramer, & Stout, 1991, for a more thorough description of the study methods and study rationale). Recall that Axelrod had individuals design strategies that would play other strategies in a "classic" Prisoner's Dilemma game (PDG; i.e., a deterministic, binary-choice form of the game with 0 uncertainty or "noise"). Because we were interested in studying how uncertainty regarding others' intentions and actions affects decision-making, we modified Axelrod's procedures in several important ways. First and foremost, we introduced uncertainty (noise) into the communication channel between the players. In the classic Prisoner's Dilemma, after players decide whether they wish to cooperate with the other person, they learn with perfect certainty what their partners chose to do as well. In most real-world trust dilemma situations, of course, people typically experience some degree of uncertainty regarding what their partners did. Accordingly, to introduce such uncertainty into our tournament, participants' cooperation levels were obscured by adding or subtracting a small random amount of noise to their feedback during each period of play. Because of this noise factor, participants in our tournament (or, more accurately stated, the computer programs of the strategies they designed) could receive feedback that their partners (strategies) had behaved either more or less cooperatively than they actually had. This allowed us to explore how decision-makers adjust strategically to the noise.

From the standpoint of coping with uncertainty, the participants' strategies had to explicitly solve two problems. The first is how much presumptive trust in the other to manifest initially (i.e., as the first-trial cooperation level). For example, should one extend full effort (maximum trust) to the other initially in the hope that the other will reciprocate with full effort? Extending full aid initially will help sustain a mutually productive trust relationship with a similarly inclined other. On the other hand, it opens one up to early exploitation if one happens to encounter a competitive individual who lacks trustworthiness. Thus, given the uncertainty inherent in the situation before the first decision trial, a high initial offer demonstrates a high level of presumptive trust in the other. Alternatively, one could decide to withhold much aid to the other until it was clear from their first move what they intended to do. A cautious first move provides protection against initial exploitation but risks damaging a relationship with someone who might be perfectly willing to fully cooperate.

The second important decision each participant had to make in designing his or her strategy was how to respond to feedback regarding the other's initial (and subsequent) decisions — especially when one knows that such feedback is inherently uncertain (i.e., contaminated by the noise). Stated differently, how much sensitivity should one display to indications that the other might be reciprocating less than fully, given that those indications are inherently ambiguous because of the noise in the communication channel? For example, how reactive or punishing should one be to the suspicion that the other might not be cooperating fully?

Rather than use inexperienced or novice undergraduate students who might be playing a PDG for the first time, we intentionally sought out participants who were sophisticated, expert decision-makers (i.e., individuals who were intimately familiar with theory and research on the Prisoner's Dilemma). Thus, the participants in our study included leading game theorists, economists, political scientists, and social psychologists — most of whom had actually published research in this area.

Thirteen strategies were submitted to the tournament, reflecting a variety of different intuitions and beliefs regarding how decision-makers should cope with social uncertainty. For the purposes of the present chapter, I will focus my discussion on the performance of just two strategies. In particular, I wish to compare and contrast the performance of a strategy called Vigilant and Reactive (or Vigilant for short) with that of a strategy called Benign and Underreacting (or Benign for short).

In terms of the individual decision rules embodied within this strategy, Vigilant was a "nice" strategy in the Axelrodian sense of that term (i.e., it always started out by extending maximum initial cooperation to its partner). It was therefore open or receptive to the possibility that it was dealing with a trustworthy player. However, as its name suggests, it was extremely attentive to any signs that its partner was not reciprocating fully. In particular, if Vigilant detected what it believed was less than full effort from any of its partners on any trial, it retaliated by completely withdrawing effort on the next trial (i.e., giving 0 points to its partner). The aim of this extreme reactivity was, of course, to deter further acts of perceived exploitation in an attempt to induce the other to cooperate more fully. Because Vigilant was determined not to be exploited, it was biased toward assuming the worst about its partner whenever it received a low offer of effort. In other words, whenever it received low-effort feedback, it acted as if its partner had intentionally tried to shortchange it.

Presuming that its interpretation was valid, Vigilant then retaliated to the maximum level. Thus, Vigilant was a highly reactive strategy that left no slap unanswered.

There are different ways of dissecting Vigilant's performance in our tournament. One simple metric is to assess how well it did in its pair-wise encounters (i.e., how well it did against each player it was pitted against). When looked at from this perspective, the data analyses revealed a very simple and seemingly straightforward finding: Vigilant always received on average more than it gave away. In other words, it walked away from every one of its encounters a clear winner in terms of relative or comparative gain. If we think about Vigilant as a motivated decision-maker trying to optimize her performance in a socially uncertain world, we would have to conclude that she would more than likely be rather satisfied with her performance. After all, no one she meets does better than she does.

A second strategy submitted to our tournament, called Benign, embodied a more gentle view of the world. As was Vigilant, Benign was nice in that it always began each relationship by extending maximum possible aid to its partner. However, it differed from Vigilant in several ways. First, Benign tended to be generous, returning more effort on a subsequent trial than it had received from its partner on the previous trial. Benign's generosity took the form of what might be construed as a benign sort of indifference to the other's payoffs (as long as its partner's observed effort level exceeded 80, Benign would continue to help its partner fully; i.e., give 100% of the possible points to it). Second, although Benign was provocable (i.e., would retaliate if its partner's aid dipped below 80), it reverted to full cooperation again on subsequent rounds, as long as the partner satisfied this threshold of acceptable behavior (i.e., its observed cooperation level was at least 80). Thus, Benign could be provoked, but it was also forgiving. It was thus less reactive than Vigilant and quicker to forgive.

When we compared how well Benign did in the tournament, we found that Benign lost out in its encounters with every player. In other words, it consistently gave away to its partners more than it got back from them. It appeared, at first glance at least, to be far too generous, consistently over-benefitting its partners and seemingly at its own expense. As long as it was getting at least 80% of the possible payoffs, it tended to underreact to unfavorable returns from its partner, and this underreaction seemed rather costly, allowing this strategy to be bested not only by more suspicious or wary players such as Vigilant but in fact by every other strategy in the tournament.

At first glance, a comparison of the performance of these two strategies would seem, therefore, to support just one conclusion: In an uncertain world, a certain amount of initial wariness about others' trustworthiness — coupled with a willingness to react strongly to even ambiguous evidence of that untrustworthiness — is both prudent and beneficial. In short, Vigilant appeared to be the superior strategy.

When we inspected the tournament results using a slightly different metric, however, this conclusion turned out to be less obvious. In fact, the story became quite a bit more complex — and more interesting. In particular, when we compared the overall or net performance of the strategies (i.e., examined their total earnings in the tournament by summing their average payoffs across all encounters with all strategies), a dramatically different inference suggested itself. It turned out that Benign emerged as the tournament winner (highest performer). In fact, Benign earned an average per trial payoff of 17.05 points, whereas Vigilant garnered only an unimpressive 8.99 points. Yet, recall that Vigilant outperformed Benign in their "face-to-face" encounters with each other, and every other player as well, whereas Benign lost out against every player. Thus, we seem to confront a perplexing, if not paradoxical, set of results: How could Vigilant do better in every encounter with every player it meets, and nonetheless end up losing the tournament, coming in dead last, while Benign got the short end of the stick in every encounter with every player and yet ended up accumulating more resources than any other player in the tournament?

The answer was found by inspecting the absolute payoffs each strategy obtained from its interactions with the other strategies, rather than just looking at its comparative (relative) payoffs. In particular, when we compared the absolute means of Benign's payoffs from its encounters with each player to those garnered by Vigilant, we discovered that Benign walked away from each relationship with rather high average payoffs. Indeed, many times it managed to elicit a benefit that was in fact quite close to the maximal average mean of 20 points. In contrast, Vigilant earned much less in absolute terms from these same encounters.

As an additional note, it is instructive to examine how well another strategy submitted to the tournament — a strict reciprocator called Naïve Realist — fared in this tournament. Naïve Realist adjusted to the noise factor by simply returning to its partner whatever it received from it on the previous trial. Since the average value of the noise term was 0, it assumed on average that this was a reasonable stance to take toward social uncertainty. Naïve Realist, I should note, is therefore logically equivalent to Axelrod's (1984) Tit-for-Tat. Recall that Axelrod's results had demonstrated the power of strict reciprocators such as Tit-for-Tat in a deterministic (noiseless) game (Tit-for-Tat came in first in Axelrod's tournament). Yet, in a tournament climate clouded by uncertainty, this strategy suffered a sharp decline in performance — both absolutely and relative to other players. Indeed, Naïve Realist placed a distant eighth in the final rankings, earning only 75% of the maximum symmetric payout. Thus, in a world of uncertainty, strict reciprocity gets one in trouble rather quickly.

What accounts for such degraded performance? Stated differently, why did Benign do better than a more realistic social auditor? Part of the answer to this question can be gleaned by observing how a strict reciprocator such as Naïve Realist behaves when it plays itself in the presence of uncertainty. Because Naïve Realist is nice, it starts off by extending full effort to its partner. Sooner or later, however, an unlucky ("bad") realization of the random error term occurs. Because Naïve Realist is provocable, it retaliates in the next period and retaliates with maximum punishment. Its partner, being similarly provocable, does the same, leading to a series of ongoing cycles of counterproductive mutual punishment. In contrast, a more generous strategy such as Benign effectively dampens this degradation by returning more than an unbiased estimate of its partner's effort level.

Why does Benign's generosity tend to work better than strict reciprocity in noisy worlds? As Axelrod (1984) noted in his original analysis, envy (in the form of social comparison) can get decision-makers in trouble if it sets off cycles of mutual discontent and retaliation. By setting an absolute (i.e., nonsocial comparative) standard for what it considers a reasonable rate of return on its relationships, Benign does not pay any attention to what its partners get. In contrast, Vigilant displays a great deal of concern about such comparisons — at least, it does not wish to grant full aid to others when it suspects it is not getting full aid back from them in return. Over the long haul, it pays a steep price for its insistence on never getting the short end of the stick in its relationships. In our world of unknown unknowns, it ends up safe but sorry.

Note also that Benign accomplishes something else by underreacting to the noise — something that is enormously important but easy to overlook in interdependence settings. It solves the other actor's trust dilemma. In other words, by keeping its effort levels high, its partner never has to decide whether or not to punish Benign. Recall that receiving any aid from the other above 80% is coded as justifying or warranting returning full aid back to the other. This point is important because in much of the trust dilemma literature, the focus is often on how social actors can solve their own trust dilemma (they worry only about assessing the other's trustworthiness). Little attention has been given to the importance of solving the other person's trust dilemma (i.e., demonstrating your own trustworthiness to them).

USING SURVEYS TO PROBE DECISION-MAKERS' INTUITIONS REGARDING THE COMPARATIVE EFFICACY OF DIFFERENT DECISION RULES FOR MANAGING INTERDEPENDENCE AND UNCERTAINTY

The study described in the previous section documented some counterintuitive findings with respect to the efficacy of different intentionally adaptive adjustments to uncertainty. Going forward, it is interesting to consider how well people's a priori intuitions and beliefs regarding the effectiveness of different decision rules correspond to the empirical conclusions suggested by our noisy tournament. Recall that we had recruited leading game theorists, psychologists, economists, and political scientists for this study. These were very smart people who were also quite adept at thinking about the complex interactive properties of these situations. Yet, even for this elite sample, their strategies often did not perform well. Interestingly, they often did not even do well when pitted against a clone of their own strategy. This point merits mention because it suggests that even a fairly simple first-order mental simulation of strategic interaction under noise was apparently quite difficult.

Accordingly, to explore decision-makers' intuitions or "naïve theories" regarding the efficacy of different heuristic rules, we investigated MBA students' beliefs about Benign, Vigilant, and Naïve Realist. We gave study participants complete information about all of the parameters for our noisy computer tournament. In fact, their information was identical to the information given to the entrants in the original computer simulation study. We then asked them to predict how well the three strategies (Naïve Realist, Benign, and Vigilant) would do; i.e., to predict the average payoff of each entry. As an alternative measure, we also asked students in a second study to predict the relative performance or ranking of the three strategies.

The results of this survey demonstrated that participants' intuitions regarding the comparative efficacy of these three strategies closely parallel the findings of Axelrod's (1984) original tournament. They clearly expected Naïve Realist to be the most efficacious in terms of their expectations about both absolute and relative performance. Vigilant was viewed as a strong second-place winner and hence a fairly effective strategy. Significantly, Benign ran a distant third when it came to students' expectations and predictions.

To probe further into people's intuitions regarding these rules — and how they operate — I asked another group of individuals (participants in an executive program) to write short paragraphs describing their beliefs about how each of these strategies would perform and why. One participant noted about Benign that, "If you're [this] generous, you probably will get screwed [out of your payoffs] too much. You'd be out of business in no time." In commenting on the attractiveness of Naïve Realist, in contrast, another wrote, "The nice thing about [this strategy] is that it keeps the playing field level — and that's important over the long term." "By far, Naïve Realist is the fairest strategy." And in thinking about the advantages of Vigilant, a participant stated, "In many situations … you've got to cover your back side."

In conclusion, these studies reveal some provocative and even counterintuitive insights regarding the kinds of decision rules people might use to cope with social uncertainty. Focusing only on how people think about and respond to social uncertainty within the context of experimental games or computer simulations, however, begs the question of how decision-makers in real-world settings might think about such issues. We might wonder, for example, how professional decision-makers and their clients might think about how to manage the trust dilemmas that arise in their relationship. In the next section, I present some results from a recent study designed to explore such issues.

ADAPTING TO SOCIAL UNCERTAINTY IN REAL-WORLD INTERDEPENDENCE DILEMMAS: A FIELD STUDY OF PATIENT–PHYSICIAN RELATIONSHIPS

This final study represents an effort to explore how uncertainty affects judgment and decision in a real-world interdependence dilemma setting — viz., the relationship between physicians and patients in the managed care setting of a large university hospital.

To set the stage for a discussion of this study, I should note a few important features regarding the relationship between physicians and their patients. First, the physician–patient relation is a classic (albeit complex) form of hierarchical interpersonal relationship because of the substantial asymmetries in dependence, information, knowledge, expertise, role, responsibilities, etc., that exist between the participants in the relationship. As researchers have long noted, hierarchical relations of this sort are particularly interesting arenas in which to explore issues of social uncertainty and trust (Kramer, 1996, 1999). From the standpoint of those who occupy the position of lower power (and therefore greater dependence) in the relationship, concerns about the motives, intentions, and actions of those individuals who control their fate ("those on top" in the relationship) are likely to be substantial. Patients have to worry, for instance, whether their physician is giving their case sufficient attention and whether they are motivated to do everything possible for them.

For individuals in the position of higher relative power and lower dependence in the relationship, in contrast, concerns about the commitment, compliance, deference, and trustworthiness of those below them are critical as well. Physicians have to worry that patients may be noncompliant and/or litigation prone should things take a turn for the worse. Because of these asymmetries, consequently, trust clearly matters to both parties. However, the substantive content of their trust-related concerns is likely to vary as a function of their location in the relationship. In this sense, the relationship is psychologically more complex than the sort of equal-status dyadic relationships typically studied in the laboratory.

With such considerations in mind, my collaborators and I investigated how individuals respond to the uncertainties inherent in physician–patient relationships (Cook et al., 2004). We selected this population to study for several reasons. First, there are few interpersonal relationships where concerns about trust and trustworthiness loom larger than in the relationship between patients and their physicians. Patients' emotional well-being and physical health — even their very lives — are quite literally in the hands (and heads and hearts) of the physician who provides their care. Second, although much less often studied or even acknowledged in the literature is the fact that physicians also care a great deal about the trustworthiness of their patients and the extent to which they should (and can) trust them. As noted above, patients can sue physicians for perceived breaches in performance; they can tarnish their reputations using blogs, and they can be stressful to manage. Thus, the physician's professional standing, livelihood, and even emotional well-being depend on making good judgments about which patients to trust and how to build trust.

Given the significant uncertainties they confront, on what basis do patients and physicians make judgments regarding trust and trustworthiness in their relationships? How, for example, do they go about assessing the others' trustworthiness? Relatedly, how do they go about demonstrating their own trustworthiness to the other person? To investigate such questions, we conducted a series of focus groups and semistructured interviews with a group of physicians and their patients. In contrast to the experimental studies described above — where we manipulated the variables of interest — in the present study our aim was to inductively explore the kinds of cognitive considerations and behavioral approaches individuals in a real-world trust dilemma utilized.

Content analysis of our transcribed and coded interviews identified a wide range of specific cues that individuals use to form impressions of trustworthiness. Among the larger categories of cues that both patients and physicians emphasized are behavioral cues that are construed as diagnostic of caring, concern, and empathy. Implicitly, these cues are perceived as correlates or manifestations of underlying trustworthiness. These cues include both verbal and nonverbal behaviors. Numerous patients, for instance, cited the importance of minor transactional behaviors and gestures that physicians engage in — such as eye contact and physical touching — during an interview or examination. For example, one patient observed generally, "I think it [trust] depends on the doctor ... on the way they [sic] treat you ... *are they looking at you* [italics added] when they examine you and how they treat you as a person, not only as a patient" (Patient 38, quoted in Cook et al., 2004, p. 71). Another patient elaborated, "When she [my physician] is done, she puts her pen down, and she will make eye contact with me immediately after she's done writing. Her eye contact starts when she enters the room," (Patient 36, p. 71). One patient asserted even more strongly, "I think eye contact is *one of the most important things* [italics added] when you're talking to a doctor so that you don't feel like they [*sic*] are ignoring you" (Patient 38, p. 71).

In addition to caring and concern, perceived competence emerged as another important and highly salient dimension to patients when assessing their physician's trustworthiness. As trust researchers have long noted, people's judgments regarding trustworthiness reflect not only their attributions regarding others' benign intentions and motives but their judgments regarding their competence at enacting trustworthy behavior. In other words, in order for someone to be judged trustworthy, we not only need to know they have our interests at heart (i.e., that their intentions are good) but that they are competent to act on those benign intentions. Consistent with this argument, we found patients in our study attached considerable importance to the apparent knowledge and competence of their physicians. As one patient put it, "He's pretty confident about his decisions. So that helps. He seems to know what he's talking about. I'm not a doctor, so I couldn't tell you if what he's telling me is right, but it sounded pretty good" (Patient 37, quoted in Cook et al., 2004, p. 75).

In addition to discovering that patients and physicians possessed many beliefs regarding the perceived determinants of trustworthiness, we identified a variety of cues that contributed to lack of perceived trust and trustworthiness. Some of the most damning (in the sense of trust-eroding or destroying) cues were subtle nonverbal behaviors that physicians seemed not to even notice — and certainly do not intend — when they were dealing with their patients. Patients, nonetheless, afforded considerable importance to them. One patient, for instance, described how she was sitting on the examination table wearing only a paper hospital gown and awaiting her first visit with her surgeon. "So, when I was on the table ... feeling pretty vulnerable, he comes in, mumbles something ... [he] stood at the foot of my bed, with his arms crossed ... You know, you belong at my bedside, not the foot of my bed. Uncross your arms; get your hands out of your pockets ... and look me in the eye ... as soon as he walked in the door and stopped at the foot of my bed, that set the tone" (Patient 36, quoted in Cook et al., 2004, p. 77).

Among the other important findings that emerged from our study was the extent to which both patients' and physicians' judgments about trust and trustworthiness were adversely influenced by contextual factors that added to the perceived uncertainty in the relationship. By *contextual factors* I mean the specific institutional norms and practices governing physician–patient relationships within a given setting or organizational culture. In this particular study, for example, the patient–physician relationships all occurred within the context of the new "managed care" mileau. Managed care systems are supposed to provide efficient, state-of-the-art, multidisciplinary team care to patients. As desirable and laudable as those goals might be, the managed care setting injects some unintended features into the trust relationship. For example, in sharp contrast to the warm-and-fuzzy images we might still retain of the family physician personally attending the loyal patient (picture Dr. Marcus Welby here), the physician–patient transactions in our study were embedded in a setting in which (a) teams of physicians shared responsibilities for patients, (b) physicians' decisions were constrained by a host of institutional and provider regulations, and, importantly, (c) patients' stereotypes regarding the impact of managed care on their physicians' ability to provide direct, responsive personal care all directly impacted judgments of trust and trustworthiness.

We found, for instance, that the managed care setting cast a rather large and often ominous shadow over the development and maintenance of trust in the doctor–patient relationship in several ways. First, the time constraints imposed by managed care systems were often perceived as adversely impacting the depth and quality of the trust relationship between doctors and their patients — and that negative impact cut both ways. For example, patients and physicians both drew attention to the deleterious impact of perceived time urgency and time scarcity on trust development. One patient described her physician as "no smile, no sense of humor, just 'quick, quick, let's get the job done'" (Patient 21, quoted in Cook et al., 2004, p. 77). Relatedly, patients reported that the tendency for busy physicians to give incomplete or hurried explanations often undermined trust. One patient complained, for example, that "I get very frustrated because so many doctors take an authoritative position … 'I'm going to tell you what to do, I don't have to explain it, I don't have to pay any attention to your knowledge or your awareness'" (Patient, 22, p. 79).

As one physician — coming at this problem from her perspective — added, "… there are time constraints in the sense that if I spend longer than [the allotted 15 minutes recommended] with a patient, then I'm getting later and later, and I know I'm going to keep other patients waiting. … So it's a constant tension between trying to respond to the needs that people have and give as much time as necessary but knowing … that it's going to affect everything that happens for the rest of the day" (Physician 5, quoted in Cook et al., 2004, p. 84). This same physician was acutely aware of the erosion of trust associated with the constant and unrelenting pressures to juggle the clock for the sake of efficiency and profitability. "I often feel like I'm spending a lot of saved-up goodwill with my patients. Making little withdrawals and spending it … but it's as if we're gradually depleting it and I'm not so sure how long that could go on without them saying … 'You're not the same physician I used to know'" (p. 84).

Another way in which the managed care setting affects trust pertains to the perceived lack of continuity and fragmentation of care within the relationship. Because physicians in managed care settings are part of a multidisciplinary team, diffusion of responsibility in providing patient management may result. Patient care, for example, is often allocated to multiple physicians treating the patient at different times, depending on schedule, availability, and need. Relatedly, patients often assume that physician mobility and turnover are likely to be high in managed care settings. Thus, over time patients themselves may be less likely to make the same level of investment and commitment to their relationship, because they believe it will be short lived (and they are correct: physician turnover in the relationships we studied was substantial). Physicians are cognizant of this same reality. As one physician lamented, "I've had to move around much more than I expected … I didn't think I'd be 'starting over' with patients quite so often."

Finally, we found that the perceived economic realities of the managed care environment cast a shadow over the relationship as well. In particular, physicians and patients both expressed concerns regarding the perception (if not the reality) that insurance and other economic considerations were driving physician recommendations and decisions. For example, patients sometimes expressed concerns about confidence in a physician's drug or treatment recommendations because they assumed there were external pressures on physicians that might affect their judgment (e.g., concerns about costs of generic versus brand-name drugs; "cozy" relationships between physicians or hospitals and drug companies).

To summarize, the results of this final study revealed some of the finer grained psychological complexity associated with people's judgments about trust and trustworthiness, especially when some of the social uncertainty is endemic to the institutional context in which the interpersonal relationships happen to be embedded. People's judgments often reflected a host of idiosyncratic cues. This study also illustrates how stereotypes or beliefs about a given setting or context can color such judgments independent of the actual behavior of the interacting parties. One implication of this latter finding is that both patients and physicians might facilitate the trust-building process and strengthen their mutual trust by explicitly acknowledging and discussing such factors. Consistent with this idea, we found that some physicians were able to build trust by "hanging a lantern on" (openly acknowledging) the many problems created by managed care settings. These physicians made it a point to emphasize that they only prescribed drugs they personally knew about and in which they believed, adding that insurance company guidelines or allowances would not influence their ultimate judgment. Other physicians reassured patients that, whenever necessary, they would allocate the extra time needed to deliver high-quality care or answer questions, even if that meant getting behind with their other patients.

IMPLICATIONS AND CONCLUSIONS

This chapter summarizes the results of a programmatic series of empirical investigations into the nature and impact of social uncertainty on judgment and choice in various forms of interdependence dilemmas. Viewed in aggregate, the results from these studies reveal the significant extent to which decision-makers' construals of their interdependence with other people are affected by both psychological and situational factors. In particular, whether decision-makers perceive social opportunity or risk in their encounters with others is largely influenced by a variety of basic cognitive processes — such as the initial construal of their interdependence, the framing of their choices, and the salience of various individual or social identities. The experiments also implicate a variety of situational factors, including the salience feedback about others' decisions, the structure of opportunity, and vulnerability (e.g., institutional norms and constraints on choice).

The results of these studies also reveal some of the creative responses decision-makers make when attempting to cope with such interdependence and uncertainty. One way of thinking about these responses is that they represent intentionally adaptive or compensatory actions. In other words, they reflect decision-makers' explicit "online" assessments as to how best to manage the inherent trade-offs between perceived risks and perceived opportunities in situations involving uncertainty about others' motives and intentions. In this respect, these results accord nicely with prior arguments by Messick and his students regarding the utility of what he termed *social decision rules* for solving various kinds of interdependence dilemmas (e.g., Allison & Messick, 1990; Samuelson & Messick, 1995).

In the case of interdependence dilemma situations, the present research suggests at least two different kinds of adaptive rules are important in helping decision-makers respond to interdependence and uncertainty (see Figure 6.1). One subset of rules can be thought of as predominantly

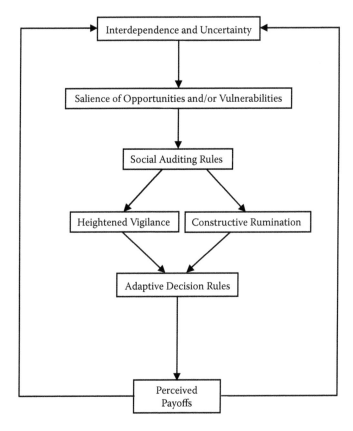

FIGURE 6.1
Social information processing effects of interdependence and uncertainty.

cognitive in nature and pertain to the social auditing heuristics individuals use when trying to assess opportunity and vulnerability in a given situation. This includes the search for evidence that individuals rely on when trying to assess others' trustworthiness and cooperativeness. These cognitive rules constitute, in a fashion, "social auditing" rules that decision-makers employ to facilitate sense-making in dilemma situations. Such social auditing rules presumably reflect individuals' beliefs regarding what different behaviors by other people mean (e.g., how verbal and nonverbal behaviors should be interpreted or decoded). The social auditing rules people use reflect, in this sense, their a priori beliefs regarding the expressive attributes presumably correlated with, and predictive of, others' trustworthiness and cooperativeness.

A second subset of rules might be characterized as more behavioral in nature and operate as prescriptive guidelines that support intentionally adaptive decision-making. In other words, these prescriptive rules guide decision-makers who are trying to determine how they ought to respond to a given situation, given their construal of it. These behavioral rules can be viewed as intentionally adaptive in the sense that their use presumably helps decision-makers reap the benefits of trust and cooperation when they happen to be dealing with trustworthy and cooperative others. At the same time, they help minimize the costs of misplaced trust and cooperation when they happen to be interacting with untrustworthy or uncooperative others. As noted throughout this chapter, research by many scholars has documented the versatility and power of even very simple decision rules for navigating social dilemmas (see Axelrod, 1984; Gigerenzer, 2000, for a recent overview). The framework depicted in Figure 6.1 implies that decision-makers are attentive (vigilant and ruminative) when it comes to monitoring evidence and consequences, leading to cycles of experiential learning over time.

The results from these studies further indicate there is sometimes a rather sharp disparity between people's beliefs regarding the efficacy of different auditing and behavioral rules and their actual usefulness or effectiveness. One reason why people's beliefs regarding the effectiveness of such rules may be error prone is that they may overweight — and therefore worry too much about — the prospects of being exploited while underestimating the mutual benefits that would accrue from more benign attributions and less reactive behaviors (Kramer, 1998). As prior research has shown, the prospect of losses often looms larger, and is more aversive to, decision-makers than the prospect of gains of comparable magnitude (Kahneman & Tversky, 1984). Moreover, getting the so-called sucker's payoff in dilemma situations is often experienced as extremely aversive. When these two pieces of the puzzle are put together, it is perhaps understandable why many people would rather be safe than sorry when dealing with others about whom they know little.

One of the major goals of these studies has been to explicate some of the cognitive processes associated with social judgment in the face of interdependence and uncertainty. We can conceptualize decision-makers' judgments in these dilemma situations as forms of embedded or "situated" cognition. Situated cognitions locate our choices about whom to trust and cooperate with within a much larger class of judgments that have been extensively studied by behavioral decision theorists. Their prior research takes as a starting point the recognition that human beings are imperfect information processors who must often render judgments before all of the relevant and desired facts are known. This fundamental idea was first articulated by Simon (1957) in the notion of *satisficing*. In contrast to conceptions of decision-making that presumed thorough and exhaustive search, Simon argued that people often are satisfied with alternatives that are perceived as acceptable or good enough under the prevailing circumstances.

This core insight regarding the utility of satisficing solutions led, in turn, to the subsequent identification of numerous heuristics — simple judgmental rules — that could replace and approximate normatively optimal rules. In advocating the value of such heuristic reasoning, Polya (1945) noted that there are many situations where "we may need the provisional before we attain the final" (p. 112). As did other decision theorists subsequently, Polya viewed heuristic reasoning from a functionalist perspective: the use of such heuristics could lead to the generation of plausible hypotheses, sensible hunches, and reasonable solutions.

Stimulated largely by the pioneering and imaginative work of Kahneman and Tversky (1984), the study of heuristic reasoning enjoyed a period of considerable vogue. It then, however, went through a period of spirited scrutiny. In particular, a number of decision theorists — most notably Hogarth (1981) and von Winterfeld and Edwards (1986) — began to suggest that the contemporary focus on the ways in which heuristic processes led to judgmental biases misrepresents reality and constitutes "a message of despair" (von Winterfeld & Edwards, 1986, p. 531). To be sure, the predominant emphasis of experimental research for several decades did seem to be the documentation of judgmental shortcomings. However, some responded, perhaps the baby had been thrown out with the bath water. In this spirit, a variety of studies have undertaken the task of rehabilitating the notion of heuristic information processing (e.g., Allison & Messick, 1990). Of particular note, there has been a movement away from thinking that heuristics are necessarily sources of biased or flawed cognition and instead toward thinking of heuristics as adaptive cognitions (Gigerenzer, 2000; Gigerenzer & Todd, 1999). These studies, and many others, converge on the proposition that in some contexts even very simple decision heuristics can produce highly efficient and satisfactory results for a variety of important information processing tasks.

From the perspective of such work, it would be easy to construe such heuristic-based modes of judgment as somewhat shallow or "quick and dirty." They might seem to occur in the blink of an eye or, more literarily perhaps, a blink of the mind (Gigerenzer, 2007; Gladwell, 2005). But there are many circumstances where judgments about who to trust or cooperate with must be rendered swiftly, even if not all of the relevant or desired information is available to decision-makers (Gambetta & Hamill, 2005; Meyerson, Weick, & Kramer, 2006).

One interesting question for future research to engage, therefore, is under what circumstances people are likely to give other people the benefit of the doubt in such situations. Research provides some suggestive possibilities. First, empathy — defined here as simply the ability to take the other party's perspective into account and to care about their outcomes — may influence individuals' willingness to engage in trusting behavior. In support of this intuition, Arriaga and Rusbult (1998) found that the experience of "standing in a partner's shoes" increased constructive responses to a dilemma. As noted earlier in this chapter, there is also some evidence that the salience of shared or common social identities among decision-makers may also influence the perceived efficacy of different decision rules. In a series of experiments, several collaborators and I have shown that the salience of common (ingroup) versus uncommon (intergroup) identities dramatically affects trusting behavior in various dyadic dilemmas, including ultimatum bargaining games (Kramer et al., 1995) and multi-issue negotiations (Thompson, Valley, & Kramer, 1995).

Decision-makers are probably more willing to entertain benign assumptions about others and give them the benefit of the doubt when they share a perceived social tie or bond. For example, when decision-makers from the same neighborhood meet face to face, they may presumptively trust each other more and cooperate more willingly than they would otherwise (cf. Ostrom, 1998). Further, common identification with an ongoing inter-action partner along some salient dimension — such as a common group identity — may affect which strategy is viewed as most fair and/or most effective (Kramer et al., 1993).

These are only first steps, of course, on the road to a more complete under-standing of how decision-makers think about and respond to social inter-dependence and uncertainty. Ultimately, however, whether decision-makers perceive two, eight, or even ten psychological horns to the dilemmas they con-front starts inside their own heads. In the final analysis, therefore, I remain optimistic about people's prospects for solving such dilemmas. If people can think their way into dilemmas, they can also think their way out of them.

REFERENCES

References marked with an asterisk indicate studies included in the meta-analysis.

Allison, S., & Messick, D. (1990). Social decision heuristics in the use of share resources. *Journal of Behavioral Decision Making, 3*, 195–204.

Arriaga, S. B., & Rusbult, C. E. (1998). Standing in my partner's shoes: Partner perspective taking and reactions to accommodative dilemmas. *Personality and Social Psychology Bulletin, 24*, 927–948.

Axelrod, R. (1980a). Effective choice in the prisoner's dilemma. *Journal of Conflict Resolution, 24*, 3–25.

Axelrod, R. (1980b). More effective choice in the prisoner's dilemma. *Journal of Conflict Resolution, 24*, 379–403.

Axelrod, R. (1984). *The evolution of cooperation.* New York: Basic Books.

Bendor, J., Kramer, R. M., & Stout, S. (1991). When in doubt: Cooperation in the noisy prisoner's dilemma. *Journal of Conflict Resolution, 35*, 691–719.

*Brewer, M. B., & Kramer, R. M. (1986). Choice behavior in social dilemmas: Effects of social identity, group size, and decision framing. *Journal of Personality and Social Psychology, 50*, 543–549.

Cialdini, R. B. (1980). Full circle social psychology. In L. Bickman (Ed.), *Applied social psy-chology annual* (Vol. 1, pp. 21–47). Beverly Hills, CA: Sage.

Cook, K. S., Kramer, R. M., Thom, D. H., Stepanikova, I., Mollborn, S. B., & Cooper, R. M. (2004). Trust and distrust in patient-physician relationships: Perceived determinants of high- and low- trust relationships in managed care settings. In R. M. Kramer & K. S. Cook (Eds.), *Trust and distrust in organizations: Dilemmas and approaches* (pp. 65–98). New York: Russell Sage Foundation.

Ezard, J. (2003, December 2). Rumsfeld's unknown unknowns takes the prize. *The Guardian*, p. A3.

Gambetta, D. (1988). Can we trust trust? In D. Gambetta (Ed.), *Trust* (pp. 213–238). New York: Blackwell.

Gambetta, D., & Hamill, H. (2005). *Streetwise: How taxi drivers establish their customers' trustworthiness*. New York: Russell Sage Foundation.

Gigerenzer, G. (2000). *Adaptive thinking: Rationality in the real world*. New York: Oxford University Press.

Gigerenzer, G. (2007). *Gut feelings: the intelligence of the unconscious*. New York: Viking.

Gigerenzer, G., & Todd, P. M. (1999). Simple heuristics that make us smart. New York: Oxford University Press.

Gladwell, M. (2005). *Blink*. New York: Penguin.

Hogarth, R. M. (1981). Beyond discrete biases: Functional and dysfunctional aspects of judgmental heuristics. *Psychological Bulletin, 90*, 197–217.

Hotchner, A. E. (2008). *The good life according to Hemingway*. New York: HarperCollins.

Kahneman, D., & Tversky, A. (1984). Choices, values, and frames. *American Psychologist, 39*, 341–350.

Kelley, H. H., Holmes, J. G., Kerr, N. L., Reis, H. T., Rusbult, C. E., & Van Lange, P. (2003). *An atlas of interpersonal situations*. New York: Cambridge University Press.

Kelley, H. H., & Thibaut, J. W. (1978). *Interpersonal relations: A theory of interdependence*. Reading, MA: Addison-Wesley.

Kramer, R. M. (1987). Cooperation in security dilemmas. *Social Science, 72*, 144–148.

Kramer, R. M. (1989). Windows of vulnerability or cognitive illusions? Cognitive processes and the nuclear arms race. *Journal of Experimental Social Psychology, 25*, 79–100.

Kramer, R. M. (1991). Intergroup relations and organizational dilemmas: The role of categorization processes. In L. L. Cummings and B. M. Staw (Eds.), *Research in organizational behavior* (Vol. 13, pp. 191–228). Greenwich, CT: JAI Press.

Kramer, R. M. (1994). The sinister attribution error. *Motivation and Emotion, 18*, 199–231.

Kramer, R. M. (1996). Divergent realities and convergent disappointments in the hierarchic relation: The intuitive auditor at work. In R. M. Kramer & T. R. Tyler (Eds.), *Trust in organizations: Frontiers of theory and research* (pp. 216–245). Thousand Oaks, CA: Sage.

Kramer, R. M. (1998). Paranoid cognition in social systems. *Personality and Social Psychology Review, 2*, 251–275.

Kramer, R. M. (1999). Trust and distrust in organizations: Emerging perspectives, enduring questions. *Annual Review of Psychology, 50*, 569–598.

*Kramer, R. M., & Brewer, M. B. (1984). Effects of group identity on resource use in a simulated commons dilemma. *Journal of Personality and Social Psychology, 46*, 1044–1057.

Kramer, R. M., McClintock, C. G., & Messick, D. M. (1986). Social values and cooperative response to a simulated resource conservation crisis. *Journal of Personality, 54*, 576–592.

Kramer, R. M., & Messick, D. M. (1995). Negotiation in social contexts. In R. M. Kramer & D. M. Messick (Eds.), *Negotiation as a social process* (pp. 1–4). Thousand Oaks, CA: Sage.

Kramer, R. M., & Messick, D. M. (1996). Ethical cognition and the intuitive lawyer: Organizational dilemmas and the framing of choice. In D. M. Messick & A. Tenbrunsel (Eds.), *Codes of conduct: Behavioral research and business ethics* (pp. 59–85). New York: Russell Sage Foundation.

Kramer, R. M., &, Messick, D. M. (1998). Getting by with a little help from our enemies: Collective paranoia and its role in intergroup relations. In C. Sedikides, J. Schopler, & C. Insko (Eds.), *Intergroup cognition and intergroup behavior* (pp. 233–255). Hillsdale, NJ: Lawrence Erlbaum.

Kramer, R., Meyerson, D., & Davis, G. (1990). How much is enough? Psychological components of "guns versus butter" decisions in a security dilemma. *Journal of Personality and Social Psychology, 58*, 984–993.

Kramer, R. M., Newton, E., & Pommerenke, P. (1993). Self-enhancement biases and negotiator judgment: Effects of self-esteem and mood. *Organizational Behavior and Human Decision Processes, 56*, 110–133.

Kramer, R., Pommerenke, P., & Newton, E. (1993). The social context of negotiation: Effects of social identity and accountability on negotiator judgment and decision making. *Journal of Conflict Resolution, 37*, 633–654.

Kramer, R. M., Pradhan-Shah, P., & Woerner, S. (1995). Why ultimatums fail: Social identity and moralistic aggression in coercive bargaining. In R. M. Kramer & D. M. Messick (Eds.), *Negotiation as a social process* (pp. 123–146). Thousand Oaks, CA: Sage.

Lim, E. T. (2008). *The anti-intellectual presidency*. New York: Oxford University Press.

Messick, D. M., & Kramer, R. M. (2001). Trust as a form of shallow morality. In K. S. Cook (Ed.), *Trust in society* (pp. 89–118). New York: Russell Sage Foundation.

Messick, D. M., Wilke, H., Brewer, M. B., Kramer, R. M., Zemke, P., & Lui, L. (1983). Individual adaptations and structural change as solutions to social dilemmas. *Journal of Personality and Social Psychology, 44*, 294–309.

Meyerson, D., Weick, K., & Kramer, R. M. (2006). Swift trust and temporary groups. In R. M. Kramer (Ed.), *Organizational trust: A reader* (pp. 415–444). New York: Oxford University Press.

Ostrom, E. (1998). A behavioral approach to the rational choice theory of collective action. Presidential address, American Political Science Association, 1997. *American Political Science Review, 92*, 1–22.

Polya, G. (1945). *How to solve it*. Princeton, NJ: Princeton University Press.

Samuelson, C. D., & Messick, D. M. (1995). Let's make some new rules: Social factors that make freedom unattractive. In R. M. Kramer & D. M. Messick (Eds.), *Negotiation as a social process* (pp. 48–68). Thousand Oaks, CA: Sage.

Simon, H. A. (1957). *Models of man*. New York: Wiley.

Stepanikova, I., Cook, K. S., Kramer, R. M., Thom, D, & Mollborn, S. B. (in press). Trust development and maintenance in patient-physician relationships. In K. S. Cook, R. Hardin, & M. Levi (Eds.), *Capstone volume on trust*. New York: Russell Sage Foundation.

Thompson, L., Valley, K. L., & Kramer, R. M. (1995). The bittersweet feeling of success: An examination of social perception in negotiation. *Journal of Experimental Social Psychology, 31*, 467–492.

von Winterfeldt, D., & Edwards, W. (1986). *Decision analysis and behavioral research*. Cambridge, UK: Cambridge University Press.

Section II

Social Values, Social Control, and Cooperation

7

Nonverbal Communication and Detection of Individual Differences in Social Value Orientation

Gregory P. Shelley
Kutztown University

Madeleine Page
University of Delaware

Peter Rives
Center Point Human Services, North Carolina

Erin Yeagley
University of Delaware

D. Michael Kuhlman
University of Delaware

By definition, a social dilemma is a situation of social interdependence requiring a choice between Defection (D), or maximizing one's own outcomes at some expense to others, and Cooperation (C), or maximizing collective outcomes at some expense to self. The most commonly studied two-person dilemma is known as the Prisoner's Dilemma (PD), and the most common PD research paradigm presents participants with a payoff matrix of the sort shown in Figure 7.1.

As can be seen in Figure 7.1, the D choice strictly dominates C in terms of classic game theory and so it is reasonable to expect that D choices should be common and C rare. Yet from the early research of Rapoport and Chammah (1965) through the present, findings show just the opposite: in the aggregate, people choose C quite often.

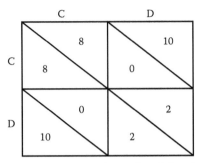

Notes: (1) The row chooser's payoffs are below the diagonal. (2) The D choice "dominates" C for both players; regardless of the partner's choice, each player will receive a higher payoff by choosing D rather than C.

FIGURE 7.1
Example of a Prisoner's Dilemma payoff matrix.

David Messick recognized that such findings indicated the need for psychological theories of interdependent choice that go beyond the normative prescriptions of formal game theory. One of his lasting theoretical and empirical contributions to social psychology was to show that people are not necessarily attempting to maximize their own outcomes as displayed in the payoff matrix, but rather transformations of displayed outcomes to self *and* other. We emphasize "and" in the previous sentence because it points to the fundamentally important point of Messick's theoretical work: the motivations (not the strategies employed to satisfy them) guiding interdependent behavior can have a social as well as an egocentric component. As easy as we find it to accept that we are genuinely concerned with what happens to us in social relationships, Messick is saying that we should allow for the possibility that we may also be just as genuinely concerned with what happens to our partner, and that the desires and goals underlying social choice are social motivations.

Messick and McClintock (1968) published a classic paper in which a set of three social motivations was proposed, each being a different combination of matrix payoffs to self and other. *Cooperation* was defined as the social motive that is satisfied by maximizing joint gain, or the sum of payoffs to self and other. *Individualism*, most like the motive deemed rational by classic game theory, is the motive to maximize own gain, or payoffs to self, with no regard to the other's outcomes. *Competition* is the social motive to maximize relative gain, or outcomes to self minus outcomes to other. Over the decades of research inspired by this paper, it has become common to refer to "cooperation" as J (for joint gain), "individualism" as O (for own gain), and "competition" as R (for relative gain). Also, since the time of their original paper, the phrase *social motivation* has been replaced by *social value orientation* (SVO), with no change in the definition of J, O, and R.

Recognizing the important difference between motives and the strategies employed to satisfy them, Messick and McClintock developed a paradigm for assessing SVO that maintained social interdependence while minimizing strategic influences. The paradigm consists of a simple decision task called the *decomposed game*, in which two participants make decisions with no information concerning the partner's identity or decisions. This no-feedback procedure was intended to minimize attempts to influence the partner and/or be influenced by him/her, thereby making choices a less ambiguous expression of motivation.

Examples of two decomposed games are given in Figure 7.2. Each SVO (J, O, R) leads to a different set of choices across the two games. For J (maximize the sum), choices would be A in both games, for O (maximize points to self), choices would be B in Game 1 and A in Game 2, and for R (maximize self minus other) choices would be B in both games.

Messick and McClintock's participants played a set of no-feedback decomposed games, and clear evidence was found for the existence of all three SVOs. They analyzed participants' choices with a stochastic choice

	Decomposed Game 1	
	Choice A	**Choice B**
Your Points	6	7
Other's Points	4	2
	Decomposed Game 2	
	Choice A	**Choice B**
Your Points	7	6
Other's Points	3	0

Notes: (1) Joint gain is maximized by Choice A in both games. Own gain is maximized by Choice B in Game 1 and Choice A in Game 2. Relative gain is maximized by Choice B in both games.

FIGURE 7.2
Examples of two decomposed games.

model that assumes the decision-maker to be in one of four motivational states; namely, J, O, R, or indifference, with probabilities w, x, y, and z, respectively. Estimates of the four probabilities were made assuming that they were the same for all participants. Importantly, w, x, and y were found to be greater than zero, indicating the existence of J, O, and R motives. And just as importantly for many researchers inspired by this work, Messick and McClintock report further results suggesting that w, x, and y are not necessarily the same for all participants. That is, they suggest individual differences in SVO.

Their suggestion led to research focused on measuring such differences and demonstrating their importance to an increased understanding of socially interdependent behavior and cognition. In terms of behavioral differences, studies have shown that Js, Os, and Rs tend to employ different strategies (e.g., Kuhlman & Marshello, 1975; McClintock & Liebrand, 1988) and show different levels of helping in real-world settings (McClintock & Allison, 1989). In terms of cognition, studies show that Js, Os, and Rs have different beliefs regarding the levels of the three SVOs in the general population (Kuhlman, Brown, & Teta, 1992; Kuhlman & Wimberley, 1976), assign different meaning to cooperative and competitive behavior (Liebrand, Jansen, Rijken, & Suhre, 1986), and are differentially responsive to framing effects (De Dreu & McCusker, 1997). These differences are temporally stable and covary with a wide variety of behaviors both inside and outside the laboratory, such as trust (Kuhlman, Camac, & Cuhna, 1986) and judgments concerning public transportation (Joireman, Van Lange, Kuhlman, Van Vugt, & Shelley, 1997). Furthermore, and of direct relevance to the present chapter, Js, Os, and Rs appear to be perceived differently by their friends (Bem & Lord, 1979). These studies are hardly a comprehensive review of the SVO literature; the interested reader is referred to Van Lange (2000).

There is an extensive literature on behavioral and cognitive differences in SVO; nonetheless, there is very little work focused on its nonverbal/emotional aspects, despite very good theoretical justification for doing so. The remainder of this chapter outlines the theoretical issues, reviews relevant research, and presents the results of five studies we have conducted concerning SVO and nonverbal behavior.

As mentioned above, research on the Prisoner's Dilemma game finds levels of C choices higher than would be expected, based on the formal game theoretic expectation of high levels of D. In addition, it is a common finding in the SVO literature that Js are the modal SVO group, followed by smaller numbers of Os and Rs. The facts from both PD and SVO research make the happy suggestion that we are more cooperative than was originally believed. Nevertheless, they also raise an important question concerning the mechanisms by which our cooperativeness is maintainable.

Theorists with an evolutionary approach (Dawkins, 1989; Frank, Gilovich, & Regan, 1993) have argued that cooperation in a PD is facilitated to the extent that individuals with a cooperative predisposition, whom we will call Js, are able to detect such predispositions in others and to selectively form relationships with them. These theorists acknowledge nonverbal behavior as a potentially important channel through which this accurate identification might be achieved.

Prior research suggests that people are able to detect cooperative predispositions of others. For example, in a PD game study by Frank et al. (1993), participants were asked to take 30 minutes to "get to know" each of a set of partners before guessing how they would choose. Participants were able to predict their partners' choices at a rate significantly better than chance. For participants given no opportunity to interact, predictive accuracy did not exceed chance level. Nonetheless, it is not clear from these results whether the information signaling cooperation was verbal, nonverbal, or a mixture of both.

Other research suggests that a tendency toward prosocial behavior may be communicated through nonverbal cues. Specifically, Brown, Palameta, and Moore (2003) showed that videotapes of self-reported altruists were rated more "helpful," "concerned," and "attentive" than those of self-reported non-altruists. Takahishi, Yamagishi, Tanida, Kiyonari, and Kanazawa (2006) showed that photographs of males who had defected in a variety of experimental games were rated as more attractive than males who had cooperated. Verplaetse, Vaneste, and Braeckman (2007) took photos of participants at the time they were choosing between C and D in a PD game. They found that judges could discriminate photos of cooperative choosers from those of competitive ones. Thus, there is evidence supporting the idea that nonverbal behavior covaries with prosocial motivation, and that it is detected and used by others.

According to Frank (1988), emotional aspects of nonverbal cues may be very important in the communication of cooperative predisposition, and several studies show that the emotional facial display of a partner leads to different levels of cooperation. Scharlemann, Eckel, Kacelnik, and Wilson (2001) showed their participants a photo of their ostensible partner who was either smiling or emotionally neutral. For males, levels of cooperation in a one-shot trust game were higher with a smiling than a non-smiling partner. Krumhuber et al. (2007) show that not all smile expressions are equal in terms of eliciting cooperation. They presented participants with a computer-generated display of an ostensible partner who showed a smile that was either "authentic" or "fake" in terms of characteristics of the dynamic smile expression. A partner displaying a neutral expression was presented in the control condition. Cooperation in a trust game was highest for the authentic smile compared to the fake smile and neutral display. Mehu, Grammer, and Dunbar (2007) found a positive correlation between frequency of participants' Duchenne smiles during an interaction involving sharing and self-reports of the amount of financial help they would give a friend in need. No such associations were found for other types of smiles.

The above research provides support for the idea that facial expressions of emotion may signal cooperative intent and elicit different levels of cooperative behavior. It also suggests that the type of emotional expression necessary may be limited to positive affect, and perhaps even more specifically to genuine smiles. However, with the single exception described next, we know of no research that has specifically examined nonverbal behavior of Js, Os, and Rs. Although it was done years before the nonverbal research described above, its findings are consistent with the more recent literature. Specifically, work done by Peter Carnevale (1977) as an undergraduate psychology major at the University of Delaware demonstrated that an individual's nonverbal affective style is, in part, a function of his SVO. Weeks after their SVOs were measured with decomposed games, subjects were videotaped recalling happy, angry, and sad stories from their lives. These videotapes were shown (without audio) to another group of participants who were to decide whether the story being told by the subject was happy, angry, or sad. Js were thought to be telling happy stories more often than non-Js, who were more likely to be viewed as telling negative stories. The following year, Carnevale's results were replicated in a senior's honor thesis conducted by Jay Mills (1978). Participants were shown silent videos of J, O, and R targets recounting happy, angry, and sad stories from their own lives and were asked to indicate how much happiness, anger, and sadness they saw in each story. Averaged over the three stories, Js appeared to be generally happy storytellers, whereas Os and Rs were seen as generally angry and/or sad.

Thus, people with a cooperative predisposition (Js) appear to differ nonverbally from those with a noncooperative predisposition (ORs) in terms of positive affect. It nevertheless remains to be seen whether the SVO of a stranger can be detected from his/her nonverbal behavior and, if so, what type(s) of nonverbal cues are responsible for its communication. These are the goals of the studies reported in the present chapter. The first two studies examine the nonverbal behavior of Js, Os, and Rs during casual conversation. Thus, nonverbal behavior is spontaneously generated by the participant him/herself in a setting that creates no external demand for emotional display; the participants just talk. The last three studies ask participants to pose a variety of emotions. Here we can see whether the possible differences in how Js, Os, and Rs attempt to display emotional states act as cues for the detection of SVO.

OVERVIEW OF STUDIES 1 AND 2

Because most of our interactions with strangers involve relatively innocuous as opposed to emotionally charged conversation, it seems desirable to sample nonverbal behavior in such relaxed settings. Studies 1 and 2 focus on the nonverbal behaviors of Js, Os, and Rs in a setting designed to elicit more casual talking than the emotionally explicit happy, angry, and sad storytelling used in the work of Carnevale (1977) and Mills (1978). Specifically, in these studies, Js, Os, and Rs are asked simply to tell a stranger what they did on the previous day, from the time they woke up until they went to sleep.

Study 1 performs a general analysis of the facial nonverbal styles of Js, Os, and Rs by means of Ekman and Friesen's (1978) Facial Affect Coding System (FACS). Thus, Study 1 seeks to discover at least some the specific nonverbal behaviors that are encoded, rather than limiting its focus to anger, happiness, and sadness.

Study 2 asks whether a target's SVO can be detected (decoded) by strangers on the basis of a short (30-second) silent videotape of that target talking about what he/she did yesterday.

OVERVIEW OF STUDIES 3, 4, AND 5

Although the video segments used in Studies 1 and 2 are short, they contain a great deal more nonverbal information than the stimuli used in Studies 3, 4, and 5, which are still photographs. Study 3 examines the remote possibility that SVO may be communicated by facial structure, or physiognomy, by presenting participants with photos of Js, Os, and Rs posing a neutral expression. As pointed out by Zebrowitz (1997), there are several non-mutually exclusive ways in which a personality trait might be correlated with what the target "looks like." The first is based on differential life experiences of Js, Os, and Rs, which might exert cumulative effects on the face. Kelley and Stahelski (1970) suggest the social interaction history of competitors is consistently more conflicted and aversive (Messick & Thorngate, 1967; Steigleder, Weiss, Cramer, & Feinberg, 1978) than are cooperators' histories. A second mechanism described by Zebrowitz (1997) is along the lines of a self-fulfilling prophecy. Here, individual differences in genetically based facial morphology can lead to initially incorrect, stereotype-based judgments of a competitive or cooperative predisposition, which in turn leads to differential treatment from others. Finally, if SVO is heritable, there is the possibility that the genes responsible may also exert influence on facial morphology. Study 3 was not designed to provide a basis for choosing between these three possibilities but rather to simply see whether physiognomy relates to judgments of SVO.

Studies 4 and 5 also use still photos of Js, Os, and Rs, but in this case the targets are posing emotions. Study 4 presents judges with photos of Js, Os, and Rs posing happiness. A recent study (Harker & Keltner, 2001) suggests that the way a person smiles for the camera is correlated with self-reported personality descriptions and judgments of others. Using the FACS coding system, Harker and Keltner (2001) classified the yearbook photos of 114 college women according to whether or not they expressed "genuine" smiles (Duchenne, 1990). Duchenne smilers gave higher self-reports of affiliation and competence and were judged by others as more desirable interaction partners. Remarkably, Duchenne smiling predicted positive outcomes in personal well-being and marriage some 30 years after the photos were taken. Thus, there is some empirical evidence, albeit indirect, that allows for the possibility that SVO might communicated by information as minimal as a single smiling photograph.

Study 5 explores the possibility that providing the judge with more than one emotional expression will affect the detection of SVO. In this study, judges are shown a set of seven different posed emotions: happiness, anger, sadness, surprise, disgust, fear, and friendliness. If judges pay selective attention to happiness, then there should be little difference between judgments in Studies 4 and 5. To the extent that SVO is validly communicated by posed emotions other than happiness, we might see an improvement in detection accuracy. Finally, if judges hold incorrect implicit personality theories concerning emotional expression and SVO, we might find that increased (but in some instances worthless) nonverbal information makes things worse.

Studies 3, 4, and 5 are preliminary and exploratory. If their results suggest accurate detection of SVO, future research will be needed to determine just what aspects of the photos are driving judgments.

STUDY 1: METHOD

Generation of Stimulus Tapes

Thirty-two targets (students enrolled in introductory psychology) whose SVOs had been assessed with three-choice decomposed games about 4 weeks earlier (16 males and 16 females; 6 Js, 5 Os, and 5 Rs of each sex) were videotaped to provide the stimuli used in Studies 1 and 2. The sixth male J and sixth female J were videotaped in order to provide a male and female "practice" target. Participants were not aware of the practice nature of these two targets, but the data gathered on them were not analyzed.

The participants were videotaped while they described to the experimenter (blind to the target's SVO) what they did on the previous day, from the time they woke up to the time they went to sleep. Pilot tests of this task indicated that it easily engages participants and allows for the expression of a variety of nonverbal behaviors typical of those that occur during a casual interaction with a stranger.

After all 32 targets had been recorded, 30-second segments of each target's story were created by combining two unique (nonoverlapping) 15-second video-only segments of each target from his/her raw interview tape. These

15-second segments were selected according to the following criteria: (a) The target talked during the entire 15 seconds, and (b) one segment came before the midpoint of the story, as close to the midpoint as possible, and the other came after the midpoint, as close to the midpoint as possible.

The order of target persons on the resulting stimulus tape was random, given two constraints. (a) The two practice persons were presented first. (b) The remaining 30 target persons were presented at random given that, for every block of 6 target persons, each gender and social orientation pairing was presented once. Two stimulus videotapes were created in order to test for target presentation order effects. On each tape, the same 30 targets were present in a different random order given the same constraints noted above.

Facial Action Coding

The nonverbal (facial) behavior of the targets was coded using the Facial Action Coding System, or FACS (Ekman & Friesen, 1978). Each 30-second video segment was coded using complete FACS coding by a trained, experienced FACS coder (Greg Shelley), blind to the SVO of the targets. Another trained coder (Nina Kulkarni) coded 10 randomly selected segments (1/3 of the 30) in order to assess interrater agreement. Interrater agreement (calculated from each scoreable facial event by dividing the number of Action Units [AUs] where each coder agreed by the total number of AUs scored by each rater) was .72. There were six FACS codes that had emotional interpretations: enjoyment smiles, non-enjoyment smiles, anger expressions, disgust expressions, total negative expressions (anger, contempt, and disgust), and total scoreable expressions (including those with no emotional interpretation). These six measures were analyzed as a function of target SVO, gender, and the SVO × Gender interaction.

FACS Coding Results

As predicted, a significant multivariate effect was found when comparing J with OR targets (Wilks' lambda = .211, $F[6,19]$ = 11.827, p <.001, effect size = .789). Analysis of the univariate effects for each coded behavior suggests that J targets displayed significantly more enjoyment smiles (M = 3.5) than ORs (M = 0.5; $F[1,24]$ = 55.710, p < .001, eta^2 = .699). Js did not differ from ORs on any of the other FACS measures. No multivariate or univariate effects comparing O with R targets were obtained (all *p* values ranged from .126 to .680).

A significant multivariate effect for target gender was also found (Wilks' lambda = .507, $F[6,19]$ = 3.083, *p* =.028, effect size = .493). Examination of the univariate effects revealed that female targets displayed more enjoyment smiles (*M* = 2.75) than males (*M* = 1.2; $F[1,24]$ = 11.594, *p* = .002, eta^2 = .326) as well as a larger total number of scoreable facial expressions ($F[1,24]$ = 6.685, *p* = .016, eta^2 = .218).

It is noteworthy that the size of the main effect for J vs. OR was larger than that for gender, given that the gender of the target was explicit and obvious to the FACS coder, whereas his/her social orientation was not. Furthermore, the experimental setting in which the videos were recorded made no mention of cooperation or SVO, nor was it emotionally evocative. These results suggest that enjoyment smiles may be a generally valid indicator of SVO in casual social interaction with strangers.

Although no multivariate interaction effects between target's social orientation and gender were obtained (*p* values ranged from .080 to .881), a significant univariate interaction between target gender and social orientation (Js vs. ORs) on the total number of enjoyment smiles did reach significance ($F[1,24]$ = 7.014, *p* = .014, eta^2 = .226).

Figure 7.3 shows the means associated with this interaction and clearly demonstrates that the J vs. OR difference was largest in female targets. It is

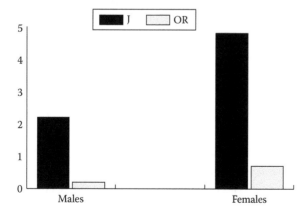

FIGURE 7.3

Means associated with the Target Sex × Target SVO interaction on enjoyment smiles in Study 1.

hard to know whether this difference is general, given that the interviewer for all recordings was a male.

These results suggest one nonverbal signaling system through which a stranger's SVO might be communicated to and perhaps accurately decoded by others. The next study examines such accuracy in a large group of observers naïve with respect to the target's SVO.

STUDY 2: METHOD

In Study 2, participants (35 males, 96 females) were Introductory Psychology students satisfying a research participation requirement, run in small groups of 13 to 17 students. At the beginning of the study, participants (henceforth referred to as "judges") played a set of decomposed games, allowing for assessment of their SVOs. At the end of this task, judges were told that prior research had shown that people tend to follow one of six choice rules when making their decisions. The rules were described in terms of the decision-maker's concern for him/herself and for the partner when making choices. For example, the Cooperative (J) choice rule was called "+Self,+Other" and described as choosing the column that provides the largest sum of points to self and other. Individualism was called "+Self,0Other" and described as choosing the largest number of points for self with no concern for the other. Competition was "+Self,–Other" and described as choosing the alternative in which the difference between self and other was the largest. The three remaining choice rules were (a) altruism, or "0Self,+Other," (b) aggression, or "0Self,–Other," and (c) equality, described as choosing the column in which the absolute difference between self and other was smallest. In these instructions, the words *altruism*, *cooperation*, and the like were never used in describing the choice rules. Following the description of the rules, the judges were shown a series of decomposed games and asked to indicate what alternative would be selected if a person was following each rule. Performance on this test was very good; only a few (less than 5%) of the judges were eliminated for failure to demonstrate that they understood the rules.

Following the description of the choice rules, judges were shown the 32 silent videotapes. After viewing each recording, the judges were asked to indicate the likelihood that the target just seen would follow each of the six rules. Judgments were made on a 7-point scale, where 1 = *definitely not*, and 7 = *definitely yes*. Thus, each judge made six ratings for each of the videos.

Study 2: Main Effects for Sex and SVO of Target

Not surprisingly, the multivariate effect for target gender was significant (Wilks' lambda = .582, $F[6,120] = 14.348$, $p < .001$, eta^2 = 0.42). Figure 7.4 displays the average likelihood ratings received by males and females for each rule.

Consistent with sex-role stereotypes, females were judged more likely to follow equality, altruistic, and cooperative choice rules, and males to follow individualistic, competitive, and aggressive choice rules. The univariate p values for all rules but aggression were less than 0.001; for aggression, $p = 0.0374$.

A significant global multivariate effect was obtained for judges' ratings of targets with different SVOs (Wilks' lambda = .591, $F[12,144] = 6.583$, $p < .001$, eta^2 = 0.33). This effect was found to be due to differences in J versus OR targets (Wilks' lambda = .67, $F[6,120] = 9.833$, $p < .001$). Consistent with the findings of Study 1, differences between O and R targets were not observed.

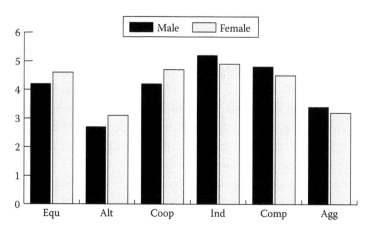

Notes: (1) Eq is Equality, Alt is Altruism, Coop is Cooperation, Ind is Individualism, Comp is Competition, and Agg is Aggression.

FIGURE 7.4
Average likelihood ratings given to Male and Female targets for each choice rule in Study 2.

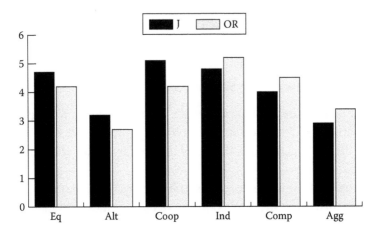

Notes: (1) Eq is Equality, Alt is Altruism, Coop is Cooperation, Ind is Individualism, Comp is Competition, and Agg is Aggression.

FIGURE 7.5
Average likelihood ratings given to J and OR targets for each choice rule in Study 2.

Figure 7.5 displays the average likelihood ratings of J and OR targets for each of the six choice rules. The figure shows that J targets received higher ratings on equality, altruism, and cooperation, whereas OR targets received higher ratings on individualism, competition, and aggression. Univariate analyses showed the differences suggested by Figure 7.5 to be significant ($p < 0.003$) for each rating.

Thus, it appears that our judges were able to discriminate between J and OR strangers based on a small sample of their nonverbal behavior during casual conversation. Of course, we cannot tell from these results just what cue (or cues) was guiding judgments, but we find it reasonable to suggest that they were at least in part guided by the differences in the level of enjoyment smiles between J and OR targets.

Our judges also judged females as more likely to be prosocial (altruistic, equality, cooperative) and males more likely to be antisocial (individualism, competition, aggression). Unlike the FACS results for enjoyment smiles presented above, the effect size for target sex was larger than for target SVO. Results presented next, for the interaction of SVO and target sex, appear to support the notion that enjoyment smiles are important in the judgment of SVO and help to provide an explanation for the larger main effect for sex than for SVO.

Study 2: Interaction Between Target Sex and Target SVO

We found a significant global interaction between target sex and SVO (Wilks' lambda = .653, $F[12,114]$ = 5.054, $p < .001$). Analysis of the 1-df components of this global effect revealed a significant Target J versus OR × Target Gender interaction (Wilks' lambda = .716, $F[6,120]$ = 7.923, $p < .001$). Examination of the means associated with this component of the interaction as well as univariate significance tests show the main effects for SVO (J targets received higher prosocial ratings and lower non-prosocial ratings than did ORs) holds for both male and female targets but appears to be larger for female targets. That is, although judges were accurate in their perceptions of targets with different SVOs independent of the target's gender, they were especially accurate in their perceptions of SVO within female targets.

This interaction is structurally quite similar to the Sex × J vs OR interaction found in FACS coding results for enjoyment smiles. To the extent that enjoyment smiles are important to SVO judgment, we might expect the sort of interaction on judgments observed here. Also, to the extent that enjoyment smiles are important to SVO judgment, we could expect that judges would be biased to give females (who have a higher base rate of enjoyment smiling than males) higher prosocial ratings than males. In combination with biases driven by sex role stereotypes, this could lead to a stronger main effect size for target sex than for target SVO.

Effects for SVO of Judges

In addition, between-subject effects for the social orientation of the judge were examined. These effects were consistent with the structured assumed similarity bias found by Kuhlman and Wimberley (1976). Judges rated targets (collapsed across target SVO and gender) as overall more likely to employ strategies consistent with their own SVO. Similar effects for judges' SVOs were also found in Studies 3, 4, and 5, which used still photographs.

There were also significant higher order interactions that are not readily interpretable. For example, the interaction between judge's SVO and target gender suggests that the difference in altruism (0,+) and cooperation (+,+) ratings assigned to male versus female targets is larger for OR judges than for J judges. In addition, the difference between cooperation (+,+) likelihood ratings assigned to male versus female targets (females were rated as more likely to be cooperative) appeared to be larger in R judges. Also, R judges rated male targets as especially low on cooperation.[1]

To summarize, the first two studies show differences in the base rates of enjoyment smiles in J and OR targets (Study 1), which appear at least in part to provide a basis for a valid discrimination of a stranger's predisposition to cooperate (Study 2). Though these studies are quite different from the earlier work of Carnevale (1977) and Mills (1978) described in the beginning of this chapter, they underscore the important role of emotional expression in the processes of encoding and decoding SVO.

In addition, Studies 1 and 2 suggest that the important SVO distinction, both in terms of encoding and decoding, is in terms of cooperative (J) vs non-cooperative (O or R) motives. Although Os and Rs in fact attempt to achieve different kinds of outcomes in interdependent relationships, there is good reason to believe that in many situations their behaviors will be very similar, particularly in situations with the structure of a social dilemma. In social dilemmas, joint gain (the goal of a J) is maximized by one choice, whereas both own gain and relative gain (the goals of Os and Rs, respectively) are maximized by another. This could lead to behavioral and experiential similarities between Os and Rs that might tend to blur the underlying motivational distinction.

The remaining studies reported in this chapter were inspired by Study 2, which shows that a rather minimal amount (30 seconds) of nonverbal behavior provides information sufficient to detect differences between Js and ORs. This prompts the question of just how minimal the nonverbal information necessary to decode SVO might be. Research cited in the Introduction suggests that under some circumstances, a single still photograph is sufficient to make distinctions related to the trustworthiness and/or cooperative behavior of targets. In addition, this research suggests that neutral photographs are less likely to produce accurate judgments than emotional (happy) ones. The next three studies were conducted by Peter Rives (Study 3) and Madeleine Page (Studies 4 and 5). Each asks judges to make SVO likelihood ratings based on still photos, using the same rating task employed in Study 2.

STUDIES 3, 4, AND 5: METHOD

Generation of Photos

The targets used in these studies were students from Introductory Psychology satisfying a research participation requirement and were selected on the basis of their responses to decomposed games administered in class approximately 4 weeks prior to the photograph session. At the photograph session, each participant was asked to pose the following expressions: neutral, happy, angry, sad, afraid, disgusted, surprised, and friendly. The expressions were video-recorded by Peter Rives, who was blind with respect to the SVO of the target. Recording continued until 30 targets (5 male and 5 female Js, Os, and Rs) had given their signed consent to use the videos in research concerning the judgment of personality, including predispositions to cooperate.

In the following semester, two undergraduate research assistants (blind to target SVO) used a video capture device to select a single frame of the video recording, which was saved as a JPEG image. Criteria for selection were (a) the frame should be near the center of the video segment, and (b) the target should be looking into the camera. After the research assistants had completed their selections, one was chosen at random for use in subsequent judgment studies.

Common Procedure for Studies 3, 4, and 5

Groups of Introductory Psychology students (about 50% were male) reported to a large lecture hall. In the first task, the students' SVOs were assessed via decomposed games. For the second task, as in Study 2, the students were told (truthfully) that they were going to see photos of earlier students (targets) who had been asked to pose an expression. Judges were also told that these targets had completed the same decomposed game measure that they had just completed. The researcher told the judges their task was to indicate the likelihood that each target had followed each of five choice rules. As in Study 2, the rules were not described with verbal labels (such as altruism, joint gain, etc.), but rather in terms of concern with self (+ or 0), and concern with other (+, 0, or –). Judges used the same

7-point rating scale employed in Study 2. Unlike Study 2, judges did not make ratings for equality.

The three studies differed in only one way; specifically, the type of photograph(s) used. In Study 3, judges were told that the targets were posing a neutral expression and were shown only neutral photos. In Study 4, judges were told that the target was posing a happy expression and saw only happy photos. In Study 5 they were told that the targets had posed a variety of emotional expressions and were shown a gallery of seven photos: happy, angry, sad, afraid, disgusted, surprised, and friendly. The gallery was presented as a single PowerPoint slide, and under each photo was a verbal label of the emotion being posed.

Results for Studies 3, 4, and 5

In each study, each judgment was analyzed according to a factorial ANOVA in which between-subject variables were judge sex and judge SVO, and within-subject variables were target sex and target SVO.

Common Effects Across All Studies

Importantly, across all studies, target effects were not moderated by judge SVO or judge sex. That is, it appears that judges were using nonverbal information in the same way. In all three studies there was a nonsurprising and highly consistent difference (all p values less than 0.001) in male and female target ratings for each of the five SVO judgments. Female targets were judged more likely than male targets to be altruistic and cooperative; the opposite was true for judgments of own, competition, and aggression.

Finally, in all three studies and for all five judgments there were no reliable differences between O and R targets. This is very similar to results in Study 2, again suggesting that judges make cooperative/non-cooperative distinctions between strangers. As reported next, the three studies did produce different results in terms of ratings given to J and OR targets.

Effect for SVO of Target

Differences were observed between J and OR targets in Studies 4 and 5 but not in Study 3. Figure 7.6 shows the mean ratings for J and OR targets in each study. The top, middle, and bottom panels of Figure 7.6 show judgments in Study 3 (neutral faces), Study 4 (happy faces), and Study 5 (gallery of faces), respectively.

In Study 3 (neutral photo) none of the J versus OR differences were reliable. In Study 4 (happy only) differences on altruism, competition, and aggression were reliable ($p < 0.01$). Effects were marginal for cooperation

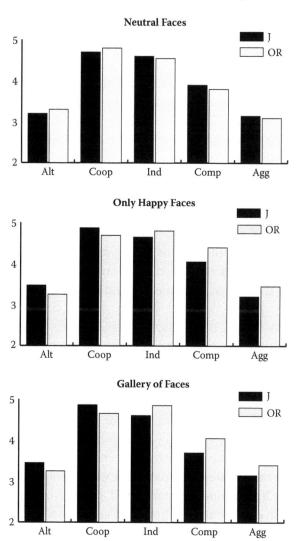

FIGURE 7.6
Average likelihood ratings given to J and OR targets for each choice rule in Studies 3, 4, and 5.

($p = 0.055$) and individualism ($p = 0.088$). Thus, posed happiness appears to have some influence on judgments of SVO. In Study 5 (gallery of 7 posed emotions), all J vs. OR differences were reliable (all p values < 0.005). Js were judged more likely to follow altruistic and cooperative choice rules and less likely to follow own, relative, and aggressive choice rules.

DISCUSSION

Since the early work of Carnevale (1977), which is really what sparked our interest in SVO and nonverbal behavior, there have been three groups of studies at Delaware dealing with this issue: (a) Mills (1978), (b) Shelley (1997), Shelley and Kuhlman (2007), and (c) Page, Rives, and Kuhlman (2007). They differ in procedures, but all lead to the same general conclusions: (a) Js and ORs differ in nonverbal displays, with Js being more positive than ORs, and (b) these differences are detectable by strangers. Shelley's work provides rather convincing and direct evidence that at least one aspect of the positivity of Js has to do with their higher (compared to ORs) base rate of "genuine" or "enjoyment" smiles during casual conversation. With regards to future research on still photos, Shelley's work suggests that the genuineness of J and OR posed happiness should be examined.

It is important to point out that in each of these three groups of studies, (a) the lab sessions in which the recordings were made were designed to avoid any suggestion of cooperation, social interdependence, etc.; (b) the person making the recordings was blind to the SVO of the target; and (c) different people made the recordings in each group of studies. Thus, it is difficult to argue that differences in nonverbal behavior resulted from demand characteristics or experimenter effects. Furthermore, in each group, SVO of the targets was assessed weeks prior to the time they were videotaped or photographed. Thus, these findings are consistent with the notion that SVO is, to some degree at least, temporally stable. And, the nonverbal stimuli (videotapes, photos) in each of the three groups of studies used different groups of Js, Os, and Rs as targets. That is, the general conclusions mentioned at the beginning of this paragraph appear to be rather robust.

These findings increase our conviction that in the real world there are important and trait-like individual differences in the predisposition to cooperate. The idea is by no means unique to us (e.g., Kelley & Stahelski, 1970; Van Lange, 2000), nor is the work presented in this chapter the only empirical demonstration of its probable truth. Rather, this chapter adds to the general literature on SVO as a trait-like variable that covaries not only with decisions in experimental games but also more real-world measures such as willingness to be helpful (McClintock & Allison, 1989) and Q-sort descriptions of Js, Os, and Rs provided by people who know them (Bem & Lord, 1979). To this list, the present chapter allows the addition of non-verbal behavior.

It is important to remember that the seminal 1968 paper by David Messick and Charles McClintock talked about social motivations and defined Js, Os, and Rs in terms of their value systems, specifically the concern they have for the well-being of others. In keeping with that definition, we can think of the differences between the above-mentioned real-world cooperators and non-cooperators in terms of how much they are predisposed to like others. Thus, it is not naïve to believe that there really are "nice" people out there whose niceness is a genuine expression of how they feel about their fellow human beings. And, the results of most SVO studies happily suggest that the nice guys are in the majority.

It is important to point out that these nice guys are not unconditionally cooperative. Indeed, one of the early studies (Kuhlman & Marshello, 1975) on SVO and the Prisoner's Dilemma game showed that Js appear to follow a Tit-for-Tat (TFT) strategy; they readily cooperate if it is mutual but are intolerant of exploitation. As demonstrated by Axelrod (1984), TFT is a viable strategy in PDG. Thus, one reason for the apparent predominance of Js in the population may have to do with their interaction strategies in ongoing relationships. However, TFT is not an evolutionarily stable strategy (ESS), in that it can be "invaded" by, for example, a strategy of unconditional cooperation. Thus, to understand how Js might maintain themselves over generations it may be necessary, as Frank (1988) and others have argued, that their relationships are formed in a manner maximizing the probability of having a J as a partner. The findings of the present chapter suggest that simple, minimal, nonverbal displays of positive affect could be helpful cues in this process.

Of course, simple recognition of a stranger's SVO is not enough. Ironically, to establish mutually cooperative relationships it is necessary that Js are highly discriminatory, seeking out Js as partners and avoiding everyone else, including altruists. This leads to an important research question, having to do with the preferences of Js (and Os and Rs) for relationship partners.

In this regard, a simple study done by Erin Yeagley (2000) in her first year of graduate school provides some provocative results. Yeagley had Js, Os, and Rs indicate how much they would want to be in a relationship with one of five different partners (Js, Os, Rs, altruists, and aggressors) differing in SVO. The partners were described in terms of concern with self (+ or 0) and concern with other (−, 0, +) in the same way that SVO was described to participants in the studies reported in this chapter. She found that Js were highly attracted to a J (+Self, +Other) partner and not at all attracted to any of the others, including altruism (0Self, +Other). Just as important, she found that O and R participants had precisely the same preferences as the Js. Thus, Js emerge as "sociometric stars," which would make it easier for them to succeed in their highly discriminatory pursuit of relationship partners. Future research will systematically replicate and extend Yeagley's findings, in the context of a general research program concerned with the evolutionary aspects of social value orientation.

We end this chapter a bit informally, but we think quite appropriately. The 1968 paper of David Messick and Charles McClintock is the fundamental inspiration of decades of research of many of their students and their students' students. It enriched the psychology of the experimental gaming paradigm and led to demonstrations of its validity as a method for increasing our understanding of socially interdependent behavior. For that paper, we say thank you very much! But the inspiration does not stop with the paper. We say thank you for calling us your intellectual children and grandchildren and for the enduring patience, support, affection, and yes, constructive criticism that fathers and grandfathers, intellectual and otherwise, freely express.

NOTE

1. Interested readers are invited to contact Greg Shelley (shelley@ kutztown.edu) for a copy of his dissertation for more information on these and other interactions involving target and judge SVO and gender.

REFERENCES

Axelrod, R. (1984). *The evolution of cooperation*. New York: Basic Books.

Bem, D. J., & Lord, C. G. (1979). Template Matching: A proposal for probing the ecological validity of experimental settings in social psychology. *Journal of Personality and Social Psychology, 37*, 833–846.

Brown, W. M., Palameta, B., & Moore, C. (2003). Are there nonverbal cues to commitment? An exploratory study using the zero-acquaintance video presentation paradigm. *Evolutionary Psychology, 1*, 42–69.

Carnevale, P. (1977). *Cooperators, competitors and individualists encode nonverbal affect*. Paper read at the Eastern Psychological Association Convention, Boston.

Dawkins, R. (1989). *The selfish gene*. Oxford, UK: Oxford University Press.

De Dreu, C. K. W., & McCusker, C. (1997). Gain-loss frames and cooperation in two-person social dilemmas: A transformational analysis. *Journal of Personality and Social Psychology, 72*, 1093–1106.

Duchenne, B. (1990). *The mechanisms of human facial expression or an electrophysiological analysis of the expression of the emotions* (A. Cuthbertson, Trans.) New York: Cambridge University Press. (Original work published 1862)

Ekman, P., & Friesen, W. (1978). *Facial action coding system*. Palo Alto, CA: Consulting Psychologist Press.

Frank, R. H. (1988). *Passions within reason: The strategic role of the emotions*. New York: W. W. Norton.

Frank, R. H., Gilovich, T., & Regan, D. (1993). The evolution of one-shot cooperation. *Ethology and Sociobiology, 14*, 247–256.

Harker, L., & Keltner, D. (2001). Expressions of positive emotion in women's college yearbook pictures and their relationship to personality and life outcomes across adulthood. *Journal of Personality and Social Psychology, 80*, 112–124.

Joireman, J., Van Lange, P. A. M., Kuhlman, D. M., Van Vugt, M., & Shelley, G. (1997). An interdependence analysis of commuter decisions. *European Journal of Social Psychology, 27*, 441–463.

Kelley, H. H., & Stahelski, A. J. (1970). Social interaction bases of cooperators' and competitors' beliefs about others. *Journal of Personality and Social Psychology, 16*, 66–91.

Krumhuber, E., Manstead, A. S. R., Cosker, D., Marshall, D., Rosin, P. L., & Kappas, A. (2007). Facial dynamics as indicators of trustworthiness and cooperative behavior. *Emotion, 7*, 730–735.

Kuhlman, D. M., Brown, C., & Teta, P. (1992). Judgments of cooperation and defection in social dilemmas: The moderating role of judge's social orientation. In W. B. G. Liebrand, D. Messick, & H. Wilke (Eds.), *A social psychological approach to social dilemmas* (pp. 111–132). Elmsford, NY: Pergamon.

Kuhlman, D. M., Camac, C. R., & Cuhna, D. A. (1986). Individual differences in social orientation. In H. Wilke, D. Messick, & C. Rutte (Eds.), *Experimental social dilemmas* (pp. 151–176). New York: Verlag Peter Lang.

Kuhlman, D.M., & Marshello, A. F. J. (1975). Individual differences in game motivation as moderators of pre-programmed strategy effects in prisoner's dilemma. *Journal of Personality and Social Psychology, 32*(5), 922–931.

Kuhlman, D. M., & Wimberley, D. L. (1976). Expectations of choice behavior held by cooperators, competitors, and individualists across four classes of experimental games. *Journal of Personality and Social Psychology, 34*, 69–81.

Liebrand, W. B. G., Jansen, R. W. T. L., Rijken, V. M., & Suhre, C. J. M. (1986). Might over morality: Social values and the perception of other players in experimental games. *Journal of Experimental Social Psychology, 22,* 203–215.

McClintock, C. G., & Allison, S. T. (1989). Social value orientation and helping behavior. *Journal of Applied Social Psychology, 19,* 353–362.

McClintock, C. G., & Liebrand, W. B. G. (1988). Role of interdependence structure, individual value orientation, and another's strategy on social decision making: A transformational analysis. *Journal of Personality and Social Psychology, 55,* 396–409.

Mehu, M., Grammer, K., & Dunbar, R. I. M. (2007). Smiles when sharing. *Evolution and Human Behavior, 28,* 415–422.

Messick, D. M., & McClintock, C. G. (1968). Motivational basis of choice in experimental games. *Journal of Experimental Social Psychology, 4,* 1–25.

Messick, D. M., & Thorngate, W. B. (1967). Relative gain maximization in experimental games. *Journal of Experimental Social Psychology, 3,* 85–101.

Mills, J. A. (1978). *Social motivations and encoding and decoding of nonverbal affect.* Unpublished undergraduate thesis, University of Delaware.

Page, M., Rives, P., & Kuhlman, D. M. (2007). *Still photos as cues for social value orientation.* Poster session presented at the 12th International Conference on Social Dilemmas, Seattle, WA.

Rapaport, A., & Chammah, A. M. (1965). *Prisoner's Dilemma.* Ann Arbor: University of Michigan Press.

Scharlemann, J. P. W., Eckel, C. C., Kacelnik, A., & Wilson, R. K. (2001). The value of a smile: Game theory with a human face. *Journal of Economic Psychology, 22,* 617–640.

Shelley, G. (1997). *Encoding and decoding social value orientation: Evidence for consensus and achievement.* Unpublished doctoral dissertation, University of Delaware.

Shelley, G. P., & Kuhlman, D. M. (2007). *The detection of social value orientation of strangers based on nonverbal behavior.* Poster session presented at the 12th International Conference on Social Dilemmas, Seattle WA.

Steigleder, M. K., Weiss, R. F., Cramer, R. E., & Feinberg, R. A. (1978). Motivating and reinforcing functions of competitive behavior. *Journal of Personality and Social Psychology, 36,* 1292–1301.

Takahashi, C., Yamagishi, T., Tanida, S., Kiyonari, T., & Kanazawa, S. (2006). Attractiveness and cooperation in social exchange. *Evolutionary Psychology, 4,* 315–329.

Van Lange, P. A. M. (2000). Beyond self interest: A set of propositions relevant to interpersonal orientation. In W. Stroebe M. & Hewstone (Eds.), *European review of social psychology* (Vol. 11, pp. 297–330). Chichester, UK: Wiley.

Verplaetse, J., Vaneste, S., & Braeckman, J. (2007). You can judge a book by its cover— The sequel: A kernel of truth in predictive cheating detection. *Evolution and Human Behavior, 28,* 260–271.

Yeagley, E. (2000). *Preferences of Js, Os and Rs for relationship partners of varying social value orientation.* Unpublished first year graduate project, University of Delaware.

Zebrowitz, L. A. (1997). *Reading faces: Window to the soul? New directions in social psychology.* Boulder, CO: Westview Press.

8

Persons, Organizations, and Societies: The Effects of Collectivism and Individualism on Cooperation

Terry L. Boles
University of Iowa

Huy Le
University of Central Florida

Hannah-Hanh D. Nguyen
California State University, Long Beach

In 1984, as an undergraduate in social psychology at the University of California at Santa Barbara, I (the first author) stepped into Dave Messick's research lab. It was a step that began a long, fruitful, and continuing education with a marvelous man and mentor. Graduate students working in his lab at the time included Charlie Samuelson and Scott Allison (see Chapters 2 and 12 of this volume), who were heavily involved in Dave's social dilemma research, which he had begun in collaboration with Marilynn Brewer and Rod Kramer (who had departed for UCLA by that time, but who continued to be important research colleagues — Rod coedited this volume and contributed Chapter 6). During this time, others visited this lab, including Wim Liebrand, a social psychologist from the University of Groningen in the Netherlands, and his student at the time, Paul Van Lange (see Chapter 4), who also participated in social dilemma and social value research with Dave and Chuck McClintock. The excellent repartee, critical thinking, and complete joy in doing research in that lab convinced me that UCSB was the place to stay and pursue my graduate studies. Although my own research interests tended toward judgment and decision-making as regards understanding the effects of foregone alternatives on outcome evaluation (Boles & Messick 1995), I never forgot my early immersion in the social dilemma research group. Thus, I am pleased to have the opportunity to present in the chapter that follows how Dave Messick's replenishable resource paradigm was employed in a study that examined the effects of collectivism and individualism (personal, organizational, and societal) on cooperation. This work was done in collaboration with Huy Le, formerly a Ph.D. student at the University of Iowa and now on the faculty at the University of Central Florida, and Hannah-Hanh D. Nguyen, formerly a Ph.D. student at Michigan State and now on the faculty at California State University, Long Beach. As such, Dave's social dilemma work continues to influence another generation of researchers.

Social dilemma research has demonstrated that in situations of interdependence, mutually cooperative behavior improves both collective and individual outcomes in the long run (Dawes, 1980; Van Lange, Liebrand, Messick, & Wilke, 1992). Regrettably, when such dilemmas present themselves, people are often self-interested and myopic and, as such, do not always make the cooperative choice. Messick and his colleagues (Messick & Brewer, 1983) have contributed immensely to our understanding of social and resource dilemmas and in particular have focused on the structural and normative constraints that can promote cooperative behavior.

We argue that people's propensity to engage in cooperative behavior is multiply determined. Specifically, we aver that examining the constructs of collectivism and individualism at three different levels — personal, organizational, and societal — will further our understanding of determinates of cooperative choice in resource dilemmas. We are not the first to examine collectivism and individualism as constructs that determine cooperative behavior; others have explored their effects in workgroups (Chatman & Barsade, 1995; Chatman, Polzer, Barsade, & Neale, 1998; Eby & Dobbins, 1997; Wagner, 1995) as well as across internal and external organizational borders (Gratton, 2005).

However, what exactly the constructs of collectivism and individualism (C-I) involve is often obfuscated, as researchers often operationalized them differently. Some researchers conceptualize C-I as a cultural characteristic of societies (e.g., Boone & Witteloostuijn, 1999; Gelfand & Christakopoulou, 1999; Parks & Vu, 1994; Wade-Benzoni et al., 2002); others consider it as a personal (individual)[1] characteristic (e.g., Chatman & Barsade, 1995; Earley, 1989, 1993; Probst, Carnevale, & Triandis, 1999; Wagner, 1995); and some have examined it as an organization-level construct (e.g., Chatman & Barsade, 1995; Chatman et al., 1998; Robert & Wasti, 2002).

Although these three different levels of C-I (societal, organizational, and personal) generally produce similar results with respect to cooperation when studied separately, each is evidently distinct, just as an organizational culture may be distinct from the national culture (cf. Schneider, 1990). Accordingly, we argue that a comprehensive understanding of the effects of C-I on cooperation requires examining all three levels of the construct concurrently. Failure to do so is likely to result in contextual fallacies (Rousseau, 1985). However, to date, no extant studies have included all three levels of C-I simultaneously. In the study presented in this chapter, we endeavor to extend the literature by examining the impact of the three C-I levels on cooperation concurrently. Specifically, we examine the relationship between C-I and cooperative behaviors as a function of personal dispositions, within the context of organizational cultures, and in different societal cultures.

LEVELS OF COLLECTIVISM-INDIVIDUALISM AND COOPERATION

Societal Level

C-I has been a popular topic for research in cross-cultural psychology since the seminal work of Hofstede (1980). Hofstede (1991) defines C-I as follows:

> Individualism pertains to *societies* [italics added] in which the ties between individuals are loose: everyone is expected to look after himself or herself and his or her immediate family. Collectivism as its opposite pertains to *societies* [italics added] in which people from birth onward are integrated into strong, cohesive ingroups, which throughout people's lifetime [*sic*] continue to protect them in exchange for unquestioning loyalty. (p. 51)

Similarly, Earley (1989) suggests that the essential attribute of a collectivistic society is that individuals will subordinate their personal interests to the goals of the groups to which they belong. Collectivistic cultures emphasize attending to the needs of other members of a group, fitting in, and harmonious interdependence (Markus & Kitayama, 1991). On the other hand, individualistic cultures value personal independence, uniqueness, and attending to oneself (Markus & Kitayama, 1991). These definitions clearly refer to C-I as a societal-level construct. Further, implicit in the definitions is the fact that C-I is conceptualized as a unidimensional, bipolar construct and that societies can be ranked along a continuum, with individualism at one end and collectivism at the other.

It might also be inferred from the definitions that cooperation among ingroup members is generally higher in collectivistic societies where people are expected to work harmoniously with others in groups, compared with individualistic societies where pursuing individual interests, sometimes at the cost of the group goals, is the norm. Such logic was confirmed by studies showing that societal culture indeed determines people's cooperative behaviors within groups (Boone & Witteloostuijn, 1999; Cox, Lobel, & McLeod, 1991; Gelfand & Christakopoulou, 1999; Parks & Vu, 1994; Wade-Benzoni et al., 2002).

Person Level

It has been recognized that individual members within a society may also differ in their respective C-I characteristics. Accordingly, researchers have suggested that the construct be studied at the personal level (Schwartz, 1990). Triandis, Leung, Villareal, and Clack (1985) use the terms *allocentric* and *idiocentric* to denote people with collectivistic and individualistic dispositions, respectively, independent of the societal culture in which they live. In his study of collectivistic and individualistic people within an individualistic society (the United States), Wagner (1995) defines individualists as people who look after themselves and tend to ignore group interests if such interests conflict with their own personal desires. Collectivists, viewed as the opposite of individualists, are those who let the demands and interests of groups take precedence over their own personal desires and needs.

Research examining the link between person-level C-I and cooperation have indicated that collectivists are likely to cooperate better in groups (Chatman & Barsade, 1995; Wagner, 1995) and in social dilemma games (Probst et al., 1999) than are individualists. Similarly, Earley (1989, 1993) showed that trait-like collectivism is negatively correlated with social loafing. In sum, collectivists are generally found to demonstrate more cooperative behaviors than are individualists.

Though researchers studying the C-I construct at the societal level generally treat it as a bipolar construct (i.e., collectivism vs. individualism) in accordance with Hofstede's original conceptualization, there appears to be disagreement as to the dimensionality of C-I at the person level. Some researchers view individualists as being at the opposite end of the continuum from collectivists (e.g., Chatman & Barsade, 1995), whereas others suggest that collectivism and individualism represent two relatively independent factors (Earley & Gibson, 1998; Triandis, 1995; Triandis, 1996). The latter conceptualization of the construct has gradually gained empirical and theoretical support (cf. Earley & Gibson, 1998; Oyserman, Coon, & Kemmelmeier, 2002). In the study described here, we chose to adopt the view that collectivism and individualism at the person level represent distinct factors. As demonstrated later in the section Cross-Level Collectivism-Individualism Interactions, this view helps explain some seemingly inconsistent findings in the literature regarding the effects of C-I on cooperation and enables us to formulate hypotheses about the interplay of C-I levels in determining behavior.

Organizational Level

Though there is a general consensus that C-I can be studied at both the societal and personal levels (Earley & Gibson, 1998), there has been relatively less empirical work at the intermediate level (i.e., workgroups, organizations) although it has been argued that this level is theoretically relevant and deserves more attention (Dansereau, 1989; Earley, 1993; Earley & Gibson, 1998; Wagner & Moch, 1986). Of a handful of studies that empirically examined the effects of organizational-level C-I (e.g., Chartman & Barsade, 1995; Robert & Wasti, 2002), it was indeed found that this level of C-I is related to important organizational outcomes, including cooperative behavior.

Organizational-level C-I is a dimension of organizational cultures (Robert & Wasti, 2002), which either emphasize individualistic values of placing priority on pursuing individuals' goals and rewarding members based on their individual achievements or highlight collectivistic values of prioritizing collective goals and rewarding members for joint contributions to organizational accomplishments (Chatman & Barsade, 1995; Earley & Gibson, 1998). As such, organizational-level C-I is embodied in the values and practices adopted by organizations (Calori & Sarnin, 1991; Gelfand & Christakopoulou, 1999; Hofstede, Neuyen, Ohavy, & Sanders,

1990). Because cooperative mechanisms — organizational practices reflecting the type of cultures adopted by an organization — can effectively influence people's cooperative behavior (Chatman & Barsade, 1995; Chen, Chen, & Meindl, 1998), it is important that organizational-level C-I be studied along with the societal and personal levels, particularly as it applies to studying cooperative behavior within an organizational setting. The few studies that have examined the effect of C-I on cooperation at either the group level (Eby & Dobbins, 1997) or the organizational level (Chatman & Barsade, 1995; Chatman et al., 1998; Morris, Avila, & Allen, 1993) have indeed demonstrated the importance of this intermediate level as a predictor of behavior in workgroups.

Organizational-level C-I has mainly been operationalized empirically as a bipolar construct (e.g., Chatman & Barsade, 1995; Eby & Dobbins, 1997; Morris et al., 1993). More recently, Robert and Wasti (2002) suggested that, just as at the personal level, organizational-level C-I should be considered as a multidimensional construct with individualism being independent of collectivism. Nevertheless, these two factors are highly correlated at the organizational level (Robert & Wasti, 2002); therefore, in this study we treat organizational-level C-I as a bipolar, unidimensional construct in order to be consistent with past research that empirically examined its effects on cooperation (e.g., Chatman & Barsade, 1995; Eby & Dobbins, 1997).

CROSS-LEVEL COLLECTIVISM-INDIVIDUALISM INTERACTIONS

Although C-I levels generally produce similar main effects on cooperative behavior when examined separately, the levels may interact when they are combined in one setting. Researchers have realized this possibility but have tended to overlook it, implying that the confounding is inconsequential (Chen et al., 1998). However, when two levels have actually been combined in a single study, their effects on cooperative behavior have often been complex. For example, Gelfand and Realo (1999) found an interaction effect between person-level C-I and accountability (an organizational practice, which can be seen as an embodiment of organizational culture) on cooperative behavior. Specifically, high accountability enhanced cooperation among collectivists yet enhanced competition among individualists. That is, accountability accentuated the person-level tendencies on the C-I construct.

Earley (1989) and Wagner (1995) also found interaction effects between person-level C-I and accountability on social loafing and cooperative behavior, respectively. In these studies, individualists were more likely to adjust their behaviors in response to changes in organizational practices (accountability). Collectivists, on the other hand, appeared to be more consistent and less likely to change their behavior across organizational conditions.

In another study that directly examined the effects of the two levels of C-I (personal and organizational) on cooperation, Chatman and Barsade (1995) found that collectivists, who were very cooperative under collectivistic organizational cultures, behaved uncooperatively when placed in organizations where individualistic cultures dominated. Yet, the behavior of individualists was not significantly different across organizational cultures. These findings are consistent with the early work of Kelly and Stahelski (1970).

The empirical results so far seem to converge on the finding that organizational-level C-I moderates the relationship between person-level C-I and cooperative behavior. Yet, the specifics of such interaction effects are not consistent across studies. These seemingly contradictory findings may be reconciled if individualism and collectivism at the person level are considered as two distinct, relatively independent constructs, rather than as two poles on a continuum. Accordingly, based upon empirical evidence in the extant literature, it might be hypothesized that people who are high in either collectivistic or individualistic dispositions are likely to adapt their behaviors to organizational cultures. Highly individualistic people (compared with those low in individualism), who are motivated by self-interest, may realize that by complying with the organizational culture (i.e., behaving cooperatively under collectivistic organizational cultures and competitively under individualistic cultures) they will facilitate the achievement of their own personal goals (cf. Earley, 1989). That is, they would change their work behaviors accordingly. Similarly (but for different reasons), highly collectivistic people (compared with those low in collectivism), who value harmony with social contexts, might be more likely to adapt their behaviors to the context defined by their organizational culture (Markus & Kitayama, 1991).

Not surprisingly, the effects discussed thus far are largely based on research conducted within an individualistic society (the United States). Chen et al. (1998) suggested that individualistic societies and collectivistic societies differ in the types of mechanisms they may use to encourage cooperative behavior. For example, an equity-based reward distribution system as a cooperation mechanism might be more effective in an individualistic culture than in a collectivistic culture, which would favor an equality-based mechanism. (See Messick & Schell, 1992, for discussion of equality as a social decision-making heuristic.)

It is quite possible that the interaction effects between organizational and personal levels of the C-I construct found in individualistic societies will be different in collectivistic societies. In other words, societal-level C-I may further moderate the interaction effects between organizational-level and person-level C-I in predicting cooperation. Conceivably, in a collectivistic society, people with a high collectivistic disposition may seek harmony with social "cues" (social norms) provided by the society. Such cues may attenuate the effects of the organizational culture on cooperative behavior. As such, high collectivists may attend to social cues that emphasize cooperation with other ingroup members and behave consistently cooperatively. In other words, highly collectivistic people would be less likely to change their behavior in response to the organizational culture. Taken together, we expect that there may be a three-way interaction effect among societal, organizational, and personal levels of the C-I construct (with collectivism representing the person level). Figure 8.1 shows our hypothesized interaction effects among levels of the C-I constructs in predicting cooperation, and we state these more formally below.

Hypothesis 1

Societal-level C-I will moderate the interaction effect between person-level collectivism and organizational-level C-I. Specifically, (a) in an individualistic society, highly collectivistic people are more likely than those low in collectivism to behave cooperatively in a dominantly collectivistic organization. In a dominantly individualistic organization, people high on collectivism will behave as competitively as do those low on collectivism (see Figure 8.1a). On the other hand, (b) in a collectivistic culture, people high on collectivism will consistently cooperate with others regardless of the organizational culture (see Figure 8.1b).

Unlike people high on collectivism, we argue that those high on individualism are less likely to be influenced by societal culture. As we discussed earlier, high individualists, compared with those who are low in this disposition, tend to adjust their behavior in accordance with the organizational

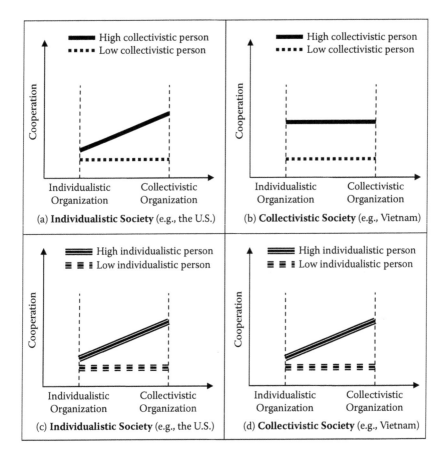

FIGURE 8.1
The hypothesized effects of three levels of collectivism-individualism on cooperation.

culture in order to achieve their personal goals. Because societal culture is unlikely to affect such perceived link between behavior and outcomes, we do not expect that the interaction effect between person-level individualism and organizational-level C-I will be moderated by societal-level C-I. Accordingly, we hypothesize that the same interaction effect between person-level individualism and organizational-level C-I will be found in both individualistic and collectivistic societies.

Hypothesis 2

In both individualistic and collectivistic societies, the relationship between the personal level of individualism and cooperation will be similarly moderated by organizational culture, such that highly individualistic persons, compared to those who are low in this disposition, are more likely to behave cooperatively under collectivistic organizations and competitively under individualistic organizations (see Figure 8.1c and Figure 8.1d).

Note that while we do not hypothesize any main effects for C-I levels, empirical evidence consistently shows that collectivism at all levels is likely to be related to cooperation in workgroups (e.g., Boone & Witteloostuijn, 1999; Chatman & Barsade, 1995; Earley, 1989, 1993; Gelfand & Christakopoulou, 1999; Probst et al., 1999; Wagner, 1995). Such effects are also reflected in Figure 8.1.

Another important issue is the potential combined effect between societal and organizational levels of C-I on cooperative behavior. As mentioned above, Chen and colleagues (1998) proposed that cooperative mechanisms, which are organizational practices, are different across societal cultures. Therefore, it is possible that societal-level C-I moderates the relationship between organizational-level C-I and cooperation. Finding such an interaction may have important implications for organizational practices across cultures. Because there is no clear theoretical reason to predict the precise nature of this interaction effect, we examined it for exploratory purposes only in the current study.

THE STUDY

Undergraduate business students from a large Midwestern public university in the United States (n = 153; 54% female) and undergraduate business students from a large public university in southern Vietnam (n = 207; 40% female) participated in a computerized social dilemma game. Previous research suggests that the American societal norm is generally individualistic, whereas the Vietnamese society is collectivistic (e.g., Parks & Vu, 1994). In both samples, participants were randomly assigned to one of two organizational cultural conditions — either collectivistic or individualistic. Local experimenters were involved in the data collection in both countries (although an American researcher of Vietnamese descent monitored the process in Vietnam).

The organizational C-I manipulation was embedded in the social dilemma game instructions, which consisted of a description of the organization and its culture, the rules of the game, and how each participant's performance would be evaluated (described in the next section). Upon finishing this role-play exercise, participants were asked to respond to a questionnaire consisting of the C-I inventories and other measures.

We used two language versions of the game instructions and questionnaires (i.e., English and Vietnamese). The Vietnamese version had been translated and backtranslated by two of the authors (Le, Nguyen), who are bilingual and fluent in both languages. A third bilingual local collaborator, unaware of the purposes of the current research, also backtranslated the experiment materials and these translations were later checked again for accuracy and pilot-tested with a small group of Vietnamese research assistants and college students to check for readability and connotation.

THE REPLENISHABLE RESOURCE GAME

Social dilemma games have been widely used to study the cooperative behavior (or lack thereof) of individuals within groups (e.g., Wade-Benzoni et al., 2002). Such games are especially useful for our experimental purposes because they provide an objective measure of cooperation. We used an adapted version of the Replenishable Resource Game described in Samuelson, Messick, Rutte, and Wilke (1984). Specifically, each participant was asked to play the role of a manager from one of three divisions of a transportation organization. The "managers" were allowed to determine the amount of the quarterly budget for each of their divisions by harvesting money from a common resource (the organization's available capital). After all managers had received their budgets for the quarter, the balance in the common resource was multiplied by 1.10 (representing a quarterly profit gain of 10% from the organization's investment activity). Managers were given feedback about the size of the replenished resource pool (but not the amount the other two managers harvested) after each payout and then decided on their budgets for the following quarter. There were 12 rounds in the game, representing 3 years. Obviously, the more money the managers took for their own division in each round, the smaller was the common resource that remained to be replenished.

Given the substantially stronger buying power of the U.S. currency compared with the Vietnamese, we were cautious about converting the U.S.

dollar amounts in the American version directly into Vietnamese "dongs" in the Vietnamese version because this fact might cause subgroup differences in the perception of the company budget. Instead, based on the feedback of an economics faculty member in Vietnam, we chose an equivalent and more realistic budget figure for the Vietnamese game version (i.e., 12 million dongs; equivalent to US$800,000, which was the then-average operating budget of Vietnamese companies).

Participants believed that they were interacting with the other two managers in their organization via computers. Unknown to the participants, the other two managers' activities (i.e., budget allocating decisions) were simulated by a computer program. This manipulation was necessary to ensure that all participants received similar responses from the other imaginary players, thereby eliminating the potential confounding influence of variable behavior by other group members.

MANIPULATION OF ORGANIZATIONAL COLLECTIVISM-INDIVIDUALISM CULTURES

Organizational cultures were manipulated by giving participants a description about their respective organizations. Participants read stories about the founder of the organizations, the founder's personal values and policy, and the company's reward system. For example, an excerpt of the collectivistic organization description reads

> United Transportation Co., Ltd. is a regional trucking company. The company has been in the business for twenty years and considered one of the leading transporters in the region. The founder of United Transportation, Alain Smith, has set up the company from a small family business. All the company employees then were members of the same family. United Transportation has grown quickly and it now has about 300 employees. Despite its current size, the company remains a big family. Almost all the employees know one another on the first name basis. Alain Smith attributes the successes of his company to the cooperation of all of the employees and their dedication for the company's goals. He strongly emphasizes the value of cooperation among the employees. Everyone in the company is expected to place the company goals and interests over his/her individual interests.

Part of the description of an individualistic company culture reads

> Independence Transportation Co., Ltd. is a regional trucking company. It has been in the business for twenty years. The founder of Independence Transportation, Robert Thompson, has single-handedly started the company in 1982 with only 20 employees. Thompson often takes pride in the fact that all of his successes to date have been solely due to his own efforts. He therefore strongly emphasizes the value of independence and competition, even among the company employees. Thompson believes that only through competition can performance standards be continuously raised. Employees are expected to work independently and competitively. Jobs are organized so that everyone can work rather independently of others. People therefore are expected to be able to know their jobs well and care only about their jobs.

In addition, how participants' performances were to be evaluated and rewarded was also consistent with their assigned organizational culture. Those in the organizational collectivistic condition were told that their performance would be evaluated "by the accumulated amount *that you and the other two managers left in the company budget* (i.e., did not take) at the end of the 3 years." Meanwhile, those in the individualistic condition were told that their performance would be evaluated *"by the accumulated amount that you have obtained* (i.e., taken for your division) throughout the 3 years." Participants were in fact paid according to these criteria.

MEASURES

The following measures were included in the questionnaire administered to the participants upon completion of the social dilemma game.

Measure of Person-Level C-I

There seems to be little consensus among researchers as to the" best" measure of C-I at the person level. For reasons mentioned earlier, we followed the recent conceptualization of individual level C-I (Earley & Gibson, 1998), which suggests that the construct includes two distinct factors,

TABLE 8.1

Results of the Exploratory Factor Analysis for the U.S. Sample — Item Loadings on the Main Factors

		Factor[a]			
Item		**1**	**2**	**3**	**4**
1	If you want something done right, you've got to do it yourself.	.46			
2	Winning is everything.		.63		
3	People who belong to a group should realize that they're not always going to get what they personally want.				.49
4	In the long run the only person you can count on is yourself.	.47			
5	People should be made aware that if they are going to be part of a group, then they are sometimes going to have to do things they don't want to.				.86
6	Success is the most important thing in life.		.52		
7	Doing your best is not enough; it is important to win.		.72		
8	The well-being of my friends is important to me.			.68	
9	To me, pleasure is spending time with others.			.69	
10	I feel good when I cooperate with others.			.96	
11	Parents and children must stay together as much as possible.			.51	
12	I rather depend on myself than others.	.62			
13	I often do "my own thing."	.63			
14	I rely on myself most of the time; I rarely rely on others.	.66			

Note: N = 153.

[a] Factor 1 = Independence; Factor 2 = Competition; Factor 3 = Group belonging; Factor 4 = Individuality subordination.

collectivism and individualism. Accordingly, we used subsets of items from Wagner's (1995) and Triandis and Gelfand's (1998) measures of C-I. Table 8.1 lists the 14 items included in the study.

Measure of Cooperation

Following the tradition of replenishable social dilemma games (Samuelson et al., 1984), we used the total budget amount that each participant took for his/her division as the operational measure of cooperative behavior, such that a larger amount taken indicated a lower level of cooperation.

ANALYSIS

Measurement Equivalence

In any cross-cultural research, researchers need to ascertain that the measures used in their study similarly reflect the same constructs across cultures. Thus, it is critical to assess and establish measurement equivalence before any analysis addressing substantive research questions can be conducted (cf. Ryan, Chan, Ployhart, & Slade, 1999). According to Vandenberg and Lance (2000), metric invariance (i.e., loadings of the items on their principal factors being equal across samples) should be established before any meaningful cross-cultural analyses can be carried out. Accordingly, we first carried out an exploratory factor analysis using the U.S. sample to determine the factors underlying the C-I items. These factors were a priori used to establish a factor structure for the Vietnamese sample. We then used confirmatory factor analysis to examine the equivalency of the factor structure across cultures.

Hypothesis Testing

Moderated multiple regression analyses with cooperation (i.e., amount taken) as the dependent variable were carried out to test the hypotheses. We included both samples (U.S. and Vietnam) in our analyses. Before combining the samples, we standardized the outcome variable of cooperation and the C-I measures within each sample. This step was necessary because of concern regarding the absolute equivalence of the buying power of the currencies in the two countries, which would render the dependent variable not comparable. Standardization only affects results related to the main effect of societal-level C-I, which is not the focus of the current study.

A number of hierarchically nested multiple regression models were then examined. The first model (Model 1) includes only gender as the control variable. The second model (Model 2) adds the main effects of the C-I levels, in which dummy variables (collectivistic culture = 1, individualistic culture = 0) were created for societal-level and organizational-level C-I. Model 3 further includes all the two-way interaction terms between societal, organizational, and person levels of the C-I constructs. Finally, Model

4, which includes all the same variables as Model 3 plus the three-way interaction terms, provides the direct tests for the hypotheses.

There are two possible three-way interactions in Model 4 because the individual level C-I includes two distinct factors, individualism and dollectivism. Each three-way interaction term pertains to a hypothesis. Hypothesis 1 was tested by examining the three-way interaction term created by the person-level collectivism and the other two levels of the C-I construct. Hypothesis 2 suggests that (a) there is an interaction between organizational-level C-I and person-level individualism and (b) such an effect is not affected by societal culture. Accordingly, to test this hypothesis, we examined (a) the two-way interaction effect between person-level individualism and organizational-level C-I and (b) the three-way interaction effect created by person-level individualism and the other two levels of the C-I construct.

RESULTS

Examining the Collectivism-Individualism Factor

Using an exploratory factor analysis on the C-I items for the U.S. sample only, we extracted four factors based upon a combination of several criteria, including examination of the resulting scree plot (Cattell, 1966), parallel analysis (Thompson & Daniel, 1996), and factor interpretability. Based on the content of the included items, the resulting four factors were named as follows: independence, competition, group belonging, and individuality subordination. The factors and their item loadings are presented in Table 8.1.

We next used a multiple-group confirmatory factor analysis, sequentially specifying the same factor structure and loadings for the items in both the U.S. and Vietnamese samples, in order to examine the extent to which participants in these two countries interpreted the items similarly. This analysis involves testing hierarchically nested Confirmatory Factor Analysis (CFA) models with increasing constraints imposed on the equivalency of the parameter estimates for the models across the two groups. The first model, which specifies only the same factor structures across both samples, tested "configural invariance" (Vandenberg & Lance, 2000), which is the prerequisite for subsequent tests. This model had acceptable fit.

The next model tested metric invariance. In this model, we constrained factor loadings for all the items to be equal across samples. Compared to the previous model testing configural invariance, the current model had almost the same level of fit. Of special importance, the chi-square difference between this model and the previous model was statistically insignificant, suggesting that item loadings on the factors were likely to be similar across samples. Overall, our analytic results indicated that the C-I items similarly measured the four constructs across cultures.

As described in the Analysis section, we further sought to combine the resulting four C-I factors into higher order factors, collectivism and individualism, in order to test the hypotheses. The individualism factor includes the two first-order factors of competition and independence. The collectivism factor underlies the group belonging and individuality subordination factors. We examined this higher order factor model using a multigroup CFA. Results indicated that the model fit the data reasonably well. As we expected, collectivism and individualism are relatively independent of each other (factor correlation is estimated to be −.17 in the U.S sample and .14 in the Vietnam sample). Based on this result, we grouped the items into two general scales, individualism and collectivism. Subsequent analyses were based on these two scales.

Cross-Level Collectivism-Individualism Effects on Cooperation

Descriptive statistics and correlations among the measured variables are presented in Table 8.2. It can be seen therein that the correlation between organizational culture and the budget amount taken (the operational measure of cooperation) was significant in the U.S. sample, indicating that people in a collectivistic organizational culture tend to take less money (e.g., are more cooperative). In the Vietnamese sample, this effect was in the expected direction but was not significant. Surprisingly, all of the correlations between the person level of the C-I constructs and cooperation were small and statistically nonsignificant across samples.

As mentioned in the Analysis section, four hierarchically nested regression models were examined on the combined sample. Results of these analyses are shown in Table 8.3. For Model 2, the effect of organizational-level C-I reaches statistical significance, whereas the effects for person levels

TABLE 8.2

Correlations Among Measured Variables

	M[a]	SD[b]	Gender[c]	Org. Culture[d]	Individualism[e]	Collectivism[f]	Amount[g]
Gender	.60/.46	.49/.50	1.00	.19*	.19*	.02	-.04
Organizational Culture	.50/.50	.50/.50	-.02	1.00	.04	.03	-.08
Individualism	38.9/33.5	7.21/7.60	.26*	-.02	1.00	.28*	-.07
Collectivism	31.8/34.4	4.71/4.64	-.18*	.12	-.10	1.00	.02
Amount taken[h]	532.6/5,108	211.7/2,036	.13	-.35*	-.01	-.07	1.00

Note: Above diagonal: Vietnamese sample ($N = 207$), below diagonal: U.S. Sample ($N = 153$).

a   Mean of Vietnamese sample/Mean of U.S. sample.

b   SD of Vietnamese sample/SD of U.S. sample.

c   Female = 0; Male = 1.

d   The manipulated condition of organizational cultures to which the participants were assigned (individualistic culture = 0; collectivistic culture = 1).

e   Participants' scores on the Individualism scale (person level).

f   Participants' scores on the Collectivism scale (person level).

g   Amount of budget taken by participants (a proxy of cooperation [reversed]).

h   Unit for Vietnamese sample = million VN dong; Unit for U.S. sample = thousand U.S. dollars.

* $p < .05$.

TABLE 8.3

Effects of Collectivism-Individualism Levels on Cooperation (Combined Sample)

Independent Variables	Model 1			Model 2			Model 3			Model 4		
	β	R²	ΔR²	β	R²	ΔR²	β	R²	ΔR²	β	R²	ΔR²
		.01	.01		.04	.03*		.08	.04*		.08	.00
Control Variable												
Gender	.03			.07			.06			.06		
C-I Variables												
Societal culture (SC)				−.01			−.14*			−.14*		
Organizational culture (OC)				−.20*			−.35*			−.35*		
Individualism (person level; PI)				−.05			.12			.15		
Collectivism (person level; PC)				.01			.01			.10		
Two-Way Interactions												
SC × OC							.24*			.24*		
OC × PC							−.02			−.13		
OC × PI							−.18*			−.21*		
SC × PC							.04			−.07		
SC × PI							−.07			−.09		
Three-Way Interactions												
SC × OC × PC										.15		
SC × OC × PI										−.00		

Note: N = 360.

β = Standardized regression coefficient.

*p < .05.

do not. These results are consistent with findings we obtained from the zero-order correlations in Table 8.2.

Three-Way Interaction Effects of the C-I Levels on Cooperation

In Hypothesis 1 we suggested that societal-level C-I will moderate the interaction effect between person-level collectivism and organizational-level C-I. None of the two-way interactions involving person-level collectivism was statistically significant in Model 3. Subsequently, in Model 4, the three-way interaction involving person-level collectivism did not reach statistical significance. Therefore, Hypothesis 1 was not supported.

Interaction Effect Between Person-Level Individualism and Organizational C-I

In Hypothesis 2 we suggested that the interaction between organizational-level C-I and person-level individualism would not be affected by societal culture. In Model 3, only the hypothesized interaction between person-level individualism and organizational-level C-I was significant. This interaction effect remains statistically significant in Model 4. The direction of this effect indicates that those high on personal-level individualism are likely to change their behaviors (in terms of amount taken) across organizational cultures, compared to those low on personal-level individualism. This finding, coupled with the fact that the three-way interaction among societal C-I, organizational C-I, and person-level individualism is virtually zero, indicates that Hypothesis 2 was supported by the data.

We acknowledge, however, that nonsignificant findings do not necessarily provide support for hypotheses. Thus, we sought to corroborate these findings by conducting further analyses separately for the U.S. and Vietnamese samples. Results are shown in Table 8.4 (for the U.S. sample) and in Table 8.5 (for the Vietnamese sample). As can be seen, in both samples, the interaction effects between person-level individualism and organizational-level C-I are very similar. Both effects are statistically significant. Taken together, the evidence appears to support Hypothesis 2.

To further illustrate the interaction effect, we split each sample into three groups based upon their scores on the individualism scale. We

TABLE 8.4

Effects of the Collectivism-Individualism Levels on Cooperation (U.S. Sample)

Independent Variables	Regression Model								
	Control Variables Only			C-I Variables Added			Interaction Terms Added		
	β	R^2	ΔR^2	β	R^2	ΔR^2	β	R^2	ΔR^2
Control Variables									
Gender	.13	.02	.02	.13	.14*	.12*	.16	.17*	.03*
C-I Variables									
Organizational culture (OC)				−.35*			−.35*		
Individualism (person level; PI)				−.04			.14		
Collectivism (person level; PC)				−.01			.13		
Interaction Terms									
OC × PI							−.23*		
OC × PC							−.15		

Note: N = 153.

β = Standardized regression coefficient.

*p < .05.

TABLE 8.5

Effects of the Collectivism-Individualism Levels on Cooperation (Vietnamese Sample)

	Regression Model								
	Control Variables Only			C-I Variables Added			Interaction Terms Added		
Independent Variables	β	R²	ΔR²	β	R²	ΔR²	β	R²	ΔR²
		.00	.00		.01	.01		.03*	.02*
Control Variables									
Gender	−.04			−.01			−.01		
C-I Variables									
Organizational culture (OC)				−.07			−.07		
Individualism (person level; PI)				−.08			.05		
Collectivism (person level; PC)				.05			.02		
Interaction Terms									
OC × PI							−.19*		
OC × PC							−.06		

Note: N = 207.

β = Standardized regression coefficient.

*p < .05.

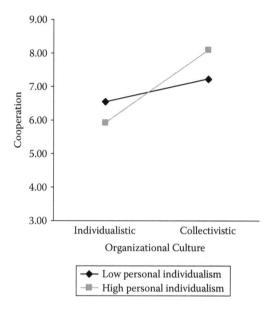

FIGURE 8.2
Cooperation (difference between maximum amount available and the total amount taken, in thousands of U.S. dollars).

then computed the average amount of money not taken by the lowest group and by the highest group across organizational cultures We plotted amount not taken so that increased cooperation is plotted in Figure 8.2 (for the U.S. sample) and Figure 8.3 (for the Vietnamese sample). The same pattern of interaction effects can be seen in both figures, such that those high on personal individualism showed much more sensitivity to organizational culture than those low on this trait. For example, in Figure 8.2, high person-level individualists behaved relatively uncooperatively under the individualistic organizational culture (i.e., average amount of total budget left was $5.92 million vs. $6.54 million from low person-level individualists). However, those high individualists behaved in a more cooperative fashion in the collectivistic organizational culture (i.e., average amount of total budget left was $8.09 million vs. $7.23 million taken by low individualists).

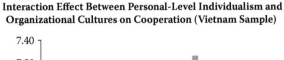

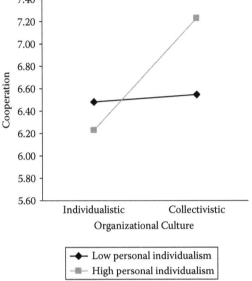

FIGURE 8.3
Cooperation (difference between maximum amount available and the total amount taken, in millions of VN dong).

Interaction Effect Between Societal and Organizational Levels of C-I

Although not hypothesized, we found an interesting interaction effect between societal and organizational levels of C-I. As shown in Model 4, this interaction effect indicates that the relationship between organizational-level C-I and cooperation is moderated by societal cultures, such that the link between organizational C-I and cooperation is weaker in collectivistic societal cultures than in individualistic societal cultures.

DISCUSSION AND CONCLUSIONS

The success of multinational organizations partly depends on how cooperatively employees work with one another in a global setting. To understand organizational and societal cultural barriers that could hinder or

promote workgroup cooperation, knowledge about the nature of cooperation within the context of corporate culture as well as within the country of operation is critical. Accordingly, organizational researchers must
answer the question: How does organizational culture interact with societal culture to affect cooperation, given person-level dispositions? This
study provides a first attempt at answering this question.

We characterized cultures (societal and organizational levels) and personal dispositions based upon the collectivism-individualism framework
and examined the combined effects of these variables on cooperation. This
framework is especially relevant to the current question because (a) the
C-I construct can be conceptualized at each of the three levels of interest, and (b) these levels have been found to be important determinants
of cooperative behavior in workgroups. Based upon current theory surrounding the C-I constructs as well as empirical evidence in the literature,
we proposed two separate interaction effects: a three-way interaction effect
for person-level collectivism and a two-way effect between organizational
C-I and person-level individualism.

The results, as they often are when three-way interactions are predicted,
were mixed. As predicted, we found that no matter to which societal culture (individualistic or collectivistic) the participants belonged, highly
individualistic persons were very adaptive compared with low individualists. In other words, the high individualists pursued their own gain when
they "worked" in an individualistic organizational culture, but under a
collectivistic organizational culture they "absorbed" the values of that
culture and behaved cooperatively. As discussed earlier, this pattern of
findings was predicted on the basis that individualists tend to follow the
modal behavior encouraged by the organization as a way to achieve their
own personal goals. Low individualists, on the other hand, did not change
their behavior in response to organizational collectivistic practices. That
is, they behaved relatively consistently across organizational cultures. This
finding regarding individualists' universal adaptation to the immediate
organizational culture is consistent with the findings of Earley (1989) and
Wagner (1995). The earlier studies, however, did not explicitly examine
organizational-level C-I and either (a) did not directly test the moderating effect of societal culture (Earley, 1989) or (b) included only samples
from the United States (Wagner, 1995). Our study therefore comple-
ments the earlier studies and allows a more conclusive understanding

as to the cross-cultural universality of the interaction effect between organizational-level C-I and person-level individualism.

Conceivably, the current finding has both theoretical and practical implications. Theoretically, it provides a contextual perspective for understanding people's behavior in workgroups by specifying an integrative framework that explains how the three levels of the C-I constructs may influence cooperation. Practically, this finding suggests that multinational organizations that have cultivated a strong culture of collectivism and team-based reward systems might benefit from specific personnel selection policies in different countries of operation in order to promote cooperation among their global staff (e.g., actively recruiting and hiring highly individualistic workers).

We further expected a high level of adaptive behavior among persons high in collectivism in an individualistic societal culture (the United States), such that they would become less cooperative in a dominantly competitive corporate culture compared to those low on collectivism. On the other hand, in a collectivistic society (Vietnam), persons high on collectivism were hypothesized to "ignore" the organizational cues and steadfastly adhere to the societal norms of collectivism. To our surprise, the data did not support our prediction. There was no difference in the extent to which American or Vietnamese collectivists engaged in the cooperative behavior of interest; nor were there any differences in cooperative behavior between persons high and low on collectivism. A possible reason for this finding is that our adapted collectivism scale was not sufficiently sensitive to detect such a three-way interaction effect. The reliability of this scale ($\alpha = .61$) was lower than that of the individualism scale ($\alpha = .73$). Future studies need to revisit this important question before any conclusions about the nature of interplay among these three levels of C-I in determining cooperative behavior can be made.

Interestingly, we found an interaction effect between societal-level and organizational-level C-I on cooperation, such that organizational C-I was positively related to cooperation in an individualistic society (United States) but not in a collectivistic society (Vietnam). As noted earlier, the effect of organizational-level C-I in individualistic societies on cooperation has often been found in the literature (e.g., Kirkman & Shapiro, 2001). In collectivistic societies, it is possible that the societal norms are so strong that any effects created by manipulation of organizational cultures are suppressed. Because there have not been many studies examining the effects of organizational cultures in collectivistic societies in the literature, the appropriateness of our speculation is subject to future cross-cultural investigations.

Some indirect evidence may shed light on this issue. For example, Pasa, Kabasakal, and Bodur (2001) examined the effects of organizational culture on managers' perceptions of leadership behavior and attributes in Turkey, a highly collectivistic society. The researchers found that, regardless of the variance in organizational norms and practices, collectivism consistently affected perceptions at multiple levels of analysis, such that an ideal leadership style was perceived as the ability to satisfy the needs of group belonging — a characteristic of collectivism. Further, Lewis and Earley (1997) found the effects of societal culture on perceptions of elements of quality across countries. The researchers thus proposed using societal cultural values to explain why the same quality improvement policies implemented in multinational organizations yield mixed results around the world. The converging empirical evidence indicates that there may be differential interaction patterns between the societal and organizational cultures on organizational behavior and attitudes (i.e., collectivistic societies provide a stronger contextual effect than individualistic societies). The current finding of the interaction between societal and organizational levels of C-I on cooperation is consistent with these earlier findings. Hence, our study provides further support for the influence of societal cultures on the links between organizational practices and organizational outcomes.

We included samples from two countries representing the two poles of the societal-level C-I spectrum, the United States and Vietnam. Using countries as proxies for societal-level C-I as in the current study means that any differential effects found in the two samples would be assumed to be entirely due to their differences in the C-I construct. This assumption may not hold in certain situations because the two countries included in the study, the United States and Vietnam, are also different in many other dimensions (e.g., power distance, femininity-masculinity, uncertainty avoidance; Hofstede, 1980). It is also quite possible that Vietnamese college students may be higher on person-level individualism than the general Vietnamese population. Nevertheless, we believe that C-I provides an initial meaningful framework to organize cross-cultural differences especially as it has been found to relate to cooperation, the criterion of interest in the current study, and note that previous studies also used countries as proxies for societal-level C-I (e.g., Boone & Witteloostuijn, 1999; Gelfand & Christakopoulou, 1999; Parks & Vu, 1994; Wade-Benzoni et al., 2002).

Another concern may involve generalizability of the study findings due to the nature of the social dilemma game utilized in manipulating organizational C-I. Though it is conceivable that corporate cultures contain nuances and richness that may not be easily induced by such a simple task, social dilemma games have been extensively used in experimental social dilemma and interaction research since the important work of Luce and Raiffa (1957). Despite the criticism that participant reactions might not accurately reflect what employees would do in a real-world situation, researchers consistently found that individual social values, or orientations toward specific goals, are predictive of resource dilemma behaviors (Kramer, McClintock & Messick, 1986; Liebrand, 1986; Liebrand & Van Run, 1985; Parks, 1994). Because we were fundamentally interested in analyzing cross-cultural behaviors in situations of interdependence and conflicts, social dilemma games were the most effective methodology. Nevertheless, field studies in other collectivistic and individualistic societies may wish to focus on the relationships between organizational culture and individuals in actual companies in order to shed further light on the current findings.

The theoretical question of how societal cultures differentially influence organizational C-I cultural norms on individuals' cooperative behavior, taking personal C-I dispositions into account, has very important implications for cross-cultural organizational research and practice. Yet addressing this question is challenging because it requires a highly demanding research design, including samples from multiple countries and organizations. The current study is among the first to directly examine this question. Thus, our study further endorses earlier calls for attention to levels of cultural constructs when studying their effects (Bond & Smith, 1996).

A relatively new theory in the management domain, cultural intelligence (Early & Ang, 2003), may be relevant to future research in this area. This theory posits that understanding the effect of an individual's cultural background on their behavior is a key component in being able to predict an individual's success in engaging in a variety of business, social, and cultural settings. Cultural intelligence is still an individual level measure, although it captures a cultural sensitivity quotient that is absent in simple individualism/collectivism scales and hence may provide a more nuanced approach to our understanding of individual behavior in cultural contexts. Though many questions remain, we believe the current findings offer intriguing and interesting implications that will stimulate more research on this important topic.

THERE AND BACK AGAIN

I'd like to close with a few final thoughts on Dave Messick and the influence he had on my career, research, and thinking. It is fascinating to ponder on the winding paths that academics take in their careers and the serendipity of how events and people lead us to places we never imagined. As a fifth-year Ph.D. student, I was on the committee charged with bringing speakers to our weekly Friday afternoon Social Psychology seminar at UCSB. Because we had essentially no budget, we looked primarily within the state and took advantage of scholars visiting the Center for Advanced Studies in the Behavioral Sciences at Palo Alto. Max Bazerman (a coeditor of this volume) was visiting the center that year and I invited him to give a talk. I remember a meeting in Dave's lab prior to the talk where both Dave and I met Max for the first time. A discussion ensued and Max encouraged me to apply for the Visiting Professor position at the DRRC at Kellogg GSM at Northwestern, an event that led to my 2-year tenure in Evanston, Illinois, and my career in a business school. During this same period I married Chuck McClintock, who followed me from UCSB to Evanston in year 2, as did Dave and Judy Messick (who Max also convinced to join the faculty at Kellogg). So we came full circle and serendipity found us all together again (along with another coeditor of this volume and coauthor of Chapter 5, Ann Tenbrunsel, who was a Ph.D. student at the time), albeit for a short time.

But this is only part of the There and Back Again story (Tolkien, 1937). Dave and I often discussed the perception of time on judgment and, in particular, how it always seems to take so much longer to get to some place that you are excited about going to than it does to come back again (think of Bilbo's long and eventful journey to Middle Earth but less dramatic trip home). We had a difficult time imagining how we could operationalize this study, yet I would still like to find a way to do it. Perhaps in his retirement Dave can come up with a design. Returning to Santa Barbara for his *festschrift* as so many of the authors of this volume did in September of 2007 was certainly a delightful journey (but was it there or back again?).

NOTE

1. We use the term *personal* or *person-level* to describe the individual level trait of C-I to avoid confusion when discussing collectivistic or individualistic individuals.

REFERENCES

Boles, T. L., & Messick, D. M. (1995). A reverse outcome bias: The influence of multiple reference points on the evaluation of outcomes and decisions. *Organizational Behavior and Human Decision Processes, 61*, 262–275.

Bond, M. H., & Smith, P. B. (1996). Cross-cultural social and organizational psychology. *Annual Review of Psychology, 47*, 205–235.

Boone, C., & Witteloostuijn, A. V. (1999). Competitive and opportunistic behavior in a prisoner's dilemma game: Experimental evidence on the impact of culture and education. *Scandinavian Journal of Management, 15*, 333–350.

Calori, R., & Sarnin, P. (1991). Corporate culture and economic performance: A French study. *Organizational Studies, 12*, 49–74.

Cattell, R. B. (1966). The scree test for the number of factors. *Multivariate Behavioral Research, 1*, 245–276.

Chatman, J. A., & Barsade, S. G. (1995). Personality, organizational culture, and cooperation: Evidence from a business simulation. *Administrative Science Quarterly, 40*, 423–443.

Chatman, J. A., Polzer, J. T., Barsade, S. G., & Neale, M. A. (1998). Being different yet feeling similar: The influence of demographic composition and organizational culture on work processes and outcomes. *Administrative Science Quarterly, 43*, 749–780.

Chen, C. C., Chen, X. P., & Meindl, J. R. (1998). How can cooperation be fostered? The cultural effects of individualism-collectivism. *Academy of Management Review, 23*, 285–304.

Cox, T. H., Lobel, S. A., & McLeod, P. L. (1991). Effects of ethnic group cultural differences on cooperative and competitive behavior on a group task. *Academy of Management Journal, 34*, 827–847.

Dansereau, F. (1989). A multiple level of analysis perspective on the debate about individualism. *American Psychologist, 44*, 959–960.

Dawes, R. (1980). Social dilemmas. *Annual Review of Psychology, 31*, 169–193.

Earley, P. C. (1989). Social loafing and collectivism: A comparison of the United States and the People's Republic of China. *Administrative Science Quarterly, 34*, 565–581.

Earley, P. C. (1993). East meets West meets Mideast: Further explorations of collectivistic and individualistic workgroups. *Academy of Management Journal, 36*, 319–348.

Earley, P. C., & Ang, S. (2003). *Cultural intelligence: Individual interactions across cultures.* Palo Alto, CA: Stanford University Press.

Earley, P. C., & Gibson, C. B. (1998). Taking stock in our progress on individualism-collectivism: 100 years of solidarity and community. *Journal of Management, 24*, 265–304.

Eby, L. T., & Dobbins, G. H. (1997). Collectivistic orientation in teams: An individual and group-level analysis. *Journal of Organizational Behavior, 18*, 275–295.

Gelfand, M. J., & Christakopoulou, S. (1999). Culture and negotiator cognition: Judgment accuracy and negotiation processes in individualistic and collectivistic cultures. *Organizational Behavior and Human Decision Processes, 79*, 248–269.

Gelfand, M. J., & Realo, A. (1999). Individualism-collectivism and accountability in intergroup negotiations. *Journal of Applied Psychology, 84*, 721–736.

Gratton, L. (2005). Managing integration through cooperation. *Human Resource Management, 44*, 151–158.

Hofstede, G. (1980). *Culture's consequences: International differences in work-related values.* Beverly Hills, CA: Sage.

Hofstede, G. (1991). *Cultures and organizations: Software of the mind.* London: McGraw-Hill.

Hofstede, G., Neuijen, B., Ohavy, D. D., & Sanders, G. (1990). Measuring organizational cultures: A qualitative and quantitative study across twenty cases. *Administrative Science Quarterly, 35*, 286–316.

Kelley, H. H., & Stahelski, A. J. (1970). Social interaction basis of cooperators' and competitors' belief about others. *Journal of Personality and Social Psychology, 16*, 66–91.

Kirkman, B. L., & Shapiro, D. L. (2001). The impact of team members' cultural values on productivity, cooperation, and empowerment in self-managing work teams. *Journal of Cross-Cultural Psychology, 32*, 597–617.

Kramer, R. M., McClintock, C. G., & Messick, D. M. (1986). Social values and cooperative response to a simulated resource conservation crisis. *Journal of Personality, 54*(3), 576–592.

Lewis, K. M., & Earley, P. C. (1997). Quality assessment across cultures. In S. Ghosh & D. B. Fedor (Eds.), *Advances in the management of organizational quality: Vol. 2. An annual series of quality-related theory and research papers* (pp. 139–168). Greenwich, CT: Elsevier Science/JAI Press.

Liebrand, W. G. B. (1986). The ubiquity of social values in social dilemmas. In H. A. M. Wilke, D. M. Messick, & C. G. Rutte (Eds.), *Experimental social dilemmas* (pp. 113–133). Frankfurt: Verlag Peter Lang.

Liebrand, W. G. B., & VanRun, G. J. (1984). The effects of social motives on behavior in social dilemmas in 2 cultures. *Journal of Experimental Social Psychology, 21*(1), 86–102.

Luce, R. D., & Raiffa, H. (1957). *Games and decisions: Introduction and critical survey.* New York: John Wiley & Sons.

Markus, H. R., & Kitayama, S. (1991). Culture and the self: Implications for cognition, emotion, and motivation. *Psychological Review, 98*, 224–253.

Messick, D. M., & Brewer, M. B. (1983). Solving social dilemmas. In L. Wheeler & P. Shaver (Eds.), *Review of personality and social psychology* (Vol. 4, pp. 11–44). Beverly Hills, CA: Sage.

Messick, D. M., & Schell, T. (1992). Evidence for an equality heuristic in social decision making. *Acta Psychologica, 80*, 311–323.

Morris, M. H., Avila, R. A., & Allen, J. (1993). Individualism and the modern corporation: Implications for innovation and entrepreneurship. *Journal of Management, 19*, 595–612.

Oyserman, D., Coon, H. M., & Kemmelmeier, M. (2002). Rethinking individualism and collectivism: Evaluation of theoretical assumptions and meta-analyses. *Psychological Bulletin, 128,* 3–72.

Parks, C. D. (1994). The predictive ability of social values in resource dilemmas and public goods games. *Personality and Social Psychology Bulletin, 20,* 431–438.

Parks, C. D., & Vu, A. D. (1994). Social dilemma behavior of individuals from highly individualist and collectivist cultures. *Journal of Conflict Resolution, 38,* 708–718.

Pasa, S. F., Kabasakal, H., & Bodur, M. (2001). Society, organisations, and leadership in Turkey. *Applied Psychology: An International Review, 50,* 559–589.

Probst, T. M., Carnevale, P. J., & Triandis, H. C. (1999). Cultural values in intergroup and single-group social dilemmas. *Organizational Behavior and Human Decision Processes, 77,* 171–191.

Robert, C., & Wasti, S. A. (2002). Organizational individualism and collectivism: Theoretical development and construct validation. *Journal of Management, 28*(4), 544–566.

Rousseau, D. M. (1985). Issue of levels in organizational research: Multi-level and cross-level perspectives. *Research in Organizational Behavior, 7,* 1–37.

Ryan, A. M., Chan, D., Ployhart, R. E., & Slade, L. A. (1999). Employee attitude surveys in a multinational organization: Considering language and culture in assessing measurement equivalence. *Personnel Psychology, 52,* 37–58.

Samuelson, C. D., Messick, D. M., Rutte, C. G., & Wilke, H. (1984). Individual and structural solutions to resource dilemma in two cultures. *Journal of Personality and Social Psychology, 47,* 94–104.

Schneider, B. (Ed.). (1990). *Organizational climate and cultures.* San Francisco: Jossey-Bass.

Schwartz, S. H. (1990). Individualism-collectivism: Critique and proposed refinements. *Journal of Cross-Cultural Psychology, 21,* 139–157.

Thompson, B., & Daniel, L. G. (1996). Factor analytic evidence for the construct validity of scores: A historic overview and some guidelines. *Educational and Psychological Measurement, 56,* 197–208.

Tolkien, J. R. R. (1937). *The hobbit or there and back again.* Boston: Houghton Mifflin Co.

Triandis, H. C. (1995). *Individualism and collectivism.* Boulder, CO: Westview Press.

Triandis, H. C. (1996). The psychological measurement of cultural syndromes. *American Psychologist, 51,* 407–415.

Triandis, H. C., & Gelfand, M. J. (1998). Converging measurement of horizontal and vertical individualism and collectivism. *Journal of Personality and Social Psychology, 74,* 118–128.

Triandis, H. C., Leung, K., Villareal, M. J., & Clack, F. L. (1985). Allocentric versus idiocentric tendencies: Convergent and discriminant validation. *Journal of Research in Personality, 19,* 395–415.

Vandenberg, R. J., & Lance, C. E. (2000). A review and synthesis of the measurement invariance literature: Suggestions, practices, and recommendations for organizational research. *Organizational Research Methods, 2,* 4–69.

Van Lange, P. A. M., Liebrand, W. B. G., Messick, D. M., & Wilke, H. A. M. (1992). Introduction and literature review. In W. Liebrand, D. Messick, & H. Wilke (Eds.), *Social dilemmas: Theoretical issues and research findings* (pp. 3–28). Oxford, UK: Pergamon.

Wade-Benzoni, K. A., Okumura, T., Brett, J. M., Moore, D. A., Tenbrunsel, A. E., & Bazerman, M. H. (2002). Cognitions and behavior in asymmetric social dilemmas: A comparison of two cultures. *Journal of Applied Psychology, 87*, 87–95.

Wagner, J. A. (1995). Studies of individualism-collectivism: Effects on cooperation in groups. *Academy of Management Journal, 38*, 152–172.

Wagner, J. A., & Moch, M. K. (1986). Individualism-collectivism: Concept and measure. *Group & Organization Studies, 11*, 280–304.

9

Attraction to Prospective Dyadic Relationships: Effects of Fate Control, Reflexive Control, and Partner's Trustworthiness

Janusz L. Grzelak
University of Warsaw, Poland

D. Michael Kuhlman
University of Delaware

Erin Yeagley
University of Delaware

Jeff A. Joireman
Washington State University

The attractiveness of interpersonal relationships has been investigated by social psychologists for decades. An impressive list of factors accounting for relationship attractiveness can be found in almost any social psychology handbook, including similarity or complementarity of needs, the kind and value of exchanged goods and services, physical attractiveness, similarity of attitudes, respect for privacy, belongingness to the same social group or category, and others. The present chapter is exclusively focused on the attractiveness of prospective dyadic relationships as a function of two general classes of variables. The first is situational and concerns the types of control over outcomes possessed by both parties. Thus, it is a feature of the relationships among the possible outcomes of the relationship, or the relationship's "structure." We readily acknowledge that the kinds and amounts of outcomes available in a relationship, the "what," play an important role in its attractiveness. However, our concern here will be with "how" the outcomes allocated to self and other (the "whats") are controlled by each party and how such control relates to relationship attractiveness. The second is more personal, namely, the trustworthiness of the prospective partner.

Von Neumann and Morgenstern's normative game theory (1944) focuses on optimal (rational) choice behavior of interdependent parties attempting to obtain outcomes of maximum subjective value, well-being, or speaking more technically of highest subjective expected utility, regardless of what utility is composed. As explained below, one important theoretical foundation for our chapter is the work of David Messick and Charles McClintock (1968), who developed a psychological theory of utility within socially interdependent relationships, which we will refer to as *social value orientation* (SVO). This theory has led to the identification of individual differences in the way people calculate the utility of interdependent outcomes. We will explore the possibility that these differences moderate the control processes that are the major focus of our chapter.

We suggest that an idea from game theory can be related to the notion of a relationship's attractiveness. Namely, games differ in their value, which is the long-term expected utility of outcomes achieved through "rational" play. However, beyond the notion of a game's value, game theory does not consider the possibility that relationships may also differ in attractiveness as a function of the types of control possessed by each party.[1] The present chapter attempts to evaluate that possibility and does so on the basis of another important theory, namely Kelley and Thibaut's (1978) interdependence theory.

The following paragraphs will describe the two above-mentioned theories on which the present chapter is based, followed by the development of four hypotheses concerning the effects of control and partner trustworthiness on relationship attractiveness.

MESSICK AND MCCLINTOCK'S THEORY OF SOCIAL VALUE ORIENTATION

A classic paper by David Messick and Charles McClintock (1968) provides a psychological theory of outcome utility in socially interdependent situations, suggesting that it is based on a weighting of outcomes to self and other. The value of outcomes depends on goals that individuals want to maximize in a given situation, such as own gain, collective welfare, or competitive advantage. Thus, the fact that people make different decisions in the same situation does not require some to be deemed rational and others irrational in terms of game theoretic prescriptions; they are simply attempting to achieve different goals (Kuhlman & Marshello, 1975). The research inspired by Messick and McClintock (1968) has shown that individuals assign weights to self and others quite consistently, revealing different SVOs. The number of orientations distinguished by researchers ranges from eight (Griesinger & Livingstone, 1973) to, in the simplest case, two: proself and prosocial. The SVOs in our study correspond to the three indentified by Messick and McClintock. *Cooperators* (Js) are positively concerned with both own outcomes and others' outcomes; others, called *individualists* (Os), are positively concerned with own outcomes; and still others, *competitors* (Rs), looking for a relative gain, are positively self-concerned but negatively concerned with others' outcomes. Furthermore, Messick and McClintock's SVO theory is a centrally important aspect of Kelley and Thibaut's (1978) interdependence theory, specifically in terms of Kelley and Thibaut's concept of the transformation of objective outcomes to subjective values (utilities).

KELLEY AND THIBAUT'S INTERDEPENDENCE THEORY

Further developments of interdependence theory (Kelley, 1997; Kelley, Holmes, Kerr, Reis, Rusbult, & Van Lange, 2003; Van Lange, 1994) go beyond the analysis of behavior within established relationships and focus on the motivation to stay in or exit from relationships, or more generally with what we will call *relationship attractiveness*.

People approach or avoid some interpersonal relationships and maintain or leave others. To the extent that they are not forced by external factors to establish new relationships or have freedom to stay in or exit from established ones, they can control their own transsituational mobility. Kelley (1997) calls this *transition control* and proposes decision rules that guide our locomotion, or movement toward or away from relationships. Because the exercise of transition control is in part guided by attractiveness of relationships, it is important to understand what makes relationships more or less attractive. The present chapter tests a set of hypotheses concerning the effects of outcome control (defined below) on the attractiveness of prospective relationships. Based on interdependence theory we ask how the attractiveness of a prospective relationship depends on who controls and to what extent he/she controls the outcome allocations it provides.

Within a given dyadic relationship each person's actions may change to some degree the outcomes of one or both parties. When outcomes to self or the partner are affected by changes in one's actions, he/she is said to have *outcome control* (Kelley, 1997). Outcome control can vary in outcome domain (i.e., whose outcomes are controlled) and in amount. Each person may control to some degree his/her own outcomes, which is called *reflexive control* (RC). In addition, each person may have some amount of *fate control* (FC) over the outcomes of the partner.[2] A fundamental assumption of our chapter is that the distribution of outcome control in a relationship is one of the major sources of our attraction to it (Grzelak, 1982, 2001). Thus, in addition to the subjective values of outcomes described above, we assume that control per se operates as a value in social relationships.

The general idea of control as a value has a long theoretical tradition. There are many theories in which the assumption of motivation for control was explicitly or implicitly made, such as reactance (Brehm, 1966), self-disclosure (Derlega & Chaikin, 1977), Machiavellianism (Christie & Geis, 1970), learned helplessness (Seligman, 1975), and many others (De Charms, 1968). More relevant to the present chapter are theories focused on motivation for self-control (e.g., Burger & Cooper, 1979) and for power (Adler, 1929; Winter, 1973). In these latter theories, control is most often defined either as generalized need to control one's own fate or a need to control (need for power) or to avoid control of others' fates (fear of power), which are conceptually similar to one's own RC and FC in a relationship.

In theories of control motivation, concepts related to RC and FC are treated as goals people might try to achieve in the relationship. For Kelly and Thibaut, RC and FC are defined as basic descriptive properties of an interpersonal relationship; in more formal terms they are features of the relationship's objective payoff structure. Importantly, a relationship's objective payoff structure is independent of the motives/goals of the relationship's members; thus, RC and FC can be regarded as features of the social environment. This chapter examines how attraction to (specifically, motivation to be in) a prospective relationship is affected by the types of control (RC,

FC) that are provided by the relationship's objective payoff structure. Thus, it can be seen as an extension of earlier theories of control motivation.

A second way we extend previous work on control is by focusing not only on the effects of one's own RC and FC but the RC and FC of the partner. The remainder of this introduction will develop our hypotheses on control and attractiveness in the context of interdependence theory. First, we provide a more detailed explanation of RC and FC.

Dyadic relationships differ in terms of the types and amount of RC and FC held by each party. For example, imagine that in Relationship A you completely control both your own and your partner's outcomes. You have both RC and FC, and your partner has none. Further imagine that in Relationship B, the situation is reversed. Which of these relationships would you most want to be in? We anticipate that you prefer Relationship A. But why? Because you have all the control and partner has none? Because your partner does not control your outcomes? Because you control his/hers?

A choice between these (and many other) answers may become easier if, as was done in the study reported here, we examine how attractiveness varies in response to a set of relationships generated by the systematic combination of the RC and FC held by one's self with the RC and FC held by one's partner. Interdependence theory gives precise definitions of RC and FC. Because a good grasp of these notions is necessary to understanding both the rationale and procedures of the present study, they are given specific attention in the following paragraphs.

In a given dyadic relationship, each person may have RC and FC, only RC, only FC, or neither. If a person has both RC and FC, they are either "concordant" or "discordant." Concordance exists when actions that are most beneficial to the self are at the same time most beneficial to one's partner (no conflict of interest situations). Discordance between RC and FC occurs when actions most beneficial to the self are not most beneficial to the partner (conflict of interests). Thus, in terms of RC and FC, each person may have one of five types of control: (a) neither (X), (b) FC only (F), (c) RC only (R), (d) FC and RC concordant (C), (e) FC and RC discordant (D). Furthermore, the type(s) of control possessed by Person A may be different from or identical to the type(s) possessed by Person B. As will be seen below, all of the combinations of the five types of Person A's control with the five types of Person B's are possible, and in this chapter all were studied.

TABLE 9.1

Design and Notation for the 25 Games

Row's Control	Column's Control				
	None (X)	Only RC (R)	Only FC (F)	Concordant (C)	Discordant (D)
None (X)	X/X	X/R	X/F	X/C	X/D
Only RC (R)	R/X	R/R	R/F	R/C	R/D
Only FC (F)	F/X	F/R	F/F	F/C	F/D
Concordant (C)	C/X	C/R	C/F	C/C	C/D
Discordant (D)	D/X	D/R	D/F	D/C	D/D

Notes: 1. For each game, the first letter shows the type of control possessed by the row player, and the second shows the type of control possessed by the column player.

   2. The nine games in the bottom right 3 × 3 submatrix cells are "socially interdependent" (Kelley & Thibaut, 1978) relationships, in that both players have fate control over their partner.

   3. The four games in the upper left 2 × 2 submatrix cells are socially nondependent (our term) in that neither player has fate control.

   4. The remaining 12 games are socially dependent (our term) in that only one player has fate control.

The five types of control for self and for partner can be completely crossed to produce the set of 25 dyadic relationships or two-person games used in the present study (see Table 9.1). Each of the 25 games can be symbolized with two letters, the first indicating the control possessed by the row player and the second indicating control possessed by column. For example, in the F/C game the row player possesses only fate control and the column player possesses both reflexive and fate control, which are concordant. In the R/X game, the row player possesses only reflexive control and the column player has no control of any type. Below, with the help of Figure 9.1 we provide a more detailed explanation of relationships varying in RC and FC. This figure is useful both in terms of understanding the theory and also the design of the present study.

Figure 9.1 provides examples of several relationships modeled as 2 × 2 payoff matrices, or experimental games. In each game, payoffs to the row player (whose choices/actions are A and B) are below the diagonal and payoffs to the column player (who chooses between X and Y) are above the diagonal. The game in Panel A models the R/R relationship in which both row and column have only reflexive control. Note that the row player guarantees him/herself 1 more point by choosing A over B. Thus, he/she has RC. Also note that the column player guarantees him/herself 1 more point by choosing column X. Column has RC as well. There is nothing

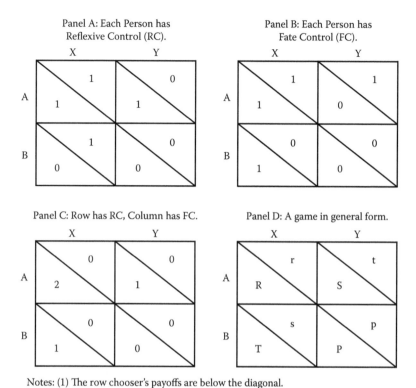

Notes: (1) The row chooser's payoffs are below the diagonal.

FIGURE 9.1
Examples of games varying in RC and FC.

the row player can do to produce a change in column's outcome. Row has no FC over column. The same is true for column's ability to produce a change in row's outcome. Furthermore, in this game, 100% of the variation in row's (column's) outcomes is due to changes in row's (column's) actions. These percentages correspond to the notion of "effect size" in the 2 × 2 analysis of variance. Indeed, interdependence theory quantifies the amount of RC and FC in precisely this way.

Panel B models the F/F relationship in which each person only has FC over the partner's outcomes. Row's choice of A guarantees his/her partner one more point than a choice of B. Column's choice of X guarantees Row 1 more point than a choice of Y. Both players have FC. Changes in row's (column's) actions produce no change in row's (column's) outcomes. Neither player has RC. In this game, 100% of the variation in row's (column's) outcomes is due to changes in the actions of the other person.

Panel C models the R/F relationship in which row has RC only, and column has FC over row. In this game, as opposed to the two just discussed, row's outcomes are not totally controlled by one of the players but partly by each. Row guarantees him/herself 1 more point by choosing A over B; row has RC. But, column guarantees row one more point by choosing X over Y; column has FC over row. In this case, 50% of the variation in row's outcomes is due to changes in his/her actions, and 50% is due to the actions of the partner. In this relationship, there is no variation in column's outcomes. Thus, of necessity column has no RC and row has no FC. Panel D in Figure 9.1 represents a relationship in general form. Figure 9.1, in combination with Table 9.2, which shows the payoffs for all 25 relationships used in this study, can be used to generate the payoff matrix for any game in which the reader is interested.

Next we develop predictions for the effects of own and of partner's control. In doing so, we will use a notational scheme in which the type of control is given in capital letters (X for no control, R for RC only, F for FC only, C for concordant RC/FC, and D for discordant RC/FC) followed by a subscript (self or partner) denoting which person possesses it. Thus, X_{self} corresponds to a relationship in which the self has no control of either sort; $R_{partner}$ indicates a relationship in which the partner possesses only reflexive control.

Our hypotheses for the effects of own control and of partner's control are based on the fundamental assumption that the overwhelming majority of people are to some degree egocentric or concerned with their own, personal control over outcomes. The phrase *to some degree* in the preceding sentence recognizes the important demonstration of individual differences in SVO, from Messick and McClintock (1968) through to the present day. Specifically, the SVO literature shows that most people are either cooperative (Js), individualistic (Os), or competitive (Rs). Although these SVOs differ in terms of concern with the other's well being, they have in common a positive self-concern.

Thus, practically everyone is asking to an important degree "What do *I* get?" Extending this to outcome control, we assume that people will also be asking "How do *I* control what happens in this relationship?" We will consider the impact of control possessed by the partner at a later point. Although we are arguing for the importance of own control based on the general self-interest demonstrated by SVO research, it is important to point out that the vast majority of these studies have been conducted on American and European populations. Thus, at the present time we feel

TABLE 9.2

Outcome Values in Each Game

	Row Player's Outcomes				Column Player's Outcomes			
Game	R	S	T	P	r	t	s	p
XX	0	0	0	0	0	0	0	0
XR	0	0	0	0	1	0	1	0
XF	1	0	1	0	0	0	0	0
XC	1	0	1	0	1	0	1	0
XD	1	0	1	0	0	1	0	1
FX	0	0	0	0	1	1	0	0
FR	0	0	0	0	2	1	1	0
FF	1	0	1	0	1	1	0	0
FC	1	0	1	0	2	1	1	0
FD	1	0	1	0	0	1	1	2
RX	1	1	0	0	0	0	0	0
RR	1	1	0	0	1	0	1	0
RF	2	1	1	0	0	0	0	0
RC	2	1	1	0	1	0	1	0
RD	2	1	1	0	0	1	0	1
CX	1	1	0	0	1	1	0	0
CR	1	1	0	0	2	1	1	0
CF	2	1	1	0	1	1	0	0
CC	2	1	1	0	2	1	1	0
CD	2	1	1	0	1	0	2	1
DX	1	1	0	0	0	0	1	1
DR	1	1	0	0	0	1	1	2
DF	2	1	1	0	0	0	1	1
DC	2	1	1	0	1	0	2	1
DD	2	1	1	0	0	1	1	2

that it would be premature to suggest that our hypotheses and findings are cross-culturally valid or general, respectively.

ATTRACTIVENESS AS A FUNCTION OF ONE'S OWN CONTROL

Our first prediction concerns relationship attractiveness as a function of the five types of control possessed by the self. First, considering only the three types of relationship in which the individual does not have both reflexive and fate control, we expect that R_{self} will be most attractive, followed by F_{self} and then X_{self}. Assuming concern with one's personal outcomes, reflexive control provides a more direct and less risky way to achieve personal viability than having only the ability to control the outcomes of others (FC). Wheras FC is less directly relevant to personal viability, controlling others' outcomes may provide some basis for inducing the other to act in the interest of the self (see Kelley & Thibaut, 1978, on the conversion of fate control to behavior control). No control whatsoever (X_{self}) leaves the individual in the most precarious and uncertain circumstances. Thus, we expect that in terms of attraction, $X_{self} < F_{self} < R_{self}$. To the best of our knowledge, there is no theory of social power or control that would contradict this predicted ordering.

Next, to the degree that both RC and FC are desirable (for reasons given above), it seems reasonable to expect that relationships providing both types of control would be preferred to those providing only one. That is, we expect that D_{self} and C_{self} relationships will be more attractive than X_{self}, F_{self}, and R_{self}. At the present we find it just as easy to imagine that $D_{self} > C_{self}$ as we do the opposite. This leads to our first hypothesis, which is an ordering of the five types of own control from least to most preferred:

Hypothesis 1: $X_{self} < F_{self} < R_{self} < \{D_{self}, C_{self}\}$

Our next predictions concern the type of control possessed by the partner. As will be seen, there is good reason to expect that effects for partner's control will be moderated by his/her trustworthiness.

ATTRACTIVENESS AS A FUNCTION OF PARTNER'S CONTROL AND TRUSTWORTHINESS

As stated above, the present study systematically manipulates the type of control possessed by the partner. Here, it seems self-evident that relationship attractiveness should depend upon whether the partner not only can but also will use his/her control to benefit or to harm the self. In other words, expectations of the partner's trustworthiness become quite important.

Since the early work of Deutsch (1958, 1960), the fundamental importance of trust in social relationships has been well documented. Yamagishi and Yamagishi (1994) argue that there are three bases for trusting others:

(a) the past history of a given relationship demonstrating that another is trustworthy, (b) a belief that people are honest and attempt to benefit rather than harm others, and (c) assurance, defined as external factors, which can be either informal (social customs, norms) or formal (law, administrative sanctions), forcing others to act to one's benefit or preventing others from acting to one's detriment. Next, we develop predictions regarding (a) a main effect for trustworthiness per se and (b) an interaction between partner's trustworthiness and his/her control.

Based on common sense and the extensive social psychological literature on interpersonal attraction, we expect that attractiveness will be in general higher for relationships with a trusted (socially attractive) partner than a non-trusted (socially unattractive) partner. This leads directly to Hypothesis 2.

Hypothesis 2: In general, prospective relationships with trusted partners will be more attractive than those with non-trusted partners.

However, we also expect that the size of the trust effect will vary as a function of partner control. In the present study, there are two levels of partner control ($X_{partner}$ and $R_{partner}$) where the partner does not have the capacity to influence outcomes to self and three ($F_{partner}$, $C_{partner}$, and $D_{partner}$) where he/she does. For $X_{partner}$ and $R_{partner}$, the structure of the relationship provides assurance that the partner can do you no harm. Thus, we expect that trust information will have a smaller effect on attractiveness in $X_{partner}$ and $R_{partner}$ relationships than in the other three. This leads to Hypothesis 3a. Hypothesis 3b also assumes an interaction between partner control and trust and will be developed following Hypothesis 3a.

Hypothesis 3a: Trust information and partner control will interact; the effect of trust will be smallest in $X_{partner}$ and $R_{partner}$ relationships, which provide structural assurance that the partner can do you no harm.

Our next hypothesis, also related to the trust and partner control interaction, is based on a study by Van Lange and Visser (1999). Van Lange and Visser had participants of varying SVO (Js, Os, and Rs) interact with a "partner" (actually, a stooge following different preprogrammed strategies) in an experimental game. Some participants played with a partner whose strategy allowed the participants to achieve their preferred type of social goal: joint gain for Js, own gain for Os, and relative gain for Rs. We'll call this the *enabling partner*. Other participants played with a nonenabling partner whose strategy did not allow for this. Following the initial interaction with the enabling or nonenabling partner, participants indicated their preferences for new games that varied in their level of interdependence. Van Lange and Visser found that participants of all three SVOs preferred highly interdependent relationships with an enabling partner but not with a nonenabling partner. Thus, beliefs/expectations concerning the partner were shown to be important in participants' relationship attractiveness. And, in their study, these expectations were based on an established, ongoing relationship with the partner.

Our study dealt with prospective relationships, so that by definition our participants had no interaction history with the prospective partner. However, even for prospective relationships, expectations regarding the partner may be based on information or opinions provided by others and/or on other situational cues. In the present study, participants were provided with information as to whether the prospective partner is trustworthy or not. Assuming that knowing a prospective partner is trustworthy leads participants to be optimistic about achieving their own relationship goals, a prediction based on the Van Lange and Visser study is possible.

Specifically, our set of 25 games can be divided into three groups that differ in terms of interdependence. Group 1 (interdependent relationships) contains all games in which both parties have FC, Group 2 (unilateral dependence) contains all games in which one party has FC but the other does not, and Group 3 (no dependence) contains all games in which neither party has FC. Hypothesis 3b predicts that attraction to these sets of games will be moderated by partner trustworthiness.

Hypothesis 3b: For the trusted partner, the most attractive are interdependent relationships, followed by unilateral dependence and then by no-dependence relationships. The opposite order is expected for the non-trusted partner.

Our fourth and final hypothesis relates to an expected interaction between one's own control and that of the partner. There are four cases in which the self has some degree of control (R_{self}, F_{self}, C_{self}, and D_{self}) and one where he/she has none (X_{self}). One way to obtain a measure of the importance of each of the four types of self-control is to compare the attraction it produces with the no-control (X_{self}) condition. For example, by this measure the importance of RC would correspond to the change in attraction between the X_{self} and R_{self} conditions, the importance of FC to the change between X_{self} and F_{self}, and so on. It seems reasonable to expect that such measures of importance should be greater when the partner controls one's own fate ($F_{partner}$, $C_{partner}$, $D_{partner}$) than when he/she does not ($X_{partner}$, $R_{partner}$). Thus, we expect an interaction between own control and partner's control of the type specified in Hypothesis 4.

Hypothesis 4: The importance of one's own control will be larger when the partner has FC ($F_{partner}$, $C_{partner}$, or $D_{partner}$) than when he/she does not ($X_{partner}$, $R_{partner}$).

ATTRACTIVENESS OF CONTROL AND SVO

The SVO literature demonstrates that choice behavior in interdependent persons is better understood if we assume that people attempt to maximize one of a variety of goals and not just the mere maximization of own personal outcomes. Although these goals are named differently in various conceptualizations and at various times (social motives, social value orientations, social orientations), the main idea remains the same: It matters to people not only what they gain (or lose) themselves but also what are the others' gains (or losses). Assessment of SVOs is based on inferring them from individuals' preferences over various outcome allocations. In words more relevant to this chapter, SVOs are inferred from individuals' evaluations of attractiveness of outcome allocation.

Are the two sources of attractiveness, outcome allocations and types of control, interrelated or, as we suspect, independent? To date, the empirical evidence suggests that people's concerns with outcome and control allocation are rather independent. In a survey (Grzelak, 2004) run in a large representative samples of Poles, a relationship between preferences for outcome allocation (SVOs) and control allocation (outcome orientations) was investigated.[3] None of the control scales correlated with social orientation at a level higher than .23, and all but one correlated at a level below .14.[4] There is a basis then to treat the two types of preferences as independent. The present study was not designed to examine this relationship directly. However, we measured SVO and so were able to examine its possible role at two levels. First, at the main effect level, viz., do Js, Os, and Rs differ in terms of their overall attraction to prospective relationships? And second, does SVO moderate the effects for outcome control and trust?

There are some questions left open. For instance, we do not develop hypotheses concerning the difference between concordant and discordant

RC/FC. Concordance is "nice" in terms of removing the conflict between self's and other's interests. But, discordance can cause your partner to think twice before attempting to exploit you. After extensive consideration we have been unable to come up with a compelling rationale for favoring one over the other. We also do not make predictions concerning interaction effects of a higher order than Hypothesis 4. The main reason for not anticipating more complex effects is that we could not find any a priori well-grounded psychological basis for hypothesizing subtler and/or more complex effects.

METHOD

Design and Participants

A 5 (Own Control) × 5 (Partner Control) × 2 (Partner Trustworthiness) × 3 (SVO, cooperator, individualist, competitor) mixed design was employed. Own control, partner control, and partner trustworthiness were within-subjects variables and SVO was a between-subjects variable. (The factorial design on control is as shown in Table 9.1.) Participants were 202 females enrolled in General Psychology at the University of Delaware, fulfilling a research participation requirement.

General Procedure

Participants were run in two different sessions and approximately half the participants came to each session. They arrived at a lecture hall, where they were asked to perform two main tasks: (a) rating their motivation to enter each of 25 relationships and (b) completing an SVO measure. In both sessions, the SVO measure came last and was not mentioned before it was administered.

All participants were given a folder with a response form and a set of instructions, which were read aloud by the experimenter. First, participants were familiarized with the relationship matrices used in the study. They were told that in any social relationship with a partner, each would receive specific outcomes as a consequence of their joint decisions. They were asked to think of outcomes as such objective things as food and money. The only word used to describe the matrices was *relationship*. It was then explained how each person in the relationship could have different types and amounts of control over their own and the partner's outcomes. Participants were told that they would be shown a set of different relationships that would differ in terms of the amount (0, 50, 100%) of control that (a) the participant had over her own outcomes, (b) the participant would have over their partner's outcomes, (c) the partner would have over her own outcomes, and (d) the partner would have over the participant's outcomes.

At this time the first example of a relationship (in the form of a 2 × 2 matrix) was shown to them, and the features of the matrix were described. This first example did not include any information about control over outcomes, in order to simplify the instructions. In this example, they and their partner could each choose between two options. The instructions described which of the four outcome possibilities resulted from different combinations of individual choices. A diagonal line divided each cell. The participant's outcome was shown in the lower half of each cell, and the partner's outcome was shown in the upper half of each cell. For reasons given below, circles represented outcomes. A large circle represented an outcome of 2, a small circle an outcome of 1, and the absence of a circle indicated an outcome of zero.

A second relationship example was shown to illustrate how information regarding control over outcomes would be presented. Figure 9.2 gives an example of what participants were shown. This second example included all of the features present in the actual 25 stimulus relationships. Each outcome circle in the relationship was shaded differently according to who had control over that outcome.

If the participant (partner) had 100% control over an outcome, it was shaded lightly (darkly). If the participant and the partner each had 50% control over an outcome, half of the circle was shaded lightly and half of the circle was shaded darkly. Below the payoff matrix were two tables. One indicated that a small circle corresponded to an outcome of 1 and a large circle corresponded to an outcome of 2. The second table summarized in words who controlled the participant's outcomes and by how much and who controlled the partner's outcomes and by how much. Before beginning the rating task, participants were shown the entire set of 25 relationships in a predetermined random order for 2 seconds each. The order was different for each session.

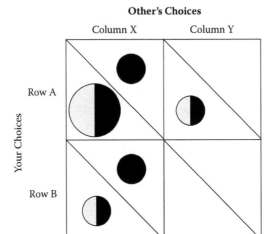

A large circle is an outcome of 2, a small circle is an
outcome of 1, and a blank is an outcome of 0.

Your Outcomes
You have 50% control of your outcomes
The other has 50% control of your outcomes

The Other's Outcomes
You have 0% control of the other's outcomes
The other has 100% control of his/her outcomes

FIGURE 9.2
Example of a relationship as shown to participants.

All participants were told that their hypothetical partner was a university student whom they had never met before and asked to imagine that each relationship would include many interactions over a long period of time. Participants rated how motivated they would be to enter each relationship on a 9-point Likert scale, where 0 indicated that they were highly motivated to avoid the relationship, and 8 indicated that they were highly motivated to be in the relationship. When making their ratings, participants were shown each relationship for approximately 10 seconds, in a random order different from the one used for the abovementioned 2-second preview of all situations.

Partner Trustworthiness Manipulation

The response forms given to each participant had one column labeled "T" for "Trusted" and one column labeled "NT" for "Not Trusted." For half of the participants in each session, the left-hand column was "T" and the right-hand column was "NT," and for the other half of participants this order was reversed. Each of the two columns contained spaces for 25 responses. Participants were told that they would rate each game twice, once for a trusted partner and once for a non-trusted partner. They were simply told that their partner "could be trusted" or "could not be trusted." Trustworthiness was not further defined for them in any way. It was emphasized that the partner's trustworthiness is only one aspect of a person, and that in any given relationship the trustworthiness of the partner may or may not influence their feelings.

The two sessions differed very slightly in the way the relationships were presented to the subjects and rated by them. We should mention that these differences in ratings procedures produced no differences in the results, which were virtually identical for the two sessions. In both sessions, every showing of the series of matrices was in a different predetermined random order.

SVO Measure

After completion of the main task, participants were introduced to the SVO measure task. They were told to imagine that their partner in this task would be someone different than in the task they had previously completed, and that they had no information about their partner for this new task.

The most common manner of assessing SVO is by means of decomposed games; however, because participants had just completed a task in which matrices were described to them, matrices were used in the SVO measure to simplify the instructions. Participants were told that this new task was similar to the one they had just completed, the main difference being that they would be making actual choices in these relationships rather than rating the relationships. A set of 12 matrices was used, with 3 games from each of four motivational dominance classes (Messick & McClintock, 1968). One class was AltJOR*Ag in which altruism (maximizing the other's outcomes), joint, own, and relative gain were maximized by the same choice, and aggression (minimizing the other's outcomes) was maximized by the other choice. The remaining three classes were AltJ*ORAg, AltJO*Rag, and AltJOR*Ag. A participant's SVO was assessed based on the consistency with which she followed a joint gain, own gain, or relative gain choice rule over the 12 games.

The standard SVO instructions were read to participants, modified only to apply to matrices rather than decomposed games.[5] After the instructions, the 12 games were shown to the participants for a few seconds each in a predetermined random order to familiarize them with the matrices. For the actual choice task, the 12 games were shown again in a different random order for about 10 seconds each. At the conclusion of the experiment, all participants were thanked and debriefed.

Attraction ratings were analyzed according to a completely crossed four factor design. One factor (SVO, with three levels) was between-subjects. The other three factors were within-subject: (a) partner's trustworthiness, with two levels; (b) participant's own control, with five levels; and (c) partner's control, with five levels.

Based on choices made in the 12 games at the end of the experimental session, participants were classified according to their SVOs. If at least 9 choices maximized joint gain, own gain, or relative gain the participant was classified as a J, O, or R respectively. In the total sample of 202, there were 18 unclassifiable participants, 61 Js, 44 Os, and 79 Rs. Unclassified participants were not included in the analyses reported here. Compared to the great majority of SVO studies, the percentage of Rs in our sample is very high; it is normal to see around 15%. We will return to this in the discussion section.

Throughout this results section, the reader will see many *F*s for which degrees of freedom are not given. For all these *F*s, $df1 = 1$ and $df2 = 181$. When the degrees of freedom differ they are provided.

RESULTS FOR HYPOTHESIS 1: OWN CONTROL

The main effect was significant. (multivariate $F[4,178] = 208.14$, $p < 0.001$, $\eta^2 = .824$). The means associated with own control are shown in Figure 9.3, which shows that attraction monotonically increases according to our prediction. The figure also makes very clear that partner

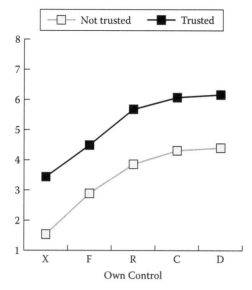

Note: "X" corresponds to No Control, "F" to Fate Control Only,
"R" to Reflexive Control Only, "C" to Concordant Reflexive and Fate
Control, and "D" to Discordant Reflexive and Fate Control.

FIGURE 9.3
Main effects for own control.

trustworthiness had no moderating effect whatsoever on own control. A set of contrasts conducted on the four adjacent pairs of means showed a significant increase for X_{self} to F_{self} ($F = 128.14$, $p < 0.0001$), F_{self} to R_{self} ($F = 179.25$, $p < 0.0001$), and R_{self} to C_{self} ($F = 42.39$, $p < 0.0001$). Though the smallest of the four changes, the increase from C_{self} to D_{self} was also reliable ($F = 8.74$, $p = 0.003$). These results provide good support for Hypothesis 1.

RESULTS FOR HYPOTHESIS 2: PARTNER'S TRUSTWORTHINESS

Not surprisingly, attraction to relationships with a trusted partner ($Mn = 5.148$) was higher than with a non-trusted partner ($Mn = 3.340$; $F = 318.84$, $p < 0.001$, $\eta^2 = 0.638$).

MAIN EFFECTS FOR PARTNER'S CONTROL

Although we made no specific prediction for partner control, we did find a significant main effect (multivariate $F[4,178] = 22.4322$, $p < 0.001$, $\eta^2 = .335$). The means for the main effect of partner's control are shown as the middle ("averaged") profile in Figure 9.4. The sequencing of the five types of partner control in Figure 9.4 goes from "high control" ($D_{partner}$ and $C_{partner}$) on the left to "less control" (only one type of control, $F_{partner}$ or $R_{partner}$) and finally to no control at all ($X_{partner}$) on the right. This "high is bad, low is good" (HBLG) ordering is based on our assumption that people may prefer situations in which the partner has no ability to affect their own outcomes ($X_{partner}$, $R_{partner}$) than when he/she does ($F_{partner}$, $C_{partner}$, and $D_{partner}$). The HBLG ordering was used for all figures displaying partner control on the x-axis.

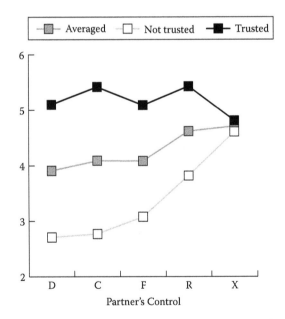

Notes: (1) "X" corresponds to No Control, "F" to Fate Control Only, "R" to Reflexive Control Only, "C" to Concordant Reflexive and Fate Control, and "D" to Discordant Reflexive and Fate Control. (2) The grey, middle profiles shows the means for the Main Effect of Partner Control. (3) The black and white profiles show the means associated with the Trust by Partner Control Interaction.

FIGURE 9.4
Main effect for Partner Control and the Partner Control × Trustworthiness interaction.

Contrasts on the four adjacent pairs of means showed that (a) $D_{partner}$ was less attractive than $C_{partner}$ ($F = 23.293$, $p < 0.0001$), (b) there was no change in attraction from $C_{partner}$ to $F_{partner}$ (F nearly zero, $p = 0.980$), (c) attraction to $R_{partner}$ was higher than to $F_{partner}$ ($F = 37.86$, $p < 0.0001$), and (d) there was no difference between $R_{partner}$ and $X_{partner}$ ($F = 3$, $p = 0.084$).

RESULTS FOR HYPOTHESES 3A AND 3B: PARTNER'S CONTROL AND PARTNER'S TRUSTWORTHINESS INTERACTION

Hypothesis 3 implies an interaction between partner's trustworthiness and partner's control, which was observed (multivariate $F[4,178] = 48.735$, $p < 0.001$, $\eta^2 = .523$). The means associated with this interaction are the top (black dots) and bottom (white dots) profiles in Figure 9.4. Note that the ordering of partner control is the HBLG sequence.

Based on the notion of assurance, Hypothesis 3a states that the partner's trustworthiness should matter more when he/she possesses fate control than when he/she does not. Figure 9.4 shows support for this anticipated assurance effect. We tested Hypothesis 3a by comparing the difference in attraction for the trusted partner ($Mn = 5.15$) and the non-trusted partner ($Mn = 2.79$) in the $D_{partner}$, $C_{partner}$, and $F_{partner}$ conditions with the difference in attraction for the trusted ($Mn = 5.13$) and non-trusted partner ($Mn = 4.17$) in the $R_{partner}$ and $X_{partner}$ conditions. In support of Hypothesis 3, the trust effect ($5.15 - 2.79 = 2.36$) in the $D_{partner}$, $C_{partner}$, and $F_{partner}$ conditions was reliably larger than the trust effect ($5.13 - 4.17 = 0.97$) in the $R_{partner}$ and $X_{partner}$ conditions ($F[1,181] = 133.82$, $p < 0.0001$).

Hypothesis 3b is based on the work of Van Lange and Visser (1999) and states that, for the trusted partner, attraction should be highest for socially interdependent relationships, followed by unilateral dependence and then by no dependence. The reverse ordering is expected for the non-trusted partner. To test this, we sorted our 25 games into three categories: (a) interdependence relationships in which both parties have fate control, either in isolation or in combination with reflexive control; (b) unilateral dependence relationships, in which one party but not both has fate control; and (c) no dependence relationships in which neither party has fate control. We performed repeated measures analysis of variance

(ANOVA) for the trusted partner condition in which SVO was a three-level between-subjects factor, and dependence was a repeated measures factor with three levels (interdependence, unilateral dependence, and no dependence). The analysis yielded a significant main effect for dependence (multivariate $F[2,180] = 84.68$, $p < 0.001$), which was not moderated by SVO. Contrasts showed that participants preferred interdependent relationships ($Mn = 5.76$) to non-interdependent (unilateral dependence and no dependence combined) ones ($Mn = 4.86$, $t[181]$, $= 10.61$, $p < 0.0001$). A smaller but significant effect was found for the unilateral dependence versus no dependence relationships ($t[181] = -2.05$, $p = 0.041$). Note that for this latter effect participants were showing a slightly higher preference for the no-dependence ($Mn = 4.97$) over the unilateral dependence ($Mn = 4.75$) relationships. A similar ANOVA was performed for the non-trusted partner condition. As before, a significant repeated measures main effect was found for dependence (multivariate $F[2,180] = 6.09$, $p = 0.003$), which was not moderated by SVO. Contrasts showed that for the non-trusted partner the most preferred relationship was that of no dependence (Mn $= 3.621$), which was preferred both to unilateral dependence ($Mn = 3.272$, $t[181] = -3.33$, $p = 0.001$) and to interdependence ($Mn = 3.307$, $t[181] = -2.18$, $p = 0.030$).

RESULTS FOR HYPOTHESIS 4: INTERACTION BETWEEN OWN AND PARTNER'S CONTROL

The interaction between own and partner's control was significant (multivariate $F[16,166] = 17.847$, $p < 0.001$, $\eta^2 = .623$). Hypothesis 4 predicts that the importance of one's own control should be higher when the partner possesses fate control than when he/she does not. We tested Hypothesis 4 as follows. "Importance" for a given type of self-control is defined as the difference between attraction when the self has it and when the self has no control at all. For example, if attraction equals 5 when self has RC only, and attraction is 2 when self has no control, the importance of RC = 5 − 2, or 3.

We conducted four contrasts, one for each of the importance measures. The first contrast, for importance of FC ($F_{partner} - X_{partner}$) was not significant ($F = 2.6$, $p = 0.108$). The remaining three contrasts were all significant:

(a) for $R_{partner} - X_{partner}$, $F = 11.39$, $p < 0.001$; (b) for $C_{partner} - X_{partner}$, $F = 31.17$, $p < 0.0001$; and (4) for $D_{partner} - X_{partner}$, $F = 39.52$, $p < 0.0001$. Thus, Hypothesis 4 receives partial support. In the interests of space, we do not report a figure detailing this interaction because it would be to some degree redundant with the figure we will report for the three-way interaction between own control, partner control, and trust, which is described below. Though not predicted, it is perhaps our most important finding.

THE TRUST BY OWN CONTROL BY PARTNER'S CONTROL INTERACTION

The interaction was significant (multivariate $F[16,166] = 6.122$, $p < 0.001$, $\eta^2 = .371$), and the associated means are shown in Figure 9.5.

Each panel of Figure 9.5 corresponds to one of the five levels of own control, specifically X_{self}, F_{self}, R_{self}, C_{self}, and D_{self}, for Panels 1 through 5, respectively. Figure 9.5 suggests that when the partner is not trusted (grey dots), attraction consistently follows the HBLG pattern for all levels of own control; for non-trusted partners, high is bad and low is good. Five tests (one for each level of own control) showed a significant linear relationship between partner's control and attraction. From Panel 1 to Panel 5, the Fs were 51.56, 133.35, 200.31, 53.73, and 34.8, respectively; all p values were < 0.0001.

For the trusted partner (black dots), Figure 9.5 suggests that attraction is generally higher than for the non-trusted partner and that own control is moderating the relationship between partner's control and attraction. That is, the own control by partner control interaction predicted by Hypothesis 4 seems to be limited to trusted partners. When own control is zero (X_{self}), partner's control appears to exert little effect. When own control involves one but not both types of control (F_{self}, R_{self}), effects for partner control tend to follow the HBLG pattern observed for the non-trusted partner. However, when own control is "high" (C_{self}, D_{self}), the relationship between partner's control and attraction is just the opposite of the HBLG pattern observed so far. In these two panels, attraction is highest when partner has high control and lowest when he/she has none.

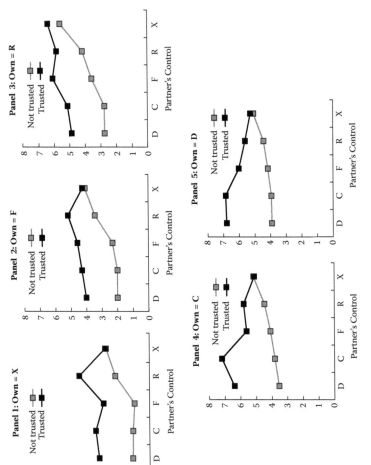

FIGURE 9.5

Means associated with the Own Control × Partner Control × Trustworthiness interaction.

Note: The X-axis is ordered according to the "High is Bad Low is Good" (HBLG) sequence. D is Discordant RC/FC, C is Concordant RC/FC, F is FC Only, R is RC Only, and X is neither type of Control.

Five tests (one for each level of own control) on the linear relationship between partner's control and attraction were performed. For Panel 1 (X_{self}) no relationship was found ($p = 0.224$). For Panel 2 (F_{self}), a significant HBLG relationship was found ($F = 11.543$, $p = 0.0008$). A similar result occurred for Panel 3 (R_{self}; $F = 88.49$, $p < 0.0001$) For high own control, Panel 4 (C_{self}) and Panel 5 (D_{self}), the relationship was also significant, though in the opposite direction. For Panel 4, $F = 55.45$, and for Panel 5, $F = 54.50$. Both p values were < 0.0001. Thus, the heart of this three-way interaction appears to be the reversal of the HBLG pattern when own control is high and the partner is trusted.

Beyond the reversal of the partner control-attraction relationship just described, Figure 9.5 shows very consistent support for the notion of assurance. For each level of own control, the effect for trust is very small when partner has no control. For each level of own control, a test of the trust effect when partner has no control was performed. With one exception (R_{self}), all tests were nonsignificant. For R_{self}, $F = 16.74$, $p < 0.0001$. Furthermore, at all levels of own control results are consistent with the "assurance" effect predicted by Hypothesis 3. Specifically, the trust effect was reliably smaller when partner had no fate control ($R_{partner}$ and $X_{partner}$) than when partner did ($F_{partner}$, $D_{partner}$, and $C_{partner}$). Moving from Panel 1 to Panel 5, results were as follows: Panel 1 ($F = 13.89$, $p = 0.00026$); Panel 2 ($F = 74.2$, $p < 0.0001$); Panel 3 ($F = 36.11$, $p < 0.0001$); Panel 4 ($F = 117.38$, $p < 0.0001$), and Panel 5 ($F = 90.9$, $p < 0.0001$).

RESULTS FOR SOCIAL VALUE ORIENTATION

We found only two effects involving SVO, which are described below. The main effect for partner trustworthiness was moderated slightly by SVO. Although Os and Rs showed no difference in their response to trust information, Js were found to differ from Os and Rs combined. In Js, the size of the trust effect (Trusted Partner – Non-Trusted Partner) in Js (1.508) was significantly smaller than the trust effect in Os/Rs (1.958; $F = 4.51$, $p = 0.035$, $\eta^2 = 0.024$.).

The effect for partner's control was moderated to a slight degree by SVO. Whereas the J versus OR contrast was not significant, the O versus R contrast was (multivariate $F[4,178] = 3.22$, $p = 0.014$, $\eta^2 = 0.067$). Only for the last pair of adjacent means ($R_{partner}$ and $X_{partner}$) was there an O vs. R difference ($F = 9.79$, $p = 0.002$). The Os found it less attractive for the partner to have RC than no control at all, whereas Rs felt just the opposite.

DISCUSSION

In the present chapter we have attempted a systematic and, to our knowledge, first empirical evaluation of hypotheses on FC, RC held by both parties and their interactions with partner's trustworthiness. Our findings support most of our predictions and yield an unpredicted but understandable three-way interaction. We discuss these findings below and conclude the chapter with some general theoretical points.

The Main Effect for Participant's Own Control

As predicted by Hypothesis 1, relationship attractiveness increased as one's own control changed from none (X_{self}) to some (F_{self}, R_{self}) to both (C_{self}, D_{self}). The size of the global effect for own control ($\eta^2 = 0.824$) was the largest obtained in the study and more than twice as large as for the global main effect of partner's control ($\eta^2 = 0.335$). In addition, the effect for own control was not moderated by the participant's SVO. It appears that the self-interest common to Js', Os', and Rs' evaluations of outcome distributions also extends to outcome control. Regardless of their SVOs, participants appear to give relatively more attention to the control they have in the relationship than the control possessed by the partner. This is demonstrated not only by the relative effect sizes just described but by the finding that attraction was higher for R_{self} than F_{self}; participants are indicating that they would rather control their own outcomes than those of the partner.

However, as is the case with the SVO literature, this self-concern is not total but, rather, larger than concern with the partner. Specifically, the highest attraction occurred for relationships in which the participant had control over the outcomes of both parties (C_{self} and D_{self}). Thus, relationship attractiveness does not exclude consideration of the partner. There are at least two reasons (not mutually exclusive) that this may be so. First, it may be that power per se is a value; and in general, the more the better.

Second, for many of us (as SVO findings show), the outcomes to the other are an important part of the utilities of our own outcomes. Thus, having control over the other's outcomes is possibly a basis for increasing control over the utilities of our own outcomes.

Effects for Partner's Trustworthiness and Partner's Control

As predicted by Hypothesis 2, prospective relationships with trusted partners were more attractive than with non-trusted ones. By itself, this finding is so straightforward that it deserves little comment.

Although we made no specific prediction of the main effects of partner's control, the results follow an interesting pattern. Specifically, in contrast to the main effect for own control which can be described as "the more the better," for partner's control it appears to be "the less the better." Though these main effects are moderated by partner's trustworthiness (as predicted by Hypotheses 3a and 3b, which are discussed below), they nonetheless have important implications for future research.

Specifically, how might partner's control affect attractiveness when we have no information about his/her trustworthiness? It may be that we adopt a form of interpersonal risk aversion, assuming the worst, and therefore preferring relationships in which partner's power is low rather than high. Or, it may be that the participant's general trust in others might moderate the effects of partner's control. Low trusters (Os and Rs?) might be more likely to show the "less the better" pattern than high trusters (Js?). In this case, we could expect to find moderating effects for SVO, which were absent in the present study. Future research employing our paradigm should investigate this possibility by withholding information about prospective partners' characteristics.

With regards to the three predicted effects involving partner's control, two involved an interaction with partner's trustworthiness (Hypotheses 3a and 3b), and the third an interaction with one's own control (Hypothesis 4). Findings relevant to these hypotheses are discussed next.

The Trust by Partner Control Interaction

Hypothesis 3a successfully predicted an interaction between partner's control and trustworthiness, based on the notion of assurance. Specifically, when the partner can control your outcomes (i.e., when he/she has FC) the effect for his/her trustworthiness should be larger than when he/she cannot control your outcomes. The detailed results for Hypothesis 3a shown in Figure 9.4 suggest that the trustworthiness effect is largest when the partner has both types of control than FC alone, and we find that the trust effect is larger in the D than in the C condition. Thus, it is not just that assurance is low when the other can hurt you; it seems that it is (sensibly) lowest when acting in one's self-interest at the same time necessarily hurts you. That trustworthiness appears to matter more in the $D_{partner}$ than $C_{partner}$ condition suggests that our subjects were in fact sensitive to concordance/discordance. This is noteworthy given that concordance/discordance information was not explicitly provided on the slides used to present the relationships, nor was it explained in the instructions.

The Partner Control × Trust interaction also relates to the work of Van Lange and Visser (1999), which led to Hypothesis 3b. Specifically, we predicted that for the trusted partner, relationship attractiveness should be highest in situations of social interdependence (both people have FC), followed by those of unilateral dependence (only one person has FC), to no dependence (neither person has FC). Trust in a prospective partner appears not only to facilitate the achievement of mutually satisfactory outcomes in ongoing interaction (Deutsch, 1958) but a preference for mutuality in control over those outcomes.

The Own Control by Partner Control Interaction and the Own Control by Partner Control by Trust Interaction

As reported in the Results section, this interaction was significant, and analyses of its structure provided some, but not total, support for our prediction (Hypothesis 4) that the importance of own control would be highest when the partner has fate control. However, the unpredicted three-way interaction shows that the effects of partner's control do change with one's own level of control but in a fashion that is qualitatively moderated by trust. For a non-trusted partner, preferences follow a high power is bad, low power is good (HBLG) pattern, regardless of the type of own control. It appears that we become cognitive misers with non-trusted partners: "If I can't trust the partner, I don't want him/her to have control, period." However, for a trusted partner, we become more discerning. When own control is low (X_{self}, F_{self}, R_{self}), the partner's control does not matter that much, and attraction is relatively high. In this case, the HBLG heuristic is replaced by generalized "trustworthiness is good" thinking. If the same thing happened at high levels of own control (C_{self}, D_{self}), the story would be simple, and the explanation (at least to us) intuitively compelling: If you can trust your partner, don't worry about anything else; go for it!

But, it's not that simple. When own control is high and the partner is trusted, participants want that partner to have high control as well. This is true even for the D/D relationship, which models the conflict between self and social interest that defines a social dilemma. Assuming that a trusted partner is also a liked partner, it seems reasonable that you would want to be able to reward him/her, either as a direct expression of your goodwill or as reciprocity for the good will he/she shows you; you would want F_{self}. And, since everyone appears to value controlling their own outcomes to some degree, you would want R_{self} as well. You would want both R_{self} and F_{self}, what we are calling high personal power. If a trusted partner is a liked partner, and you enjoy R_{self}, then why should he/she not have it as well? You would want $R_{partner}$. And if a trusted partner is someone whom you can expect to treat you well if he/she is able, you would certainly want him/her to be able; you would want $F_{partner}$. You would want your trusted partner to have both $R_{partner}$ and $F_{partner}$; you would want him/her to have high power as well.

SOCIAL VALUE ORIENTATION

We were quite surprised at the virtual absence of effects for SVO and spent a great deal of time on analyses (not reported here) attempting to find some evidence for its importance. Nothing changed. Yeagley, Kuhlman, and Grzelak (2005) replicated this study with two important methodological changes: (a) SVO was measured at the beginning rather than the end of the study, and (b) they used decomposed games rather than matrices. The proportions of Js, Os, and Rs were similar to what is usually found (rather than the very high proportion of Rs observed in the present study), and once again SVO did not matter. Thus, the absence of SVO effects in the present study does not appear to be the result of its specific procedures.

The virtual absence of SVO effects is quite consistent with the idea raised in the beginning of this chapter that control preferences and SVO are rather independent. In that regard, the present study can be viewed as a conceptual replication of Grzelak's (2004) questionnaire studies on a large Polish sample.

Some insight into the absence of SVO effects is gained with the "appropriateness" framework of Weber, Kopelman, and Messick (2004). (See the Van Lange and Joireman chapter in this volume for an extensive discussion.) According to this framework, in any given situation people ask, "What does a person like me do in a situation like this?" Our control results tell us that when people are presented with a situation asking about control in a prospective relationship, people answer in pretty much the same way: They want to control their own outcomes, are generally averse to relationships with "powerful" non-trusted partners, and generally prefer relationships with trusted ones; to us, that sounds like a rather typical human being. When presented with a situation asking about the type of outcomes (cooperative, individualistic, competitive) they would like to achieve in an ongoing relationship, people are more variable in their answers; some answer as Js, others as Os, and others as Rs. The relative homogeneity of answers to the control situation would preclude a correlation with the variability of answers to the SVO assessment situation.

Of course, another, different interpretation assumes that just as there are individual differences in SVO, so too are there individual differences in control preference. For example, perhaps people differ in terms of how much they like having fate control over the outcomes of others. That does not in itself imply whether that power is used to benefit or to harm another person. In the (nonreported) analyses described above, we used a variety of statistical techniques (e.g., conjoint analysis, cluster analysis) to measure within-subject preferences for FC, RC, and so on. The correlations between the control and SVO measures were consistently nonsignificant.

The very high proportion of Rs obtained in our study was quite surprising. One possible explanation may lie with the fact that we used matrices rather than decomposed games to measure SVO. However, the work of Doi (1990), who used matrices, does not find high levels of R. Furthermore, a dissertation by Paul Teta (1995) used both decomposed games and matrices and found, with both techniques, SVO distributions much like those typically observed. Rather, it seems to us more likely that we inadvertently created a priming effect. Perhaps making issues of control and/or partner trustworthiness prior to assessing SVO had the effect of increasing competition. Future research should systematically investigate this issue.

GENERAL CONCLUSION AND COMMENTS

Finally, let us come back to the problem we started our chapter with, the motivational bases of behavior in interdependence situations. Messick and McClintock (1968) proved that diversity of choices people make in seemingly the same social situations can be understood and seen as rational only if we assume a more complex concept of subjective utility. The utility is composed from the utility of outcomes and the utility of allocation of outcomes to self and others, the so-called structure of the relationship. Preferences for specific outcome allocations are both situation and person dependent. The attractiveness (utility) of a relationship depends not only on outcome allocations but, as our study demonstrates, on control allocations. It can be claimed that it matters to people who controls and to what extent they control outcomes to self and others, and that we can just as sensibly speak of control preferences or orientations as we can of social motives or SVO. An important direction for future research would be the continuing development of assessment techniques for individual differences in control preferences (see Grzelak, 2004). Such measures might provide additional and important information about socially interdependent behavior that is quite distinct from SVO. The value of such research will be greatest if it recognizes that individual control preferences have "plasticity" (see Van Lange and Joireman's chapter in this volume), in that they are context dependent, varying in terms of a set of conditional probabilities of attractiveness where conditions are various social settings (like home, workplace, friendships, social status). This probabilistic approach, which is becoming a rather widely held view among SVO researchers (Van Lange, De Cremer, Van Dijk, & Van Vught, 2007), does not preclude the possibility that a person may have a dominant distribution of preferences for control across different situations. In other words, people may have generalized control preferences or orientations that affect their cognitions, evaluations, choice of behavior, and choice of situations.[6]

Both our theoretical analysis and empirical study dealt exclusively with a dyadic relationship. In principle, the main distinctions between types of interdependence and their implications can be extended to *n*-person relationships. However, it would require a much more complicated theoretical instrument than already very sophisticated theory provided by Kelley and Thibaut (1978). It would also, in empirical studies, require enormously complex operationalizations, not easily understood by research participants. The issue is beyond the scope of this chapter but seems desirable as a perspective for further explorations because so many real-life relationships have more than two actors.

We close our chapter with a small tribute to David Messick and a test of the reader's comprehension of our findings. By definition, a social dilemma is an interdependent relationship in which both parties have discordant reflexive control and fate control. If you look at Figure 9.3, Panel 5, you will see that for a certain kind of partner, people are very happy to "locomote" to a social dilemma relationship, as long as the partner is trustworthy, which in our study is about the nicest thing you could say about the partner. Would you be happy to be in a social dilemma relationship with Dave? We would.

NOTES

1. This is not a criticism of game theory, which limits itself to normative prescriptions for rational choice within established relationships.
2. Note that we do not include the third type of control proposed by Kelley and Thibaut (1978), called *behavioral control*. Inclusion of behavioral control would greatly enlarge the set of relationships. Furthermore, reflexive and fate control are directly related to control over outcomes, which is the focus of our chapter. Behavior control is related to one's ability to control the partner's actions.
3. An inferential Warsaw technique, similar in its logic to the methods developed by Kuhlman and Marshello (1975) and Liebrand and McClintock (1988), was used to measure social orientations. Assessment of control orientations was based on a questionnaire composed of reliable scales, each corresponding with different type of control.

4. The most recent, not yet published studies (surveys run in representative samples of Polish persons in 2004 and 2007) does not show correlations higher than those in in the earlier studies.
5. For a description of decomposed games, see the chapter by Shelley, Page, Yeagley, Rives, and Kuhlman in the present volume.
6. The results of preliminary studies on differential effects of generalized control orientations are mentioned in Grzelak (2001).

ACKNOWLEDGMENTS

This work was supported by a grant from the Ministry of Education in Poland (KBN 1 H01F 021 27) and by the University of Delaware.

REFERENCES

Adler, A. (1929). *The science of living*. New York: Greenberg.

Brehm, J. W. (1966). *A theory of psychological reactance*. Oxford, UK: Academic Press.

Burger, J. M., & Cooper, H. M. (1979). The desirability of control. *Motivation and Emotions, 3*, 381–393.

Christie, R., & Geis, S. L. (1970). *Studies in Machivellianism*. New York: Academic Press.

De Charms, R. (1968). *Personal causation: The internal affective determinants of behavior*. New York: Academic Press.

Derlega, V. J., & Chaikin, A. L. (1977). Privacy and self-disclosure in social relationships. *Journal of Social Issues, 33*, 102–115.

Deutsch, M. (1958). Trust and suspicion. *Journal of Conflict Resolution, 2*, 265–279.

Deutsch, M. (1960). The effect of motivational orientation on trust and suspicion. *Human Relations, 13*, 123–139.

Doi, T. (1990). An experimental investigation of the validity of the characteristic space theory and the measurement of social motivation. *The Japanese Journal of Experimental Social Psychology, 29*, 15–24.

Griesinger, D. W., & Livingston, J. W. (1973). Toward a model of interpersonal motivation in experimental games. *Behavioral Science, 18*, 173–188.

Grzelak, J. (2001). Control Preferences. In J. A. Bargh & D. K. Apsley (Eds.), *Unraveling the complexities of social life* (pp. 141–154). Washington, DC: American Psychological Association.

Grzelak, J. (2004). Social motivation: Are we better now than then? *International Journal of Sociology, 34*(4), 60–82.

Grzelak, J. L. (1982). Preferences and cognitive processes in social interdependence situations. In V. Derlega & J. Grzelak (Eds.), *Cooperation and helping behavior: Theory and research* (pp. 97–127). New York: Academic Press.

Kelley, H. H. (1997). Expanding the analysis of social orientations by reference to the sequential-temporal structure of situations. *European Journal of Social Psychology, 27*, 373–404.

Kelley, H. H., Holmes, J. G., Kerr, L. R., Reis, H. T., Rusbult, C. E., & Van Lange, P. A. M. (2003). *An atlas of interpersonal situations.* New York: Cambridge University Press.

Kelley, H. H., & Thibaut, J. W. (1978). *Interpersonal relations: A theory of interdependence.* New York: Wiley.

Kuhlman, D. M., & Marshello, A. (1975). Individual differences in game motivation as moderators of preprogrammed strategic effects in prisoner's dilemma. *Journal of Personality and Social Psychology, 32*, 922–931.

Liebrand, W. B. G., & McClintock, C. G. (1988). The ring measure of social values: A computerized procedure for assessing individual differences in information processing and social value orientation. *European Journal of Personality, 2*, 217–230.

Messick, D. M., & McClintock, C. G. (1968). Motivational bases of choice in experimental games. *Journal of Experimental Social Psychology, 4*, 1–25.

Seligman, M. E. (1975). *Helplessness: On depression, development, and death.* San Francisco: W. H. Freeman.

Teta, P. (1995). *Structural and interpersonal influences on decision making in 2 × 2 symmetric matrix games.* Unpublished doctoral dissertation, University of Delaware.

Van Lange, P. A. M. (1994). Toward more locomotion in experimental games. In W. U. Schulz, W. Albers, & U. Mueller (Eds.), *Social dilemmas and cooperation* (pp. 25–43). New York: Springer Verlag.

Van Lange, P. A. M., De Cremer, D., Van Dijk, E., & Van Vugt, M. (2007). Self-interest and beyond: Basic principles of social interaction. In A. W. Kruglanski & E. T. Higgings (Eds.), *Social psychology: Handbook of basic principles* (2nd ed., pp. 540–561). New York: Guilford.

Van Lange, P. A. M., & Visser, K. (1999). Locomotion in social dilemmas: How we adapt to cooperative, tit for tat, and noncooperative partners. *Journal of Personality and Social Psychology, 77*, 762–773.

Von Neumann, J., & Morgenstern, O. (1944). *Theory of games and economic behavior.* Princeton, NJ: Princeton University Press.

Weber, J. M., Kopelman, S., & Messick, D. M. (2004). A conceptual view of decision making in social dilemmas: Applying a logic of appropriateness. *Personality and Social Psychology Review, 8*(3), 281–307.

Winter, D. G. (1973). *The power motive.* New York: Free Press.

Yamagishi, T., & Yamagishi, M. (1994). Trust and commitment in the United States and Japan. *Motivation and Emotion, 18*, 129–166.

Yeagley, E. L., Kuhlman, D. M., & Grzelak, J. (2005). *Attraction to dyadic relationships as a function of outcome control and partner trustworthiness.* Paper presented at the 11th International Conference on Social Dilemmas, Kraków, Poland.

Section III

Ethical Judgments, Fairness, and Equality

10

See No Evil: When We Overlook Other People's Unethical Behavior

Francesca Gino
University of North Carolina

Don A. Moore
Carnegie Mellon University

Max H. Bazerman
Harvard University

It is common for people to be more critical of others' ethical choices than of their own. This chapter explores those remarkable circumstances in which people see no evil in others' unethical behavior. Specifically, we explore (a) the motivated tendency to overlook the unethical behavior of others when recognizing the unethical behavior would harm us; (b) the tendency to ignore unethical behavior when ethicality erodes slowly over time; (c) the tendency to ignore unethical behavior unless it is clear, immediate, and direct; and (d) the tendency to assess unethical behaviors only after the unethical behavior has resulted in a bad outcome, but not during the decision process.

> We believe that we are fairer than others because we think that we do fair things more often and unfair things less often than others. (Messick, Bloom, Boldizar, & Samuelson, 1985, p. 497)

Since 1985, when David Messick and his colleagues showed that people think they are fairer than others, a great deal of research has documented the broad and powerful implications of their work. Among the findings: People are routinely more willing to be critical of others' ethics than of their own. People are more suspicious of others' motives for committing good acts (Epley & Caruso, 2004; Epley & Dunning, 2000). People assume that others are more self-interested than they are and more strongly motivated by money (Miller & Ratner, 1998; Ratner & Miller, 2001). People believe that they are more honest and trustworthy than others (Baumhart, 1968; Messick & Bazerman, 1996) and that they try harder to do good (Alicke, 1985; Baumeister & Newman, 1994). But people are not always eager to shine a critical moral light on others. Indeed, there are systematic and predictable circumstances under which people look the other way when others engage in unethical conduct. This chapter concerns those circumstances.

Our work relies heavily on Messick's pioneering contributions to the field of business ethics (1995; 1996; Messick & Bazerman, 1996; Messick & Sentis, 1979, 1983; Messick & Tenbrunsel, 1996; Tenbrunsel & Messick, 1996). Prior to Messick's ethics research, most writing on business ethics was rooted in philosophy. The limited empirical work conducted was descriptive, lacking a specific focus on how to change behavior. Messick's work identified individual decisions as the most important entry point for changing and improving ethical behavior in business contexts. In particular, his research focused on psychological patterns of behavior that could predict how natural patterns of human judgment would lead to unethical behaviors.

A second critical input to the ideas presented in this chapter is research on bounded awareness (Bazerman & Chugh, 2006). Bounded awareness refers to systematic patterns of cognition that prevent people from noticing or focusing on useful, observable, and relevant data. Human beings constantly make implicit choices about what information to attend to in their environment and what information to ignore. Bazerman and Chugh (2005) argue that we make systematic errors during this process.

Messick's psychological perspective on ethics has joined with work on bounded awareness to create the concept of *bounded ethicality* (Banaji, Bazerman & Chugh, 2003; Banaji & Bhaskar, 2000; Murnighan, Cantelon, & Elyashiv, 2001). Just as *bounded rationality* refers to the fact that people have cognitive limitations that affect the choices they make based on their own preferences (Simon, 1947), bounded ethicality refers to the tendency of people to engage in behavior that is inconsistent with their own ethical values. That is, bounded ethicality refers to situations in which people make decision errors that not only harm others but are inconsistent with their own consciously espoused beliefs and preferences — decisions they would condemn upon further reflection or greater awareness (Bazerman & Moore, 2008). Banaji et al. (2003) have discussed implicit discrimination, ingroup favoritism, and overclaiming credit as examples of bounded ethicality.

This chapter seeks to map a subcategory of bounded ethicality. Rather than focusing on the unethical behaviors of a focal decision-maker, we are interested in the conditions under which the focal decision-maker over-looks the unethical behavior of others. When does it become easier for us to overlook others' unethical behavior? When that behavior serves our own interests. Indeed, under the predictable circumstances described in this chapter, people look the other way so that others can engage in ethically questionable acts on their behalf. For example, members of organizations routinely delegate unethical behavior to others in their organizations. This occurs when managers tell their subordinates to "do whatever it takes" to achieve production or sales goals, leaving open the possibility of aggressive or even unethical tactics. It happens when U.S. companies outsource production to offshore subcontractors that are inexpensive because they are less constrained by costly labor and environmental standards. It happens when partners at accounting firms remind junior auditors about the importance of retaining a client that has inappropriate accounting practices. In these and many other situations, people are motivated to overlook the problematic ethical implications of others' behavior.

One vivid example of the tendency to encourage others to perform our own dirty work comes from the National Football League's 2007 season. Many have argued that the New England Patriots were one of the greatest football teams of all time. But the team's coach, Bill Belichick, scarred the team's reputation by cheating. During the Patriots' game against the New York Jets (a weak team) early in the 2007 season, Belichick had an assistant film the Jets' private defensive signals. During the previous NFL season, the same assistant had been caught taping unauthorized video during the Patriots' game against the Green Bay Packers, but the Patriots were not punished ("Belichick Draws $500,000 Fine, but Avoids Suspension," 2007). For the 2007 offense, NFL commissioner Roger Goodell fined Belichick $500,000, fined the Patriots $250,000, and eliminated their first draft choice for the 2008 team. The Patriots' owners, the Kraft family, who had hired Belichick and encouraged him to win, offered no criticism of the coach after the incident. Their silence suggests that the coach's behavior was acceptable to them. Yet the ethics of the Kraft family largely were unquestioned by the media, and Patriots' fans did not seem overly concerned about the behavior of either Belichick or the Kraft family.

Why does it matter whether people condone others' unethical behavior? In recent years, ethics scandals have cost the owners, investors, and employees of firms such as Enron, WorldCom, Global Crossing, Tyco International, Parmalat, and Arthur Andersen billions of dollars. We believe that these scandals would not have occurred if leaders and employees within these firms had taken note of the unethical behavior of their colleagues rather than overlooking such behavior. Clearly, a greater understanding of this issue is a matter of real practical importance (Trevino & Youngblood, 1990). In addition, the issue is important to the psychological study of ethical judgment, because it highlights an important exception to the general conclusion that people are especially critical of others' ethics.

In this chapter, we explore the psychological processes at work in the ethical perception of others' behaviors. We begin by discussing what we call *motivated blindness*: the tendency for people to overlook the unethical behavior of others when recognizing that the unethical behavior would harm them. Second, we review recent evidence suggesting that gradual moral decay leads people to grow comfortable with behavior to which they would otherwise object. Third, we explore how readily people forgive others who benefit from delegating unethical behavior. Fourth, we examine how the tendency to value outcomes over processes can affect our assessments of the ethicality of others' choices. When predicting or judging the intentions and actions of a decision-maker, information about that person's decision process is much more relevant than information about the outcome of the decision. Yet people often use outcomes in a heuristic manner that reduces the likelihood of identifying obvious patterns of unethical behavior.

We should note two streams of prior research that has investigated issues related to the notion of noticing others' unethical behavior. The first is on informal systems and ethical climates within organizations (Tenbrunsel, Smith-Crowe, & Umphress, 2003; Trevino, 1990). Both informal systems and ethical climates can influence individuals' ethical behaviors within an organization by making salient to individuals what ethical norms and standards are valued by the organization's founders or leaders. The biases related to bounded ethicality discussed in this chapter might have relevant implications for the ethical culture supported within an organization. If such culture is built around biased ethical preferences of the organization's leaders, then ethical standards might exacerbate individuals' failures to notice others' unethical behavior within the organization.

The second stream of research is on organizational whistle-blowing (e.g., King, 1997; Miceli, Dozier & Near, 1991; Near & Miceli, 1986). Whistle-blowing is defined as the disclosure by organizational members of wrongdoing within an organization to the public or to those in position of authority (Near & Miceli, 1985). The literature on whistle-blowing focuses on explaining individuals' reactions to acts of perceived unethical behavior (Gundlach, Douglas, & Martinko, 2003) and has identified individual, organizational, and situational factors (Near & Miceli, 1995). One of the premises of the literature on whistle-blowing is that both whistle-blowers and inactive observers do in fact notice others' unethical behaviors. However, the research described in this chapter calls into question this premise and suggests that people might not blow the whistle because they fail to identify others' problematic behaviors as unethical in the first place.

MOTIVATED BLINDNESS

Psychologists have known for some time that individuals who have a vested self-interest in a situation have difficulty approaching the situation without bias, even when they view themselves to be honest (Ross & Sicoly, 1979). In other words, when Party A has an incentive to see Party B in a favorable light, Party A will have difficulty accurately assessing the ethicality of Party B's behavior. Though this point is obvious to psychologists, it is regularly ignored by those who set up organizations and regulatory structures (Moore, Tetlock, Tanlu, & Bazerman, 2006). Similarly, when discussing the conflict between what managers are obligated to do versus what they are individually rewarded for doing, the business press frequently presents such decisions as intentional, conscious choices, overlooking the role of unconscious bias.

Continuing with another example from the world of sports, Barry Bonds has surpassed Hank Aaron to become the all-time leader in career home runs, perhaps the most valued record in Major League Baseball (MLB). Many people now question whether Bonds' performance truly surpasses that of Aaron, given allegations that Bonds used steroids or hormones to enhance his physique. Far more interesting, in our view, is the failure of the MLB commissioner, the San Francisco Giants team, and the players' union to investigate the rapid changes in Bonds' physical appearance, his enhanced strength, and his increased power at the plate when they occurred. Because the MLB and the players' union benefited (at least in the short term) from the steroid use of players such as Bonds, this interest prevented them from taking action on the steroid issue for at least a decade.

A much more serious threat to our society comes from the incentives of auditors to please their clients (Bazerman, Morgan, & Loewenstein, 1997). Accounting firms have numerous motivations to view their clients' books in a positive light, including the auditing and consulting fees they receive from the hiring companies. Thus, auditors face a conflict between acting in their own self-interest and acting ethically (Bazerman, Moore, Tetlock, & Tanlu, 2006; Moore et al., 2006). Bazerman, Loewenstein, and Moore (2002) tested the strength of this conflict of interest by giving study participants a complex set of information about the potential sale of a fictional company. The participants' task was to estimate the company's value. Participants were assigned to different roles: buyer, seller, buyer's auditor, or seller's auditor. All participants read the same information about the company, including information that could help them estimate the worth of the firm. After reading about the company, auditors provided estimated valuations of its worth to their clients. As the literature on self-serving biases would suggest, sellers submitted higher estimates of the company's worth than prospective buyers (Babcock & Loewenstein, 1997). Even more interesting, the "auditors" who were advising either the buyer or the seller were strongly biased toward the interests of their clients: The sellers' auditors publicly concluded that the firm was worth more than did buyers' auditors. Was the auditors' judgment intentionally biased, or was bounded ethicality at play? To answer this question, Bazerman et al. (2002) asked the auditors to estimate the company's true value, as assessed by impartial experts, and told the auditors that they would be rewarded for the accuracy of their private judgments. Auditors who had been serving sellers reached estimates of the company's value that, on average, were 30% higher than the estimates of auditors who served buyers. It appears that, due to the influence of self-serving biases, participants assimilated information about the target company in a biased way. As a result, they were unlikely to provide accurate and unbiased estimates when their private judgments were submitted. This study suggests that even a purely hypothetical relationship between an auditor and a client distorts the judgments of those playing the role of auditor. It seems likely that a longstanding relationship that involves many thousands or even millions of dollars in ongoing revenues would have an even stronger effect. Bazerman et al. (2002) conclude that bias is likely to be a far greater and much more entrenched problem in corporate auditing than outright corruption.

This evidence is consistent with broader research suggesting that people evaluate evidence in a selective fashion when they have a stake in reaching a particular conclusion or outcome. Humans are biased to selectively see evidence supportive of the conclusion they would like to reach (Holyoak & Simon, 1999; Koehler, 1991; Lord, Ross, & Lepper, 1979), while ignoring evidence that goes against their preferences or subjecting it to special scrutiny (Gilovich, 1991). Though some scholars have suggested that professional auditors might be less subject to these biases due to their special training and knowledge, research has found professionals to be vulnerable to the same motivated biases that affect novices (Buchman, Tetlock, & Reed, 1996; Cuccia, Hackenbrack, & Nelson, 1995; Moore et al., 2006).

Consider the case of Enron, one of the most famous business collapse of our time. How was it possible for Arthur Andersen, Enron's auditor, to vouch for the firm's financial health during the time that Enron was concealing billions of dollars in debt from its shareholders? Arthur Andersen had strong reasons to be afflicted by motivated blindness. First, having earned millions from Enron ($25 million in auditing fees and $27 million in consulting fees in 2001), Andersen was motivated to retain and build on these lucrative contracts. In addition, many Andersen auditors hoped to be hired by Enron, as a number of their colleagues had been. Cases such as this shed light on an important weakness of the current auditing system in the United States: it allows motivated blindness to thrive.

To summarize, motivated blindness refers to situations in which individuals see no evil in others' behaviors because they have a vested self-interest in the outcome. Research on motivated blindness has focused on conflict of interests and on the role of self-serving biases across various contexts (such as relationships between buyers and sellers or between plaintiffs and defendants).

UNETHICAL BEHAVIOR ON A SLIPPERY SLOPE

Research on visual perception has shown that people frequently fail to notice gradual changes that occur right in front of their eyes (Simons, 2000). It is often the case that people cannot report that a change has happened or what that change was. Nevertheless, it is not the case that they have no memory trace of what happened, because study participants generally are able to remember, at least in part, what they saw before a change occurred. For example, in one study investigating change detection, an experimenter holding a basketball stopped pedestrians to ask for directions (Simons, Chabris, Schnur, & Levin, 2002). While the pedestrian was in the process of giving directions, a group of confederates walked between the experimenter and the pedestrian. As the group was passing by, the experimenter handed the basketball to one of the confederates. Once the pedestrian was done giving directions, the experimenter asked her if she noticed any sort of change while she was talking. Most pedestrians in the study generally did not notice any change. However, when they were asked directly about a basketball, many recalled it, and some even recounted specific characteristics of the ball. So, while the participants failed to explicitly notice that a change took place, it was possible that they could have done so, had they been attuned to it.

In this study, as in many others by Simons and his colleagues, the information people miss is visual, and the mental processes that might explain this failure to notice changes are perceptual. Recent decision-making research investigated how these processes operate when the information is not visual and the processes are not perceptual. Gino and Bazerman (2008) found that other types of changes also go unnoticed, leading to important decision-making errors with ethically relevant consequences. Investigating the implications of "change blindness" for unethical behavior, for example, they showed that individuals are less likely to notice others' unethical behaviors when it occurs in small increments than when it occurs suddenly. Their findings suggest that bounded awareness extends from perceptual processes to decision-making processes in ethically relevant contexts.

Gino and Bazerman's work was motivated by the intuitive concept of a "slippery slope," which predicts that decision-makers are less likely to notice small changes in behavior and to code them as unethical than they are to notice and code a dramatic change as unethical (Tenbrunsel

& Messick, 2004). This idea can be used to explain real-world examples of unethical behavior, such as that of some auditors (Bazerman et al., 2002). Suppose that an accountant with a large auditing firm is in charge of the audit of a large company with a strong reputation. For 3 years in a row, the client's financial statements were extremely ethical and of high quality. As a result, the auditor approved the statements and had an excellent relationship with its client. This year, however, the company committed some clear transgressions in its financial statement — stretching and even breaking the law in certain areas. In such a situation, the accountant likely would refuse to certify that the financial statements were acceptable according to government regulations.

By contrast, what would happen if the corporation stretched the law in a few areas one year but did not appear to break the law? The auditing firm might be less likely to notice the transgressions than in the previous condition. Now suppose that the next year, the firm stretches the ethicality of its returns a bit more, committing a minor violation in federal accounting standards. The following year, the violations are a bit more severe. The year after that, the auditing firm might find itself facing the type of severe violations described above, where the client crossed the ethical line abruptly. Based on the evidence presented by Gino and Bazerman (2008), we believe auditors would be more likely to notice and refuse to sign the statements in the first version of the story than in the second one, even if the unethical behavior is the same in the last year described in both stories.

To summarize, research on the slippery slope phenomenon has demonstrated that people are less likely to perceive changes in others' unethical behaviors if the changes occur slowly over time rather then abruptly. This work has investigated the influence of gradual versus abrupt changes in others' unethical behaviors on judges' likelihood to stop such behavior. The findings of this research suggest that many of us fail to notice gradual changes in unethical standards, in part because our bounded awareness leaves us better equipped to notice abrupt rather than gradual changes.

FAILURE TO SEE THROUGH INDIRECTNESS

In August 2005, pharmaceutical manufacturer Merck sold off a cancer drug named Mustargen that it had developed to Ovation, a smaller pharmaceutical firm, along with a second cancer drug called Cosmegen (Berenson, 2006). So far, this transaction seems ordinary enough. After all, why should a firm as large as Merck bother with the complexities of manufacturing small lots of drugs used by fewer than 5,000 patients and generating annual sales of only about $1 million?

There is more to the story, however. After selling the product rights, Merck continued to manufacture the drugs for Ovation. If small-market products were a distraction, why would Merck continue to produce the drugs? Indirect evidence on the topic might help us identify a possible answer to this question. Soon after completing its deal with Merck, while the drugs were still being produced by Merck, Ovation raised the wholesale price of Mustargen by approximately tenfold and raised the price of Cosmegen by even more. It turns out that Ovation is generally in the business of buying small-market drugs from large firms that have public relation concerns and then dramatically increasing the price of the drugs. For example, Ovation purchased Panhamtic from Abbott Laboratories, increased the price nearly tenfold, and Abbott continued to manufacture the drug. Why didn't Merck keep the two drugs and raise their sales prices itself? One possible answer is that the company wanted to avoid the headline, "Merck Increases Cancer Drug Prices by 1,000%," but was less concerned about the headline, "Merck Sells Two Products to Ovation."

In this section we focus on organizations that create harm indirectly through the use of an additional organization. Consider the following context created by Paharia, Kassam, Greene, and Bazerman (2008) to mirror the environment of the Merck story presented earlier:

> A major pharmaceutical company, X, had a cancer drug that was minimally profitable. The fixed costs were high and the market was limited. But, the patients who used the drug really needed it. The pharmaceutical was making the drug for $2.50/pill (all costs included) and was only selling it for $3/pill.

One group of study participants was asked to assess the ethicality of the following action:

> A: The major pharmaceutical firm raised the price of the drug from $3/pill to $9/pill.

Another group was asked to asses the ethicality of a different course of action:

B: The major pharmaceutical X sold the rights to a smaller pharmaceutical. In order to recoup costs, company Y increased the price of the drug to $15/pill.

Interestingly, participants who read Action A judged the behavior of pharmaceutical firm X more harshly than did participants who read Action B, despite the smaller negative impact of Action A on patients. Notably, participants made these assessments the way the world normally comes to us — one option at a time. Paharia et al. (2008) went on to ask study participants in a third condition, who saw both possible actions, to judge which was more unethical. In this case, preferences reversed. When they could compare the two scenarios, people saw Action B as being more ethically problematic than Action A.

In further studies, Paharia et al. (2008) replicated this result in the realms of contaminated land and pollution controls. In each case, when study participants were judging one option, they significantly discounted the unethicality if the focal firm acted through an intermediary. But when asked to compare an indirect and a direct action, they saw through the indirectness and made their assessments based on the magnitude of the harm created by the action.

To test the robustness of their demonstrated effect, Paharia et al. (2008) examined how transparent the intent of pharmaceutical X needs to be for the effect to disappear. Even in the case of extraordinary transparency, they were able to replicate the basic effect reported above. They created four conditions. In one condition (raise price), study participants were told that "… The pharmaceutical firm raised the price of the drug from $3/pill to $9/pill, thus increasing the value of the drug to company X by $10 million." In a second condition (sell without knowledge), participants were told that "… The major pharmaceutical X sold the rights to a smaller pharmaceutical, Y, for $10 million. In order to recoup costs, company Y increased the price of the drug to $9/pill." In a third condition (sell with knowledge), participants were told that "… The major pharmaceutical X sold the rights to a smaller pharmaceutical, Y, for $10 million. In order to recoup costs, company Y increased the price of the drug to $9/pill. Company X was aware that company Y would raise the price to $9/pill before the sale of the drug." Finally, in a fourth condition (sell through Y), participants were told that "… Rather than brand and distribute the drug themselves incurring a cost of $100,000 to company X, they made a contract with company Y for this service. Under the contract, company Y agreed to sell the product under company Y's name and through their distribution channels for $9/pill. Company X paid company Y $100,000 for this service and increased the value of the drug to company X by $10 million." As the transparency of pharmaceutical X's intent increased, participants rated the firm as less ethical. However, even in the transparent "sell through Y" condition, the indirect strategy was not perceived as being as unethical as in the "raise price" condition.

Finally, Coffman (2008) created an experimental economics demonstration of the same core effect found in Paharia et al. (2008), using a four-player game adapted from the dictator game. In the standard dictator game, Player A is given a fixed amount of money and faces a choice between giving none, some, or all of this money to Player C. Player C is a passive recipient of Player A's decision. In the Coffman (2008) study, as in the standard version of the game, Player A is given $24 to allocate between Player A and Player C. However, in his version, Player A has an alternative option: selling the rights to the game to Player B (at a price negotiated in a double auction). If Player A decides not to sell, then the game resembles the traditional dictator game between Player A and Player C (with Player A being the dictator). If Player B buys the game from Player A, Player B then assumes the role of the dictator in a game played with Player C (as in the traditional dictator game). Then, as the last step, Player D, who is given a separate allotment of funds, has the opportunity to punish Player A (but not Player B) for his or her actions by reducing Player A's final payoff. Player D, however, must pay one cent (money that is detracted from Player D's final payoff) for every 3 cents that s/he wants to punish Player A. Not surprisingly, the smaller the amount of money that Player B gives to Player C, the larger the punishment that Player D administers to Player A. More interestingly, when Player A sells the rights to the game to Player B, the amount of punishment decreases dramatically. These results are consistent with the results of Paharia et al. (2008) and the Merck/Ovation story.

Unfortunately, we do not sufficiently hold people and organizations accountable for the type of indirect unethical behavior described in this section, even when the unethical intent is clear. Notably, we are not intending with this argument to condemn market forces or the ethicality of overtly increasing prices. Rather, we are raising a red flag concerning the practice of some individuals and organizations to intentionally create opaqueness when they believe the public may have ethical qualms with their actions. Assuming that companies such as Merck know that a tenfold price increase on a cancer drug would attract negative attention, we believe that it is manipulative and unethical to hide this increase through the use of an intermediary such as Ovation. We also believe that this strategy works — that the public and the press fail to condemn people and firms that use an intermediary to do their dirty work.

Our argument builds on the insightful work of Royzman and Baron (2002), who show that people do not view indirect harms to be as problematic as direct harms. For example, Royzman and Baron (2002) document that some Catholic hospitals would rather give an endangered pregnant patient a hysterectomy than use a simple abortion process, even though the hysterectomy will abort the fetus, if indirectly, while also eliminating the possibility of future pregnancies. We view this preference pattern as illogical and as taking advantage of the irrational manner in which people judge ethical harm.

In sum, research on the failure to see others' unethical behaviors through indirectness has demonstrated that individuals tend to discount the unethicality of a target's actions if the target acted through an intermediary. This work has also shown that such discounting can be eliminated if judges make their assessments of ethicality by comparing an indirect and a direct action at the same time. In such a case, people judging the actions of others see through the indirectness and base their ethical judgments on the magnitude of the harm created by the action.

THINKING THERE'S NO PROBLEM — UNTIL SOMETHING BAD HAPPENS

In this section, we describe people's tendency to evaluate unethical acts only after the fact — once the unethical behavior has resulted in a bad outcome but not during the decision process. We start this section with a few stories. Read each of them and then assess the magnitude of the unethical behavior in each:

A) A pharmaceutical researcher defines a clear protocol for determining whether or not to include clinical patients as data points in a study. He is running short of time to collect sufficient data points for his study within an important budgetary cycle within his firm. As the deadline approaches, he notices that four subjects were withdrawn from the analysis due to technicalities. He believes that the data in fact are appropriate to use, and when he adds those data points, the results move from not quite statistically significant to significant. He adds these data points, and soon the drug goes to market. This drug is later withdrawn from the market after it kills six patients and injures hundreds of others.

B) An auditor is examining the books of an important client, a client that is not only valuable for their auditing fees, but also buys lucrative advisory services from the auditor's firm as well. The auditor notices some accounting practices that are probably illegal, but it would take multiple court cases to be sure about whether the action was legal or not. The auditor brings up the issue with the client, who insists that there is nothing wrong with their accounting. The client also threatens to withdraw their business if the auditor withholds their approval. The auditor agrees to let it go by for one year and encourages the client to change their accounting practices over the next year. Six months later, it is found that the client was committing fraud, their corporation goes bankrupt, the bankruptcy is connected to the issue that the auditor noticed, and 1,400 people lose their jobs and their life savings.

C) A toy company finds out that the products that they were selling, manufactured by another firm in another country, contains lead, which can be extremely hazardous to children. The toy company had failed to test for lead in the product, since testing is expensive and is not required by U.S. law. The lead paint eventually kills six children and sends dozens more to emergency room for painful treatment for lead poisoning.

How unethical did you find the actions of the pharmaceutical researcher, the auditor, and the toy company to be? Now consider the following (related) stories:

A1) A pharmaceutical researcher defines a clear protocol for determining whether or not to include clinical patients as data points in a study. He is running short of time to collect sufficient data points for his study within an important budgetary cycle within his firm. He believed that the product was safe and effective. As the deadline approaches, he notices that if he had four more data points for how subjects are likely to behave, the analysis would be significant. He makes up these data points, and soon the drug goes to market. This drug is a profitable and effective drug and years later shows no significant side effects.

B1) An auditor is examining the books of an important client, a client that is not only valuable for their auditing fees but also buys lucrative advisory services from the auditor's firm as well. The auditor notices clearly fraudulent practices by their client. The auditor brings up the issue with the client, who insists that there is nothing wrong with their accounting. The client also threatens to withdraw their business if the auditor withholds their approval. The auditor agrees to let it go by for one year and encourages the client to change their accounting practices over the next year. No problems result from the auditor's decision.

C1) A toy company sells products made by another firm, manufactured in another country. The toy company knows that the toys contain lead, which can be extremely hazardous to children. The toy company successfully sells this product, makes a significant profit, and no children are injured by the lead paint.

Imagine that you had only read A1, B1, and C1 (and not A, B, and C). How would you have reacted? We asked a group of participants to read the first set of stories, and asked a second group to read A1, B1, and C1 (Gino, Moore, & Bazerman, 2008). The results showed that people were more critical of the researcher, the auditor, and the toy company in A, B, and C than of those in A1, B1, and C1. Specifically, people rated the behaviors described in A, B, and C as more unethical than the behaviors described in A1, B1, and C1. They also said that such behavior should be punished more harshly.

Yet, if you compare A and A1, it is clear that the pharmaceutical researcher's behavior was more unethical in A1 than A. The same holds true for the next two pairs. We confirmed this intuition by asking participants to rate the ethicality of the actions described in all the scenarios above without giving information about the outcomes (see Gino et al., 2008). A different group of participants read the stories described in A, B, and C, and a second group read the stories described in A1, B1, and C1. As expected, participants rated the actions described in A1, B1, and C1 as more unethical than the ones described in A, B, and C.

Why do people exposed to the full versions of A, B, and C judge these decision-makers more harshly than the decision-makers in A1, B1, and C1? The answer may lie in what Baron and Hershey (1988) call the *outcome bias*: the tendency to take outcomes into account, in a manner that is not logically justified, when evaluating the quality of the decision process that the decision-maker used. Baron and Hershey have found that people judge the wisdom of decision-makers, including medical decision-making and simple laboratory gambles, based on the outcomes they obtain. Marshall and Mowen (1993) found the same effect in cases in which people are asked to judge the decisions of salespeople.

Bringing this research to an ethical context (Gino et al., 2008), we found that people too often judge the ethicality of actions based on whether harm follows rather than on the ethicality of the choice itself. We replicated the results from the two studies reported above with a different set of stories and a within-subjects design. In a third study, participants first evaluated the quality of each decision without knowing its outcome. Then participants learned the outcome and evaluated the decision again using the same criteria. This within-subjects design allowed us to test the contention that the outcome bias results from differences in how people believe they would have evaluated the choice in the absence of outcome knowledge. Consistent with the results of the two studies described above, we found that even when participants have seen and rated the ethicality of a decision prior to learning its outcome, their opinions change when they learn the outcome: they decide that decisions with negative outcomes were unethical, even if they did not think so before.

Our research also investigated the mechanisms that can be used to eliminate the outcome bias in ethical judgment. We found that the differential impact of outcome information on ethical judgments is stronger when individuals make their judgments based on intuitive, gut feelings of right and wrong than when they use a rational, analytic mode of thought.

One problem with the influence of outcome information on ethical judgments is that it can lead us to blame people too harshly for making sensible decisions that have unlucky outcomes. We believe this is one reason why people are often too slow to be outraged by a pattern of unethical behavior. Too often, we let problematic decisions slide before they produce bad outcomes, even if bad outcomes are completely predictable. Thus, the outcome bias may partially explain why we so often fail to take notice of unethical behavior — and condemn it only after a harmful outcome occurs.

One prime example of this pattern lies in the area of auditor independence. For decades, auditing firms provided both auditing and consulting services to their clients and engaged in other activities that logically and psychologically compromised the independence of their audits (Frankel, Johnson, & Nelson, 2002; Moore et al., 2006). Despite evidence of the failure of auditor independence (Levitt & Dwyer, 2002) and the belief that independence was core to auditing (Berardino, 2000; *Burger, W. United States v. Arthur Young & Co.*, 1984), the U.S. government refused to address the issue until auditor conflicts of interest were glaringly obvious in the failures of Enron, WorldCom, Tyco, and other firms (Moore at al., 2006). Long before the bad outcomes, ample evidence was available that the existing structure compromised the ethics of the auditing profession (Bazerman & Watkins, 2004). But only bad outcomes motivated our legislative representatives to address the problem.

Similarly, many now question the ethics of the Bush administration's decision to invade Iraq, including its misrepresentation of the "facts" that prompted the war. Yet criticism of the Bush administration was muted in much of the United States when victory in Iraq appeared to be at hand. Once the difficulties in Iraq became obvious, more people questioned the administration's pre-war tactics, such as unfounded claims of evidence of weapons of mass destruction in Iraq. Why didn't these critics and the public at large raise such ethical issues when the United States appeared to be winning in Iraq? One possibility is the outcome bias and its effects on judgments of ethicality.

In another sphere, we see a connection between the outcome bias in ethical contexts and research on identifiable victims (Small & Loewenstein, 2003, 2005; Kogut & Ritov, 2005a, 2005b). The "identifiable victim effect" suggests that people are far more concerned with and show more sympathy for identifiable victims than statistical victims. Simply indicating that there is a specific victim increases caring, even when no personalizing information about the victim is available (Small & Loewenstein, 2003). Similarly, on a psychological continuum, the same unethical action could harm an identifiable victim, an unidentifiable victim, or no victim at all. We predict that people would see more unethicality when identifiable victims are affected than when victims are statistical, and that even weaker perceptions of unethicality will occur when there are no victims. Across this continuum, we predict that differences in judgments of unethicality will depend on the outcome of the unethical behavior, even though the actions of the perpetrator of the unethicality remain the same.

One fascinating example of this prediction comes from our industry, higher education. Schmidt (2007), deputy editor of the *Chronicle of Higher*

Education, documents that, at many excellent universities, the leading form of affirmative action is "legacy admits" — the policy of admitting subpar children of alumni, children of donors, and other well-connected individuals. The obvious consequence of legacy admission policies is that elite institutions end up favoring unqualified, less capable applicants from privileged social groups over more qualified, unconnected applicants. Amazingly, this racist and elitist behavior was largely ignored for many decades. Even today, very few have raised their voices in objection to legacy admits. We believe that lack of concern over these ethically questionable practices results from a combination of two factors: the difficulty in identifying the victims of such practices (those who are denied admission) and lack of perception that the practices cause harm. In essence, even when we do recognize the negative outcome of unethical behavior, we are often dulled by the lack of vividness of the harmful outcomes.

To summarize, research on the effects of outcome information on ethical judgments has found that individuals judge behaviors as less ethical, more blameworthy, and to be punished more harshly when such behaviors led to undesirable rather than desirable consequences, even if they saw those behaviors as acceptable before they knew its consequences. The findings of this work also demonstrate that a rational, analytic mindset can override the effects of one's intuitions in ethical judgments.

CONCLUSIONS

> The moral virtues, then, are produced in us neither by nature nor against nature. Nature, indeed, prepares in us the ground for their reception, but their complete formation is the product of habit. (Aristotle, from *Nicomachean Ethics*)

Aristotle wrote that developing a moral virtue requires one to practice the choices and feelings appropriate to that virtue. Indeed, the psychological evidence strongly supports the notion that most people value ethical decisions and behavior and strive to develop the habit of ethicality. Yet, despite these beliefs, people still find themselves engaging in unethical behavior because of biases that influence their decisions — biases of which they may not be fully aware. This is true in part because human ethicality is bounded: Psychological processes sometimes lead us to engage in ethically questionable behaviors that are inconsistent with our own values and ethical beliefs. And, as we have discussed, human awareness is also bounded: unconsciously, our minds imperfectly filter information when dealing with ethically relevant decisions. As a result of these limits, we routinely ignore accessible and relevant information.

Deliberative, systematic thought (Kahneman & Frederick, 2002; Stanovich & West, 2000) in ethically relevant contexts is often insufficient to avoid unethical decisions, judgments, or behaviors. The clarity of evidence on bounded awareness and bounded ethicality places the burden on management schools to make students aware of the possibility that even good people sometimes will act unethically without their own awareness. In addition, organizational leaders must understand these processes and make the structural changes necessary to reduce the harmful effects of our psychological and ethical limitations. Similar to the development of moral virtues described by Aristotle, considering the critical information that is typically excluded from decision problems should become a habit. Our legal system typically requires evidence of intent in order to prove someone guilty of wrongdoing; fraud, for instance, usually requires that an individual knew that a statement was false when he made it. We believe that executives should face a higher hurdle. They should be held responsible for the harms that their organizations predictably create, with or without intentionality or awareness.

SUMMARY AND RESEARCH AGENDA

The research presented in this chapter relies on Messick's work in the business ethics literature. Though traditionally ethics has been a topic studied by philosophy researchers who used a descriptive approach, Messick's research stressed the importance of studying how psychological factors influence human judgment and behavior in the ethics realm. Building on Messick's insightful contributions to business ethics research, this chapter described those remarkable circumstances in which people see no evil in others' unethical behavior. We identified four such situations: (a) the motivated tendency to overlook the unethical behavior of others when we recognize that the unethical behavior would harm us; (b) the tendency to ignore unethical behavior when ethicality erodes slowly over time; (c) the tendency to ignore unethical behavior unless it is clear, immediate, and direct; and (d) the tendency to assess unethical behaviors only after the unethical behavior has resulted in a bad outcome but not during the decision process.

We believe that further research is warranted to uncover the boundary conditions of the tendencies described here, as well as novel factors that might lead us astray in ethical domains. More generally, research in this area should not only identify conditions under which our ethical judgments and behaviors are biased but examine the mechanisms through which our systematic errors can be corrected and eliminated.

REFERENCES

Alicke, M. D. (1985). Global self-evaluation as determined by the desirability and controllability of trait adjectives. *Journal of Personality and Social Psychology, 49*(6), 1621–1630.

Aristotle (350 BC). *Nicomachean ethics. Book II: Moral virtue. Chapter 1*. Retrieved March 11, 2009, from http://www.virtuescience.com/nicomachean-ethics.html

Babcock, L., & Loewenstein, G. (1997). Explaining bargaining impasse: The role of self serving biases. *Journal of Economic Perspectives, 11*, 109–126.

Banaji, M. R., Bazerman, M. H., & Chugh, D. (2003, December). How (un)ethical are you? *Harvard Business Review, 81*(12), 56–64.

Banaji, M. R., & Bhaskar, R. (2000). Implicit stereotypes and memory: The bounded rationality of social beliefs. In D. L. Schacter & E. Scarry (Eds.), *Memory, brain, and belief* (pp. 139–175). Cambridge, MA: Harvard University Press.

Baron, J., & Hershey, J. C. (1988). Outcome bias in decision evaluation. *Journal of Personality and Social Psychology, 54*, 569–579.

Baumeister, R. F., & Newman, L. S. (1994). Self-regulation of cognitive inference and decision processes. *Personality and Social Psychology Bulletin, 20*, 3–19.

Baumhart, R. (1968). *An honest profit: What businessmen say about ethics in business*. New York: Holt, Rinehart and Winston.

Bazerman, M. H., Loewenstein, G., & Moore, D. A. (2002, November). Why good accountants do bad audits. *Harvard Business Review, 80*(11), 96–102.

Bazerman, M. H., & Moore, D. A. (2008). *Judgment in managerial decision making* (7th ed.). New York: Wiley.

Bazerman, M. H., Moore, D. A., Tetlock, P. E., & Tanlu, L. (2006). Reports of solving the conflicts of interest in auditing are highly exaggerated. *Academy of Management Review, 31*(1), 1–7.

Bazerman, M. H., Morgan, K., & Loewenstein, G. (1997, Summer). The impossibility of auditory independence. *Sloan Management Review, 38*, 89–94.

Bazerman, M. H., & Watkins, M. D. (2004). *The disasters you should have seen coming and how to prevent them.* Boston: Harvard Business School Publishing.

Belichick draws $500,000 fine, but avoids suspension. (2007, September 14). Retrieved July 1, 2008 from ESPN.com: http://sports.espn.go.com

Berardino, J. F. (2000). Hearing on auditor independence. Retrieved July 1,2008 from http://www.sec.gov/rules/proposed/s71300/testimony/berardi2.htm

Berenson, A. (2006, March 12). A cancer drug's big price rise is cause for concern. The New York Times. Retrieved March 11, 2009, from http://www.nytimes.com/2006/03/12/business/12price.html

Buchman, T., Tetlock, P. E., & Reed, R. O. (1996). Accountability and auditors' judgments about contingent events. *Journal of Business Finance and Accounting, 23,* 379–398.

Burger, W. United States v. Arthur Young & Co., 82-687 S. Ct. (1984).

Coffman, L. (2008). Personal conversation. Unpublished raw data.

Cuccia, A. D., Hackenbrack, K., & Nelson, M. (1995). The ability of professional standards to mitigate aggressive reporting. *The Accounting Review, 70,* 227–249.

Epley, N., & Caruso, E. M. (2004). Egocentric ethics. *Social Justice Research, 17,* 171–187.

Epley, N., & Dunning, D. (2000). Feeling "holier than thou": Are self-serving assessments produced by errors in self- or social prediction? *Journal of Personality and Social Psychology, 79*(6), 861–875.

Frankel, R. M., Johnson, M. F., & Nelson, K. K. (2002). The relation between auditors' fees for nonaudit services and earnings management. *The Accounting Review, 77*(Suppl.), 71–105.

Gilovich, T. (1991). *How we know what isn't so: The fallibility of human reason in everyday life.* New York: The Free Press.

Gino, F., & Bazerman, M. H. (2008). *Slippery slopes and misconduct: The effect of gradual degradation on the failure to notice other's unethical behavior.* (Working paper.)

Gino, F., Moore, D. A., & Bazerman, M. H. (2008). No harm, no foul: The outcome bias in judging unethical behavior.

Gundlach, M. J., Douglas, S. C., & Martinko, M. J. (2003). The decision to blow the whistle: A social information processing framework. *Academy of Management Review, 28*(1), 107–123.

Holyoak, K. J., & Simon, D. (1999). Bidirectional reasoning in decision making by constraint satisfaction. *Journal of Experimental Psychology - General, 128,* 3–31.

Kahneman, D., & Frederick, S. (2002). Representativeness revisited: Attribute substitution in intuitive judgment. In T. Gilovich, D. Griffin, & D. Kahneman (Eds.), *Heuristics and biases: The psychology of intuitive judgment* (pp. 49–81). New York: Cambridge University Press.

King, G. (1997). The effects of interpersonal closeness and issue seriousness on blowing the whistle. *Journal of Business Communication, 34,* 419–436.

Koehler, D. J. (1991). Explanation, imagination, and confidence in judgment. *Psychological Bulletin, 110,* 499–519.

Kogut, T., & Ritov, I. (2005a). The "identified victim" effect: An identified group, or just a single individual? *Journal of Behavioral Decision Making, 18,* 157–167.

Kogut, T., & Ritov, I. (2005b). The singularity effect of identified victims in separate and joint evaluations. *Organizational Behavior and Human Decision Processes, 97,* 106–116.

Levitt, A., & Dwyer, P. (2002). *Take on the street.* New York: Pantheon.

Lord, C. G., Ross, L., & Lepper, M. R. (1979). Biased assimilation and attitude polarization: The effects of prior theories on subsequently considered evidence. *Journal of Personality and Social Psychology, 37*, 2098–2109.

Marshall, G. W., & Mowen, J. C. (1993). An experimental investigation of the outcome bias in salesperson performance evaluations. *The Journal of Personal Selling & Sales Management, 13*(3), 1–16.

Messick, D. M. (1995). Equality, fairness, and social conflict. *Social Justice Research, 8*, 153–173.

Messick, D. M. (1996). Why ethics is not the only thing that matters. *Business Ethics Quarterly, 6*, 223–226.

Messick, D. M., & Bazerman, M. H. (1996). Ethical leadership and the psychology of decision making. *Sloan Management Review, 37*(2), 9–22.

Messick, D. M., Bloom, S., Boldizar, J. P., & Samuelson, C. D. (1985). Why we are fairer than others. *Journal of Experimental Social Psychology, 21*, 480–500.

Messick, D. M., & Sentis, K. P. (1979). Fairness and preference. *Journal of Experimental Social Psychology, 15*, 418–434.

Messick, D. M., & Sentis, K. P. (1983). Fairness, preference, and fairness biases. In D. M. Messick & K. S. Cook (Eds.), *Equity theory: Psychological and sociological perspectives* (pp. 61–94). New York: Praeger.

Messick, D. M., & Tenbrunsel, A. E. (Eds.). (1996). *Codes of conduct.* New York: Russell Sage Foundation.

Miceli, M. P., Dozier, J. B., & Near, J. P. (1991). Blowing the whistle on data fudging: A controlled field experiment. *Journal of Applied Social Psychology, 21*, 271–295.

Miller, D. T., & Ratner, R. K. (1998). The disparity between the actual and assumed power of self-interest. *Journal of Personality and Social Psychology, 74*(1), 53–62.

Moore, D., Tetlock, P. E., Tanlu, L., & Bazerman, M. (2006). Conflicts of interest and the case of auditor independence: Moral seduction and strategic issue cycling. *Academy of Management Review, 31*, 10–29.

Murnighan, J. K., Cantelon, D. A., & Elyashiv, T. (2001). Bounded personal ethics and the tap dance of real estate agency. In J. A. Wagner, J. M. Bartunek, & K. D. Elsbach (Eds.), *Advances in qualitative organization research* (Vol. 3, pp. 1–40). New York: Elsevier.

Near, J. P., & Miceli, M. P. (1985). Organizational dissidence: The case of whistle-blowing. *Journal of Business Ethics, 4*, 1–16.

Near, J. P., & Miceli, M. P. (1986). Retaliation against whistleblowers: Predictors and effects. *Journal of Applied Psychology, 71*, 137–145.

Near, J. P., & Miceli, M. P. (1995). Effective whistleblowing. *Academy of Management Review, 20*, 679–708.

Paharia, N., Kassam, K., Greene, J., & Bazerman, M. H. (2008). Washing your hands clean: Moral implications of indirect actions in business decisions. (Working paper.)

Ratner, R. K., & Miller, D. T. (2001). The norm of self-interest and its effects on social action. *Journal of Personality and Social Psychology, 81*(1), 5–16.

Ross, M., & Sicoly, F. (1979). Egocentric biases in availability and attribution. *Journal of Personality and Social Psychology, 37*, 322–336.

Royzman, E. B., & Baron, J. (2002). The preference for indirect harm. *Social Justice Research, 15*, 165–184.

Schmidt, P. (2007, September 28). At the elite colleges—dim white kids. The Boston Globe. Retrieved March 11, 2009, from http://www.boston.com/news/globe/editorial_opinion/oped/articles/2007/09/28/at_the_elite_colleges___dim_white_kids/

Simon, H. A. (1947). *Administrative behavior: A study of decision-making processes in administrative organization.* New York: Macmillan.

Simons, D. J. (2000). Current approaches to change blindness. *Visual Cognition, 7*(1–3), 1–15.

Simons, D. J., Chabris, C. F., Schnur, T., & Levin, D. T. (2002). Evidence for preserved representations in change blindness. *Consciousness & Cognition: An International Journal, 11*(1), 78–97.

Small, D. A., & Loewenstein, G. (2003). Helping the victim or helping a victim: Altruism and identifiability. *Journal of Risk and Uncertainty, 26*(1), 5–16.

Small, D. A., & Loewenstein, G. (2005). The devil you know: The effect of identifiability on punitiveness. *Journal of Behavioral Decision Making, 18*(5), 311–318.

Stanovich, K. E., & West, R. F. (2000). Individual differences in reasoning: Implications for the rationality debate. *Behavioral & Brain Sciences, 23*, 645–665.

Tenbrunsel, A. E., & Messick, D. M. (1996). Behavioral research, business ethics, and social justice. *Social Justice Research, 9*(1), 1–6.

Tenbrunsel, A. E., & Messick, D. M. (2004). Ethical fading: The role of self deception in unethical behavior. *Social Justice Research, 17*(2), 223–236.

Tenbrunsel, A. E., Smith-Crowe, K., & Umphress, E. E. (2003). Building houses on rocks: The role of ethical infrastructure in the ethical effectiveness of organizations. *Social Justice Research, 16*, 285–307.

Trevino, L. K. (1990). A cultural perspective on changing and developing organizational ethics. *Research in Organizational Change and Development, 4*, 195–230.

Trevino, L. K., & Youngblood, S. A. (1990). Bad apples in bad barrels: A causal analysis of ethical decision-making behavior. *Journal of Applied Psychology, 75*, 378–385.

11

From Theory to Practice: Messick and Morality

Kevin W. Gibson
Marquette University

J. Keith Murnighan
Northwestern University

High-stakes business decisions present unique challenges, including the need to balance rationality, relevance, and, occasionally, ethics and morality. Practically speaking, decision-makers must be able to identify both pertinent information and defensible choices. General observations of this process suggest that decision-makers often appear to use unsophisticated and sometimes inconsistent moral reasoning. We show that insights from recent social psychology can help to resolve this potential conundrum. More specifically, our chapter addresses the underpinnings of rational choice theory, identifies some of the conditions when and some of the reasons why decision-makers are so fallible, and, finally, illustrates how a set of initial assumptions can lead to more systematic business decisions.

Human commerce, both business and social, requires innumerable decisions. When ethical issues entered the mainstream of business education much of the early literature had the approach of "add theory and stir" with the assumption that theory and practice could be married straightforwardly. However, there were lingering tensions between the business impulse to maximize returns and philosophical admonitions to promote general welfare. With the emergence of stakeholder theory, managers became aware that they needed to take account of not only the interests of investors but those of everyone likely to be in a position to help or harm the company, both in the near and long term. As Mackey (2005) put it, "The enlightened corporation should try to create value for *all* of its constituencies. From an investor's perspective, the purpose of the business is to maximize profits. But that's not the purpose for other stakeholders — for customers, employees, suppliers and the community ... and each perspective is valid and legitimate."

Thus, the ethical reasoning involved in business decisions had to become more comprehensive and sophisticated, and this has been reflected in current academic literature (e.g., Greene & Haidt, 2002). At the same time, though, empirical research shows that most managers tend to operate at a fairly low level of moral reasoning (Rest, 1986; Weber, 1990). We contend that bridging this gap between academic theory and practice will require taking ethical issues seriously and addressing them with sufficient time and diligence.

People tend to make expedient decisions based on rough-and-ready ethical justifications (Jones, 1991). The merit of their decisions in large part depends on the coherence and consistency of their underlying principles. In general, principles demand deliberative effort and reflection to accurately reflect an individual's values. Moreover, even the best moral intentions must deal with a number of confounding psychological dynamics that can lead to suboptimal decisions. Hence, the moral manager has a double task: accurate assessment of his best beliefs, all things considered; and dealing with the normal tendencies to follow our biases instead of relying on objective reasoning.

In this chapter, we try to show how a moral theory embraces a wide range of concerns that are consistent with a multiple-stakeholder approach. To be practical, we also try to provide wide-ranging methods that reveal both the complexity of the model and the value of psychological insights, particularly the psychology of David Messick, in resolving some apparent inconsistencies in applying theory to day-to-day decisions. Specifically, we move from a brief description of principled reasoning to an account of one particular moral theory, utilitarianism. We have chosen utilitarianism because it is sometimes thought of as the theory most akin to business, with its demand to calculate the good and bad effects of an action, à la cost/benefit analysis. In developing the analysis we show that the theory actually demands consideration of a wide range of concerns. Thus, though it may initially seem that people take on different moral theories as their thinking moves from business to personal and societal matters, it turns out that what is going on is an ever more sophisticated application of a consistent moral theory as the circle of ethical concern widens. We illustrate this by looking at two cases that involve business decisions about the environment, because they show the complex range of issues that can be incorporated in a sophisticated analysis. We go on to say that knowing moral theory is insufficient, and that practical calculation and application require an awareness of the psychological dynamics that affect our decisions. We conclude that moral decisions would do well to blend ethical theory with insights from social psychology. This theme, not coincidentally, is completely consistent and follows the Messick approach to ethical decision-making.

PRINCIPLED REASONING

We make decisions all the time, even high-stakes decisions, without much conscious effort. At the same time, if we are called on to justify our choices, we usually appeal to principled reasoning to show that they were not merely intuitive or haphazard. We can think of the principles like grammar in speech: We all speak the language routinely, but there may be times when difficult or novel cases require reference to grammatical rules to reveal the correct usage. The grammar itself is, of course, evolving over time, but it nevertheless provides a syntax that orders linguistic content. Similarly, we rely on ethical rules to guide our behavior, even though we may not always be able to articulate them well when asked. When we do explain our behavior, though, we typically point to underlying principles. That is, rational action is more than reaction to stimuli but behavior guided by principles. However, although the principles may be fairly straightforward, their real-time manifestation is inevitably nuanced and pulls on a wider set of fundamental working assumptions. Therefore, the insights of social psychology and philosophy can be useful in parsing what may initially seem to be paradoxical or inconsistent, specifically in how businesspeople appear to deal with their own interests compared to those of third parties and the environment.

Many decisions need not involve a moral dimension: a manager, for example, may face an investment decision that involves balancing a high-risk, high-yield deal with one that has lower risk but correspondingly less risk. The associated reasoning would typically involve the projection of possible outcomes via a cost/benefit analysis in which the optimal course of action maximizes the difference between benefits and costs.

Many business decisions have limited or no moral content: they are devoid of immediate or subsequent moral implications. Instead, decision-makers act as if their decisions can be made by well-constructed algorithms that, once followed, will recommend a best available course of action. It is natural to expect that the repeated and frequent use of numerical calculations to make business decisions might become a habit. When taken to a habitual extreme, however, business decisions that do include moral implications will then fail to incorporate a careful consideration of their moral consequences. Dennis Koslowski, the former CEO of Tyco, represents one of many extreme examples. He was convicted, with his chief financial officer, of 22 of 23 counts of grand larceny, conspiracy, and securities fraud totaling $600 million. When Koslowski was asked what it was like to be paid so much — his average Tyco compensation was $100 million a year for the 4 years prior to his resignation — he did not invoke morality in any way but instead indicated that, "It's a way of keeping score, I guess."

Similar stories have repeatedly surfaced after the Enron scandal. It was not so much that the actors at Enron were greedy; instead, they were hypercompetitive — always looking at ways to quantitatively better their counterparts in competitive companies. Sadly, the predominately economic, quantitative approaches to business problems that prevail in most business schools and MBA programs reinforce these kinds of calculative mindsets.

Business decisions that include a moral element should, however, lead to what we have described elsewhere as an expanding circle of concern. Consider the case of a manager who must choose between two competing suppliers; e.g., a cheaper overseas bid versus a local company that is marginally more expensive. Although information that the local company employs mentally and physically challenged workers in its assembly plant should have no impact in a strictly economic, calculative approach to the choice, we might expect moral individuals to be affected by issues that are, strictly speaking, beyond the numbers.

A prevailing message in business has been that a manager should look solely to corporate profitability and treat other issues as secondary (Friedman, 1970). Although a singular drive to increase efficiency may seem clear, straightforward, and compelling, it subsumes a number of unspoken assumptions: it focuses on short-term results; it tends to ignore externalities; and it promotes the welfare of a specific group of stakeholders — investors. Although the basic axioms are straightforward, in practice it achieves its apparent clarity by concentrating on some results and necessarily diminishing the importance of others. In effect, it presents a complex picture more simply but only by omission. This point of view also suggests that managers can compartmentalize their psychological interests; for instance, separating what they would do as individuals from what they would do at work.

Though this approach has merit, its exclusions lead to conclusions that regard issues like the impact of business on the environment as an extraneous consideration. A more expansive, inclusive approach would consider business issues in terms of many stakeholders and their potential to help or hurt the firm (e.g., Freeman, 1994). This expanded reasoning now integrates the potential impact of a decision on other parties and brings in nonfinancial factors. The decision procedure has not changed — it still focuses on outcomes — but we now expand the factors that a decision-maker must consider.

Take another case, for example, of a construction firm that has invented a device that increases the safety of using cranes. It then faces the dilemma of whether it should share its invention with its competitors: Patenting the device would be profitable but slow; i.e., taking over 2 years before they can market the new device. Alternatively, it could share the design immediately with its competitors and forego the profits but save lives without delay. A singular motive to profit maximize would suggest patenting the device. Overall societal welfare, in contrast, would trump these potential profits. The broader perspective raises more moral issues, and even the decision to ignore questions that go beyond the short-term bottom line manifests a clear moral stance.

We now consider a specific form of moral theory — utilitarianism — as an illustration of the increasing complexity of moral thinking. We then turn to two business cases that have an environmental component, chosen because they involve a wide array of moral concerns and many stakeholders. They also demonstrate well how practical matters such as assessing valuation embedded in the theory are subject to psychological dynamics and how we need to integrate those findings.

UTILITARIANISM

Utilitarianism maintains that the moral worth of an action should depend on its outcome (rather than, say, the motives involved). Utility is a measure of human welfare. Bentham (1789/1970) sought an empirical model of morality that could be useful in comparing alternative courses of action. He created what he termed the *hedonic calculus*, where we look at the amount of pleasure created in seven different dimensions: intensity; duration; certainty (the probability of it coming about); propinquity (how accessible it is); fecundity (the ability to generate other pleasures); purity (the freedom from associated pains); and extent (the number affected by it). In a crude example, we might think of attending a football game in winter. The pleasures involved will vary in intensity; for instance, when a field goal is scored. Moreover, the game may give many people pleasure, and they will have the added ability to benefit in recalling the plays. At the same time, the physical discomfort and commute to the game will detract from the enjoyment. Bentham's focus on assessments of intensity presaged current discussions of the importance of moral intensity (Jones, 1991) in ethical decision-making, which psychological research suggests has considerable influence over our decisions.

The more well-known philosopher of utilitarianism is John Stuart Mill (1806–1873; 1863/2001), who refined and popularized the theory. Mill's greatest happiness principle suggested that we should act to bring about the maximum good for the maximum number:

> Actions are right in proportion as they tend to promote happiness, wrong as they tend to produce the reverse of happiness. By happiness is intended pleasure, and the absence of pain; by unhappiness, pain and the privation of pleasure. (p. 7)

In short, decision-makers should anticipate potential outcomes and select the alternative that gives greatest happiness or least pain. Thus, utilitarianism provides a convenient, reliable, and defensible ethical directive; it also is completely consistent with familiar cost/benefit analyses.

Mill viewed happiness broadly, as an intrinsic good. For him, even an excited student who works to the point of exhaustion might qualify as being happy, because the activity brings personal fulfillment. The language of maximizing happiness, pleasure, or good has recently been replaced by assessments of utility: Maximizing utility means assessing individuals' preferences and selecting the option that, in the aggregate, gives most people as much utility as possible.

An important part of a practical, more readily implementable approach to maximizing benefit adds the concept of benign self-interest. For example, risky, short-term cooperation in a mutual venture might still proceed when it is accompanied by an expectation of future reciprocal benefits. Thus, donating blood may result from a logic that supporting an institution now facilitates its long-term survival, which can provide direct benefits to a current donor if, in the future, they too need more blood than they can personally produce. Even more abstractly, it may also be more pleasant for a donor to live in a community where people are charitable.

A key assumption of utilitarianism, then, is that morality does not arise solely from moral impulses but from reasoned strategies in the context of human community. Indifference to others unless it affects us personally ignores the fact that we live in communities and exchange goods and services; i.e., we may be best served by mutual cooperation. A challenge that it has to confront, though, is whether self-interested action will lead to destructive competition or cooperation.

Thomas Hobbes (1588–1679; 1651/1929) assumed that self-interest in an unregulated competitive environment would necessarily lead to destructive behavior:

> Every man is enemy to every man, the same consequent to the time wherein men live without other security than what their own strength and their own invention shall furnish them withal. In such condition there is no place for industry, because the fruit thereof is uncertain: and consequently no culture of the earth…no arts; no letters; no society; and which is worst of all, continual fear, and danger of violent death; and the life of man, solitary, poor, nasty, brutish, and short. (p. 97)

His proposed response was to organize society to impose potentially horrific sanctions on wrongdoers, so that people are effectively compelled to cooperate.

Other, less self-directed options, however, can also emerge, especially if we assume that many (if not most) interactions are non-zero-sum; i.e., greater payoffs result from working together. Even direct competitors — if they expect each other to exist for some time — are not served by unmitigated competitive acts but rather by knowing the range of potential bargaining outcomes and acting rationally. Numerous empirical studies document how, in situations that can be either cooperative or competitive, the competitive actions of one party not only stimulate competition by the other, to their mutual disbenefit, but make restoring future cooperation increasingly difficult (e.g., Bottom, Gibson, Walker, & Murnighan, 2002).

Contemporary philosophers — e.g., David Gauthier in his *Morals by Agreement* and Peter Danielson in his *Artificial Morality* — have used these kinds of game theoretic, empirical findings to underpin a morality of benign self-interest. Gauthier (1986) starts with the standard rational, economic assumption that people are most concerned with their own personal welfare and will work to maximize it. He also suggests that we will be indifferent to the welfare of others, unless it affects our personal benefit (Gauthier, 1986). He follows standard economics even further by suggesting that we rationally respond to others' anticipated actions, what he terms the *centroid utility-maximizing response*. He gives credence to empirical results by suggesting that people will constrain their short-term behaviors to satisfy their long-term interests, and that two parties could potentially enhance each other's utility at no cost, but "the structure of some interactions leads to a formal selfishness. ... [Parties] could maximize each other's utility at no personal cost, but it would seem that neither has reason to do so ..." (Gauthier, 1986, p. 73). His focus, then, is directly oriented toward self-interest with little incentive to go beyond personal advantage.

Danielson, in contrast, suggests that cooperation should only result from reciprocity. Gauthier presumes that others will realize the long-term benefits of initial cooperation; Danielson (1992) warns that it is crucial that we are able to "identify other cooperators, or similarly constrained players, or, in Chicken, unreasoning threateners. ... One way to do this is by means of transparently public principles, which others can test and copy" (p. 196) A correlate of this view is that morality need not be an exclusively human activity: We could potentially program a computer to make our decisions; or, as Danielson indicates, if organizational decision processes were transparent, corporations would naturally act to maximize their returns, their actions would be thoroughly predictable, and they might very well be more moral than their individual human counterparts.

Although these models appear to presume that moral agents are thoroughly rational and are capable of accurate and comprehensive calculation, humans are often subrational and fallible in their decision-making. This fact does not undermine normative morality, of course. Rather, it means that any theory of applied ethics needs to consider the subtleties of individuals' psychological dynamics, the fallibility of our assessments and projections, and, as we shall see, the complexities of human motivation, all of which are immensely difficult to reduce to a crude algorithm. Thus, game theoretic findings are only as robust as the psychological models they incorporate. Without a sophisticated model of ethical thinking and psychological forces that affect rationality, game theoretic models like Gauthier's will inevitably be somewhat crude. Thus, for example, subjects in prisoner dilemma games quite routinely go against instructions that tell them to maximize profits above all considerations, especially when their most rational strategies contradict their personal sense of fairness or justice.

A further feature that distinguishes the strategic and the moral distinction considers whether to consider unintended consequences in our moral assessments. Utilitarianism is forward-looking and therefore projects our best assessment of likely outcomes. However, as is often apparent, unfortunate or unseen consequences are common events. A *consequentialist* view criticizes utility theory because it is mainly prescriptive in telling us what we should do based on probabilities; when the focus is primarily on all of the consequences, rather than just those the decision-makers projected, they become morally responsible for every result, even those that are unforeseen. In short, a consequentialist view claims that our moral approach should not only be about right and wrong but about praise and blame; advocates contend that any adequate moral theory must incorporate the psychology of motives and intentions (Anscombe, 1958).

David Messick (1998) has distinguished "specific outcome consequentialists" and "a priori expected utility consequentialists": The former consider an immediate result; the latter consider decisions "based on the expected utility created across the possibilities of the set of possible outcomes, based on the value system of the decision maker" (p. 477). Going beyond immediate, specific outcomes suggests that managers have a moral duty to consider the wide-ranging effects of their actions before they act. After due consideration a manager may feel that immediate, self-interested results matter most; at the same time, it seems morally wrong to make choices without deliberating about values and the effects of actions. Yet social psychology tells us that people can be particularly short-sighted; that is, not intentionally but inadvertently wrong, due to normal human omissions (e.g., Bazerman & Banaji, 2004; Murnighan, Cantelon, & Elyashiv, 2001).

INTERNAL AND EXTERNAL BENEFITS

Benefits do not have to be commodities — we might enjoy a sunset, and that experience cannot be transferred to others except via the description of an internal mental state. Indeed, people might pay for the opportunity to have that experience, but it is inevitably private. (We could contrast this to a fictional memory implant, where the experience is a commodity, but we are far from that technology and the morality it might engender.) People are willing to pay for many mental experiences; e.g., giving money to preserve penguins in their native habitat. In this case, contributors receive a positive feeling and knowledge of their own beneficence even though they never see a penguin in the wild.

Many economic theories can account for this behavior: *Homo economicus* is not defeated by nonfungible rewards — paying for mental experiences can be completely rational. At the same time, however, these examples focus on the need for a better idea of what constitutes a benefit in the calculus of utilitarianism. In his seminal paper, Amartya Sen (1985) critiques rational choice theory by distinguishing (a) self-interest, (b) sympathy, and (c) commitment (Peter & Schmid, 2005). For Sen, sympathy describes the beneficial feelings that result from incorporating others' welfare in our decision processes; e.g., when we donate to charity. (In social psychological terms, the same concept is termed *social utility*; Loewenstein, Thompson, & Bazerman, 1989). Commitment represents a spur to action that is unrelated to our personal welfare; e.g., when we get involved in activities that do not provide us direct benefits and might even lead us to incur losses.

Including commitment in a rational choice model confounds the direct link between choice and welfare; it also means that people's choices do not always exclusively consider their own personal objectives. Sen (2005) analyzed rational choice as using the self in three different ways, via "self-centered welfare," a "self-welfare goal," and "self-goal choice":

Self-centered welfare: Personal welfare depends only on an individual's own consumption, which eliminates sympathy or antipathy toward others as well as the effects of processes and relational concerns on one's own welfare.

Self-welfare goal: A person's only goal is to maximize his or her own welfare, which eliminates other considerations (such as the welfare of others) *unless they influence the person's own welfare.*

Self-goal choice: Choices must be based on the pursuit of an individual's own goals, which eliminates any effect of the recognition of others' goals *unless they influence the person's own goals.* (p. 6)

Sen's concept of commitment gives explanatory force to behaviors that conflict with contemporary rational choice theory. Essentially, he challenges the assumption that people will make rational choices and then act on them as standard economic theory suggests. Thus, he describes people who neglect commitments and concentrate only on personal welfare as "rational fools." A particularly apt application of these concerns is an issue that has captured considerable attention for current business decisions; i.e., how to incorporate environmentally aware thinking, given both strategic and moral concerns.

BUSINESS AND THE ENVIRONMENT

At the time of writing this chapter (mid-2008), the American retail industry is awash with concerns that they be "green"; i.e., environmentally aware. Popular discourse in the media presents a clear, strong conclusion: a more aware, more caring public will reject products and services that are created and promoted without attending to environmental concerns. This makes careful consideration of environmental issues important for business decisions and strategies; it also provides a useful topic to test our ethical assumptions, because the harm to people from not considering the environment carefully may be remote for a business's daily concerns and deliberations.

People's normal concerns are generally anthropocentric: we care about the welfare of animals and the planet because they can affect our future welfare. Thus "The Ethical Framework of Economics: Utilitarianism" section of *Technology, Humans and Society: Towards a Sustainable World* (Dorf, 2001) states:

> As a starting point, economics analysts are concerned with *human* welfare or well-being. From the economic perspective, the environment should be protected for the material benefit of humanity and not for strictly moral or ethical reasons. To an economist, saving the blue whale from extinction is valuable only insofar as doing so yields happiness (or prevents tragedy) for present or future generations of people. The existence of the whale independent of people is of no importance. This human-centered ... moral foundation underlying economic analysis, which has as its goal human happiness or utility, is known as utilitarianism. (p. 53)

Another example: the slogan of the National Forests, "Land of Many Uses," implies a consideration of multiple factors and trade-offs: Preservation may have human value, but it can be balanced against other interests, including recreation and resource extraction. At this point, let us turn to two examples that show how the interplay between business and environmental interests demand nuanced moral theory tempered by psychological findings.

CASE #1: GETTYSBURG

The Gettysburg battlefield in Pennsylvania is preserved as a national park, monument, and educational center, commemorating the American Civil War battle that killed 51,000 in 1863. The park has about 2 million visitors annually. A recent proposal to build a new museum and visitor center, costing some $125 million, has provoked considerable controversy: opponents of the plan note that the expanded facilities will have a negative impact on the environmental integrity of the site; proponents counter by arguing that the Park Service will be better able to attract and educate visitors. If net benefit maximization is the goal, then operating Gettysburg as a Disney theme park becomes a realistic option.

The difficult question is how to frame the debate. If we accept that battlefields are not inherently immune from development (for example,

Bunker Hill in Boston is highly developed and sought-after real estate), then the central utilitarian issue becomes how to best gauge public preferences. With complete and perfect information, people will be aware of the proposed development and can indicate whether they would invest in it, ignore it, or pay to stop it. How much they are willing to pay for the two alternatives could then provide a good indicator of the strength of their support or their opposition. At some payment point, each side should express indifference between paying more or conceding to the other side. By this economic approach, values and monetary commitments are directly correlated.

The amount that people would be charged at the battlefield, however, may not reflect the willingness to pay of people who are not completely aware of the issue. This necessitates a method that will approximate their desires and interests by extrapolating the preferences of a sample of informed people to a more general group (Krutilla, 1967).

The U.S. government provides a recent example of this approach, addressing the regulation of development to preserve fish habitat in the Four Corners region in the American West. A survey asked respondents how much they would be willing to pay to support the habitat. All U.S. taxpayers in the area would be solicited; if a majority would contribute, the fish would be protected from extinction. Respondents were also told that if most people voted against the proposal, four species of fish would very likely become extinct. Those voting for the proposal were asked to put down an amount that they would be willing to contribute. When the survey was sent to a sample of 1,600 households, the average amount pledged was just under $200 each. Extrapolating this amount nationally gives a figure that outweighs the local benefits of development (Barrens, Ganderton, & Silva, 1996; Brookshire, McKee, & Watts, 1994).

In the case of the Gettysburg battlefield, then, the controversy could be resolved in purely economic terms: those who support development can be bought off. Supporters of preserving the area can either muster financial support directly or make their case based on contingent valuation. Making the argument monetary allows both sides the opportunity to generate data to support their claims, and the overall policy can be decided on a purportedly objective basis dealing with the amount of anticipated benefit or costs against the normative backdrop that we should always seek to maximize benefits. A strictly monetary approach, however, ignores a host of intangible benefits, including the educational benefits for visiting students, the pride that might be felt by ancestors of the soldiers involved, and a sense of national heritage in a historic site.

CASE #2: INDIAN SHRIMP FISHING

A second example — one that provides a more easily identified set of criteria — involves shrimp fishing in equatorial regions, specifically in India. Shrimp used to be considered a delicacy in many parts of the world, but modern farming methods have increased their supply and reduced their cost: worldwide shrimp production has quadrupled between 1985 and 2005 (Food and Agriculture Organization of the United Nations, 2007). The coastline of India is one of the world's richest sources of shrimp, especially large tiger shrimp. In the early 1990s, the Indian government was eager to promote economic development, and with assistance from the World Bank actively recruited international companies to harvest seafood (Lewis, Philipps, Cough, & Macintosh, 2003). Currently India produces about 3 million tons of shrimp annually, about 80% of its seafood exports (Ramalingam, 1990). The offshore catch of shrimp by mechanized vessels including trawlers was initially high but dropped significantly as stocks were depleted. This led to the development of shrimp farms in the mangrove swamps, where the brackish water proved to be an ideal environment. The areas were cleared of vegetation to create ponds, which were then stocked with shrimp larvae.

In business terms, the enterprise has been a success for both the companies and the host nation — that is, the industry has been profitable and a significant source of hard currency. As the publicity materials from one producer (Siam Canadian Foods, 2004) note:

> As there is a growing demand for India shrimp in the markets abroad, farmers in Kerala have converted uneconomical paddy fields into farms by taking them on lease. ... This helps the livelihood of the poor, through food supply, employment and income. ... The shrimp culture has boomed in India mainly because of the liberalization of the economy, high profitability and a good international market. The government has highlighted

shrimp culture of India shrimp because it increases exports and brings in foreign exchange reserves. ... Industrialists can now lease vast land areas along the coast on favorable terms. Along with this, financial institutions give liberal credit and the government also gives subsidies.

The case of Indian shrimp illustrates just how carefully we need to apply a utilitarian calculus. Although the data clearly indicate that the investors, the government, and the ultimate consumers all stand to gain financially, and the land may be better utilized as well, these numbers do not tell the whole story.

Shrimp are bottom-feeders: harvesting them requires churning up the water bed. Farmed shrimp are inefficient eaters: they consume fish bycatch and protein pellets, but they eat less than 20% of a farmer's offerings, leaving rotting protein in the water (Shiva, n.d.). This leads to the need to add antibiotics to the water, along with pesticides and detergents. The water also needs to be aerated to prevent bacterial growth, resulting in greater evaporation and increased salinity that is then counteracted by adding more fresh water. Prior to the intrusion of shrimp farms, a single hectare of mangrove forest could sustain 10 equatorial families. In contrast, a 110-hectare shrimp farm employs six people during the year and five more during harvest (Shanahan, 2003). Thus, the shrimp farms have displaced local farmers and traditional sustenance activities have become untenable.

The shrimping industry can be highly lucrative, because most shrimp are exported to Japan and the United States. At the same time, the new farms have displaced coastal populations, destroyed traditional livelihoods, polluted wells with chemicals and salt, and decimated local fish stocks. The saline water also renders surrounding areas infertile, and because of the buildup of chemical sludge in the bottom of the ponds, they have to be abandoned after about 10 years. Workers in the ponds also spend hours in brackish water. In 1996 the Indian courts heard cases on behalf of dislodged people and ruled to curtail the industry; those verdicts have never been enforced.

These two examples show what we earlier called the *expanding circle of ethical concern*. Both cases could be treated with straightforward cost/benefit analyses, without any apparent normative dimension; this would give primacy to economic efficiency, narrowly understood. In many cases this is entirely appropriate. Yet issues that have a wider range of consequences require more sophisticated moral models. Treating Gettysburg simply as undeveloped real estate ignores the significant cultural and historical value it has for many people; analyzing shrimp farms without incorporating their effects on the local population, the environment, and its sustainability risks serious utility miscalculations. Capturing these wider effects requires a more subtle moral theory. At the same time, enacting more comprehensive moral judgments creates psychological dynamics that can lead to irrational or hasty decisions.

SOCIAL PSYCHOLOGY AND THE UTILITARIAN DEBATE

Initially it might seem that a utilitarian approach would support development in both Gettysburg and in India: the rational calculus of economic benefits is completely consistent with the reasoning behind a purely business decision. Insights from social psychology, however, suggest that the issues are considerably more nuanced. As Messick (Bazerman & Messick, 1998) puts it: "[Our work] offers a precise definition of rationality. It embodies the consistency principles that underlie expected utility maximization, and reflects neoclassical micro-economics. *It is also consistent with what subjects would desire with more insight, thought and reflection* [italics added]" (p. 478). Messick's (2004) utilitarian decision-maker would consider the issues broadly, including its non-commodifiable aspects: "*I suggest the most fundamental element ... may be the tendency of humans and other species to experience the world in evaluative terms* [italics added]" (p. 129) It is not necessarily that managers use different kinds of thinking for different cases but more that the reflective and evaluative elements become more or less immediate as factors in some of their decisions but not others.

It is not surprising that many individuals making business decisions focus on calculative forms of utility maximization. Before crowning them as thoroughgoing utilitarians, however, they need to satisfy two significant criteria that are often overlooked, especially when utilitarianism is conflated with cost/benefit analysis: the first is impartiality; the second is sympathy.

Mill (1863/2001) and his philosophical compatriots viewed people as truly equal; i.e., the good of any other person is equal to my own. This approach to utilitarianism deemphasizes the target of economic allocations and focuses solely on increasing the amount of good in the world. It also includes an implicit value; i.e., a true concern for others, who all count as moral equals. In practical terms, this means that we cannot give our friends and families moral preference: a worker in an apparel factory in an undeveloped country should have the same standing and entitlements as our own child.

In addition, the theory assumes that decision-makers have an obligation to everyone who is affected by a moral decision. Thus, we cannot benefit a few well-off consumers if it means that a larger group will suffer. Mill (1863/2001) also believed that we have a natural sympathy to one another and that we are capable of distancing ourselves sufficiently to make impartial moral decisions. Adam Smith agreed. (He also objected to the purchase of unnecessary luxury goods for personal use; Smith, 1970.) This makes it clear that a well-developed view of rational choice and utilitarianism should incorporate Sen's (2005) concepts of self-interest and sympathy.

This distinction also helps to explain the apparent subrational responses that some players choose in prisoners' dilemma games, which we would characterize as being complex rather than irrational or ignorant. Hence we would disagree with Rapoport and Chammah (1965) when they say, "Evidently the run-of-the-mill players are not strategically sophisticated enough to have figured out that the Defect/Defect strategy is the only rationally defensible strategy, and this intellectual short-coming saves them from losing" (p. 29).

At this point we can see how philosophical distinctions will be useful. The repeated, habitual approach to business decisions — careful, cost-benefit calculations — simplifies and accelerates decision-making in a speed-driven, cost-focused world. This is perfectly appropriate for non-moral business decisions but is overutilized when morality surfaces in business contexts.

In other contexts, however, decision-makers are quite adept at incorporating moral concerns and moral philosophy into their decisions; i.e., when they categorize their decisions as personal rather than as business decisions. Another, better way of saying this is that people use crude utilitarianism for their business decisions but a more sophisticated version when they deal with issues that affect them personally. When social situations activate social concerns, individuals are naturally more likely to consider the social impact of their decisions.

Messick and Sentis (1979), for instance, astutely noted that individuals' preferences precede their rational calculations. Thus, particularly when situations put them into disadvantaged positions, their expanded personal concerns naturally connect to issues of fairness, in addition to immediate concerns for impersonal, everyone-is-equal costs and benefits.

Lawrence Kohlberg's (1981) famous framework has provided excellent insight into the way that people make moral judgments and the reasons that they use for their actions. Kohlberg suggests that, as people mature, they move through four developmental stages, from preconventional to conventional to postconventional morality, which includes considerations of fairness and individual rights and, finally, to universal principles in the pursuit of democratic justice.

It is important to note, however, that Kohlberg (1987) specifically encouraged his respondents to answer at the highest level of moral development that they had reached. People make most of their moral decisions, in contrast, within a particular situational context and often under pressure. Recall, too, that Bentham (1789/1970) pointed out that we should look at both the overall effects of our actions and the intensity of our internal psychological experience in determining morality. Accordingly, we must not only consider Kohlberg's vertical levels of moral deliberation that move from pure self-interest to considerations of the welfare of all; we should also examine the horizontal axis, i.e., the vividness of personal experience associated with any value-based decision.

When we apply this reasoning to work contexts, we must consider at least two critical factors, because people do not always act at their own highest level of moral maturity. A manager's job is to manage, to make decisions, to get things done, to solve problems. Under normal conditions of time and other pressures, people act to expedite solutions and minimize hassle. When people have the opportunity to answer interview questions deliberately, they can easily provide an artificial picture of what they would like to think that they would do. As a result, their interview responses may not reflect what they would actually do or what they know they should do in realistic, hectic, time-pressured, real-life predicaments. Moreover, in an organizational context, organizational loyalty and a desire for job security can also be influential. Weber (1991), for instance, found that as a managerial dilemma became more abstract and removed from everyday experience, deliberation became more elaborate and, conversely, if people thought they were familiar with the situation, they became far less reflective. He also found that, in answer to questions about morality and the organization, people's predicted actions adjusted to the context but not always positively: with increased understanding and increasing external pressures, they indicated that they would become more subservient and deliberated less. The simple lesson here is that careful moral judgments are particularly difficult: common psychological dynamics constantly work against us doing what we know to be best.

Many other psychological influences can add to this problem, further skewing ethical decision-making. The following sections are selective rather than exhaustive.

Framing Effects

The Gettysburg case centers on the notion of valuation: both sides of the debate accept that we can put a price on preservation and development; the focus is on how to best determine the appropriate numbers. An examination of the proponents' claims, however, indicates that they typically ignore whether the change is perceived as a gain or a loss. Consider an example in which one company decreases its salaries 7% in a recession with no inflation, whereas another increases salaries 5% when there is 12% inflation. Objectively the effects are the same, but in a survey of managers 60% thought the actions in the first case were unfair but only 22% had similar judgments in the second case (e.g., Kahneman, Knetsch, & Thaler, 1986).

Kahneman and Tversky (1979) have taught us that the framing or presentation of a problem can substantially affect our judgments about utility. For instance, the government asked individuals how much they would be willing to contribute to preserve fish from extinction. In this question, the question framed the issue as a monetary contribution versus a loss of fish. If the question had been reframed, say, as a loss of money and a gain in the tax base — e.g., "You will each have to pay an additional $200 environmental tax" — there might have been an altogether different result.

Clearly, evaluative terms can influence utility calculations; Messick (2004) notes that evaluations are both inevitable and fundamental to the way that we see the world. The apparent objectivity of valuation claims, however, is subject to their contextual framework, which can lead to a shift in our estimates of value. Consequently, people react more to dramatic, well-publicized, singular events (for example, when pictures of a child stuck in a pipe are on the front page of newspapers) than they do to data that documents which course of action truly benefits the maximum number (e.g., Small, Loewenstein, & Strand, 2006).

How issues are presented and understood can also be critical to moral decisions: If we consider the shrimp industry through the lens of a country desperate to boost foreign investment we are likely to come to one answer; if we see it in terms of its long-term effects on communities and the environment we may come to another.

Commitment

Sen's (1985) insights on commitment also apply directly to the psychological barriers to optimal decision-making. The standard economic view is that people will not incur a cost without obtaining at least a commensurate benefit. Adding a sense of commitment to the equation, however, makes it clear that people will pay for projects and causes, with no demand for direct benefit at all. This sort of reaction is often discounted as irrational or ignorant even though it may signify a deep expression of personal values.

Cultural and religious sites such as Gettysburg provide perfect examples: people support their protection even when their costs far outweigh any direct, measurable gains. So a billionaire may want to purchase the picture *Whistler's Mother* to use it as fuel for his fireplace, but concerned individuals would likely mobilize the political process to prevent the sale or raise sufficient funds to make the buyer indifferent to the purchase — even though a facsimile of the painting might provide the same aesthetic pleasure and many donors might never see the original in person. In sum, we often value heritage in terms other than our personal welfare and this may not be irrational.

Preference Adaptation

One of Aesop's fables clearly describes the concept of preference adaptation. As the story goes, a fox spies some juicy grapes hanging on a vine, but despite his efforts, he is unable to reach them. This leads him to retire, making the resentful comment that they were probably sour anyway. They were attractive when he thought that he could reach them, but he reactively devalued them once he realized that he could not (Ross & Stillinger, 1991). The same may be true of our own preferences. Many students have expressed strong desires to become medical doctors, and many have worked hard to achieve this goal. When they encounter seemingly insurmountable obstacles, however, like a class in organic chemistry, some readjust their preferences to accommodate their new, fresh perspective, and an alternate career path suddenly seems more attractive.

Thus, preferences are rarely fixed; framing can easily change them, as can the contextual background, leading to a shift in our perspectives. Responsible users of individual valuations, especially contingent valuations, then, need to consider these psychological facts; using a crude, "one-size-fits-all" conception of personal utility functions can lead to biased, unrepresentative decisions.

Challenges to Impartiality — Ingroup Biases

As noted, morality often requires impartiality. Sometimes this demand can be relaxed in favor of other considerations: it might be appropriate to save your mother rather than a stranger from a burning building, for example, based on the utility we all gain from familial bonds. At the same time, we must ask whether we are favoring a person or group (or conversely, handicapping them) for sound reasons: It may be fine to save your mother in this case but morally suspect if you favor someone of your race or gender on those grounds alone.

There has been a considerable amount of work done in social psychology on ingroup bias (e.g., Messick, 1974). As Sumner described the phenomenon in 1906:

> The insiders in a we-group are in a relation of peace, order, law, government, and industry, to each other. Their relation to all outsiders, or others-groups, is one of war and plunder. ... Sentiments are produced to correspond. Loyalty to the group, sacrifice for it, hatred and contempt for outsiders, brotherhood within, warlikeness without — all grow together, common products of the same situation. (p. 12)

One consequence of looking at the world in terms of social categories is that ingroup members are thought of and treated more favorably than outgroup members. As Messick and others have argued, a more even-handed solution would extend ingroup membership rather than eliminating group differentiation completely. Hence, companies are better off creating more inclusive, superordinate categories; this can also increase feelings of identity among previously ignored social categories. In local terms, this may equate to an emphasis on being a team member or associate of the corporation.

This approach may run into considerable difficulty, however, overcoming the entrenched differentiation between, say, a middle-class American and a coastal villager in India (Messick, 1998). Social categorizations are often unconscious and automatic. Hence, moral appeals to our common humanity, although a philosophical ideal, may encounter significant resistance that will be difficult to overcome (Porter, 1987).

Temporal Traps

As noted, utilitarian theory must realistically assess future costs to make appropriate decisions. Many of our actions have a temporal component: current decisions often have delayed effects. Without immediate negative feedback, though, people naturally discount future costs (Loewenstein, 2006). This appears to be true not only for hard-to-imagine cases (a smoker thinking of the prospect of cancer or individuals trying to fathom the wide-ranging possibilities of global climate change) but for straightforward tasks and events.

Messick and McLelland (1983) has described the effect of ignoring long-term effects as a "temporal trap" (p. 105). In their review of social dilemmas, Messick and Brewer (1983) surveyed how experimental participants regarded the harm that would come to a common good through excessive harvesting over time. One result was that individuals tended to overestimate the amount they could acquire in the near term without depleting the common pool and then underestimated the individual contributions that would be needed to achieve sustainability (Messick & McLelland, 1983). If we extrapolate this finding to our case of shrimp farming, we can see how even rational agents are liable to mistake the impact of industrial aquaculture for the overall good. Messick (1983) also noted that the effect is magnified for groups compared to individual decision-makers. Thus, at the corporate level, even with the best of intentions, projections that promote sustainability may fall short — even when a business plan consciously considers overall welfare and sustainability.

CONCLUSION — THE MORAL MANAGER

We started with the observation that decision-makers seem to invoke different sorts of reasoning when making moral choices. Expedient decisions can be based on rough-and-ready ethical justifications, whereas principled ethical action requires deliberative reflection that can be difficult to put into action. Although people seem to use convenient, pluralistic moral models when they face moral decisions, we may in fact be observing a natural progression to more sophisticated reasoning as decision situations become more personal.

Several forces promote abbreviated moral choices: assumptions of familiarity, restriction of information, time pressure, and various psychological heuristics and biases that delimit (even unconsciously) consideration to only a limited number of salient factors, making it look as if we are drawing on different principles at different times. The Gettysburg case, for example, indicates how reducing a decision to a consideration of costs and benefits fails to do justice to personal commitments. Expanding the range of issues under consideration, although seemingly subrational in economic terms, may actually result in principled moral decisions based on a more comprehensive understanding of a fully articulated utilitarian theory. Similarly, in the case of shrimp farms in India, reasoning that encourages large-scale development, though not necessarily wrong, is clearly liable to the traps of insufficient information and psychological biases that hinder thinking at the highest, broadest levels of moral deliberation.

To actively consider moral principles and an individual's own basic values demands deliberative effort and reflection. Merely realizing what we ought to do has almost never been sufficient; ethicists have long been aware of the gap between what we know we should do and the way we actually behave. Social psychology has built an impressive knowledge base that has repeatedly demonstrated that we are also subject to a number of confounding psychological dynamics that can hamper optimal decision-making. Hence, a manager who intends to be moral has a sizable task: accurate assessment of his best beliefs, careful consideration of diverse social effects, plus conscious adjustments to counteract our natural biases. The fact that many decisions are made in haste, or in a context in which we think we are familiar with the situation and its contingencies, means that sophisticated ethical reasoning may be exceedingly unlikely.

These findings are not altogether negative, though, and are not a recipe for moral despair in the face of difficult decisions. Ethical choices, especially in business settings, require substantial time and effort. Time is a precious commodity, especially when it is devoted to moral reflection, but wisdom resists urgency and equips decision-makers with the opportunity to make hard moral choices, even under pressure. Philosophical insights alone will not be sufficient to guarantee moral action. Instead, ethical awareness must be allied with a keen awareness of the psychological dynamics illustrated by empirical research.

REFERENCES

Anscombe, G. E. M. (1958). Modern moral philosophy. *Philosophy, 33*, 1–19.

Barrens, R., Ganderton, P., & Silva, C. (1996). Valuing the protection of minimum instream flows in New Mexico. *Journal of Agricultural and Resource Economics, 21*(2), 294–309.

Bazerman, M., & Messick, D. M. (1998). On the power of a clear definition of rationality. *Business Ethics Quarterly, 8*(3), 477–480.

Bazerman, M. H., & Banaji, M. R. (2004). The social psychology of ordinary ethical failures. *Social Justice Research, 17*, 111–115.

Bentham, J. (1970). *An introduction to the principles of morals and legislation*. In J. H. Burns and H. L. A. Hart (Eds.), Collected Works (pp. 38–41). London: Athlone. (Original work published 1789.)

Bottom, B., Gibson, K., Walker, S., & Murnighan, J. K. (2002). When talk is not cheap: Substantive penance and expressions of intent in the reestablishment of cooperation. *Organization Science, 13*(2), 497–513.

Brookshire, D., McKee, M., & Watts, G. (1994). Economic analysis of critical habitat designation in the Colorado River Basin for the razorback sucker, humpback chub, colorado squawfish and bonytail. Retrieved August 2, 2008, from http://www.ecosystemvaluation.org

Danielson, P. (1992). *Artificial morality*. London: Routledge.

Dorf, R. C. (2001). *Technology, humans and society: Towards a sustainable world*. New York: Elsevier.

Food and Agriculture Organization of the United Nations. (2007). *Fish utilization*. Retrieved November 12, 2007, from http://www.fao.org/docrep/005/y7300e/y7300e05.htm

Freeman, R. E. (1994). A stakeholder theory of the modern corporation. In T. Beauchamp & N. Bowie (Eds.), *Ethical theory and business* (pp. 66–76). Englewood Cliffs, NJ: Prentice-Hall.

Friedman, M. (1970, September). The social responsibility of business is to increase its profits. *New York Times Magazine*, pp. 32, 33, 122, 124, 126.

Gautier, D. (1986). Morals by agreement. New York: Oxford University Press.

Greene, J., & Haidt, J. (2002). How (and where) does moral judgment work? *Trends in Cognitive Sciences, 6*(12), 517–523.

Hobbes, T. (1929). *Leviathan*. Oxford, UK: Oxford University Press. (Original work published 1651)

Jones, T. M. (1991). Ethical decision making by individuals in organizations: An issue-contingent model. *The Academy of Management Review, 16*(2), 366–395.

Kahneman, D., Knetsch, J. L., & Thaler, R. H. (1986). Fairness and the assumptions of economics. *The Journal of Business, 59*, S285–S300.

Kahneman, D., & Tversky, A. (1979). Prospect theory. *Econometrica, 47*(2), 263–292.

Kohlberg, L. (1981). *Essays on moral development, Vol. 1*. San Francisco: Harper & Row.

Krutilla, J. (1967). Conservation reconsidered. *The American Economic Review, 57*, 777–786.

Lewis, R., Philipps, M. J., Cough, B., & Macintosh, D. J. (2007). *Thematic review on coastal wetland habitats and shrimp aquaculture*. Retrieved November 12, 2007, from World Bank/NACA/WWF/FAO Consortium Program on Shrimp Farming and the Environment Web site: http://library.enaca.org/Shrimp/Case/Thematic/FinalMangrove.pdf

Loewenstein, G. (2006). *Intertemporal choice*. New York: Oxford University Press.

Loewenstein, G., Thompson, L., & Bazerman, M. H. (1989). Social utility and decision making in interpersonal contexts. *Journal of Personality and Social Psychology, 57*(3), 426–441.

Mackey, J. (2005, October). Rethinking the social responsibility of business. *Reason*, 15–23.

Messick, D. M. (1974). When a little "group interest" goes a long way. *Organizational Behavior and Human Performance*, (12), 331–334.

Messick, D. M. (1998). Social categories and business ethics. In R. E. Freeman (Series Ed.) & P. H. Werhane (Vol. Ed.), *Ruffin series in business ethics: Vol. 1. New approaches to business ethics*. Charlottesville, VA: Philosophy Documentation Center, 149–172.

Messick, D. M. (2004). Human nature and business ethics. In R. E. Freeman (Series Ed.) & P. H. Werhane (Vol. Ed.), *Ruffin series in business ethics: Vol. 4. Business, science, and ethics*. Charlottesville, VA: Philosophy Documentation Center, 129–133.

Messick, D. M., & Brewer, M. B. (1983). Solving social dilemmas: A review. In L. Wheeler & P. Shaver (Eds.), *Review of Personality and Social Psychology* (Vol. 4, pp. 11–44). Beverly Hills: Sage.

Messick, D. M., & McLelland, C. (1983). Social traps and temporal traps. *Personality and Social Psychology Bulletin, 9*(1), 105–110.

Messick, D. M., & Sentis, K. P. (1979). Fairness and preference. *Journal of Experimental Social Psychology, 15*, 418–431.

Mill, J. S. (2001). *Utilitarianism*. Indianapolis: Bobbs-Merrill. (Original work published 1863)

Murnighan, J. K., Cantelon, D. A., & Elyashiv, T. (2001). Bounded personal ethics and the tap dance of real estate agency. In J. A. Wagner III, J. M. Bartunek, & K. D. Elsbach (Eds.), *Advances in qualitative organizational research* (Vol. 3, pp. 1–40). New York: Elsevier/JAI.

Peter, F., & Schmid, H. B. (Eds.). (2005). Symposium on rationality and commitment. *Economics and Philosophy, 21*, 1–3.

Porter, R. H. (1987). Kin recognition: Functions and mediating mechanisms. In C. Crawford, M. Smith, & D. Krebs (Eds.), *Sociobiology and psychology* (pp. 175–203). Hillsdale, NJ: Erlbaum.

Ramalingam, V. (1990, April). *Future of Indian shrimp exports depends on better aquaculture*. Retrieved September 3, 2008, from http://www.allbusiness.com/wholesale-trade/merchant-wholesalers-nondurable/123086-1.html

Rapoport, A., & Chammah, A. M. (1965). *Prisoner's dilemma: A study in conflict and cooperation*. Ann Arbor, MI: University of Michigan Press.

Ross, L., & Stillinger, C. (1991). Psychological barriers to conflict resolution. *Negotiation Journal, 7*, 389–404.

Sen, A. (1985) Goals, commitment and identity. *Journal of Law, Economics, and Organization, 1*, 341–355.

Sen, A. (2005). Why exactly is commitment important for rationality. *Economics and Philosophy, 21*, 5–13.

Shanahan, M. (2003, March 22). Appetite for destruction. *The Ecologist Magazine.* Retrieved August 2, 2008, from http://www.theecologist.org/pages/archive_detail. asp?content_id=170

Shiva, V. (n.d.). Freedom from the margins. Retrieved November 12, 2007, from http://www.navdanya.org/articles/acquaculture.htm

Siam Canadian Foods, Co., Ltd. (2004). Exports of Indian shrimp. Retrieved November 12, 2007, from http://www.siamcanadian.com/india-shrimp/exports.htm

Small, D., Loewenstein, G., & Strnad, J. (2006). Statistical, identifiable and iconic victims and perpetrators. In Ed McCaffery and Joel Slemrod (Eds.), *Behavioral public finance: Toward a new agenda* (pp. 32–46). New York: Russell Sage Foundation Press.

Smith, A. (1759/1970). *The theory of moral sentiments.* Cambridge, UK: Cambridge University Press. (Original work published 1759.)

Sumner, W. G. (1906). *Folkways.* Boston: Ginn.

Weber, J. (1990). Managers' moral reasoning: Assessing their responses to three moral dilemmas. *Human Relations, 43*, 687–702.

Weber, J. (1991). Adapting Kohlberg to enhance the assessment of managers' moral reasoning. *Business Ethics Quarterly, 1*(3) 293–318.

12

Fairness and Preference for Underdogs and Top Dogs

Scott T. Allison and Jeni L. Burnette
University of Richmond

A prominent recurring theme in the work of David M. Messick is the idea that people are not indifferent to the outcomes that others receive. The title of the present chapter pays homage to one of Messick's classic articles on this theme, a piece coauthored with Keith Sentis entitled "Fairness and Preference," published in 1979 in the *Journal of Experimental Social Psychology* (Messick & Sentis, 1979). This article was but one of many in a large and influential program of research by Messick and his colleagues on social interdependence, and it provided convincing data showing that interdependent choices made on the basis of fairness can lead to different choices compared to those made without fairness considerations. Borrowing from this theme, we argue in the current chapter that fairness considerations also color our judgments of underdogs and top dogs, and that our preferences for these social entities can be swayed by simple manipulations of perceiver, target, and situational characteristics.

PLEASURE AND DISPLEASURE WITH OTHERS' OUTCOMES

We begin with Messick's (1985) theoretical formation that two qualitatively different psychological processes govern our reactions to the outcomes received by others. The first of these processes focuses on the importance of social comparison, referring to the idea that other people's good fortune brings us displeasure, whereas their bad fortune brings us pleasure. According to Messick (1985), "we compare our outcomes to others and register pleasure or satisfaction if the comparison is favorable [to us] and dissatisfaction if it is not" (p. 92). This first comparison process is supported by a long history of social psychological research on equity theory (Adams, 1965; Messick & Cook, 1983), distributive justice (Homans, 1961; Tyler, 1994), social comparison theory (Festinger, 1954), comparison level theory (Thibaut & Kelley, 1959), competition (Messick & Thorngate, 1967), and relative deprivation (Crosby, 1982).

The second process proposed by Messick (1985) to describe people's reactions to others' outcomes refers to the "sympathetic or empathetic process in which one vicariously registers the pleasure or the pain of others" (p. 88). To illustrate this process, he resurrected a very telling quote from Adam Smith's *The Theory of Moral Sentiments*, in which Smith (1759/1976) proposed the idea of *fellow-feeling*:

> How selfish soever man may be supposed, there are evidently some principles in his nature, which interest him in the fortune of others, and render their happiness necessary to him, though he derives nothing from it except the pleasure of seeing it. Of this kind is pity or compassion, the emotion which we feel for the misery of others, when we either see it, or are made to conceive it in a very lively manner. That we often derive sorrow from the sorrow of others, is a matter of fact too obvious to require any instances to prove it; for this sentiment, like all the other original passions of human nature, is by no means confined to the virtuous and humane, though they perhaps may feel it with the most exquisite sensibility. The greatest ruffian, the most hardened violator of the laws of society, is not altogether without it. (p. 7)

In short, fellow-feeling refers to the pleasure that we experience when others receive good fortune and to the displeasure that we feel when others obtain misfortune. Unlike the first process in Messick's model, which implies a comparison between one's own and others' outcomes, this second process features a simple vicarious identification with others' good or bad circumstances. People's ability and willingness to experience others' outcomes vicariously are supported by a long history of social psychological research on promotive tension, empathy, and altruism (Batson & Powell, 2003; Hornstein, 1972; Krebs, 1975).

Although Messick (1985) proposed his dual-process model with the goal of explaining people's affective responses as actors in socially interdependent situations, we believe his formulation also has broader applications. As Messick suggests, actors care about the outcomes that they and others with whom they are interdependent receive, but in many situations mere observers of interdependent outcomes also care about the recipients of those outcomes. Thus, we argue that the simple act of observing others' outcomes may elicit pleasure or displeasure, even if those outcomes have no direct bearing on one's personal well-being. More specifically, we propose that Messick's two processes shed important light on people's responses to two unevenly matched social entities engaged in competition, namely, underdogs and top dogs.

Table 12.1 illustrates how Messick's (1985) dual-process model, focusing on actors in interdependent situations, compares to our model of how these two processes operate from the perspective of observers of interdependent situations. Consistent with Messick's (1985) first process, we suggest that people engage in a comparison of the projected outcomes that others are likely to receive in competitive settings. Messick's analysis suggests that, as actors, people prefer competitions in which their outcomes are likely to exceed those of their opponents, insofar as self-benefiting comparisons of outcomes bring pleasure. Our extrapolation of Messick's first process to the realm of the observer begins with the assumption that observers of competition compare the likely outcomes of participants and show a preference for contests that are evenly matched. For example, a sporting event between two comparably skilled teams provides more entertainment and appeals to our sense of fair play. Because we prefer equality of outcomes in most social situations (Allison, McQueen, & Schaerfl, 1992; Messick, 1995), we prefer closely contested competitions featuring an even

TABLE 12.1

Messick's (1985) Dual-Process Model From the Perspective of Actors and Observers

	Messick's (1985) Two Social Processes	
	Companion Process	**Vicarious Process**
Self as Actor	• Pleasure when self-other comparison is favorable	• Pleasure when another obtains positive outcome
	• Displeasure when self-other comparison is unfavorable	• Displeasure when another obtains negative outcome
Self as Observer	• Pleasure when others' outcomes are roughly equal	• Pleasure directed toward underdog
	• Displeasure when others' outcomes are clearly unequal	• Displeasure directed toward top dog

playing field where there are no clear underdogs or top dogs and where equal opportunity for success reigns.

If we are witness to an upcoming competition that is projected to yield a lopsided outcome in favor of one competitor, then we suggest that Messick's second process will be activated, such that people will feel sympathy or fellow-feeling toward the disadvantaged competitor (the underdog) and dissatisfaction with the advantaged competitor (the top dog; see Table 12.1). The idea that people associate good feelings with an underdog is reflected in the common belief that "everyone loves an underdog." Moreover, the negativity associated with top dogs is revealed in the sentiment that "the bigger they come, the harder they fall." But as with many pithy social truisms, these expressions are misleadingly simple, and in fact our research program on perceptions of underdogs and top dogs suggests that there are layers of counterintuitive complexity in our feelings for competitive entities. As we shall see below, there are circumstances under which we do not always love an underdog, and at times we do show greater preference for top dogs over underdogs. Our analysis will begin, however, with the general principle that underdogs engender our affection and top dogs our enmity, and we will point out exceptions and qualifications to this general rule where appropriate.

SYMPATHY AND LIKING: OUR AFFINITY FOR UNDERDOGS

Do people love an underdog? Until recently, most social psychological research focused only on the love people have for winners (Cialdini et al., 1976). This research identified people's tendencies to prefer an affiliation with winners and to feel a strong attraction for competent, successful others (Rosenfeld, Stephan, & Lucker, 1981). Cialdini and his colleagues called this phenomenon *basking in reflected glory* (Richardson & Cialdini, 1981).

Although top dogs no doubt attract our admiration and respect, there is also little doubt that underdogs capture our hearts and engender supportive emotions. Recent research underscores the idea that people sympathize and identify with underdogs, and that these vicarious processes elicit our emotional affection and preference for underdogs (Kim et al., 2008; Vandello, Goldschmied, & Richards, 2007). Any social entity that faces difficult challenges against a strong opponent or a demanding situation seems to inspire our support. The publishers of the children's classic *The Little Engine That Could* (Piper, 1930) suggest that the phrase "I think I can" is as pervasive in Western culture as "I have a dream" and "One small step for man."

What are the origins of our love for underdogs? Across many cultures underdog stories abound. Children in particular are educated about exciting and inspiring tales of people and animals who overcome great adversity, characters such as Cinderella, The Ugly Duckling, Popeye, and Bambi, to name but a few. We believe that such narratives reflect an archetype of struggle which elicits sympathy and support. Similarly, "The American Dream" and the Horatio Alger stories of "rags to riches," embodied by individuals such as Andrew Carnegie, captivate our dreams to overcome the imposed limitations of underdog status (Scharnhorst, 1980). Cultural icons featured in films such as *Rocky*, *The Karate Kid*, *Erin Brockovich*, *Seabiscuit*, and *Million Dollar Baby* provide sympathetic and inspiring portrayals of successful underdogs. These heroic accomplishments of underdogs inspire us and may underscore our hope that the world can be a fair place in which all individuals have the potential to succeed.

To demonstrate the underdog phenomenon, Kim et al. (2008) conducted several studies showing that people are significantly more likely to root for and sympathize with underdog entities (e.g., teams, artists, and businesses) than they are to root for and sympathize with top dog entities. Most importantly, Kim et al. found that sympathy for the underdog statistically mediates the effect of the underdog's status on people's tendency to root for the underdog.

One of Kim et al.'s (2008, Study 3) most revealing studies underscored the psychologically powerful effect of underdogs on human judgments. Employing a methodology reminiscent of that used by Heider and Simmel (1944), the study involved showing participants clips of animated shapes that appeared to chase or bump other shapes. Heider and Simmel's participants inferred causality from the movement of these shapes and also assigned dispositional attributes to the shapes as a result of their behavior toward each other. The beauty of Heider and Simmel's work is that it illustrated just how pervasive and natural the attribution process is, emerging in judgments of simple lifeless objects. Kim et al. presented their participants with moving shapes to determine whether people naturally bestow underdog status and underdog qualities upon shapes that move

FIGURE 12.1
The position of a circle as it struggles to traverse an obstacle.

more slowly than others. The study included four conditions: (a) a single non-struggling geometric shape, as shown in Figure 12.1; (b) a single struggling geometric shape; (c) a struggling geometric shape together with a benign non-struggling shape; and (d) a struggling geometric shape together with a "malicious" non-struggling shape that appeared to intentionally block the struggling shape, as shown in Figure 12.2.

The results of this study showed that people provided more emotional support for a single struggling shape than for a single non-struggling shape. This finding suggests that an entity's struggle, by itself, is enough to engender support, even when the entity is by itself. Kim et al. also found that the introduction of the social context heightened participants' emotional support for the struggling entity, such that participants were especially likely to root for a struggling entity when paired with a non-struggling one.

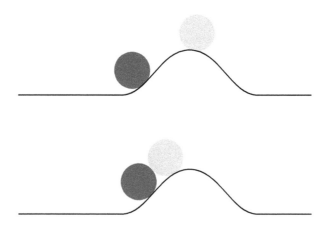

FIGURE 12.2
The position of two circles, one struggling (in this instance, dark grey) and the other non-struggling (light grey). The top panel shows the non-struggling circle after it easily passes the struggling one. The bottom panel shows the non-struggling circle reversing course and bumping the struggling circle down the hill.

Finally, the strongest underdog effect emerged when participants viewed a struggling shape whose progress toward achieving its apparent goal was overtly thwarted by a non-struggling shape (see Figure 12.2). Even more importantly, for the purposes of this chapter, Kim et al. found that participants were more likely to sympathize with the single struggling shape than with the single non-struggling shape. Moreover, participants showed the greatest degree of sympathy for the struggling shape paired with the malicious circle that impeded the struggling shape's progress.

Additional research has shown that sympathetic figures can capitalize on their underdog status by becoming exceptional leaders (Allison & Goethals, in press). For example, Allison and Heilborn (2008) found that people sympathize more with underdog leaders than with top dog leaders and that they like and respect underdog leaders more than top dog leaders. Moreover, people are significantly more inspired by the underdog leaders, more motivated to work for underdog leaders, more inspired by the underdog leader's vision, and more convinced that the underdog leaders would achieve long-term success. When asked to generate a list of real-world underdog and top dog leaders, Allison and Heilborn's participants most often listed Muhammad Ali, Steve Jobs, Martin Luther King, Jr., Nelson Mandela, and Oprah Winfrey as underdogs, and Bill Gates, George Steinbrenner, Donald Trump, George Bush, and Michael Bloomberg as top dogs. These 10 individuals were then rated by other participants on dimensions of sympathy, liking, respect, competence, and inspiration. The results showed that, compared to the group of top dog leaders, the group of underdog leaders were significantly more sympathized with, liked, respected, and inspiring.

In summary, consistent with Messick's (1985) theoretical analysis, the results of several studies support the notion that vicarious sympathy for the plight of others applies to our feelings toward underdogs. People vicariously feel the struggles that underdogs encounter, and this high degree of fellow-feeling is associated with increased sympathy for, identification with, and emotional support toward underdogs (Allison & Heilborn, 2008). Moreover, people tend to view underdogs with whom they sympathize as powerful and inspirational leaders. These underdog leaders derive their power from their ability to attract respect and admiration from followers who emotionally connect to underdog leaders' success in overcoming difficult circumstances.

Do people give underdogs their unconditional support? The results from our program of research on underdogs suggests that the answer to this question is no. There is no doubt that underdogs attract our sympathy, but the results of several of our studies indicate that our love for underdogs is limited and qualified by a number of factors, each of which we now turn to below.

JUDGMENTS OF CONSEQUENCES

Many of our most powerful underdog stories, told in books and movies, unfold within athletic contexts. Emotionally moving tales of underdog victories feature underdog participants in basketball (*Hoosiers*), baseball (*The Bad News Bears*), martial arts (*The Karate Kid*), horse-racing (*Seabiscuit*), and boxing (*Rocky*). We suspect that the prevalence of athletic underdogs in our cultural lore may stem from the fact that our goal in viewing athletic competitions is to be entertained. Rarely are there life or death consequences in athletics, and so rooting for the underdog carries with it few costs.

But what if there are significant monetary or life consequences associated with the outcome of a competition? Would we abandon the underdog and support the top dog when the consequences of the outcome of the competition go far beyond mere entertainment? To answer this question, Kim et al. (2008) presented participants with a situation in which they assumed the role of a government agency that was charged with the task of hiring a construction company to build either a life-size decorative gingerbread house (low consequences condition) or high-traffic bridge over a river (high consequences condition). Participants were told to consider bids from two construction companies, one a small and new company (underdog condition) and the other a large and established company (top dog condition). The results showed that although participants in both consequence conditions were more likely to root for the underdog construction company to succeed, they were nevertheless only likely to hire the underdog company when the consequences were low. When the consequences were high — the bridge-building condition in which lives were at stake — participants were more likely to hire the top dog company than the underdog company.

This finding suggests that although underdogs attract our sympathy, we really only pull for underdogs when the outcome of the competition has minimal impact on us or others. In general, we give underdogs our emotional support, but when our physical or material interests are at stake we are quick to abandon the underdog and give top dogs our behavioral and financial support. Why might this be so? One possibility is that top dogs are perceived as especially skillful, and when the consequences of a competitive outcome are high, we prefer to have such a skillful top dog as an ally. Conversely, when consequences are low, skillfulness in a top dog becomes less important than offering support to an underdog.

JUDGMENTS OF DESERVINGNESS

People may love an underdog, but this love is not unconditional, nor does it come without strings attached. Underdogs may be expected to "earn" our support by expending maximum effort to overcome their underdog status. Burnette, Allison, Goethals, Eylon, and Beggan (2008) found exactly this result. Participants were informed of a tennis player who was projected to lose an upcoming competition to a more accomplished opponent. Half the participants were told that the underdog player was training her hardest to prepare for the match, whereas the other half were told that the underdog was only applying about 50% effort to prepare. The results showed that participants rooted for the underdog only when they believed that she was clearly doing everything in her power to perform at her highest level in the competition. When the underdog was perceived to be coasting, participants actually indicated a higher degree of liking and respect for the top dog and were more likely to root for the top dog to prevail over the underdog.

Our research has also identified an important individual difference in perceptions of how worthy we believe underdogs and top dogs are of our support (Burnette et al., 2008). We asked participants to indicate their political affiliations (Republican or Democrat) and their degree of liberalism or conservatism. Our hypothesis was that there would be some degree of truth to the stereotype of liberals as "bleeding hearts," such that liberals would show a greater affinity for socioeconomic underdogs than would conservatives. The results showed that although there was no difference between liberals and conservatives in their degree of sympathy for economic underdogs, there was a significant tendency for liberals to indicate a greater intention to offer behavioral and monetary support for underdogs. In contrast to liberals, who displayed an unconditional desire to help underdogs, conservatives indicated that their behavioral support for underdogs was dependent on the availability of resources and on the degree to which the underdog expended effort to improve her lot.

JUDGMENTS OF EFFICACY

If our support for underdogs is contingent on their level of effort, it could also be dependent on our beliefs about the likelihood of their success. An underdog, by definition, is unlikely to prevail over the top dog, but what if the odds of success are so remote that rooting for the underdog becomes an exercise in futility?

Burnette et al. (2008) tested this hypothesis by experimentally manipulating the probability that an underdog would enjoy success in an upcoming competition. Participants were informed that a football team had either a 45, 30, 15, 2, or .1% chance of triumphing in their next game, according to a panel of football experts. The dependent variables were how much participants liked and rooted for the underdog on a 1 to 7 scale with higher number indicating greater liking and rooting. The results are depicted in Figure 12.3. As this figure shows, participants showed the strongest rooting for the underdog team when it was unlikely — but not impossible — to prevail. Liking and rooting were lowest when the underdog's chances of winning were either too high or too low, suggesting that we love an underdog most when the odds are stacked against it to a moderate degree. A moderate degree of success would seem to assure us, as observers who desire to be entertained, of a sufficiently high emotional payoff if the underdog triumphs while also providing some reasonable possibility that such a payoff could occur.

JUDGMENTS SKEWED BY FRAMING EFFECTS

Decision theorists have known for decades that people's choices are sensitive to the manner in which decision problems are framed (McElroy

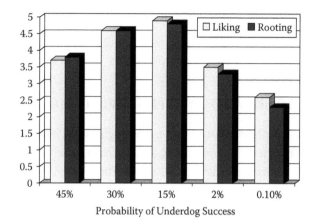

FIGURE 12.3
Liking and rooting for an underdog football team as a function of its probability of success.

& Seta, 2003; Tversky & Kahneman, 1981). We tested whether framing effects can emerge in perceptions of underdogs by informing participants of an upcoming basketball game between two teams, one of which was heavily favored to defeat the other. In the negative frame condition, participants read a scenario that focused on the plight of the underdog. They learned that the underdog team was shorthanded and overmatched by their opponents and that the team was predicted to lose by 20 points. In the positive frame condition, participants read a scenario that focused on the strength of the top dog. They were told that the top dog was a highly polished machine running at full strength, and that the team was predicted to win by 20 points.

Despite the fact that in both conditions participants read about a competition featuring one team that was projected to defeat another team by 20 points, participants' judgments about the teams differed significantly. Participants in the negative frame condition, which focused on the underdog's disadvantage, were significantly more likely to like the underdog and to root for the underdog than were participants in the positive frame condition. This finding suggests that fellow-feeling may be sensitive to simple manipulations of framing and perspective-taking. If the protagonist in the tale of competition is the beleaguered or disadvantaged underdog, we will sympathize with the underdog and give it our emotional support. But if the protagonist in the tale is the strong and successful top dog, a different type of fellow-feeling may kick in; we may admire the top dog as a hero deserving of further success.

JUDGMENTS SKEWED BY SELF-SERVING MOTIVES

Most of us would prefer not to be an underdog in competition. We want to finish ahead of others, because doing so satisfies a number of self-oriented motives such as competitive desires (Messick & Thorngate, 1967), self-improvement (Sedikides & Strube, 1997), self-verification (Swann, 1987), self-esteem (Mruk, 2006), and self-enhancement (Brown & Kobayashi, 2002).

Ironically, although we covet the advantage in competition, there are times when we prefer to be disadvantaged. Some people prefer to avoid having high expectations heaped upon them (Shepperd & Arkin, 1991), whereas others engage in self-handicapping as an impression management strategy (Berglas & Jones, 1978). When people self-handicap, they are essentially positioning themselves in the role of underdogs, announcing to others that they are disadvantaged and thus deserve great credit should they succeed and great compassion should they fail.

One interesting possibility, yet to be tested, is that observers of competition may project themselves into the role of either underdog or top dog, depending on the role with which they typically identify in that situation. From this perspective, situational cues or personal predispositions that trigger a projection into the role of underdog (or top dog) may lead an observer to take the perspective of the underdog (or top dog).

JUDGMENTS OF PERFORMANCE QUALITY

People may root for underdogs, but this emotional support may belie a disrespect for underdogs' competence level. To test this idea, Kim et al. (2008) showed both novice and expert artists a painting submitted for an art competition by either an unknown or established artist. Replicating the underdog effect, the results revealed that participants rooted for the unknown artist to win the competition more than they rooted for the successful artist. However, evaluations of the quality of the painting revealed the opposite effect. Despite the fact that all participants viewed the same painting, the painting was judged to be higher in quality when it was believed to have been produced by the top dog artist than when it was believed to have been the work of the underdog artist. Moreover, evaluations of novice and expert participants' quality ratings showed the same bias; top dogs were judged to have produced better artistic output.

We can conclude that people's emotional affinity for underdogs does not carry over to their evaluations of the quality of the underdogs' work. It does not appear to matter whether one is an expert or a novice on the dimension being evaluated; we carry with us a bias against underdogs that belies our emotional support for them. This interpretation is consistent with our earlier analysis of the perceived consequences of a competition. If top dogs are viewed as inherently more skillful than underdogs, then we top dogs may be judged as a threat when we are competitively disadvantaged or when someone we care about is disadvantaged.

SUMMARY

Messick's (1985) dual process conceptualization is largely supported by recent research on people's affective responses to the outcomes that underdogs and top dogs are projected to receive in impending competitions. The first process in Messick's (1985) model is a comparison process that emerges when people compare the outcomes that participants in competition are projected to receive. As a general rule, people prefer evenly matched competitions, but when the playing field is deemed to be uneven people extend their sympathy and support to underdogs. This extension of emotional feelings toward competitive entities represents Messick's second process at work. We have shown that people's sympathy and support for underdogs is genuine but it is also qualified by a number of variables that underscore the fragility of the underdog effect. Indeed, the underdog effect pervades our culture but is surprisingly malleable; it can be viewed as a mile wide but an inch deep (Kim et al., 2008).

Envy and Resentment: Our Dislike for Top Dogs

We now turn to fellow-feeling toward top dogs. As we have already noted, although there is a general tendency to love underdogs and to root against top dogs, our affective responses to underdogs and top dogs can be sensitive to many contextual variables. For example, we may love underdogs, but we may not necessarily respect them (Kim et al., 2008). In this same vein, we may respect top dogs, but we may also resent their success or we may form judgments that undermine them. Below we consider how and why people craft anti–top dog sentiments.

Judgments Biased by *Schadenfreude*

Although there has been little social psychological research on the underdog effect, there has been considerable research that sheds light on our disliking for top dogs. Foremost among these lines of research is work on the phenomenon of *Schadenfreude*, defined as a malicious joy that we experience upon learning of another's misfortune and suffering (Heider, 1958). The concept of *Schadenfreude* has received significant attention from social scientists (Feather & Sherman, 2002; Leach, Spears, Branscombe, & Doosje, 2003). According to Feather and his colleagues (Feather, 1999; Feather & Sherman, 2002), the key component of *Schadenfreude* is deservingness. Specifically, people's beliefs that the high status of a top dog is undeserved contribute to feelings of resentment, and this resentment fuels the individual to experience *Schadenfreude* when the undeserving top dog suffers a fall or experiences misfortune.

Similar to *Schadenfreude* is a concept developed by Feather (1989) called the *tall poppy syndrome*. This phenomenon refers to the criticism that successful people receive for their arrogant, attention-seeking behaviors. The tall poppy effect is reminiscent of the well-known Japanese proverb stating that "the nail that sticks out gets hammered down." Feather argues that the tall poppy effect stems from both envy and resentment directed toward those who enjoy great success, and that it may be more prevalent in collectivistic cultures than in individualistic ones.

People may not only experience joy when top dogs fail, they may take pleasure from preventing top dogs from experiencing additional success. For example, it is not uncommon to read news stories involving a small community's fierce opposition to the construction of a new Wal-Mart store in the area (Hicks, 2006). In these instances, local residents and community leaders usually decry the arrival of the Wal-Mart, arguing that the giant retail store will ensure the collapse of small locally owned businesses that cannot offer the same low prices or product selection that Wal-Mart can.

The resistance movement usually (but not always) fails, and the Wal-Mart facility is eventually built. Within a year or two, the Wal-Mart store is flourishing, thanks in no small part to the fact that the store attracts the business of many of the same people who initially opposed its construction (Fishman, 2006).

Why do people dislike Wal-Mart and yet admit to shopping there? The love–hate relationship that people have for Wal-Mart is well documented (Centrella, 2004; Fishman, 2006). The "love" component of the relationship refers to people's affinity for lower prices and one-stop shopping. The "hate" component refers to people's disdain for any large, highly successful entity that threatens the well-being of smaller, less successful entities. Although there are, in fact, some Wal-Mart detractors who stick to their principles and refuse to shop at Wal-Mart, many others support underdog businesses in their hearts but not with their wallets. Just as we are quick to abandon the underdog when it suits our interest (Kim et al., 2008), we are also quick to shed our dislike for top dogs if it serves our interests.

Recent research on "moral hypocrisy" supports the idea that people will quickly abandon a moral principle if it suits their own interests (Batson & Thompson, 2001). Batson and his colleagues showed that people will eschew what they know to be a fair procedure (such as flipping a coin) when distributing resources between themselves and others (Batson et al., 1997, Study 2). We might call this phenomenon *moral myopia* rather than moral hypocrisy because people who behave this way may not preach the relevant moral principle. Rather they may hold to it, but not apply it, perhaps because it is not cognitively accessible when their interests are at stake.

Judgments Revealing a Double Standard

When there is a heated battle between two intense rivals, it is not unusual for each competitive entity to try to cast itself in the role of the underdog. Doing so may take pressure off the competitor, because underdogs are not expected to prevail, but it may also represent a strategy to elicit sympathy and support from outsiders. A prominent example can be found in the ongoing conflict between Israel and Palestine. Each side in this conflict often uses the media as a tool for claiming their underdog status. Israel advertises itself as an underdog because of its relatively small geographical size and minority status in the Arab world, whereas Palestine portrays itself as the underdog because of its relative poverty and weak military capability compared to that of Israel (Dershowitz, 2003).

Besides receiving the benefit of added sympathy and support, competitors who are portrayed as underdogs often know that such a portrayal affords them the benefit of the doubt should they perform a morally questionable act. Palestinians may know that outsiders may forgive their acts of suicide bombing if Palestinians are perceived as an exploited underdog, and Israel, too, may be aware that its military actions against the Palestinians are more likely to be forgiven if Israelis are perceived as underdogs fighting back against a bully top dog.

One implication of these considerations is that a double standard may exist in people's evaluations of the actions of underdogs and top dogs. Do we judge top dogs more harshly for performing a negative action than we would judge underdogs for performing the same action? To test this hypothesis, we informed participants that a member of a football team accidentally stumbled upon the playbook of his team's opponent a few days before the game. Participants were not told whether this discovery was ever used to his team's advantage, because we wanted the action of finding the playbook to be ethically ambiguous. Participants only knew that the potential for exploiting the opponent existed. Half the participants were told that it was a member of the top dog team that found the underdog's playbook, whereas the other half were told that it was a member of the underdog team that found the top dog's playbook. We asked participants to evaluate the actions of the finder of the playbook, the fairness of the act of finding the book, and the ethics of the finder's team.

The results provided very strong and clear evidence in support of the double standard in evaluations of underdogs and top dogs. When participants believed that the finder of the playbook was a member of the top dog team, they judged this individual and his team to be significantly more unethical compared to when they believed the finder was an underdog. Moreover, the situation was described as significantly more unfair when a member of the top dog team was believed to have found the playbook. What is perhaps most surprising about these findings is that the scenarios read by participants said nothing about whether the information in the playbook was ever used to the finder's team's advantage. Simply being given the opportunity to exploit the underdog, even through serendipitous circumstances, was deemed to be unacceptable to participants. Overall, these results strongly suggest that a double standard exists in people's evaluations of underdogs and top dogs. People tend to hold top dogs to a higher ethical standard than we do underdogs.

We should acknowledge that in our studies, it is difficult to distinguish between sympathy for the underdog and disliking for the top dog. These two processes may be operating individually or in tandem to produce the effects we have reported. As noted earlier, we suspect that observers of competition may naturally (and possibly unconsciously) project themselves into the role of either underdog or top dog, or they may show tendencies to focus more emotional and judgmental energy on one "dog" over another, depending on situational cues or personal predispositions. Future research is needed to clarify the exact nature of the processes involved.

JUDGMENTS AFFECTED BY ACTOR/OBSERVER EFFECTS

Are our perceptions of fairness regarding underdogs sensitive to whether we are the underdog versus being mere observers of the underdog? We recently examined whether actor-observer differences emerge in judgments of fairness and justice in underdog settings (Burnette et al., 2008). We manipulated individuals' top dog or underdog standings in a job application process and whether the participant was the actor or observer. Specifically, participants in the actor condition read a scenario in which they were competing for a job in which they personally were either richer (top dog condition) or poorer (underdog condition) than their competitor for the position. Participants in the observer condition read a scenario in which someone else was either the top dog or underdog in a job application situation. Participants then indicated the extent to which they agreed whether it was fair for the top dog to be advantaged relative to the underdog (e.g., "The underdog deserves to beat the top dog," and "It is unfair for people to ever be disadvantaged compared to others").

Burnette et al.'s (2008) results revealed a self-centered view of the fairness of the situation. Actors' evaluations of the need for equality and fairness changed as a function of their underdog status, with actors reporting greater injustice and unfairness for their underdog standing relative to observers (see Figure 12.4). In short, participants in the actor condition perceived an underdog standing to be unfair compared to those in the observer condition. In contrast, participants in the observer condition

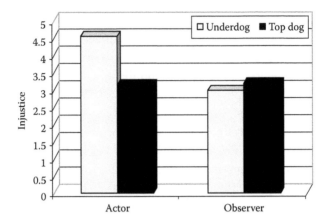

FIGURE 12.4

Perceptions of injustice as a function of underdog/top dog standing and actor/observer position.

made fairness judgments that were not as strongly based on underdog or top dog status.

What about feelings of sympathy for the underdog based on our actor and observer manipulation? Consistent with the idea that others' negative or unfair outcomes can elicit sympathy, observers reported that the top dog would feel bad about getting the job given the other applicant's disadvantaged standing. However, actors report that they personally would not feel bad about getting the position when in the top dog position (see Figure 12.5). This result suggests that people forecast a much different affective reaction to relatively positive outcomes for others compared to oneself. Others should feel pain when outperforming others, whereas we should bask in the glow of our victories. In summary, two findings have emerged from our recent work on actor-observer differences. First, actors judge their underdog status to be more unfair than the equivalent underdog status of others; and second, actors believe that any shame associated with top dog status should be felt by others but not by oneself.

SUMMARY AND FUTURE DIRECTIONS

We began this chapter with an overview of Messick's (1985) insight that two different processes appear to govern actors' reactions to others' outcomes

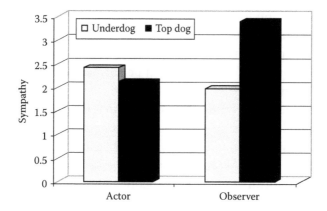

FIGURE 12.5
Sympathy (assessed by how badly one would feel about being advantaged) as a function of underdog/top dog standing and actor/observer position.

in interdependent situations. Messick argued that another's positive outcomes can either makes us feel wretched in comparison, or they can make us feel vicariously happy, and that another's negative outcomes can either make us feel great in comparison, or they can elicit sympathy. Our thesis in the present chapter was that both these processes — a comparison process and a vicarious process — also characterize people's affective responses as observers of interdependent outcomes. Observers make comparisons of the outcomes that competitors are projected to receive in impending competitions, and they prefer projected outcomes that are roughly equal over ones that are heavily imbalanced. When compared outcomes are expected to be unequal, people vicariously feel the pain of the underdog, and these various feelings translate to sympathy for underdogs and resentment directed toward top dogs.

Messick (1985) speculated that these two processes were contradictory and required theoretical reconciliation. He stated that "the general problem in the study of preferences in interdependent contexts is to understand not only the dynamics of fellow feelings, on the one hand, and competitive impulses, on the other, but also to create a general theory that incorporates both of these components with other elements as well" (p. 94). Shortly after Messick challenged scholars to reconcile the two processes, Tesser (1988) developed a self-evaluation maintenance model that made significant headway toward accomplishing precisely that goal. According to Tesser's model, whether a person feels good or bad about another's outcomes is determined by the degree to which the dimension of comparison is self-relevant to the perceiver. For example, a basketball player may feel resentment if another person has superior basketball skills (high self-relevance) but may feel joy if another person has superior sewing skills (low self-relevance).

One of the most interesting and perhaps surprising findings from our research on underdogs is the extent to which our affinity for underdogs is fragile and sensitive to numerous contextual factors. Underdogs are not unconditionally loved. As we have shown, we love underdogs when the consequences of them winning a competition are low, when they expend maximum effort, when their chances of winning are neither too high nor too low, when the problem is framed a particular way, and when we are asked about our support for them but not our assessment of the quality of their work. With all these conditions attached to our love for underdogs, one must wonder about the role of dominant cultural narratives about underdogs (e.g., *The Little Train That Could*, Horatio Alger, *Rocky*, innumerable Disney stories and fairy tales, etc.). We propose the possibility that the proliferation of these powerful underdog stories in our culture may not necessarily reflect our natural love for underdogs. Rather, they may serve as reminders that despite our belief that underdogs are inferior to most of us, we cannot forget them and they are deserving of our support.

There is also still much to be learned about how our feelings for underdogs ebb and flow as a function of the passage of time, outcomes received, and group status. Our support for underdogs would seem to be sensitive to natural changes in an underdog's fortunes. The Boston Red Sox were perennial baseball underdogs, having endured an 86-year drought in terms of World Series victories until their championships of 2004 and 2007. How much success must an underdog enjoy before it sheds its underdog status? At what point does an underdog become a top dog, and at what point do top dog setbacks transform a top dog into an underdog? Perceived momentum swings in the fortunes of competitors, and how these swings alter our fellow-feeling toward those competitors, would seem to represent a promising area for future investigations.

Another question that remains unanswered is the degree to which a group's underdog status interacts with feelings of ingroup identification we may have toward a team or organization. Prior to 2004, Bostonians had two reasons to root for their team: its underdog status and its affiliation with the city of Boston. Outside of Boston, many observers no doubt rooted for

Boston due to its underdog status, unless possibly these observers resided in New York City, home of the Yankees and Boston's intense baseball rival. Winners of more World Series than any other team, the Yankees have been baseball's top dogs since 1920 and thus attract both admirers and feelings of *Schadenfreude*. At this time we do not know how specifically how our feelings for the good or bad fortunes received by ingroups and outgroups interact with underdog or top dog status. We do know that identification with ingroups is strong (Brewer, 1999), as is identification with underdogs (Kim et al., 2008), and thus it would be interesting to see how observers of competition resolve any conflicts that may arise between these two strong identification processes. Also, building on the actor and observer differences in perceptions of fairness, of interest would be research examining the role of self-serving motives in perceptions of fairness (Messick, Bloom, Boldizar, & Samuelson, 1985) in judgments of underdogs.

Another question that would benefit from future research centers on an issue near and dear to Dave Messick, namely, the interplay of fairness considerations and self-interest. These two processes would seem to be crucial to a fuller understanding of the central motivating mechanism in the underdog phenomena we have reported. Do we enjoy equal competition because it is fair? Or does watching an evenly matched game of tennis serve our self-interest; that is, our desire to be entertained? Context would seem to be extremely important; we may want a close tennis match because of the entertainment value, but we may prefer an evenly matched competitive environment in business because of a desire for economic fairness.

This chapter was written with the intention of honoring Dave Messick's contributions to our understanding of perceived fairness in social situations. We have seen, in this chapter, only a glimpse of how Messick's theoretical analyses can have broad and meaningful applications to many domains of interest to social psychologists. On more than one occasion during his storied career, Messick pointed out that research often raises more questions than it answers (e.g., Messick & Brewer, 1983). We believe that the underdog phenomenon represents a classic example of this pattern. As we have shown, the simple notion that people love an underdog turns out to be not so simple after all. We also have no doubt that a closer reading of Messick's entire body of work on social interdependence will continue to shed additional insights into the underdog effect for years to come.

REFERENCES

Adams, J. S. (1965). Inequity in social exchange. In L. Berkowitz (Ed.), *Advances in experimental social psychology* (Vol. 2, 267–299). New York: Academic Press.

Allison, S. T., & Goethals, G. R. (in press). Deifying the dead and downtrodden: Sympathetic figures as exceptional leaders. In Goethals, Forsyth, & Hoyt (Eds.), *Social psychology and leadership*. Praeger.

Allison, S. T., & Heilborn, J. (2009). *The smaller they come, the better they lead: Underdogs as inspirational leaders*. Unpublished manuscript, University of Richmond.

Allison, S. T., McQueen, L. R., & Schaerfl, L. M. (1992). Social decision making processes and the equal partitionment of shared resources. *Journal of Experimental Social Psychology, 28*, 23–42.

Batson, C. D., Polycarpou, M. P., Harmon-Jones, E., Imhoff, H. J., Mitchener, E. C., Bednar, L. L., et al. (1997). Empathy and attitudes: Can feeling for a member of a stigmatized group improve feelings toward the group? *Journal of Personality and Social Psychology, 72*, 105–118.

Batson, C. D., & Powell, A. A. (2003). Altruism and prosocial behavior. In T. Millon & M. Lerner (Eds.), *Handbook of psychology: Personality and social psychology* (Vol. 5, pp. 444–467). Hoboken, NJ: Wiley.

Berglas, S., & Jones, E. E. (1978). Drug choice as a self-handicapping strategy in response to a noncontingent success. *Journal of Personality and Social Psychology, 36*, 405–417.

Brewer, M. B. (1999). The psychology of prejudice: Ingroup love or outgroup hate? *Journal of Social Issues, 55*, 429–444.

Brown, J. D., & Kobayashi, C. (2002). Self-enhancement in Japan and America. *Asian Journal of Social Psychology, 5*, 145–168.

Burnette, J. L., Allison, S. T., Goethals, G. R., Eylon, D., & Beggan, J. K. (2008). *Associating with both winners and losers: Underdog and BIRGing effects reconciled*. Unpublished manuscript, University of Richmond.

Centrella, H. R. (2004). National researchers study Wal-Mart's impact on consumers. *The Journal Record (Oklahoma City)*. From http://www.highbeam.com/doc/IPZ-2108343.html

Cialdini, R. B., Borden, R. J., Thorne, A., Walker, M., Freeman, S., & Sloan, L. (1976). Basking in reflected glory: Three (football) field studies. *Journal of Personality and Social Psychology, 34*, 366–375.

Crosby, F. J. (1982). *Relative deprivation and working women*. New York: Oxford University Press.

Dershowitz, D. (2003). *The case for Israel*. New York: Wiley.

Feather, N. T. (1989). Attitudes towards the high achiever: The fall of the tall poppy. *Australian Journal of Psychology, 41*, 239–267.

Feather, N. T. (1999). Judgments of deservingness: Studies in the psychology of justice and achievement. *Personality and Social Psychology Review, 3*, 86–107.

Feather, N. T., & Sherman, R. (2002). Envy, resentment, *Schadenfreude*, and sympathy: Reactions to deserved and undeserved achievement and subsequent failure. *Personality and Social Psychology Bulletin, 28*, 953–961.

Festinger, L. A. (1954). Theory of social comparison processes. *Human Relations, 7*, 117–140.

Fishman, C. (2006). *The Wal-Mart effect*. New York: Penguin.

Heider, F. (1958). The *psychology of interpersonal relations*. New York: John Wiley & Sons.

Heider, F., & Simmel, M. (1944). An experimental study of apparent behavior. *American Journal of Psychology, 57*, 243–259.

Hicks, M. (2006). *Transportation and infrastructure, retail clustering, and local public finance: Evidence from Wal-Mart's expansion* (MPRA paper 52). University Library of Munich, Germany.

Homans, G. C. (1961). *Social behavior: Its elementary forms.* New York: Harcourt, Brace, & World.

Hornstein, H. A. (1972). Promotive tension: The basis of prosocial behavior from a Lewinian perspective. *Journal of Social Issues, 28*, 191–218.

Kim, J., Allison, S. T., Eylon, D., Goethals, G., Markus, M., McGuire, H., et al. (2008). Rooting for (and then abandoning) the underdog. *Journal of Applied Social Psychology, 38*, 2550–2573.

Krebs, D. (1975). Empathy and altruism. *Journal of Personality and Social Psychology, 32*, 1132–1146.

Leach, C. W., Spears, R., Branscombe, N. R., & Doosje, B. (2003). Malicious pleasure: Schadenfreude at the suffering of another group. *Journal of Personality and Social Psychology, 84*, 932–943.

McElroy, T., & Seta, J. J. (2003). Framing effects: An analytic-holistic perspective. *Journal of Experimental Social Psychology, 39*, 610–617.

Messick, D. M. (1985). Social interdependence and decision making. In G. Wright (Ed.), *Behavioral decision making* (pp. 87–110). New York: Plenum.

Messick, D. M. (1995). Equality, fairness and social conflict. *Social Justice Research, 8*, 153–173.

Messick, D. M., & Brewer, M. B. (1983). Solving social dilemmas: A review. In L. Wheeler & P. Shaver (Eds.), *Review of Personality and Social Psychology* (Vol. 4, pp. 11–44). Beverly Hills: Sage.

Messick, D. M., Bloom, S., Boldizar, J., & Samuelson, C. D. (1985). Why we are fairer than others. *Journal of Experimental Social Psychology, 21*, 480–500.

Messick, D. M., & Cook, K. S. (Eds.). (1983). *Equity theory.* New York: Praeger.

Messick, D. M., & Sentis, K. P. (1979). Fairness and preference. *Journal of Experimental Social Psychology, 15*, 418–434.

Messick, D. M., & Thorngate, W. (1967). Relative gain maximization in experimental games. *Journal of Experimental Social Psychology, 3*, 85–101.

Mruk, C. (2006). *Self-esteem research, theory, and practice: Toward a positive psychology of self-esteem* (3rd ed.). New York: Springer.

Piper, W. (1930). *The little engine that could.* New York: Platt & Munk.

Richardson, K. D., & Cialdini, R. B. (1981). Basking in reflected glory. In J. Tedeschi (Ed.), *Impression management theory and social psychological research* (pp. 41–53). New York: Academic Press.

Rosenfeld, D., Stephan, W., & Lucker, G. (1981). Attraction to competent and incompetent members of cooperative and competitive groups. *Journal of Applied Social Psychology, 11*, 416–433.

Scharnhorst, G. (1980). *Horatio Alger, Jr.* Boston: Twayne Publishers.

Sedikides, C., & Strube, M. J. (1997). Self-evaluation: To thine own self be good, to thine own self be sure, to thine own self be true, and to thine own self be better. In M. P. Zanna (Ed.), *Advances in experimental social psychology* (Vol. 29, pp. 209–269). New York: Academic Press.

Shepperd, J. A., & Arkin, R. M. (1991). Behavioral other-enhancement: Strategically obscuring the link between performance and evaluation. *Journal of Personality and Social Psychology, 60,* 79–88.

Smith, A. (1976). The theory of moral sentiments. Oxford: Clarendon Press. (Original work published in 1759.)

Swann, W. B., Jr. (1987). Identity negotiation: Where two roads meet. *Journal of Personality and Social Psychology, 53,* 1038–1051.

Tesser, A. (1988). Toward a self-evaluation maintenance model of social behavior. In L. Berkowitz (Ed.), *Advances in experimental social psychology* (Vol. 21, pp. 181–227). New York: Academic Press.

Thibaut, J. W., & Kelley, H. H. (1959). *The social psychology of groups.* New York: Wiley.

Tversky, A., & Kahneman, D. (1981). The framing of decisions and the psychology of choice. *Science, 211,* 453–458.

Tyler, T. R. (1994). Psychological models of the justice motive: Antecedents of distributive and procedural justice. *Journal of Personality and Social Psychology, 67,* 850–853.

Vandello, J. A., Goldschmied, N. P., & Richards, D. A. R. (2007). The appeal of the underdog. *Personality and Social Psychology Bulletin, 33,* 1603–1616.

13

Meaner Managers:
A Consequence of Income Inequality

Sreedhari D. Desai
University of Utah

Arthur P. Brief
University of Utah

Jennifer M. George
Rice University

In this chapter, we examine how the widening income gap in the United States between top managers and their employees contributes to an increase in concentration of power at the top, resulting in dysfunctional consequences within organizations. We argue that this growing power concentration at the top causes managers to distance themselves from lower level workers through the use of various disengagement mechanisms such as objectification of those with less power, stereotyping, and automatic information processing. It also causes managers at the top be disinhibited in their pursuit of self-interest and rewards to the detriment of those beneath them and society as a whole. Ultimately, we propose that power consolidation at the very top of organizations as a result of escalating income inequality in the United States leads top managers to feel more comfortable indulging in behaviors that exploit their employees.

Our best bet is that when Dave Messick reads this chapter he will like it. And, we care about his assessment, because the chapter was written in Dave's honor. We suspect that he will like it more on a personal than professional level. It is just darn difficult to live up to Dave's exacting scholarly standards. Personally, however, we have a better chance, because our topic, mean managers, will appeal to him for his sense of fair play, honesty, and compassion that is evident to all who know him.

That is not to say that our topic is far from Dave's scholarly interests. His work, for example, on ethics (e.g., Darley, Messick, & Tyler, 2001; Messick & Bazerman, 1996; Messick & Tenbrunsel, 1996; Tenbrunsel & Messick, 1999, 2004) provides a setting in which our work on mean managers can be set. Enough of this foreplay; it is time meaner managers took center stage. This one is for you, Dave.

Plato told Aristotle that no one in a community should earn more than five times the pay of the lowest paid worker[1] (Crystal, 1991). He envisioned a society free of the perils wrought by extreme inequalities in income. Plato's vision has not come to pass. Income inequality is at an all-time high in the United States (Neckerman & Torche, 2007). Between 1979 and 2005, the top 5% of American families have seen their real incomes increase 81%; over the same period, the bottom 5% have seen their real incomes decrease 1% (U.S. Census Bureau, 2006). The numbers are equally dismal if we take a look at income inequality within American organizations. Chief executive officers (CEOs) of publicly traded firms in the U.S. earned 411 times as much as average workers in 2005, up from 42 times in 1979 (Dvorak, 2007; Frank, 2007). What is truly remarkable is that the disparity in income between chief executives and average workers in the United States has occurred at a time when overall economic growth has been unprecedented. In real dollars, the gross domestic product (an economic measure of national income and output) has tripled since 1960 but workers' hourly compensation has remained flat, barely keeping up with inflation (Burtless, 2003). The gap is even greater in some other sectors of the economy. According to *Forbes* magazine, the top 20 private equity and hedge fund managers pocketed an average $657.5 million last year, or 22,255 times the pay of an average U.S. worker (Shell, 2007). In other words, to make what these managers made in one day, the average American worker would have to toil for 61 years.

In this chapter, we offer a first look at how income inequality influences top managers and their behavior toward ordinary workers or wage earners. Specifically, we explore how income concentration at the top leads these executives to see themselves as more powerful and thus to behave in meaner ways toward those at lower levels of the organization. We first outline the relationship between increased CEO compensation and power. We then examine how increasing power at the top causes chief executives to experience changes in how they think of their work, think of themselves, and think of others; process information;

and, consequently, make decisions and behave. We believe that through the processes of objectification of lower level workers and self-disinhibition, CEOs with relatively greater compensation, and hence more power, view lower level employees in unfavorable ways and treat them as inferior human beings. We also present a study that examines the relationship between CEO compensation and a firm's adherence to human rights. The empirical findings, although somewhat tangential to our thesis, support our arguments. We conclude by addressing the implications of our arguments, offering possible solutions to the problem of income inequality.

CEO WEALTH — POWER

The topic of executive compensation has garnered a great deal of attention from researchers in the past two decades (e.g., Gomez-Mejia, 1994; Gomez-Mejia & Wiseman, 1997; Zajac & Westphal, 1995). As CEO wages have soared, so have the number of articles published on the subject (Murphy, 1999). Whereas many scholars have investigated possible links (or lack thereof) between executive compensation and performance (e.g., Aggarwal & Samwick, 1999; Gilson & Vetsuypens, 1993), here we investigate the link between CEO compensation and resulting power. We view "power" simply to be the capacity to influence or control other people (French & Raven, 1959). Though we recognize that some forms of power such as that arising out of expertise may influence managerial compensation, we argue that in turn that this compensation adds to the economic, political, and social power of the CEO.

The Perks of Wealth: Economic and Political Advantages

That wealth leads to power clearly is not a new idea as is evidenced across the social sciences and history. In fact, some would suggest that the notion that wealth leads to power is part and parcel of conventional wisdom, as is attested by popular sayings such as, "He who has the gold makes the rules" (Pfeffer, 1981). But exactly how does power arise from wealth? There are several ways through which wealth leads to power (Ackerman, Goodwin, Dougherty, & Gallagher, 2000). First, those with more wealth have more power over allocation of resources in a market economy. The wealthy, just by being wealthy and participating in a consumer economy, channel resources into the production of whatever goods and services they happen to currently desire. In this way, the wealthy exert economic power over what goods society manufactures. Second, lenders favor those who can pledge collaterals or establish somehow that they are capable of repaying a debt (Bowles & Gintis, 1992). As a result, credit is unequally made available to those who already have assets, thereby reinforcing existing inequalities. Third, wealth imparts security by protecting the rich from any temporary halts in income flow or expensive emergencies (Spilerman, 2000).

Wealth is also a purveyor of political power. At the end of the day, money plays a big part in elections because high-income constituents have more voice to advocate for policies that favor them than do low-income constituents (Campbell & Skinner, 1976). The wealthy gain this voice through their contributions to candidates and causes and thereby exert control over political processes (Clawson, Neustadtl, & Weller, 1998). This is true also for wealthy CEOs (Lordon, 2002). For instance, in 2003, highly compensated CEOs each raised at least $100,000 for either George W. Bush or John Kerry in the U.S. presidential campaign (Ackman, 2004). CEOs' political power is further evidenced by the presence of tax loopholes that permit corporations to deduct excessive pay packages as a business expense (S. Anderson, Cavanagh, Collins, Pizzigati, & Lapham, 2007). Their power also is evidenced by their successfully lobbying for reform of labor laws and the welfare and tax systems (Bebchuk & Fried, 2003). For example, they have been more successful in bringing about reductions in the marginal tax for high income brackets than the less privileged have been in mobilizing support in favor of redistributive measures. Whereas the effective federal tax rate for the average American family has been nearly constant since 1980, there has been a lowering of the tax rate for millionaires and the top 1% of the wealthiest households (Phillips, 2002).

The economic and political power experienced by CEOs outside of their work sphere also makes itself known in their work domain. Galinsky, Gruenfeld, and Magee (2003) demonstrated that the recollection of power experienced in a past situation caused people to behave as if they were powerful in the situation at hand. What makes this finding fascinating is that even though the context in which people had felt powerful in the past was unrelated to the situation at hand, people felt powerful in the current situation. This finding leads us to believe that the economic and political power experienced in a non-work domain can serve as reminders of power that lead CEOs to behave as if they were more powerful at work.

Compensation as a Signal of Power

Whistler, Meyer, Baum, and Sorensen (1967) were among the first to argue that pay differentials provide information regarding the relative power of managers. Finkelstein (1992) and Hambrick and D'Aveni (1992) advocated that executives' compensation is an indicator of their standing in an organization and, as such, compensation is an important indicator of the formal power of CEOs. Their argument in favor of viewing compensation as a source of power is that compensation committees set pay scales both across and within hierarchical levels and intentionally create pay differentials that indicate a manager's position and power within the firm. According to the "figurehead" view of CEOs, a CEO's compensation also sends signals about the CEO's power across organizations (Steers & Ungson, 1987; Ungson & Steers, 1984). Henderson and Frederickson (1996) provided support for this view. They suggested that CEO compensation is a mechanism to send a message to organizational stakeholders that the CEO is powerful. That is, by investing more of the firm's money in the CEO, according to Henderson and Frederickson, the board of directors signals to the rest of the organization and the business community at large that the CEO is especially powerful in terms of determining organizational outcomes. The relationship between chief executives' compensation and power has been empirically documented in other studies as well (e.g., Barkema & Pennings, 1998; Finkelstein & Hambrick, 1988, 1989, 1996; Wade, O'Reilly, & Chandradat, 1990). For instance, using a sample of 303 large publicly traded U.S. firms, Lambert, Larcher, and Weigelt (1993) tested their "managerial power model" according to which managerial compensation and power should be positively correlated. Their data, which included manufacturing and service firms spanning a large number of industrial sectors, supported the hypothesis that the higher the compensation, the higher is managerial power.

As CEOs' compensation increases, so does their perceived power. And, the CEOs' self-perceptions of this increased power likely cause them to act as if they were indeed more powerful. Finkelstein (1992), in fact, demonstrated that structural power, operationalized in part by compensation, was strongly associated with executives' perceptions of their power. Moreover, Pfeffer (1981) argued that beliefs and practices associated with those in power may become institutionalized. That is, if a CEO perceives himself/herself to be powerful and acts accordingly, then organizational members view the CEO's coercive actions as a matter of course and nothing out of the ordinary, with the CEO's power going unquestioned. Thus, compensation can be seen to trigger a process in which perceptions of power come to be realized.

That higher income concentration at the top leads to increased power at the top is clear, based on the evidence and arguments presented above. Moreover, as CEOs accumulate wealth from their high incomes, cumulative advantage processes likely operate whereby CEOs' wealth and income inequality further escalate over time (DiPrete & Eirich, 2006) with concomitant effects on CEOs' power. Now we turn to how this experience of power and the self-perception of it change the way that top managers think of themselves, their work, their subordinates, and, consequently, the way they act. In doing so, we address how exaggerated power differences between the corporate elite and wage earners cause CEOs to objectify workers and issue self-licenses to exploit them.

CEO POWER — MEANNESS

There are numerous examples of powerful executives behaving meanly toward lower level employees. An example of corporate meanness is the controversial and unethical strategy adopted by powerful FedEx executives toward their workers, whereby FedEx drivers are misclassified as independent contractors (Greenhouse, 2008). This ruse allows FedEx to get out of paying social security for its workers and at the same time requires workers to pay for their trucks, insurance, repairs, gas, and tires. The so-called independent contractors are required to wear the FedEx uniform, are given specific instructions about what to do, when to do it, how to do it, and when to take breaks. In addition, FedEx claims that its 15,000 drivers have no right to unionize because they are independent contractors. Another example of powerful executives behaving meanly is the case of a Koch Foods poultry plant in Tennessee (Greenhouse, 2008). The managers were so keen to keep the assembly line operating nonstop that workers were ordered not to go to the restroom except during their lunch and coffee breaks. If workers expressed a dire need to go to the toilette, they were publicly humiliated. Not only is there anecdotal evidence that power differences lead to mean behavior, systematic research has also found power to be related to a variety of negative effects such as selfish and corrupt behavior (C. Anderson & Galinsky, 2006; Chen, Lee-Chai, & Bargh, 2001; Galinsky et al., 2003; Kipnis, 1972); reduced empathy and less openness to the perspectives, emotions, and attitudes of others (C. Anderson, Keltner, & John, 2000; Galinsky, Magee, Inesi, & Gruenfeld, 2006; Van Kleef, De Dreu, Pietroni, & Manstead, 2006); and a tendency to objectify and stereotype others[2] (Goodwin, Gubin, Fiske, & Yzerbyt, 2000; Gruenfeld, Inesi, Magee, & Galinsky, 2008). Power has also been recognized as a catalyst that might trigger sexual harassment (Bargh, Raymond, Pryor, & Strack, 1995).

What is it about power that causes people to behave in mean and selfish ways? Below, we outline philosophical and psychological perspectives that speak to the ways in which possessing high amounts of relative power can alter the way people think of themselves and others and consequently causes people to behave meanly toward those with low power. We first discuss how the experience of power causes people to objectify others and treat them as inferior beings. We then examine Kipnis's (1972) classic conception of powerholding. Lastly, we examine power-as-control and power-as-threat theories, which offer additional insight into psychological mechanisms that lead the powerful to behave meanly toward those with low power.

Philosophers have discoursed on how being in a position of power leads those in power to view the powerless as objects to be used for personal gratification (e.g., Nussbaum, 1999). Broadly defined, "objectification" is a process of instrumentality that involves viewing people as means to an ends, as objects to be used and discarded, without according them the rights and respect due to beings with moral worth (e.g., Bartky, 1990; Frederickson & Roberts, 1997). Instrumentality, arising out of power differences, explains a broad range of mean behaviors, from sexual objectification (Dworkin, 1974, 1987; MacKinnon & Emerson, 1979) to Marx's notion of economic objectification under capitalism (Marx, 1884/1983).

Psychological research has shown that power directs the attention of the power holder toward those features of a target that are most relevant to the goals of the powerful (Overbeck & Park, 2001, 2006; Vescio, Gervais,

Snyder, & Hoover, 2005; Vescio, Snyder, & Butz, 2003) and that being in a position of power, in fact, causes people to objectify those in positions of low or no power (Gruenfeld et al., 2008). Being in power tends to promote objectification by reducing the power holder's awareness of others and their individuating features, unless those features are instrumental for power-holders to accomplish their goals (Van Kleef et al., 2006). Zimbardo (2007) argued that as a result of objectification and dehumanization, an environment with exaggerated power asymmetry can cause even normal people without any apparent prior psychological problems to become brutal and abusive toward those with low power. Consistent with this reasoning, Keltner, Gruenfeld, and Anderson (2003) propose that high levels of power lead the powerful to engage in automatic information processing and pursue self-rewards in a disinhibited manner. As such, those with high power may be more likely to view others in instrumental self-interested ways and may be less motivated to think of the needs and aspirations of the less powerful (Keltner et al., 2003).

The objectification of those who are weaker is consistent with Kipnis's (1976) classic conception of power holding. He identified four corrupting influences of power affecting power holders and those in subordinate relationships with them. He postulated that power becomes an end in itself, to be acquired at any cost. Furthermore, the experience of power results in a desire to influence subordinates, and once influence has been exerted, power-holders begin to believe that the actions of subordinates are not self-controlled. They attribute a subordinate's effort to the exertion of managerial power rather than to the subordinate's ability or motivation. Consequently, power-holders begin to devalue the worth of subordinates and develop a desire to maintain social and psychological distance from them. Power-holders' self-evaluations change to the point where they develop an exalted sense of themselves and believe that common moral standards are not applicable to them. Over the course of time, the more powerful see the powerless as inferior human beings and feel that the moral values that affirm the intrinsic worth of each person are not applicable to the less powerful. Consistent with this reasoning, a meta-analysis of 25 studies focused on the relation between power and superiors' evaluations of subordinates (Georgesen & Harris, 1998) found that as power levels increase, evaluations of subordinates become increasingly negative and self-evaluations grow increasingly positive. All in all, the experience of power metamorphoses power holders into meaner people.

Fiske's (1993) "power as control" theory offers another possible explanation why powerful people stereotype and abuse their subordinates. According to this theory, power-holders often do not perceive any repercussions of incorrectly evaluating subordinates. On the contrary, they feel motivated to denigrate their subordinates to justify and protect their power. Stereotyping subordinates justifies individual and group power differentials and helps minimize threats to power roles (Fein & Spencer, 1997; Jost & Banaji, 1994). Georgesen and Harris (2000) further developed this idea in their "power as threat" theory, wherein they suggested that the powerful often feel insecure about their positions. As such, the powerful are likely to misperceive their subordinates' actions as threats to their own position and, consequently, derogate them as a preemptive strike. Kramer and Gavrieli (2004) discussed the prevalence of leader paranoia and how those in power are predisposed to view others as a potential source of opposition or even danger. They went on to say that the powerful feel safer if those with less power are stripped of whatever little power they have. Paranoid leaders justify their mean behavior and rationalize it by overemphasizing the dangers and costs of misplaced trust in low power individuals. Their frame of mind can be summed best in the words of Intel's former CEO, Andrew Grove, "Only the paranoid survive" (Kramer & Gavrieli, 2004).

The theorizing and research discussed above suggest that when individuals have high levels of power, they tend to treat those with low levels of power in a negative and dehumanizing fashion. That is, the powerful tend to self-interestedly pursue personal goals without concern for the social consequences of their actions and the needs and well-being of the less powerful. Ultimately, wide power disparities can lead to social exploitation of those with low levels of power. So far, the story that increased CEO compensation leads to increased power asymmetries and, consequently, meaner managers is based on theoretical arguments. Below, we report a crude first test of our arguments.

A PRELIMINARY STUDY

The unit of analysis for our study was the organization. We investigated the relationship between the total compensation of an organization's CEO and the organization's adherence to human rights. The sample of organizations was drawn from Kinder, Lydenherg, Domini & Co. (KLD) Company Profiles, a database that has been used by several researchers in the past (e.g., Graves & Waddock, 1994; Johnson & Greening, 1949; Kane, Velury, & Ruf, 2005; Turban & Greening, 1996). For each year starting from 1991, KLD compiles the top 100 best corporate citizens. In our study, we focused on the publicly available list of the top 100 best corporate citizens for the year 2006. This list was compiled by KLD after screening approximately 650 companies that comprised the S&P Index, the Domini 400 Social Index, the Russell 1000, and the Russell 3000 for the year 2006. Of the 650 companies, only those with superior ratings in environmental, social, and governance performance were rank-ordered and included in the final 100 list. In our sample, we included only those firms that were listed in the 100 best corporate citizens list for 2006 and for whom information regarding executive compensation was available in the Compustat database for the previous year. Our sample size was 85 firms.

Our dependent variable was the human rights performance of the firm. In the KLD database, each firm receives a rating of its strengths and weaknesses with respect to observance of human rights. In our analysis, we chose to focus on the variable human rights as an indicator of meanness (the lower the rating, the more meanness) and a very crude proxy for how lower participants may be treated in the organization. We computed CEO compensation as salary plus bonus. Compensation was measured for the lag year because we expected income inequality effects to take time to set in. Because firm size might be correlated with CEO compensation, we used it as a control in our analysis. Firm size was operationalized as the total market value of equity and was measured for the lag year.

Sample means, standard deviations, and correlations for the indicator variables are presented in Table 13.1. The first thing to note is that the average compensation of the CEOs in our sample is below the average CEO compensation for 2005. This suggests that the companies that made it to the top 100 best corporate citizens' list paid their CEOs less than the going rate. To examine if CEO compensation affected subsequent human rights, we conducted a regression analysis (Cohen & Cohen, 1983) on human rights. The results are presented in Table 13.2. Of greatest importance, the hypothesized CEO compensation–human rights relation was significant ($b = -.35$, $t = -2.79$, $p < .01$). This finding suggests that the higher the

TABLE 13.1

Correlation Analysis of Predictor Variables

	Mean	SD	1	2	3
1. Human rights	—	—	1.00		
2. CEO compensation (in thousands of 2005 USD)	7,641.51	2,567.21	−0.41[**]	1.00	
3. Firm size	6.79	6.55	−0.31[*]	0.61[**]	1.00

Note: All tests of variables are two-tailed ($N = 85$).
[*]$p \leq .01$, [**]$p \leq .001$.

TABLE 13.2

Summary of Hierarchical Regression Analysis of Variables, Human Rights[a]

	Step 1	Step 2
Main Effects		
Firm size	−0.31**	−0.10
CEO compensation		−0.35**
R^2	0.10**	0.17**
ΔR^2		0.07*
Adjusted R^2	0.09**	0.15**

Note: All tests of variables are two-tailed ($N = 85$).
[a] Beta coefficients are standardized.
[*]$p \leq .05$; [**]$p \leq .01$.

level of CEO compensation, the less the human rights were upheld by the organization.

Our study, as we have mentioned before, is crude. For example, we did not gauge either income inequality within organizations or meanness directed toward lower level organizational participants; rather we studied CEO compensation and the humanitarian posture of the organization. Moreover, our sample was highly skewed — America's 100 best companies in terms of corporate citizenship. But such skewness could be interpreted as contributing to a more conservative test of our hypothesis. Future research should attend to these issues. Additionally, researchers may want to examine the inequality-meanness relation from a cross-cultural perspective. Yet another possibility might be to examine this relationship across countries with varying levels of income inequality to determine whether employees are treated better in countries that have less income inequality (e.g., Denmark).

CONCLUSIONS

In sum, we propose that escalating income inequality in the workplace results in a greater concentration of power at the top and a widening disparity in power levels between top managers and rank-and-file workers. The ramifications of this inequity for worker welfare in corporate America are exceedingly negative. Though varying degrees of power have always existed in the workplace, of late the gap between the top and the bottom has become exaggerated. The powerful are getting more powerful at the expense of the powerless and in the process they are experiencing increased psychological distance from lower level employees, valuing them less, and divesting them of human qualities. Dehumanizing lower level employees strips decision-making situations of ethical implications and offers disinhibited executives a pass to pursue self-interest without regard to the needs and well-being of those at the bottom; through both deliberate and automatic processes that accompany possessing very high levels of power, there is the very real potential for the powerful at the top to treat those at the bottom in an increasingly mean and selfish fashion.

We have painted a bleak picture of the consequences of income inequality in the corporate world, but what is the solution? Bebchuk and Fried (2003) and Crystal (1991) suggested that one possible solution might be to make the board of directors, who determine CEO pay, more independent of the executives they supervise and more dependent on shareholders instead. This would encourage the board of directors to bear in mind possible repercussions from shareholders if they set the CEO compensation unwisely. In 2007, then-Senator Barack Obama sponsored the Shareholder Vote on Executive Compensation Act, which was strongly supported by the U.S. House of Representatives but was defeated in the U.S. Senate (LaBolt, 2007). If such a piece of legislation is passed, it would be a step in the right direction. In October 2007, the Securities and Exchange Commission (SEC) published results of a review that examined how companies disclose to their shareholders information about the procedure through which CEO compensation is determined. The SEC's report concluded that such disclosure is made in a vague and imprecise manner and recommended that in the section regarding compensation discussion and analysis, companies' reports should be more specific and precise regarding how and why a company arrives at a particular executive compensation decision. Also, the SEC recommended that companies should cater their reports to both the lay reader and the professional.

Yet another solution may be modifying how executive income is taxed. Currently, executive deferred pay plans allow unlimited tax deferrals whereas the standard 401(k) plans, the only tax-deferral tool available to rank-and-file corporate employees, are constrained by strict deferral limits. Putting a cap on tax-free deferred executive pay may help reduce the wealth disparity between CEOs and lower level employees. Also, managers of private equity and hedge funds (who made 22,255 times the compensation of ordinary workers last year) currently pay taxes on a large portion of their income at the 15% capital gains rate as opposed to the standard 35% rate that would apply if their compensation were treated as ordinary earnings (S. Anderson et al., 2007). Legislation that puts an end to such tax loopholes and an increase in the top marginal tax rate on high incomes are essential to redistribute tax burdens fairly across executives and ordinary workers. Lastly, tax loopholes that allow corporations to deduct excessive pay packages as a "business expense" should be eliminated if businesses are to be forced to consider lowering CEO pay packages (S. Anderson et al., 2007).

We started this chapter by stating Plato's recommendation that no one in a community should make more than five times the wages of the lowest paid worker. Plato referred to income inequality as the greatest of all plagues. His solution to the problem was to set limits for poverty as well as riches. J. P. Morgan, who is no stranger to capitalism, voiced a similar solution. He stated that CEOs should earn no more than 20 times the wages of an average worker (Crystal, 1991). An alternative solution would be to require CEOs and other people with exorbitantly high incomes to donate earnings in excess of a set amount to a charity of their choice. This way, CEOs would still be able to "compete" for the status and prestige that accompanies high-paying jobs.

In closing, compensation for top executives has grown at an unprecedented rate in the past two decades, resulting in unprecedented income inequality between executives and rank-and-file employees. The rising income inequality between CEOs and ordinary workers, in turn, is creating extreme power asymmetries in the workplace. We propose that these power differences can lead to CEOs behaving in a mean and selfish fashion toward lower level employees. Corporate and public policies sorely need to respond before workers rebel, leading America into a perhaps long overdue class struggle that speaks to the downsides of corporate capitalism (e.g., Kasser, Cohn, Kanner, & Ryan, 2007).

NOTES

1. Our reading of Plato's *Laws* led us to understand that no one should earn more than five times the pay of the lowest paid worker.
2. Handgraaf and colleagues have shown that in delta ultimatum bargaining games, as the power asymmetry between allocators and recipients increases, allocators make increasingly unfavorable offers to recipients (Handgraaf, Van Dijk, Vermunt, Wilke, & De Dreu, 2000). However, when the recipient is completely powerless, allocators make offers that are slightly better than the offers they make in situations in which the recipient has at least a little power. Thus, if one could conceive of a case in which workers are completely powerless, then our reasoning may not hold.

REFERENCES

Ackerman, F., Goodwin, N. R., Dougherty, L., & Gallagher, K. (2000). *The political economy of inequality*. Covelo, CA: Island Press.

Ackman, D. (2004, August 31). CEOs who outsource jobs are paid better. *Forbes*. Retrieved June 25, 2008 from http://moneycentral.msn.com/content/invest/forbes/P93373.asp.

Aggarwal, R. K., & Samwick, A. A. (1999). Executive compensation, strategic competition, and relative performance evaluation: Theory and evidence. *The Journal of Finance, 54*, 1999–2043.

Anderson, C., & Galinsky, A. D. (2006). Power, optimism, and risk-taking. *European Journal of Social Psychology, 36*, 511–536.

Anderson, C., Keltner, D. J., & John, O. P. (2003). Emotional convergence between people over time. *Journal of Personality and Social Psychology, 84*, 1054–1068.

Anderson, S., Cavanagh, J., Collins, C., Pizzigati, S., & Lapham, M. (2007). *Executive excess 2007: The staggering social cost of U.S. business leadership*. Retrieved June 5, 2008, from http://www.faireconomy.org/files/pdf/ExecutiveExcess2007. pdf

Bargh, J. A., Raymond, P., Pryor, J. B., & Strack, F. (1995). Attractiveness of the underling: An automatic power-sex association and its consequences for sexual harassment and aggression. *Journal of Personality and Social Psychology, 68*, 768–781.

Barkema, H. G., & Pennings, J. M. (1998). Top management pay: Impact of overt and covert power. *Organization Studies, 19*, 975–1003.

Bartky, S. L. (1990). *Femininity and domination: Studies in the phenomenology of oppression.* New York: Routledge.

Bebchuk, L. A., & Fried, J. M. (2003). Executive compensation as an agency problem. *Journal of Economic Perspectives, 17*, 71–92.

Bowles, S., & Gintis, H. (1992). Power and wealth in a competitive capitalist economy. *Philosophy and Public Affairs, 21*, 324–353.

Burtless, G. (2003). Has widening inequality promoted or retarded US growth? *Canadian Public Policy/Analyse de Politiques, 29*, S185–S201.

Campbell, R. H., & Skinner, A. S. (1976). General introduction. In A. Smith (Ed.), *An inquiry into the nature and causes of the wealth of nations.* Indianapolis, IN: Liberty Press.

Chen, S., Lee-Chai, A. Y., & Bargh, J. A. (2001). Relationship orientation as a moderator of the effects of social power. *Journal of Personality and Social Psychology, 80*, 173–187.

Clawson, D., Neustadtl, A., & Weller, M. (1998). *Dollars and votes: How business campaign contributions subvert democracy.* Philadelphia: Temple University Press.

Cohen, J., & Cohen, P. (1983). *Applied multiple regression/correlation analysis for the behavioral sciences.* NJ: Erlbaum.

Crystal, G. S. (1991). *In search of excess: The overcompensation of American executives.* New York: W. W. Norton.

Darley, J. M., Messick, D. M., & Tyler, T. R. (Eds.). (2001). *Social influences on ethical behavior in organizations.* Mahwah, NJ: Lawrence Erlbaum.

DiPrete, T. A., & Eirich, G. M. (2006). Cumulative advantage as a mechanism for inequality: A review of theoretical and empirical developments. *Annual Review of Sociology, 32*, 271–297.

Dvorak, P. (2007, April 9). Theory and practice — Limits on executive pay: Easy to set, hard to keep. *Wall Street Journal*, p. B.1

Dworkin, A. (1974). *Woman hating.* New York: Dutton.

Dworkin, A. (1987). *Intercourse.* London: Secker & Warburg.

Fein, S., & Spencer, S. J. (1997). Prejudice as self-image maintenance: Affirming the self through derogating others. *Journal of Personality and Social Psychology, 73*, 31–44.

Finklestein, S. (1992). Power in top management teams: Dimensions, measurement, and validation. *Academy of Management Journal, 35*, 505–538.

Finkelstein, S., & Hambrick, D. C. (1988). Chief executive compensation: A synthesis and reconciliation. *Strategic Management Journal, 9*, 543–558.

Finkelstein, S., & Hambrick, D. C. (1989). Chief executive compensation: A study of the intersection of markets and political processes. *Strategic Management Journal, 10*, 121–134.

Finkelstein, S., & Hambrick, D. C. (1996). *Strategic leadership: Top executives and their organizations.* Minneapolis: West Publishing Company.

Fiske, S. T. (1993). Controlling other people: The impact of power on stereotyping. *American Psychologist, 48*, 621–628.

Frank, R. H. (2007). *Falling behind: How rising inequality harms the middle class.* Berkeley, CA: University of California Press.

Frederickson, B. L., & Roberts, T. A. (1997). Objectification theory. *Psychology of Women Quarterly, 21*, 173–206.

French, J. R. P., & Raven, B. (1959). The bases of social power. In D. Cartwright (Ed.), *Studies in social power* (pp. 150–167). Ann Arbor: University of Michigan Press.

Galinsky, A. D., Gruenfeld, D. H., & Magee, J. C. (2003). From power to action. *Journal of Personality and Social Psychology, 85,* 453–466.

Galinsky, A. D., Magee, J. C., Inesi, M. E., & Gruenfeld, D. H. (2006). Power and perspectives not taken. *Psychological Science, 17,* 1068–1074.

Georgesen, J. C., & Harris, M. J. (1998). Why's my boss always holding me down? A meta-analysis of power effects on performance evaluations. *Personality and Social Psychology Review, 2,* 184–195.

Georgesen, J. C., & Harris, M. J. (2000). The balance of power: Interpersonal consequences of differential power and expectancies. *Personality and Social Psychology Bulletin, 26,* 1239–1257.

Gilson, S. C., & Vetsuypens, M. R. (1993). CEO compensation in financially distressed firms: An empirical analysis. *The Journal of Finance, 48,* 425–458.

Gomez-Mejia, L. R., & Wiseman, R. M. (1997). Reframing executive compensation: An assessment and outlook. *Journal of Management, 23,* 291–375.

Gomez-Mejia, L. R. (1994). Executive compensation: A reassessment and future research agenda. *Research in Personnel and Human Resource Management, 12,* 161–222.

Goodwin, S. A., Gubin, A., Fiske, S. T., & Yzerbyt, V. Y. (2000). Power can bias impression processes: Stereotyping subordinates by default and by design. *Group Processes and Intergroup Relations, 3,* 227–256.

Graves, S. B., & Waddock, S. A. (1994). Institutional owners and corporate social performance. *Academy of Management Journal, 37,* 1034–1046.

Greenhouse, S. (2008). *The big squeeze: Tough times for the American worker.* New York: Knopf.

Gruenfeld, D. H., Inesi, M. E., Magee, J. C., & Galinsky, A. D. (2008). Power and the objectification of social targets. *Journal of Personality and Social Psychology, 95,* 1450–1466.

Hambrick, D. C., & D'Aveni, R. A. (1992). Top team deterioration as part of the downward spiral of large corporate bankruptcies. *Management Science, 38,* 1445–1466.

Handgraaf, M. J. J., Van Dijk, E., Vermunt, R. C., Wilke, H. A. M., & De Dreu, C. K. W. (2008). Less power or powerless? Egocentric empathy gaps and the irony of having little versus no power in social decision making. *Journal of Personality and Social Psychology, 95,* 1136–1149.

Henderson, A. D., & Fredrickson, J. W. (1996). Information-processing demands as a determinant of CEO compensation. *Academy of Management Journal, 39,* 575–606.

Johnson, R. A., & Greening, D. W. (1999). The effect of corporate governance and institutional ownership types on corporate social performance. *Academy of Management Journal, 42,* 564–576.

Jost, J. T., & Banaji, M. R. (1994). The role of stereotyping in system-justification and the production of false-consciousness. *British Journal of Social Psychology, 33,* 1–27.

Kane, G. D., Velury, U., & Ruf, B. M. (2005). Employee relations and the likelihood of occurrence of corporate financial distress. *Journal of Business Finance & Accounting, 32,* 1083–1105.

Kasser, T., Cohn, S., Kanner, A. D., & Ryan, R. M. (2007). Some costs of American corporate capitalism: A psychological exploration of value and goal conflicts. *Psychological Inquiry, 18,* 1–22.

Keltner, D., Gruenfeld, D. H., & Anderson, C. (2003). Power, approach, and inhibition. *Psychological Review, 110,* 265–284.

Kipnis, D. (1972). Does power corrupt? *Journal of Personality and Social Psychology, 24,* 33–41.

Kipnis, D. (1976). *The powerholders.* Chicago: University of Chicago Press.

Kramer, R. M., & Gavrieli, D. A. (2004). The exaggerated perception of conspiracy: Leader paranoia as adaptive cognition. In D. M. Messick & R. M. Kramer (Eds.), *The psychology of leadership: New perspectives and research*. Mahwah, NJ: Lawrence Erlbaum.

LaBolt, B. (2007). Obama calls for hearing on bill to give shareholders vote on executive pay. Retrieved June 5, 2008, from http://obama.senate.gov/press/070530-obama_calls_for_5/

Lambert, R. A., & Larcher, D. F., & Weigelt, K. (1993). The structure of organizational incentives. *Administrative Science Quarterly, 38*, 438–461.

Lordon, F. (2002). *La Politique du capital*. Paris: Odile Jacob.

MacKinnon, C., & Emerson, I. E. (1979). *Sexual harassment of working women: A case of sex discrimination*. New Haven, CT: Yale University Press.

Marx, K. (1983). Excerpts from "Economico – Philosophical Manuscripts of 1844." In E. Eugene Kamenka (Ed.), *The portable Karl Marx* (p. 131). New York: Penguin. (Original work published 1844)

Messick, D. M., & Bazerman, M. (1996). Ethical leadership and the psychology of decision making. *Sloan Management Review, 37*, 9–22.

Messick, D. M., & Tenbrunsel, A. E. (Eds.). (1996). *Codes of conduct*. New York: Russell Sage Foundation.

Murphy, K. J. (1999). Executive compensation. In O. Ashenfelter & D. Card (Eds.), *Handbook of labor economics* (pp. 2485–2563). Amsterdam: North Holland.

Neckerman, K. M., & Torche, F. (2007). Inequality: Causes and consequences. *Annual Review of Sociology, 33*, 335–357.

Nussbaum, M. C. (1999). *Sex and social justice*. New York: Oxford University Press.

Overbeck, J. R., & Park, B. (2001). When power does not corrupt: Superior individuation processes among powerful perceivers. *Journal of Personality and Social Psychology, 81*, 549–565.

Overbeck, J. R., & Park, B. (2006). Powerful perceivers, powerless objects: Flexibility of powerholders' social attention. *Organizational Behavior and Human Decision Processes, 99*, 227–243.

Pfeffer, J. (1981). *Power in organizations*. Marshfield, MA: Pitman Publishing.

Phillips, K. (2002). *Wealth and democracy*. New York: Broadway Books.

Shell, A. (2007, August). Cash of the titans: Criticism of pay for fund execs grows. *USA Today*. Retrieved June 25, 2008, from http://www.usatoday.com/money/companies/management/2007-08-29-private-equity-pay_N.htm

Spilerman, S. (2000). Wealth and stratification processes. *Annual Review of Sociology, 26*, 497–524.

Steers, R., & Ungson, G. R. (1987). Strategic issues in executive compensation decisions. In D. B. Balkin & L. R. Gomez-Mejia (Eds.), *New perspectives on compensation* (pp. 315–327). Englewood Cliffs, NJ: Prentice-Hall.

Tenbrunsel, A. E., & Messick, D. M. (1999). Sanctioning systems, decision frames, and cooperation. *Administrative Science Quarterly, 44*, 684–707.

Tenbrunsel, A. E., & Messick, D. M. (2004). Ethical fading: The role of rationalization in unethical behaviour. *Social Justice Research, 17*, 223–236.

Turban, D. B., & Greening, D. W. (1996). Corporate social performance and organizational attractiveness to prospective employees. *Academy of Management Journal, 40*, 658–672.

Ungson, G. R., & Steers, R. M. (1984). Motivation and politics in executive compensation. *Academy of Management Review, 9*, 313–323.

U.S. Census Bureau. (2006) Household income quintiles and top 5%. Retrieved June 6, 2007, from http://pubdb3.census.gov/macro/032006/hhinc/new05_000.htm

Van Kleef, G. A., De Dreu, C. K. W., Pietroni, D., & Manstead, A. S. R. (2006). Power and emotion in negotiation: Power moderates the interpersonal effects of anger and happiness on concession making. *European Journal of Social Psychology, 36*, 557–581.

Vescio, T. K., Gervais, S. J., Snyder, M., & Hoover, A. (2005). Power and the creation of patronizing environments: The stereotype-based behaviors of the powerful and their effects on female performance in masculine domains. *Journal of Personality and Social Psychology, 88*, 658–672.

Vescio, T. K., Snyder, M., & Butz, D. A. (2003). Power in stereotypically masculine domains: A social influence strategy X stereotype match model. *Journal of Personality and Social Psychology, 85*, 1062–1078.

Wade, J. B., O'Reilly, C. A., & Chandradat, I. (1990). Golden parachutes: CEOs and the exercise of social influence. *Administrative Science Quarterly, 35*, 587–603.

Wade, J. B., O'Reilly, C. A., & Pollock, T. G. (2006). Overpaid CEOs and underpaid managers: Fairness and executive compensation. *Organization Science, 17*, 527–544.

Whistler, T. L., Meyer, H., Baum, B. H., & Sorensen, P. F., Jr. (1967). Centralization of organizational control: An empirical study of its meaning and measurement. *Journal of Business, 40*, 10–26.

Zajac, E. J., & Westphal, J. D. (1995). Accounting for the explanations of CEO compensation: Substance and symbolism. *Administrative Science Quarterly, 40*, 283–308.

Zimbardo, P. (2007). *The Lucifer effect: Understanding how good people turn evil.* New York: Random House.

Section IV

Commentary and Reflections

14

Appreciation for Professor David M. Messick: Peanuts, Ping-Pong, and Naïveté

Robyn M. Dawes
Carnegie Mellon University

Our present-day discipline of psychonomics has two historical origins: psychology and economics. These disciplines merged around the year 2030 when several leading social science theorists convinced their colleagues once and for all that everyone was indeed totally selfish and that apparent altruism, interest in fairness, and other sentimental concerns were illusory — except for those that could be related to future egoistic benefits. Moreover, consensus arose that though people are not rational in the narrow sense of being logically coherent in their thinking, they (we) are "evolutionarily rational" in the sense of embracing beneficial (not irrational) cognitive heuristics and biases that achieve selfish goals. It is, therefore, of interest to study some of the ideas of a leading theorist from roughly 20 to 60 years ago who believed in the sentimental view of humans as potentially embracing human cooperation and altruism for their own sakes. His name is David M. Messick.

First, due to some unusual circumstances, we were able to obtain a majority of his published manuscripts. Though the Library of Congress was destroyed in a counterattack against a group of aspirational terrorists, and the major branches of the University of California (he was at Santa Barbara for a while) was swept out to sea after global warming had inadvertently increased the power of Pacific tsunamis by a factor of 43.8, this man Messick also had many copies of his work at Northwestern University in Evanston, Illinois, which had not been destroyed — but only made uninhabitable — by the handcrafted nuclear device that had blown up Chicago. We were able to recover these copies from his old office at Northwestern by using a recently devised robotic thief. (We had a long correspondence before we obtained permission from what we considered the most relevant Institutional Review Board, but that is "another story," as the saying goes.) To discover whether this man Messick really had any influence, we noted the names of people to whom he referred in his papers available to us and were able to determine that many of them did, in fact, reference his work as well. So we can conclude that he was influential, despite his naïve view of "human nature." Here, we will simply outline the development of this view — together with the critique specifying how badly it is flawed. Because we do not have access to a complete set of his papers, our references will be sketchy.

Apparently, his initial impact had to do with peanuts. He would ask his sons: "Would you rather have two peanuts and he have one? Or would you rather have three peanuts and he have four?" (Someone named Dawes repeated this experiment, only using miniature cookies instead of peanuts, with his two daughters.) For quite a number of choices, both of his children (and Dawes' later) replied that they would prefer two with the other child getting one.

That is, of course, the evolutionarily rational choice. We are all competing with each other for the replication of our genes, and — except in those few cases of mutual starvation and death — having a comparative advantage in food (or sex, or status, or whatever) is preferably to having more on an absolute basis, but with a comparative disadvantage, or a tie. Nevertheless, Messick seemed to believe that the 3 versus 4 choice was the rational one to make (as apparently did Dawes, who was delighted when his older daughter started indicating this preference) — based on the naïve belief that (leaving clogged arteries aside) more is better than less. We now understand that in the competition for reproduction of our genes, it is only the comparative advantage that is important. How that obvious conclusion escaped Messick (and Dawes) is a bit of a mystery, because they both appeared to be reasonably intelligent fellows.

Messick then went on to do a lot of experimental work in situations naïvely labeled *social dilemmas*. The definition of such dilemmas was that there was a dominant strategy for each player but that these strategies converged on a "deficient equilibrium," which was an outcome that no player desired as much as some other outcome on which non-dominant strategies might converge. Again, however, what Messick failed to realize was that by eschewing the dominant strategy, people are actually hurting themselves, because unless there was some guarantee that absolutely every player would do that, the so-called cooperative player might end up with less than some other player. Again, the illusion occurred because the amount that is comparatively less might be coded as absolutely more, but that once again such an illusion fails to take account of the competitive nature of economic decision-making and gene survival. (From our current, more "sophisticated" view of game theoretic outcomes, "everybody wins" is actually no different from the outcome that "everybody loses.")

Again, the point is not to think of money or sex in absolute terms but in comparative terms. (Thus, people who belonged to the U.S. Democratic party at the time were quite rational to worry that somehow, someone might be making more money than they did, whereas people who belonged to the Republican party at the time were correct to worry that somehow, somewhere people might be having more sex — or enjoying it more — than they.) That is, with our current understanding of the true nature of human nature, we can appreciate that Messick and many colleagues framed the whole problem of joint action backwards; for example, the critical social problem is not how to enhance cooperation in a social dilemma situation but how to enlighten the chooser so that cooperation is stomped out.

Along with his concerns about what he thought was desirable in choice in social dilemma situations, Messick had an obsession with what he and others termed *fairness*. He even thought that he suffered from a "bias" when he believed that he himself was "more fair than others." With our current understanding that fairness per se is undesirable from the evolutionary perspective, we might find it hard to be sympathetic with his garbled thinking; not only did he consider fairness to be good, but that his view that he was more fair than others was somehow bad.

Moreover, Messick failed to consider the ways in which behavior that is not on its surface selfish actually is when its source is known. For example, he concluded that our responses in these situations are often rooted in "shallow rules, habitual rituals, and other processes that are not directly intended to maximize outcomes, values or utilities." But a person's intention is not the point. The point is to survive, thrive, and reproduce, whatever one's "intention."

Now there are, in fact, cultures in which his concern may appear legitimate. Consider a culture in which unenlightened people believe in public "fairness," in which case it is beneficial for an individual to appear to be fair, in hopes of harvesting later rewards from others suffering from the same cultural delusion. Whether or not desiring fairness is an illusion, it would in such circumstances be desirable for an individual to appear to be fair.

But the "more fair than others" conclusion still presents a conundrum. For example, Dawes — who shared much of Messick's sentimentality about human nature — thought that Messick's conclusions could be the result of a simple availability bias. Messick was aware of the situations in which he himself was tempted to be what he would have labeled as "unfair" but nevertheless acted in a fair manner. He did not have this privileged information for others, about whom he knew only their overt behavior. So of course he thought he was "fairer than others."

But that rather "shallow" interpretation of what is going on ignores the importance of subsequent reinforcement from social peers. If, indeed, a concern with fairness is valued by others, then what better way of encouraging oneself to be overtly fair could there be than to have an exaggerated view of the degree to which one is in fact fair? If, on the other hand, a majority of people understand that fairness is bad, then the exaggerated view of one's own fairness might create sympathy on the part of peers. After all, this was an era in which people who suffered psychologically were in fact pitied, and several professions — psychiatry, clinical psychology, social work — emerged to alleviate their alleged suffering. Even in that unenlightened era, however, we understood that "no good ever comes from guilt," and that therefore someone's exaggerated need to be fair should simply be educated — out of existence. There is no need to access the guilt-producing subconscious part of the superego to understand why somebody might feel bad about believing themselves, or believed by others, to be overly fair. Instead, once people understand that their guilt is based on an irrational reversal of an accurate assessment of what they should do, this guilt will disappear.

Messick also did apparently influential work showing that selfish preferences influence judgments of such "fairness." Of course! He claimed that such judgments were positively related to egoistic payoffs. Even finding no relationship would be inconsistent with our knowledge of human nature. So should judgments of fairness? Of course! He had concluded that such judgments were positively related to egoistic payoffs. What else could he conclude? The opposite?

Finally, in his frantic effort to justify cooperation in social dilemma situations, Messick came up with the theory of "appropriate behavior." In effect, he maintained that people ask — implicitly or consciously — "What sort of person am I, and what is the appropriate behavior for someone like me?" As part of a basic tautology, if somebody concludes that they are a "cooperative" person, then they should behave "cooperatively"; otherwise, they shouldn't.[1] Though his appropriateness explanation can be critiqued on the basis of its circularity, a far more serious critique is that "appropriateness" is better defined in terms of what garners rewards. If, for example, it is appropriate to be a gang member as an adolescent "psychopath," then the good gang member is rewarded. If it is considered appropriate for someone born into the Mormon faith to proselytize during young adulthood, then attempting during this period to convert others to Mormonism will garner social rewards. The point is that what is deemed appropriate may bear absolutely no relationship to what a sentimentalist such as Messick believed but is in fact arbitrary. (Consider, for example, the story of the three umpires in baseball calling balls and strikes. The first alleges that "I calls 'em like they is," but the second corrects him by stating: "I calls 'em like I sees 'em." The third corrects both his colleagues by pointing out that: "They ain't nothing until I calls 'em.")

It must be admitted that if we were to accept the naïveté of Messick's assumptions about human nature, then we would be impressed by the quality of his reasoning and of his experiments. Unfortunately, however, he lived before the period of the great tsunamis and of the terrorist attacks and counterattacks that killed hundreds of millions of people (not just a few thousand here and a few thousand there). As a result, he has very little insight into his own naïveté.

Finally, we should point out that Messick was quite sincere in his beliefs, which is a positive characteristic for that time and place — given that sincerity was evaluated in a positive manner. For example, the final irony of Messick's career is that he accepted a named professorship of "business ethics" — an oxymoron.

NOTE

1. Among Prof. Messick's surviving papers was a typed copy of a talk to the Society for Judgment and Decision-Making Research in which he outlines his theory of "appropriateness." He alleged that he experienced an epiphany about his own "inappropriate" behavior on a weekend retreat during his 2-year tenure as a visiting professor in Bergen, Norway. He had entered a Ping-Pong tournament and — being a fairly strong player — was on his way to winning it. He was also one of the few mature adults in the tournament. Suddenly, he claimed, it dawned on him that he was not expected to win — that it would be inappropriate for him to continue soundly defeating much younger entrants in the tournament. Consequently, he claimed in his presentation, he started playing without paying much attention to what he was doing, and a 15-year-old won the tournament. (From our currently enlightened viewpoint, he should have continued whomping all these younger players, but he may have been correct in believing that observers would find such one-sided matches inappropriate, and therefore taken some sort of retributive action against him — which he suspected that they may have been doing already, given some of what he called "negative vibrations" from his Norwegian colleagues. At the time, the Scandinavian culture was not supportive of those characterized as "high in need for achievement," if not downright hostile to them.)

15

Retrospection on a Career in Social Psychology

David M. Messick

A SHORT, BOWDLERIZED AUTOBIOGRAPHY

I was born in Philadelphia and lived in a small suburb, Sharon Hill, until I was 4. We moved back to my dad's home town of Seaford, Delaware, in 1941 and I lived there until I left to go to college at the University of Delaware in 1957. In our racially segregated high school (all the Black high school kids were bussed to the only "colored" high school in Sussex County in Georgetown). I was an above-average student, an above-average athlete (I was co-captain of our high school football team), and quite religious. When I was admitted to the University of Delaware, it was in the School of Engineering and my intent was to become an engineer. In my senior year of high school I changed my plans after deciding to enter the Methodist ministry. I changed to a psychology major, thinking this would be the better preparation for a lifetime of helping others. During my freshman year of college, I became disillusioned with religion and lost all faith in it. But I remained a psychology major.

I was a totally undistinguished student for the first 2 years. I quit school in the fall of my junior year. I did not like my courses, I did not see where I was going, and I was developing some bad habits. So I drove to Miami, Florida, where I spent a month working as an ambulance attendant until my money nearly ran out. Then I drove to Fort Worth, Texas, where I stayed with my brother, Pete, for several months while selling encyclopedias. During this time I tried to enlist in the Army to go to the language school in Monterey but I discovered that I had a medical condition that made me 4F (unacceptable) to the armed forces.

Thus, in the winter of 1958, I took the money I made from an encyclopedia sale, bought a plane ticket to Philadelphia, and hitchhiked the 100 miles south to my parents' home in Seaford. I soon found a job making blender gasoline pumps in Salisbury, Maryland, a half-hour drive from home, and I worked there until the contract was filled. That spring, when the contract was filled, I was laid off along with all the other workers in the plant. I drew unemployment compensation for a while before I took a job working with a firm that was seeding and laying sod on the local highway. It was hard, hot, dirty outdoor work that left me exhausted at the end of the day.

In the fall of 1958 I returned to the University of Delaware for another shot at my third year, and this year I did quite well. The following year, 1959–1960, I worked at the DuPont Nylon plant in Seaford, the factory at which my father was a guard, in order to make enough money to return for my senior year as an undergraduate. (In the summer of 1959, I worked in the kitchen and was the only White person working there. The dining facilities were racially segregated at the time, and I chose to eat in the dining room with the guys with whom I worked — African American chaps. One morning, close to the end of a graveyard shift at about 7:00 am, a supervisor asked to speak to me and suggested that I eat in the main dining room with the other White employees. He said that friends of my dad were embarrassed to see me eating with the "colored" workers. I thanked him for his concern but said I though it made sense for me to eat with the guys I worked with. He said he understood and several weeks later the dining facilities were "integrated." The Black guys I worked with now could, and often did, eat in the main dining room, but they always ate at the same table with each other and no other White employees joined them. Everyone continued to eat with their friends, maintaining voluntary segregation. It is quite different now.) In the fall I got a job in the plant sweeping floors. (The only Black workers in the plant at that time also cleaned the floors and did custodial work. The whole work force was integrated soon after.) I worked there for nearly a year (as a draw-twist machine operator, as a forklift driver, and as a carpet yarn baler), saving my money to complete school. I worked all the overtime I could get. It was also that year that I was asked to give a neighbor a ride to a Christmas party. I did. The neighbor's name was Judy Hassan. We fell in love that night, got married a few months later, and will soon have our 50th anniversary. I returned for my senior year the following fall (1960) and completed my B.A. Our first son, Chris, was born in January 1961, during my senior year at the University of Delaware.

We had bought a house trailer with money I had saved and we lived in that trailer during my final year at Delaware. We then had the trailer towed to Chapel Hill, North Carolina, where I went to graduate school and Judy took classes to complete her B.A. We stayed in Chapel Hill for 3 years, during which time Andrew, our second, was born. I took a job with the University of California, Santa Barbara, and in the summer of 1964 we motored across the country in a small Nash Rambler from Chapel Hill to Santa Barbara, via Ann Arbor, Michigan; Mesa Verde, Colorado; and the Grand Canyon, Arizona. We had to buy a new clutch in Des Moines, Iowa, and I thought we would fry driving across the desert in late August, but we made it. I checked into the psychology office, where I was mistaken for a new undergraduate, discovered that there was little to be done for another week or so, and, since we could not move into our rental house until mid-September, we drove, with our 3-year-old and 1-year-old, up to Yosemite Valley and had a well-deserved rest. I started teaching at UCSB a couple of weeks later.

I taught and did research at UCSB from 1964 until 1992 when I accepted a chair at the Kellogg School of Management at Northwestern University. During this 28-year stretch, I had a sabbatical leave at the University of Leiden in the Netherlands from 1969 to 1970. I was the director of the U.C. Education Abroad Office at the University of Bergen, Norway, from 1975 to 1977. I spent a half year on a Fulbright Research Fellowship at the University of Groningen in 1984 and another half a year as a research scientist at the University of Groningen in 1991. In the 1980s I was the associate editor of the *Journal of Experimental Social Psychology* for 4 years and the editor-in-chief for 3.

From 1992 to 2007, I held the Morris and Alice Kaplan Chair in Ethics and Decision in Management at the Kellogg School. I taught courses on business ethics, corporate social responsibility, and leadership and I collaborated in research on issues that lay at the intersection of psychology and ethics. I became an emeritus professor on September 1, 2007, this time from Northwestern; the first time was from UCSB in 1993.

RETROSPECTION

As I reflect on my career I realize how lucky I have been. I was born in the United States, not in a poor developing country or one that was devastated by wars or disease. I have never had to cope with a life-threatening illness, nor have I ever been injured severely enough to alter the quality of my life. My childhood was relatively uneventful — I was not molested, mistreated, or ignored. I was fed, taught, loved, and disciplined. I learned the essential tools needed to be a normal, capable adult. Later, I was lucky in a multitude of ways. I met my wife when a friend asked me to drive her to a party. I fell in love that night and my love was reciprocated and we have remained in love for nearly a half a century. How lucky is that? I had professors who encouraged me to think about graduate school when I was an undergraduate and had no clue what a graduate school was. I later had colleagues and students who encouraged me in my work and who contributed to the fun of solving research problems. We called this research, but it was actually fun. Good luck has been an astonishingly important element of my life.

A second quality I confess to is an addiction to puzzle solving. I still do Sudoku and crossword puzzles in the morning paper. When I was young I loved playing cards — bridge especially — because the game was an intellectual puzzle. I bought books of cryptograms and did them. This affliction has been part of my psyche for as long as I can remember. When I was an undergraduate I loved the logic course I took because it involved lots of riddles about "some natives always lie, some always tell the truth, ..." or "how can three cannibals row three missionaries across a river. ..." I always felt a warm sense of satisfaction when I could work out the answer, which was not as often as I would have liked. It was the same with mathematics and probability problems. The same is true today with the morning newspaper puzzles. This inclination has led to a fascination with codes, paradoxes, mathematics, and, probably, foreign languages, which seem to be codes of some sort. (This fascination nearly caused me to change my major in my last year as an undergraduate. I took a year-long course in ancient history taught by Professor Evelyn Clift and became enthralled by the work of Michael Ventris, who deciphered a written language called "Linear B" and showed that it was, despite some classical scholars' assertions to the contrary, Greek; Chadwick, 1958.) I am lucky to have some talent for and enjoyment from doing these things.

The types of scientific problems that I selected to study reflect an attraction to the incongruous, the paradoxical, the puzzling. My interest in social dilemmas arose from the apparent contradiction between individual rationality and social sanity. How can those be reconciled, if that question has any meaning? My commitment to understanding the complexities of preference and motivation sprang in part from the recognition that if attractiveness is not a quality of an object or stimulus, how can it be described and how does it work? I came to wonder why group decision rules were "transparent," in the sense that people did not take them into consideration when making inferences about the qualities of the people making a group decision. Making inferences is an essential aspect of human social activity and I questioned how that happened. How do people learn? Finally, from a very early age I puzzled about the obvious conflicts that arose between efforts to lead a moral life and efforts to lead a successful one. These four puzzles occupied a large part my professional life.

Social Dilemmas

When I was in graduate school at North Carolina, a small group of us were interested in studying decision-making. There was only one other such person in my class, Amnon Rapoport, an Israeli with whom I worked closely in graduate school. There was no formal specialization in decision-making, so the four or five of us who were interested were in different formal tracks. I was in the social psychology track, whereas most of the others were in the quantitative track. We were all interested in using mathematical models to describe behavior. The early 1960s was a heady time for psychologists studying decision-making. We worked our way through von Neumann and Morgenstern's (1944) axioms about utility theory and decision-making and we plowed through the Luce and Raiffa's (1957) classic, *Games and Decisions*. One of the early lessons I got from this work was that the analysis of rationality was very different in social and nonsocial contexts. Rationality, theoretically, a type of choice coherence or consistency, meant expected utility maximization in the nonsocial context but something much more complex in competitive or mixed motive situations. In both cases, decision-makers' outcomes depend on their choices and things that they cannot control. In nonsocial situations, states of nature — the things they cannot control — do not care what the decision-makers do or what the outcomes are. The weather does not "care" if it rains or is sunny or if one carries an umbrella or not or if one gets drenched or stays dry. In social contexts, the things decision-makers cannot control are often controlled by another party who does care about the outcomes. This party also has preferences that will guide that party's choices. Hence, rational decision must take the other's preferences into account as well as those of the decision-maker.

"Rational" inferences, on the other hand, followed Bayes' rule and people adjusted their opinions rationally. So we spent hours studying Bayesian statistical models and their applications. It was a source of great satisfaction to have made our way through a book like Raiffa and Schlaifer (1961) that was more equations than words. We also read the literature that compared human information processing to Bayes' model.

My first effort to examine the assumptions about rationality was in my dissertation (Messick, 1967), where I programmed our computer in the Psychometric Laboratory to play a simple three-choice zero-sum game against undergraduate subjects. The computer played one of three strategies: a classical minimax that chose each of its three choices with predetermined probabilities, a learning strategy that kept account of the students' choices and selected a strategy that maximized expected payoff against the inferred probability distribution, and a limited version of this latter that could only remember the last five choices of the subject. The results of this study were surprising (to me at least). First, as expected, the minimax strategy was neither exploited nor exploiter. What was interesting was that the "intelligent" programs got creamed by the students. Both of the "learning" programs could be driven into cyclical patterns that the students quickly learned to exploit, and they exploited the programs viciously, although not perfectly. The naïve students outperformed the "rational" programs by a huge margin.

This study raised doubts about the value of theoretical notions of rationality. It is one thing to propose a process and to show that the process is the best at some task, but it is a completely different thing to examine possible weakness that the process has more generally. (This skepticism about a priori notions of rationality was reinforced later by Robert Axelrod's [1984] ingenious research showing that among a population of strategies for playing a simple prisoners' dilemma game, the strategy that did the best was the simplest. Authored by Anatol Rapoport, the simple tit-for-tat [start by cooperating and then do what the other bloke did on the very last trial] strategy collected more points in a round robin tournament than any other, including clever learning strategies that could, in principle, exploit another strategy's weakness.) The axiomatic notion of rationality was almost a religious conviction for decision-making in the early days and empirical results that called the concept into question were generally discredited or ignored. Things seem a little less dogmatic today with economists like Dan Ariely (2008), for example, writing about irrationality without experiencing the convulsions of an existential crisis.

The idea of rationality in the prisoners' dilemma — and more generally in social dilemmas — is noteworthy because the simple rules that govern intelligent (or rational) choice — like don't pick an option for which an alternative has better outcomes in at least one state of the world — lead to results that are worse than less rational rules. Somehow, rational choices in these dilemmas lead to poor outcomes for all involved. There seems to be a conjunction between what we might call individual-level intelligence and collective-level stupidity. Everyone trying to do well for themselves ends up doing more poorly than they might have had done otherwise. So what sense does rationality make here?

Our study of social dilemmas then focused on two questions. First, what kinds of conditions lead to cooperative (non-rational) actions in social dilemmas? This question has led to hundreds of empirical studies investigating nearly every factor one could imagine. In collaboration with many students and colleagues, including Professor Henk Wilke and his team (Wim Liebrand, Paul Van Lange, Christel Rutte, Arjaan Wit, and others) from the University of Groningen in the Netherlands, we conducted and published many studies on this general topic. I will not say much about these studies except to say that they were fun to do. The second question was perhaps deeper and more difficult to grasp; that is, to describe the nature of the relationship between choices at the individual level and processes at the collective level. When, for instance, do decisions made by a community of fishermen lead to the collapse of the fishery? Can people be taught to curtail their use of water during a drought and, if so, how? Can people be induced to install voluntarily smog-abatement devices on their vehicles to improve air quality, or will we simply have to breathe pollution? If psychologists are interested in helping to solve social problems, these questions must be addressed.

My first published answer to this to this question arose as a result of a real decision that I had to make. In the early 1970s, there was a movement within the University of California to unionize the faculty. As a good academic, instead of making a decision, I did an analysis and published it (Messick, 1973). The analysis revealed that in order for the decision to join the union to be rational — in order for it to be the decision that maximized expected payoff — the financial return would have to be a number that was far out of the range of possibility. (I did not join.) The problem was a classic dilemma — no faculty member had a realistic incentive to join, but if all of us did join, we would all have been better off than if we all did not. I did note in this paper that there was an incentive to encourage others to join because my ideal outcome would have been to have had the benefits of the union without having had to pay the membership costs. (I made precisely this same point in my comment on Donald Campbell's APA presidential address in the context of understanding why religion and organized systems of morality evolved and exist. The answer is that it is to our benefit to persuade those around us to act morally and altruistically because we benefit from their morality and altruism, regardless of our own incentives to do so. Thus, we may espouse principles of morality and altruism in an effort to influence others while not being persuaded ourselves. This disparity in incentives is, in my view, the foundation of hypocrisy.)

To the best of my knowledge, there was only one other paper in the psychological literature at the time that examined n-person prisoners' dilemmas. That was an important article by Hal Kelley and Janusz Grezlak (1972). We were all familiar with the classic article by Garrett Hardin on the "Tragedy of the Common" (1968) that outlined the paradox clearly with a parable about shared resources. Hardin was a biologist and there were few psychologists interested in this type of situation. One of the most creative, thoughtful, and productive, was Robyn Dawes, then at the University of Oregon, whose insights, analyses, and experiments had a huge impact.

Four contributions to the understanding of the linkage between individual behavior and collective outcomes were noteworthy. The first was a mathematical paper I worked on with John van de Geer of the University of Leiden, a paper that was published in 1981 (Messick and van de Geer, 1981). We displayed a common mathematical structure underlying the prisoner's dilemma, the Simpson paradox in statistics, and group selection in the evolution of altruism. We furthermore showed that in the statistical context there was no way to determine what the "right" level of analysis was. There was something distressing about this conclusion that troubles me. We showed that, for example, though one might observe a positive relationship between two variables, it is always possible that a third variable could be discovered such that the relationship between the first two variables is negative at each level of the third variable. What then is the "right" relationship between the first two variables — positive or negative?

A few years after the Messick and van de Geer paper appeared, my then colleague Marilynn Brewer and I wrote a review of the literature in social dilemma research (Messick and Brewer, 1983). We tried to update the growing literature about social dilemmas since the excellent review by Robin Dawes in 1980. One of our important contributions in this paper was to highlight the distinction between individual and structural solutions to social dilemmas. The literature was growing pessimistic about the success of individual solutions, and we highlighted the possibility that structural solutions — solutions that involved changing the nature of the dilemma — would prove to be more successful. We were ahead of the curve in seeing that regulatory, legal, or administrative solutions were going to be required to solve these problems.

If people can see that they are in a dilemma and that their options are to (a) exercise self-restraint and be taken advantage of, on the one hand, or (b) contribute to the destruction of a common good, on the other, they may want to seek new options. One line of research that we started with graduate student Charlie Samuelson and Henk Wilke's team was to investigate empirically when it was that people would want to give up the status quo in favor of some other means of accessing a resource. It was Charlie Samuelson, working on his Ph.D. research, who took the lead in trying to figure out when folks would want to change and what they would want to change to. An important part of Samuelson's work was to broaden the conception of how people responded to social dilemmas. They do not merely choose to cooperate or defect, they can try to change the rules, to communicate with others, or finesse the whole enterprise by opting out. The work that Samuelson and I did on this problem resulted in several empirical findings of interest and a model of people's preferences for change (Samuelson & Messick, 1986, 1995). The model was a clever combination of social psychological insights and decision theory principles.

The final project that should be mentioned in this category is one I undertook in 1991 with Professor Wim Liebrand at the University of

Groningen. I had agreed to take a year leave from UCSB and to spend the year at the Kellogg School at Northwestern University in Evanston, Illinois. Judy and I left UCSB in summer of 1991 and spent a 6-month sabbatical leave at SWI (Social Wetenschapelijk Informatiekunde or Social Science Information Technology). Using computer simulation, Liebrand and I wanted to study how cooperation would evolve in large groups of interacting units, all of which behaved according to one of three simple choice rules. The choice rules were (a) tit-for-tat (in which a player repeats the last strategy that had been played against it), (b) win-stay, lose-change (in which a player repeats its last choice if it was rewarded and changes otherwise), and (c) win-cooperate, lose-defect (in which a player cooperates on the next trail if it was rewarded on the previous one and defects otherwise). We imagined an interconnected grid of 100 players, each surrounded by 9 others, in which a randomly interacting pair played a standard PDG and stored the last response they and the other made, as well as the outcome from that pair of choices. A unique component of this simulation was the way we defined rewards. We used the definition of Thibaut and Kelley (more about that later) that the valence of an outcome depends on the comparison of the outcome to a standard, the value of which is partly established by the social context. We defined the standard as the average of most recent outcomes of the 9 neighbors, so when a unit was evaluating its outcome, it compared it to the neighborhood average. If the outcome was above the average, it was coded as a win or reward; otherwise, it was coded as a loss.

Liebrand and I spent 6 months running computer simulations of these processes. I had three computers: one at home on which I would run an experiment when I went to bed at night and when I went to the institute in the morning, one that I used for running experiments in my institute office, and one that I used for writing. We generated a huge body of experimental results, doing three or four experiments a day including weekends. We knew a colossal volume of facts yet had only a glimmering of an understanding about what happened under these conditions. For instance, the global levels of cooperation of the win-stay, lose-change strategy could never generate more than 50% cooperation in the population. We could show mathematically why that was the case, but we could not offer a comprehensible verbal explanation for the fact. We published this research with only a partial understanding of the nature of the dynamics we were describing (Messick & Liebrand, 1995).

This research and the several papers that followed it convinced me of one fact: understanding individual decision mechanisms may be nearly useless in understanding global or societal level phenomena. This is a depressing thought for one who hoped to improve the human condition by studying individual behavior.

Preferences

I recently wrote a chapter about the changing concept of preferences and the complexities that accompany its study, so I will merely do a brief rehash of these issues here (Messick, 2006). It was originally taken for granted that people's preferences corresponded to abstract points or to money. (Originally the numbers in payoff matrices represented rank orders of preferences, but there was a tendency to interpret the numbers as having the properties of "normal" numbers that can be added, divided, and so on.) For me, and others I suspect, the work of Thibaut and Kelley (1959) made a qualitative change in this. They argued that the valences that we associate with outcomes derive from the comparison of the outcome's value with a standard (that they called a CL or comparison level) — an assumption that Liebrand and I employed in the simulation studies I mentioned in the last section. My first effort to examine this radical assumption was in my unpublished M.A. thesis, where I showed that if one rewarded subjects (randomly) in a problem-solving task with a set of outcomes that was increasing over time, they were much happier than subjects who got precisely the same set of rewards but in the reverse order. (They also thought they were figuring the task out, which was impossible.) My interpretation was that the CL, conceptualized as a weighted average of previous outcomes with the weights being proportional to their recency, would constitute the standard of comparison. In an increasing sequence, the outcomes would tend to be above the CL and the subjects would code them as positive. In a decreasing sequence, exactly the opposite would happen: later outcomes would tend to fall below the CL and be experienced as negative. The results were perfectly consistent with this hypothesis.

I encountered a second implication of the CL early on at USCB when I was doing a series of experiments with an undergraduate, Warren Thorngate. I thought we were doing a standard experiment on learning when the results turned out completely wrong. As I recall, Thorngate realized that our student subjects were not trying to make as many points as possible (why in heaven's name should they have been?) but rather that they were trying to beat the other person (when the other person's outcome was made known to them). We did some further studies to nail this interpretation down and we called it "relative gain maximization." Our participants appeared to be using the other's outcome as his or her standard or CL and evaluating their own outcomes relative to that standard (Messick & Thorngate, 1967).

At about the same time that Thorngate and I were rethinking our understanding of preferences, Chuck McClintock, my mentor and protector at UCSB, and I were finding that some people, some of the time, acted as if they were trying to help the group or the interacting pair. McClintock and I put this all together in a paper in 1968 that turned out to be influential (Messick & McClintock, 1968). We built a model of how people could have a mix of motives in two-choice games: sometimes choosing to get the most for themselves, sometimes choosing to beat the other person, and sometimes choosing to do what was best for the pair. We called these orientations *social motives*. (In this paper we also devised the notion of decomposed games, a development that Dean Pruitt had published at about the same time.) In this paper, McClintock and I considered this mix of motives as an intra-individual mix. Indeed, I once described the idea as a random utility choice model, although we did present evidence in the paper that the parameters for the three motives differed significantly across people. It was not until 7 years later that Kuhlman and Marshello (1975) showed that the motives could be used as individual difference measures. Mike Kuhlman was one of our ingenious graduate students who coauthored the follow-up paper, which extended the Messick-McClintock methodology to three-choice games (McClintock, Messick, Campos, & Kuhlman, 1973).

Our laboratory was busy with efforts to get a handle on social motivation. McClintock was doing studies with children to track the emergence and development of these motives. Graduate students Don Griesinger and Jim Livingston were working on formalizations of the structures (Griesinger & Livingston, 1973). Professor Ken MacCrimmon and I tried to generalize the set of possible motives to include other less obvious ones (MacCrimmon & Messick, 1976), but it was not until considerably later, working with another talented undergraduate, Keith Sentis, that we showed how it might be possible to estimate what we called *social utility functions*. We did this by having undergraduate students rank outcomes that specified monetary returns to them and to another hypothetical participant. We could actually plot utility components for money and, independently, for the disparity between the ranker's payment and that of the other, the "social" component of the utility (Messick & Sentis, 1985). It was reassuring that 4 years later, using a completely different methodology, Lowenstein, Thompson, and Bazerman (1989) replicated our findings in detail. One finding that both studies reported was that people preferred equal outcomes when they had done an equal amount of work with another, but disadvantaged inequity, when the one got less than the other, was much worse than advantaged inequity, when one got more than the other. This finding is a social version of the concept of loss aversion proposed by Kahneman and Tversky (1979). In their theory, loss aversion means that people dislike losing a fixed amount more than they like gaining the equivalent amount. If in our studies, loss and gain are defined as deviations from the other's outcome, the concepts are identical.

Our subsequent work employed the concept of social motives in many ways. We found that one could predict conservation during lean times (but not during fat ones) with the social motive measures (Kramer, McClintock, & Messick, 1986; this, incidentally, was my first collaboration with Rod Kramer, a long-term friend and collaborator). Using these measures we could predict who would display egocentric biases and who would not (Beggan, Messick, & Allison, 1988). Others have reported scores of additional findings using these measures as predictors, one of the most interesting of which is Liebrand, Jansen, Rijken, and Suhre (1986), who found that competitors thought of the cooperation/competition distinction as a power differential ("competitors win and cooperators lose"), whereas cooperators thought of it as a moral issue ("cooperating is good and competing is bad").

The final issue I want to describe with regard to preferences does not concern social motives or social dilemmas. It concerns the UCSB dissertation study of Terry Boles, now a professor at the University of Iowa. In the decision-making literature, there was a phenomenon called the *outcome bias*. This bias referred to the tendency for observers to judge that a decision was a good one if the outcome was positive and a bad one when the result was negative. So, for instance, if a surgeon decided to do a risky operation on a patient, observers tended to say the decision was a good one if the patient was cured but a bad one if the patient expired. The irrationality of this judgment is that when the decision is made, the surgeon cannot know what the outcome will be. The quality of the decision should be judged by the information and alternatives that the surgeon had at the time she made the decision, not on the basis of what followed. What followed may well have been determined by chance events and it is a mistake to confuse a good decision with a lucky one.

Terry Boles's insight was that if people judge good or bad outcomes in comparison to a reference or CL of some sort, what would happen if the references or CLs for a winning or losing outcome were different? Specifically, suppose that a choice that led to a win might have led to an even better outcome if an alternative choice had been made. The winning outcome may look poor. And suppose that a decision lost, but that the alternative choice would have led to an even larger loss. That decision might look like it led to good outcome. The key here is that each outcome, the win and the loss, evokes its own comparison reference. The winning one is compared to an even better possibility and the losing one is compared to an even worse alternative. Under these circumstances, carefully worked out by Boles, observers judged that the person whose decision lost actually did better than the person whose decision won. The losing decision was judged to be better than the winning decision. This work demonstrated just how malleable human preferences can be.

Beliefs About Others, Groups, and Ourselves

As graduate students we were engaged in understanding belief formation and change. The standard model at the time was the Bayesian approach that assumed that people have subjective probability distributions over some parameter space and that the distribution was altered by new information. The rule for updating was Bayes' rule. While a graduate student I wrote a couple of Psychometric Laboratory Reports (1963, nos. 35 and 42) that used the elegance of Bayesian models with beta prior distributions and binomial data processes to explore some aspects of group decision-making in the one case and to develop a theory for optimal stopping in sampling in the other. This same class of models turned out to be useful in formalizing the information in interpersonal relationships (e.g., how it affects the probability that Ike likes Bob if you know that Bob likes Ike). I did this work with Steve McNeel, one of our graduate students (McNeel & Messick, 1970). The basic Bayesian idea also led to investigations of the role of alternative possible causes in the inference or attribution of personal characteristics to others. The principle here was called *discounting* and the idea was that the weight associated with a particular cause of an action would be discounted if there were alternative possible causes. The discounting principle is entirely consistent with a Bayes-like model in that the posterior probability of a cause will be inversely related to the number of alternative plausible causes. The early research we did on this topic was ably led by graduate students Glenn Reeder and Eddy van Avermaet (Messick & Reeder, 1972; Reeder, Messick, & van Avermaet, 1977). Reeder followed up with a number of additional important papers.

The question of how people drew inferences about individuals' qualities led to a similar question about groups. How do people make attributions about the qualities of social groups? One of our creative graduate students, Scott Allison, was the idea leader in this line of work. He developed an idea that he called *the group attribution error*. The individual attribution error referred to the tendency for people to discount or ignore the constraints on people when they did things. For example, if someone was told by a teacher to write an essay in favor of Fidel Castro, others were likely to think that the writer actually was in favor of Castro. They attributed the favorable essay to the writer's attitudes rather than the teacher's instructions. The group attribution error works in a similar way. Observers of a group tend to ignore the decision rule that is used to generate a decision. The result is a tendency to think that there is a correspondence between the outcome of a group decision and the attitudes of the group members. Allison and I demonstrated this phenomenon in several ways in our first paper and we followed up with a number of additional studies. My colleague, Diane Mackie, did some clever studies exploring this notion and she and Allison and I wrote a review of this work in 1996 (Allison, Mackie, & Messick, 1996). One of the surprising findings we reported was that people used the group decision outcome not only to make inferences about the attitudes of others but to make inferences about their own attitudes.

An unexpected application of this idea arose in the early 1990s after I had moved from Santa Barbara to Evanston, Illinois. My wife and I were shopping for a house and we found one that we liked. In discussions with our broker, we discovered that the sellers were the three sons of the owner, who had died. We did not know what kind of a rule the three sons would use in making a decision about selling. They may have decided that any of the three could veto a sale if he was dissatisfied with the offer. They may have decided that any one could accept the offer on behalf of the three if he was satisfied that the offer was fair. Or they may have decided to vote and abide by a majority rule. The question was whether the offer we made should depend on the type of rule that the sellers had agreed upon. I discussed this problem with my friend and colleague, Professor Max Bazerman, and we did some calculations that demonstrated that the sellers' decision rule could make a major difference in size of the offer that might be accepted. As I did with the faculty union question that arose back in the early 1970s, rather than use the theory to tune our offer on the house, Bazerman and I and Don Moore, a graduate student, instead wondered if our MBA students at the Kellogg School would ignore the decision rule like the undergraduates whom Scott Allison and I tested in Santa Barbara (Messick, Moore, & Bazerman, 1997). Sure enough, they showed the same indifference to the decision rule that we had seen in our other studies. The offers they made to groups using very different acceptance rules were very much the same, whereas the ideal or rational offers would have been very different. People seem to think of groups with whom they interact as if the group were a single individual. This thought is misleading, of course. (On the housing front, my wife and I quickly agreed on a price with the sellers' broker and bought the house, probably for more money than if I had employed the ideas we learned in our experiments.)

Before leaving the issue of making judgments about groups, I want to mention one study that I did with Arlene Asuncion, another of our clever and hardworking graduate students. Will Rogers, the American humorist, is reputed to have said that the exodus of farmers from Oklahoma to California in the 1930s raised the average IQ of both Oklahoma and California. One is tempted to conclude from this that Americans got smarter, but that could not be the case since they are the same people. The principle involved in this statement is easy to illustrate. Imagine the first 10 integers, 1 through 10. Divide them into the first three (1, 2, and 3) and the top seven (4 through 10) and take the average of each subgroup (2 and 7, respectively). Now redivide the 10 numbers so that the lower group consists of the bottom 7 (1 through 7) and the upper group contains the three highest. The mean of the lower group is now 4 and the mean of the top group is 9. The means of both subgroups have gone up by 2, but the underlying scores are the precisely the same and the average of all the scores has not changed. What Dr. Asuncion and I showed was that categorizations such as the one I just demonstrated would influence people's judgments of a group's average intelligence; for instance, even when all the scores are known to the judges (Messick & Ascuncion, 1993). Taking the average of the subgroup means is a convenient but potentially misleading shortcut, particularly when the subgroups are based on different numbers of cases.

The final area in which we studied inferences and belief was with regard to one's self. One process that operates in the maintenance of beliefs about ourselves that is less present in beliefs about other things is a generic self-promotion process. In a sense this process is a fact of our metaphysical existence. I cannot see the world like anyone else and I can only see it through my senses, even when I am trying to empathize with another. Each of us is condemned to be the major actor in our respective life stories. That fact has to make us special to ourselves. In another way, we are more aware of our trials, temptations, efforts, and handicaps that anyone else can be about ourselves. We have greater access to the details of our own actions than we can ever have to those of any other. As a result, we are more likely to view our own endeavors more positively and sympathetically than those of others. In other words, we see ourselves, understandably and accurately, as being unique. Not only unique, but uniquely good. Scott Allison, George (Al) Goethals, a visiting professor from Williams College, and I ran a number of studies to elucidate this process. The typical methodology is to ask people to make judgments about themselves and then to ask them to make similar judgments about a comparison person or group; e.g., your roommate, the typical UCSB student, or UCSB students generally. As a rule, people make more favorable judgments about themselves than they do about the other(s).

Against this background we wanted to evaluate the hypothesis that reality moderated the tendency to exaggerate one's goodness relative to that of others. So we did the basic experiment using different dimensions or qualities, a key one being intelligence. Intelligence is different from morality, say, in that it is more or less easily demonstrated. There is less ambiguity about it than about generic goodness, for instance. So our hypothesis, confirmed of course, was that the tendency to exaggerate would be less extreme for intelligence judgments than for more abstract dimensions. The title of the paper describing these studies ("On Being Better but Not Smarter Than Others: The Muhammad Ali Effect") caused me some worry about potential racist connotations, but there were no unpleasant consequences (Allison, Messick, & Goethals, 1989).

Ethics and Fairness

The work that Goethals, Allison, and I did on uniqueness biases actually was more related to a line of studies we had been doing on fairness than with the processes of inference. The work on fairness actually dated back to early work we had done in the lab on social preferences. When someone learns, for instance, that she did the same amount of work as another but that the other got paid more than she did, she reacts emotionally with a sense of unfairness. So our early work on preferences was simultaneously triggering thoughts about fairness.

It is essentially impossible to study social preferences without arousing a sense of fairness or unfairness at the same time. Early on, we had the impression that unfairness was a more palpable and vivid experience than fairness. There was a good bit of research being done of the topic of distributive justice, the sense that certain arrangements of outcomes were just and that other were unjust. To investigate this sense of fairness, Keith Sentis and I ran some studies in which we explicitly asked undergraduates to tell us what they thought was fair (Messick & Sentis, 1979). We found that they were more sensitive to being underpaid than to being overpaid, a result I discussed earlier, and that they thought they should be paid more than another when the other was in an identical situation to theirs. What people wanted (preference) influenced what they judged to be fair. Though this was hardly a shocking finding, it did stand in contrast to other contemporary conceptualizations that imagined people to be ideal moral judges whose sense of justice was independent of their wishes.

We also had the impression that people generally thought that they were at least as fair as others if not more so. The tendency was part of the more general egocentric or uniqueness bias that Al Goethals, Scott Allison, and I were about to investigate (Goethals, Messick, & Allison, 1991). In one series of experiments we asked students to write lists of fair things that they or others did. We asked the same question about unfair things. For each list, if they thought they did the things more than others, they should begin the sentence with "I"; and if they thought others did the thing more than they did, they should begin the sentence "They." We ended up with four lists that were completely student generated. The first thing we did was count the number of actions that had been written in each list. The students had written many more first-person fair than unfair items and more third-person unfair than fair items. In writing the lists of items, students were associating themselves differentially with fair things and others with unfair things (Messick, Bloom, Boldizar, & Samuelson, 1985).

Perhaps the biggest surprise (to me) in this series of experiments happened when we took samples of the "I" and "They" items and switched the pronouns, making the "I" items "They" and vice versa. We then had other students rate the fairness and the frequency (how often do these behaviors occur?) of the behaviors. We fully expected that the items would be rated fairer when the pronoun was "I" than when it was "They." But that did not happen. The pronoun had no impact on the fairness rating. It was just as bad for "me" to cheat on a test as it was for "them" to do it. The pronouns made a huge difference in the frequency ratings, however. "I" do fair things more often and unfair things less often than "They." To the extent that morality consists of doing moral things often and immoral things rarely, our students were implicitly claiming greater morality than "others." To eliminate the possibility that these results were the artificial consequence of rating scales, Karen Cates, a Ph.D. student at Northwestern University, and I had undergraduate subjects select the most accurate frequentistic adverb (never, infrequently, sometimes, often, usually, always) to describe moral or immoral actions of themselves or others (Cates & Messick, 1996). The results were essentially identical to the earlier ones. For instance, with the phrase "cheat on boyfriend or girlfriend" the modal selection when the phrase was headed by "I" was "never." When the pronoun was "They," the modal adverb selected was "sometimes."

In our studies of social dilemmas and of social preferences, the idea of "equality" arose with remarkable frequency. The concept of equality was grippingly important to our students. If an arrangement was "equal" or "fair" or "equitable," it seemed acceptable to our undergraduates. It was predictable that, in an era in which there was a great deal being written about the use of "decision heuristics," that we should come to think of equality as a heuristic, a more or less simple rule that could be used to make allocation decisions in otherwise complex situations. Scott Allison and I pursued this line of thought and asked how a heuristic would differ from some other sort of decision rule (Allison & Messick, 1990). As a rule, it is simple, easily communicated, effective (it gets the job done), and objective, meaning that it does not take idiosyncratic features of the people into account. Moreover, there is a consensus that equality is crucial. But equal how?

To illustrate, Terry Schell and I published an experiment in which we showed that when asked to make an allocation of profits from a partnership business, undergraduates were asked to divide either profits or expenses in such a way as to make the results fair and equitable. When they divided expenses, they tended to do so equally (and profits unequally). When they divided profits, they did so equally (and expenses unequally). It seemed that they divided equally whatever they had to divide rather than create equitable final results via either profits or expenses (as would be implied by a theory assuming people were striving for some deeper notion of distributive justice). These results highlight an important fact about equality — when one establishes equality on one dimension (say expenses), one also establishes inequality on others (say profits). Thus, choosing equality also means choosing inequality, and therein lies the potential for conflict because different people may have different ideas about how equality ought to be implemented (Messick, 1993, 1995; Messick & Schell, 1992).

Our research on equality was important not so much for the precise results we demonstrated but rather because we took an idea from the field of ethics and moral philosophy and we looked at it from a psychological perspective. We asked, "What can we say about the psychology of equality?" Others had looked at the philosophical implications. This psychological orientation was the distinctive feature that I brought as I left the Psychology Department at UCSB and joined the Kellogg School of Management at Northwestern University. My position there was as The Morris and Alice Kaplan Professor of Ethics and Decision in Management. (This chair title is rather long and awkward and deserves a digressive comment. As a psychologist I wanted to distinguish myself from the philosophers who held chairs in Business Ethics. Because my research specialty was in decision-making, I proposed that the chair be called Ethics and Decision. Morris Kaplan, who has become a dear friend, wondered why such a chair could not be in medicine or law and he countered with the "in management" addendum. After several months of discussion and counterproposals, I agreed.) In this new role I was to develop a course in business ethics, initiate a research program relevant to business ethics, and act as the school's talking head for ethical issues. In the latter role I gave radio, newspaper, and TV interviews on issues pertaining to ethical conduct in business.

The research I started at Kellogg was in collaboration with, and with the support and advice of my good friend, Max Bazerman, and his coterie of energetic and creative graduate students. Bazerman and I published a paper in 1996 that summarized how common cognitive biases and heuristics could mimic unethical decision-making (Messick & Bazerman, 1996). Much of my later work was related to this general theme. I wrote about social discrimination in the workplace, challenges to ethical and efficient organizations, and causes of and solutions to environmental problems. To illustrate, I considered the findings of the Boston Fed having to do with racial discrimination in mortgage lending. The press was treating the differential rejection rates (minority applicants were refused much more frequently than White applicants) as if they reflected a tendency for qualified minorities to be rejected for mortgages (which is how our stereotype of discrimination works). However, the difference could also have been the result of unqualified White applicants being granted loans. How banks tried to rectify this difference could well depend on which of these processes they assumed to be the cause. Did one examine rejected minority applications to find the qualified ones that were unfairly rejected, or did one examine the granted White applications to find the unqualified ones that were awarded, or both? The moral philosophical question that we did not address was whether discrimination that worked through derogation of minorities was morally different from discrimination that worked through favorability to White persons. Psychologically, ingroup favoritism is very different from outgroup derogation. I do not know if it is different morally, but intuitively it seems to be different.

One of the ideas that our research contributed to discussions of ethical issues is the notion that processing of moral issues is often as heuristic and superficial as decision-making in other domains. The concept of equality as a decision heuristic is a very good illustration. People rarely think through all the ways in which equality may be implemented in a particular situation. In society we think about equality of opportunity, equality of taxes, equality before the law, and so on, but we rarely think about the fact that choosing equality in one dimension is also a choice of inequality in others. Often we identify a version of equality that satisfies some goal and we consider it to be the only moral or ethical manifestation of equality. People who think otherwise are stupid, self-serving, immoral, or all of the above. In other words, people tend not to think more deeply about moral or ethical matters than they do about anything else. On the contrary, people who have faith or conviction often think less deeply about what they believe than people who are skeptical. Just as faith is the enemy of empiricism, it may also be the enemy of thought. Rod Kramer and I wrote a chapter in which we argued that trust, a moral concept for many people, may be as shallow and banal as the evil that Hannah Arendt wrote about (Arndt, 1994; Messick & Kramer, 2001).

With various others I held conferences to explore themes connecting psychology to business ethics. One goal of these conferences was to motivate psychologists to think about the ethical implications of their research expertise and to expose them to management challenges. The first conference was held in 1994 and it involved not only psychologists but also philosophers who specialized in business ethics. The proceedings of this conference were published in 1996 (Messick & Tenbrunsel, 1996). We later had a vigorous conference dealing with the ethics of environmental evaluation (Bazerman, Messick, Tenbrunsel, & Wade-Benzoni, 1997), and two more dealing with barriers to the creation of ethical organizations (Darley, Messick, & Tyler, 2001; Thompson, Levine, & Messick, 1999).

Of the many talented and hard-working graduate students I had the pleasure to work with at the Kellogg School there are two that I should single out. They are Ann Tenbrunsel and Mark Weber. Ann was a student of Max Bazerman's, and Mark, considerably later, was a student of my creative friend and colleague, Keith Murnighan. These two, to a greater degree than the others, were clearly interested in applying psychological notions to business ethics. Tenbrunsel had an undergraduate degree in industrial engineering but was keenly interested in the human side of management, and Weber came out of one of the top social psychology programs in Canada. He was interested from the start. The importance of my work with these two students arose from a seminar that Bazerman and I ran in the mid-1990s. We had discussed the intriguing work of James March at Stanford University, and, in particular, his book on decision-making, entitled *A Primer on Decision-Making* (1994). March's ideas clashed loudly with the classical concepts of decision-making on which I had been raised, ideas such as the independence of preferences and beliefs. March argued that much of decision-making is a matter of figuring out what a situation means, what the appropriate rules of action are, and what it means to the decision-maker personally. A crude summary of this approach is that one asks, "What does a person like me do in a situation like this?" The three elements of this approach are identity (who am I?), situational clarity (what is this situation?), and rule-based action (what rule do I follow in this situation?) Bazerman expressed the view that though March's framework, what we will call a *logic of appropriateness*, was interesting, it was not a good scientific theory because it could explain everything. In other words, no data could embarrass or discredit the idea. I was not so sure.

In the research on social dilemmas there was a considerable body of evidence that seemed to be more consistent with a Marchian conceptualization than with the classical approach. One illustration will suffice. Very early on, in 1977, Dawes, McTavish, and Shaklee published a paper that showed that there was a sizable correlation between what a person chose in a social dilemma and what that person thought others would choose. For the classical theory to explain this correlation, it has to be a bit acrobatic in its assumptions. It must assume that the expectations came first, and that when people expected others to cooperate, they would, for some reason, be more likely to cooperate themselves. But Dawes and his colleagues did a second study in which they paired an observer with each participant in the decision-making groups, the idea being that the observer would have precisely the same information regarding the others' intents as the decision-making participant. The result was that the expectations of the observers were uncorrelated with the decisions of the participants with whom that had been linked. This evidence suggests that it is the act of making the decision that drives expectations, not the information one gleans from a group discussion. Here are several possible interpretations of this pattern. First, the classical view is that data (group discussion) create expectations, which then feed into the decision process. A second view is that when one makes a decision, one uses that information to generate expectations about what others will do. This is a sort of "false consensus" process, which may, in fact, not be false at all. The third approach is that a participant tries to figure out what this situation is about and what is appropriate and, having done so, makes a decision and assumes that others will have a similar construal. This process is the logic of appropriateness. The implication is that what one chooses is derived from a construal that simultaneously determines what one expects of others and what one thinks is right and proper and appropriate.

So in what I consider to be the last contribution that I will make to our understanding of decision-making, I tried to formalize the logic of appropriateness to render it a testable theory that can be falsified. In 1999 I outlined some of the empirical implications of this theory (Messick, 1999) that overcame Bazerman's objections. In a review paper in 2004 with Mark Weber and Shirli Kopelman, we looked back over the research literature on social dilemmas to re-interpret some puzzling findings from this perspective (Weber, Kopelman, & Messick, 2004). I still think it is the approach that has the more explanatory power about decision-making in social dilemmas (and other contexts) than any rival theory.

The most compelling data that pertain to this framework came from a study I did with Ann Tenbrunsel (Tenbrunsel & Messick, 1999). We gave business student subjects a scenario in which we asked them to play the role of a factory manager who is faced with a new regulation that requires them to install scrubbers on a factory smokestack. The installation would be expensive. We gave good reasons to proceed with the installation and some cost-related reasons to delay it. We asked them what they thought they would do and, importantly, what kind of decision they thought they were making. The latter options included "A business decision," and "An ethical decision." Also, we told some of the subjects that if they did not proceed with the installation and if they were caught they would be fined. However, the fine was not large and the likelihood of them being caught was small. What we found was that the students who said they were making an ethical decision almost always decided to install the scrubbers. Those who said they were making a business decision usually did not install. But more to the point, those who were told of the possible sanctions were much more likely to say they were making a business decision than those to whom the sanctions were not mentioned. Our interpretation of these results was that the mention of the sanctions did two things at the same time: (a) The sanctions made the decision business-like because of the need to calculate expected losses from the installation and (b) the calculation showed that the correct decision, from the business perspective, was to delay installation. So the natural follow-up was to make the fine larger and the likelihood of detection closer to a sure thing. If our reasoning about what was going on was correct, students who were told of a larger, more likely fine should also say the decision is a business decision but they should also decide to install the scrubbers. That would be the correct business decision under these new circumstances. That is precisely what we found.

The logic of appropriateness ties together decisions, beliefs about others, preferences for different outcomes, and ideas about what is ethical and correct. It took me a long time, indeed most of my career, to begin to understand these relationships and my understanding is still shallow and partial. I will have to leave it to the next generation of researchers to prove what I believe to be the case. There is still a lot that is vague and cloudy, and that is good for researchers because it is the process of clarifying the vagueness and bringing light to the cloudy regions that makes progress and is fun.

Leadership

Teaching in a business school raises questions that lie unexamined in a psychology department. One of the questions that got raised for me was the question of how a school creates an environment that produces leaders for contemporary society. Rod Kramer and I spent hours discussing this question. He taught at the business school at Stanford University (indeed he had been one of the successful models of psychologists teaching in business schools that I considered before deciding to move to the Kellogg School) and had encountered the same set of questions that I had at Northwestern. Psychological research on leadership was all but extinct. Yet there was a need for courses and research on the topic. Rod was studying leadership among U.S. presidents and I was developing a psychological model that stressed the voluntary nature of the relationship between leaders and their followers. Rod and I decided to hold a conference and we invited all the psychologists and other social scientists we knew who had interest or expertise in the subject. We held the conference in 2001 and eventually published an edited volume of the papers (Messick & Kramer, 2004). Someone once wrote that leadership was the topic about which more had been written and less understood than any other. I would not argue against this characterization and I would point out that leadership is a bewilderingly complex phenomenon, but I believe that the chapters in our book help to clarify some of the complexities.

Clarifying complexities is what a research career is all about. One has to be lucky to have asked questions whose answers make a difference. One must also be lucky to have a rewarding marriage and children of whom one can be proud. One must be lucky to truly enjoy one's work and to view doing experiments as a way of tricking nature into revealing her secrets. One has to have the good luck to stay healthy enough to be able to wrestle successfully with the puzzles that come across one's desk. With such luck and with the loyal friends and creative colleagues chronicled in this chapter, not to mention a supportive spouse, how could anyone fail?

REFERENCES

Allison, S. T., Mackie, D. M., & Messick, D. M. (1996). The outcome bias in social perception: Implications for dispositional inference, attitude change, stereotyping, and social behavior. In M. Zanna (Ed.), *Advances in experimental social psychology* (Vol. 28, pp. 53–93). San Diego: Academic Press.

Allison, S. T., & Messick, D. M. (1990). Social decision heuristics in the use of shared resources. *Journal of Behavioral Decision Making, 3*, 195–204.

Allison, S. T., Messick, D. M., & Goethals, G. R. (1989). On being better but not smarter than others: The Muhammad Ali effect. *Social Cognition, 7*, 275–295.

Arendt, H. (1994). *Eichmann in Jerusalem: A report on the banality of evil.* New York: Penguin Books.

Ariely, D. (2008). *Predictably irrational.* New York: HarperCollins.

Axelrod, R. (1984). *The evolution of cooperation.* New York: Basic Books.

Bazerman, M., Messick, D. M., Tenbrunsel, A. E., & Wade-Benzoni, K. A. (Eds.). (1997). *Environment, ethics, and behavior: The psychology of environmental valuation and degradation.* San Francisco: New Lexington Press.

Beggan, J. K., Messick, D. M., & Allison, S. T. (1988). Social values and egocentric bias: Two tests of the might over morality hypothesis. *Journal of Personality and Social Psychology, 55*, 606–611.

Boles, T. L. & Messick, D. M. (1995). A reverse outcome bias: The influence of multiple reference points on the evaluation of outcomes and decisions. *Organizational Behavior and Human Decision Processes, 61*, 262–275.

Chadwick, J. (1958). *The decipherment of linear B.* Cambridge, UK: Cambridge University Press.

Darley, J. M., Messick, D. M., & Tyler, T. R. (Eds.). (2001). *Social influences on ethical behavior in organizations.* Mahwah, NJ: Lawrence Erlbaum.

Dawes, R. M. (1980). Social dilemmas. *Annual Review of Psychology, 31*, 169–193.

DeKrey, S. J., & Messick, D. M. (2007). *Leadership experiences in Asia.* John Wiley: Singapore.

Goethals, G. R., Messick, D. M., & Allison, S. T. (1991). The uniqueness bias: Studies of constructive social comparison. In J. Suls & T. A. Wills (Eds.), *Social comparison: Contemporary theory and research* (pp. 149–176). New York: Erlbaum.

Griesinger, D. W., & Livingston, J. W., Jr. (1973). Toward a model of interpersonal motivation in experimental games. *Behavioral Science, 18*, 409–431.

Hardin, G. (1968). The tragedy of the commons. *Science, 162*, 1243–1248.

Kahnman, D., & Tversky, A. (1979). Prospect theory. *Econometrica, 47*, 263–291.

Kelley, H. H., & Grzelak, J. (1972). Conflict between individual and common interest in an N-person relationship. *Journal of Personality and Social Psychology, 21*, 190–197.

Kramer, R. M., McClintock, C. G., & Messick, D. M. (1986). Social values and cooperative response in a simulated resource conservation crisis. *Journal of Personality, 54*, 577–596.

Kuhlman, D. M., & Marshello, A. (1975). Individual differences in game motivation as moderators of preprogrammed strategic effects in prisoner's dilemma. *Journal of Personality and Social Psychology, 32*, 922–931.

Liebrand, W. B., Jansen, R. W., Rijken, V. M., & Suhre, C. J. (1986). Might over morality: Social values and the perception of other players in experimental games. *Journal of Experimental Social Psychology, 22*, 204–215.

Lowenstein G. F., Thompson, L., & Bazerman, M. H. (1989). Social utility and decision making in interpersonal contexts. *Journal of Personality and Social Psychology, 57*, 426–441.

Luce, R. D., & Raiffa, H. (1957). *Games and decisions*. New York: Wiley.

MacCrimmon, K. R., & Messick, D. M. (1976). A framework for social motives. *Behavioral Science, 21*, 86–100.

March, J. (1994). *A primer on decision-making*. New York: Free Press.

McClintock, C. G., Messick, D. M., Campos, F. L., & Kuhlman, D. M. (1973). Motivational bases of choice in three choice decomposed games. *Journal of Experimental Social Psychology, 9*, 572–590.

McNeel, S. P., & Messick, D. M. (1970). A Bayesian analysis of subjective probabilities of interpersonal relationships. *Acta Psychologica, 34*, 311–321.

Messick, D. M. (1963). *Bayesian decision theory, game theory, and group problem solving* (Rep. No. 35). Chapel Hill: University of North Carolina, Psychometric Laboratory.

Messick, D. M. (1967). Interdependent decision strategies in zero-sum games: A computer-controlled study. *Behavioral Science, 12*, 33–48.

Messick, D. M. (1973). To join or not to join: An approach to the unionization decision. *Organizational Behavior and Human Decision Processes, 10*, 145–156.

Messick, D. M. (1993). Equality as a decision heuristic. In B. A. Mellers & J. Baron (Eds.), *Psychological perspectives on justice* (pp. 11–31). New York: Cambridge University Press.

Messick, D. M. (1995). Equality, fairness, and social conflict. *Social Justice Research, 8*, 153–173.

Messick, D. M. (1999). Alternative logics for decision making in social settings. *Journal of Economic Behavior and Organization, 39*, 11–28.

Messick, D. M. (2006). Utility and the psychology of preference. In D. De Cremer, M. Zeelenberg, & K. J. Murnighan (Eds.), *Social psychology and economics* (pp. 131–147). Mahwah, NJ: Lawrence Erlbaum.

Messick, D. M., & Asuncion, A. (1993). The Will Rogers illusion in judgments about social groups. *Psychological Science, 4*, 46–48.

Messick, D. M., & Bazerman, M. H. (1996). Ethical leadership and the psychology of decision making. *Sloan Management Review, 37*, 9–22.

Messick, D. M., Bloom, S., Boldizar, J. P., & Samuelson, C. D. (1985). Why we are fairer than others. *Journal of Experimental Social Psychology, 21*, 480–500.

Messick, D. M., & Brewer, M. B. (1983). Solving social dilemmas: A review. In L. Wheeler & P. Shaver (Eds.), *Review of personality and social psychology* (Vol. 4, pp. 11–44). Beverly Hills, CA: Sage.

Messick, D. M., & Kramer, R. M. (2001). Trust as a form of shallow morality. In K. Cook (Ed.), *Trust in society* (pp. 89–117). New York: Russell Sage.

Messick, D. M., & Kramer, R. M. (Eds.). (2004). *The psychology of leadership*. Mahwah, NJ: Lawrence Erlbaum.

Messick, D. M., & Liebrand, W. B. G. (1995). Individual heuristics and the dynamics of cooperation in large groups. *Psychological Review, 102*, 131–145.

Messick, D. M., & McClintock, C. G. (1968). Motivational bases of choice in experimental games. *Journal of Experimental Social Psychology, 4*, 1–25.

Messick, D. M., Moore, D. A., & Bazerman, M. H. (1997). Ultimatum bargaining with a group: Understanding the importance of the decision rule. *Organizational Behavior and Human Decision Processes, 69*, 87–101.

Messick, D. M., & Reeder, G. (1972). Perceived motivation, role variations, and attribution of personal characteristics. *Journal of Experimental Social Psychology, 8*, 482–491.

Messick, D. M., & Schell, T. (1992). Evidence for an equality heuristic in social decision making. *Acta Psychologica, 80*, 311–323.

Messick, D. M., & Sentis, K. P. (1979). Fairness and preference. *Journal of Experimental Social Psychology, 15*, 418–434.

Messick, D. M., & Sentis, K. P. (1985). Estimating social and nonsocial utility functions from ordinal data. *European Journal of Social Psychology, 15*, 389–399.

Messick, D. M., & Tenbrunsel, A. A. (Eds.). (1996). *Codes of conduct.* New York: Russell Sage.

Messick, D. M., & Thorngate, W. B. (1967). Relative gain maximization in experimental games. *Journal of Experimental Social Psychology, 3*, 85–101.

Messick, D. M., & van de Geer, J. P. (1981). A reversal paradox. *Psychological Bulletin, 90*, 582–593.

Raiffa, H., & Schlaifer, R. (1961). *Applied statistical decision theory.* Boston: Harvard School of Business.

Reeder, G. D., Messick, D. M., & van Avermaet, E. (1977). Dimensional asymmetry in attributional inference. *Journal of Experimental Social Psychology, 13*, 46–57.

Samuelson, C. D., & Messick, D. M. (1986). Alternative structural solutions to resource dilemmas. *Organizational Behavior and Human Decision Processes, 37*, 139–155.

Samuelson, C. D., & Messick, D. M. (1995). When do people want to change the rules for allocating shared resources? In D. A. Schroeder (Ed.), *Social dilemmas* (pp. 143–162). Westport, CT: Praeger.

Tenbrunsel, A. E., & Messick, D. M. (1999). Sanctioning systems, decision frames, and cooperation. *Administrative Science Quarterly, 44*, 684–707.

Tenbrunsel, A. E. & Messick, D. M. (2004). Ethical fading: The role of self-deception in unethical behaviour. *Social Justice Research, 17*, 223–236.

Thibaut, J. W., & Kelley, H. H. (1959). *The social psychology of groups.* New York: Wiley.

Thompson, L., Levine, J., & Messick, D. M. (Eds.). (1999). *Shared cognition in organizations.* Mahwah, NJ: Lawrence Erlbaum.

Von Neumann, J., & Morganstern, O. (1944). Theory of games and economic behavior. Princeton, NJ: Princeton University Press.

Weber, J. M., Kopelman, S., & Messick, D. M. (2004). A conceptual review of decision making in social dilemmas: Applying a logic of appropriateness. *Personality and Social Psychology Review, 8*(3), 281–307.

Scholarly Bibliography for David M. Messick

Allison, S. T., Mackie, D. M., & Messick, D. M. (1996). The outcome bias in social perception: Implications for dispositional inference, attitude change, stereotyping, and social behavior. In M. Zanna (Ed.), *Advances in experimental social psychology* (Vol. 28, pp. 53–93). San Diego, CA: Academic Press.

Allison, S. T., & Messick, D. M. (1985a). Effects of experience on performance in a replenishable resource trap. *Journal of Personality and Social Psychology, 49,* 943–948.

Allison, S. T., & Messick, D. M. (1985b). The group attribution error. *Journal of Experimental Social Psychology, 21,* 563–579.

Allison, S. T., & Messick, D. M. (1987). From individual inputs to group outputs, and back again: Group processes and inferences about members. In C. Hendricks (Ed.), *Review of personality and social psychology* (Vol. 8, pp. 111–143). Newbury Park, CA: Sage.

Allison, S. T., & Messick, D. M. (1988). The feature positive effect, attitude strength, and degree of perceived consensus. *Personality and Social Psychology Bulletin, 14,* 231–241.

Allison, S. T., & Messick, D. M. (1990). Social decision heuristics in the use of shared resources. *Journal of Behavioral Decision Making, 3,* 195–204.

Allison, S. T., Messick, D. M., & Goethals, G. R. (1989). On being better but not smarter than others: The Muhammad Ali effect. *Social Cognition, 7,* 275–295.

Allison, S. T., Messick, D. M., & Samuelson, C. D. (1985). Effects of soliciting opinions on contributions to a public good. *Journal of Applied Social Psychology, 15,* 201–206.

Bazerman, M. H., & Messick, D. M. (1998). On the power of a clear definition of rationality. *Business Ethics Quarterly, 8*(3), 477–480.

Bazerman, M. H., Messick, D. M., Tenbrunsel, A. E., & Wade-Benzoni, K. A. (Eds.). (1997). *Environment, ethics, and behavior: The psychology of environmental valuation and degradation.* San Francisco: The New Lexington Press.

Beggan, J. K., Messick, D. M., & Allison, S. T. (1988). Social values and egocentric bias: Two tests of the might over morality hypothesis. *Journal of Personality and Social Psychology, 55,* 606–611.

Boldizar, J. P., & Messick, D. M. (1988). Intergroup fairness biases: Is ours the fairer sex? *Social Justice Research, 2,* 95–111.

Boles, T. L., & Messick, D. M. (1990). Accepting unfairness: Temporal influence on choice. In K. Borcherding, O. I. Larichev, & D. M. Messick (Eds.), *Contemporary issues in decision making* (pp. 375–390). Amsterdam: North Holland.

Boles, T. L., & Messick, D. M. (1995). A reverse outcome bias: The influence of multiple reference points on the evaluation of outcomes and decisions. *Organizational Behavior and Human Decision Processes, 61,* 262–275.

Borcherding, K., Larichev, O. I., & Messick, D. M. (Eds.). (1990). *Contemporary issues in decision making.* Amsterdam: North Holland.

Butcher, N. J., & Messick, D. M. (1966). Parent-child profile similarity and aggression: A preliminary study. *Psychological Reports, 18,* 440–442.

Cates, K. L., & Messick, D. M. (1996). Frequentistic abverbs as measures of egocentric biases. *European Journal of Social Psychology, 26*, 155–161.

Cook, K. S., & Messick, D. M. (1983). Psychological and sociological perspectives on distributive justice: Convergent, divergent, and parallel lines. In D. M. Messick & K. S. Cook (Eds.), *Equity theory: Psychological and sociological perspectives* (pp. 1–12). New York: Praeger.

Darley, J. M., Messick, D. M., & Tyler, T. R. (2001a). Social influence and ethics in organizations. In J. M. Darley, D. M. Messick, & T. R. Tyler (Eds.), *Social influences on ethical behavior in organizations* (pp. 1–8). Mahwah, NJ: Lawrence Erlbaum.

Darley, J. M., Messick, D. M., & Tyler, T. R. (Eds.). (2001b). *Social influences on ethical behavior in organizations.* Mahwah, NJ: Lawrence Erlbaum.

Dawes, R. M., & Messick, D. M. (2000). Social dilemmas. *International Journal of Psychology, 35*(2), 111–116.

de Hues, P., & Messick, D. M. (2004). The dynamics of trust and trustworthiness in large groups: A computer simulation. In R. Suleiman, D. V. Budescu, I. Fischer, & D. M. Messick (Eds.), *Contemporary psychological research on social dilemmas* (pp. 127–154). Cambridge, UK: Cambridge University Press.

Exline, R. V., & Messick, D. M. (1967). The effects of dependency and social reinforcement upon visual behavior during an interview. *British Journal of Social and Clinical Psychology, 6*, 256–266.

Foley, J. M., Lockhart, R. A., & Messick, D. M. (Eds.). (1970). *Contemporary readings in psychology.* New York: Harper Row.

Goethals, G. R., Messick, D. M., & Allison, S. T. (1991). The uniqueness bias: Studies of constructive social comparison. In J. Suls & T. A. Wills (Eds.), *Social comparison: Contemporary theory and research* (pp. 149–176). New York: Erlbaum.

Harris, R., Messick, D. M., & Sentis, K. P. (1981). Proportionality, linearity, parameter constancy: Messick and Sentis reconsidered. *Journal of Experimental Social Psychology, 17*, 210–225.

Klatzky, R., & Messick, D. M. (1995). Curtailing medical inspections in the face of negative consequences. *Journal of Experimental Psychology: Applied, 1*, 163–178.

Klatzky, R. L., Messick, D. M., & Loftus, J. (1992). Heuristics for determining the optimal interval between checkups. *Psychological Science, 3*, 279–284.

Kopelman, S., Weber, M., & Messick, D. (2002). Factors influencing cooperation in commons dilemmas: A review of experimental psychological research. In E. Ostrom, T. Dietz, N. Dolšak, P. C. Stern, S. Stonich & U. Weber (Eds.), *The drama of the commons* (pp. 113–156). Washington, DC: National Academy Press.

Kramer, R. M., McClintock, C. G., & Messick, D. M. (1986). Social values and cooperative response to a simulated resource conservation crisis. *Journal of Personality, 54*, 596–577.

Kramer, R. M., & Messick, D. M. (Eds.). (1995). *Negotiation as a social process.* Beverly Hills, CA: Sage.

Kramer, R. M., & Messick, D. M. (1998). Getting by with a little help from our enemies: Collective paranoia and its role in intergroup relations. In C. Sedikides, J. Schopler, & C. A. Insko (Eds.), *Intergroup cognition and intergroup behavior* (pp. 233–255). Mahwah, NJ: Lawrence Erlbaum.

Liebrand, W. B. G., & Messick, D. M. (1996a). Computer simulation of cooperative decision making. In W. B. G. Liebrand & D. M. Messick (Eds.), *Frontiers in social dilemma research* (pp. 215–234). New York: Springer-Verlag.

Liebrand, W. B. G., & Messick, D. M. (1996b). Computer simulations of sustainable cooperation in social dilemmas. In R. Hegselmann et al. (Eds.), *Modelling and simulation in the social sciences from the philosophy of science point of view* (pp. 235–247). Dordrecht, Netherlands: Kluwer Academic Publishers.

Liebrand, W. B. G., & Messick, D. M. (Eds.). (1996c). *Frontiers in social dilemma research.* New York: Springer-Verlag.

Liebrand, W. B. G., & Messick, D. M. (1996d). Game theory, decision making in conflicts and computer simulations: A good-looking triad. In K. G. Troitzsch, U. Mueller, G. N. Gilbert, & J. E. Doran (Eds.), *Social science microsimulation* (pp. 211–236). New York: Springer-Verlag.

Liebrand, W. B. G., & Messick, D. M. (1996e). Social dilemmas: Individual, collective, and dynamic perspectives. In W. B. G. Liebrand & D. M. Messick (Eds.), *Frontiers in social dilemma research* (pp. 1–9). New York: Springer-Verlag.

Liebrand, W. B. G., & Messick, D. M. (1998). Dynamic and static theories of costs and benefits of cooperation. In D. V. Budescu, I. Erev, & R. Zwick (Eds.), *Games and human behavior* (pp. 331–354). Mahwah, NJ: Lawrence Erlbaum.

Liebrand, W. B. G., Messick, D. M., & Wilke, H. A. M. (1992a). *Social dilemmas: Theoretical issues and research findings.* London: Pergamon.

Liebrand, W. B. G., Messick, D. M., & Wilke, H. A. M. (1992b). Social dilemmas: The state of the art. In W. B. G. Liebrand, D. M. Messick, & H. A. M. Wilke (Eds.), *Social dilemmas: Theoretical issues and research findings* (pp. 3–40). London: Pergamon.

Liebrand, W. B. G., Messick, D. M., & Wolters, F. J. M. (1986). Why we are fairer than others: A cross-cultural replication and extension. *Journal of Experimental Social Psychology, 22,* 590–604.

McClintock, C. G., & Messick, D. M. (1966). Empirical approaches to game theory and bargaining: A bibliography. In L. von Bertalanffy & A. Rapoport (Eds.), *General systems, 11,* 229–238.

McClintock, C. G., Messick, D. M., Campos, F. I., & Kuhlman, M. (1973). Motivational bases of choice in three choice decomposed games. *Journal of Experimental Social Psychology, 9,* 572–590.

McCrimmon, K. R., & Messick, D. M. (1976). A framework for social motives. *Behavioral Science, 21,* 86–100.

McNeel, S. P., & Messick, D. M. (1970). A Bayesian analysis of subjective probabilities of interpersonal relationships. *Acta Psychologica, 34,* 311–321.

Messick, D. M. (1963). *Bayesian decision theory, game theory, and group problem solving* (Rep. No. 35). Chapel Hill: University of North Carolina, Psychometric Laboratory.

Messick, D. M. (1964a). *Sequential information seeking: An optimal strategy and other results* (Rep. No. 42). Chapel Hill: University of North Carolina, Psychometric Laboratory.

Messick, D. M. (1964b). *Sequential information seeking: Effects of the number of terminal acts and prior information* (Rep. No. 41). Chapel Hill: University of North Carolina, Psychometric Laboratory.

Messick, D. M. (1964c). Sequential information seeking: Effects of prior information and the number of terminal acts. *Psychonomic Science, 1,* 335–336.

Messick, D. M. (1965a). [Review of the book *Contributions to mathematical psychology*]. *Educational Psychological Measurement, 25,* 897–900.

Messick, D. M. (1965b). [Review of the book *Mathematics and psychology*]. *Educational and Psychological Measurement, 25,* 625–627.

Messick, D. M. (1965c). The utility of variability in probability learning. *Psychonomic Science, 3,* 355–356.

Messick, D. M. (1967a). Interdependent decision strategies in zero-sum games: A computer-controlled study. *Behavioral Science, 12,* 33–48.

Messick, D. M. (1967b). [Review of the book *Handbook of mathematical psychology: Vol. II*]. *Journal of the American Statistical Association, 62,* 704–707.

Messick, D. M. (1968a). Choice behavior as a function of expected payoff. *Journal of Experimental Psychology, 76,* 544–549.

Messick, D. M. (Ed.). (1968b). *Mathematical thinking in the behavioral sciences: A* Scientific American *reader.* San Francisco: W. H. Freeman.

Messick, D. M. (1970a). Learning probabilities of events: A discussion. *Acta Psychologica, 34,* 172–183.

Messick, D. M. (1970b). Some thoughts on the nature of human competition. *Hypotheses, 14,* 38–52.

Messick, D. M. (1971). Logical aspects of social inference. In *Proceedings of the Third Research Conference on Subjective Probability, Utility, and Decision Making* (pp. 61–83). London: Uxbridge University Press.

Messick, D. M. (1972a). A stochastic model of preference in decomposed games. In H. Sauermann (Ed.), *Contributions to experimental economics* (Vol. 3, pp. 363–394). Tübingen Germany: Mohr.

Messick, D. M. (1972b). Decisions as transitions. *Abstract guide to 20th International Congress of Psychology.* Tokyo: Science Council of Japan, 234–235.

Messick, D. M. (1972c). [Review of the book *Small group performance*]. *Psychometrika, 37*(1), 111–112.

Messick, D. M. (1972d). Some statistical terms and concepts. In C. G. McClintock (Ed.), *Experimental social psychology* (p. 571). New York: Holt.

Messick, D. M. (1973). To join or not to join: An approach to the unionization decision. *Organizational Behavior and Human Performance, 10,* 145–156.

Messick, D. M. (1974a). Bigger and better [Review of the book *Statistics for the social sciences*]. *Instructional Science, 2,* 503–504.

Messick, D. M. (1974b). When a little "group interest" goes a long way: A note on social motives and union joining. *Organizational Behavior and Human Performance, 12,* 331–334.

Messick, D. M. (1976). Comment on Campbell. *American Psychologist, 31,* 366–369.

Messick, D. M. (1979). Rasch models and games [Book review]. *Contemporary Psychology, 24,* 587–589.

Messick, D. M. (1982). Some cheap tricks for making inferences about distribution shapes from variances. *Educational and Psychological Measurement, 42,* 749–758.

Messick, D. M. (1984). Solving social dilemmas: Individual and collective approaches. *Representative Research in Social Psychology, 14,* 72–87.

Messick, D. M. (1985). Social interdependence and decision making. In G. Wright (Ed.), *Behavioral decision making* (pp. 87–109). New York: Plenum.

Messick, D. M. (1986). Decision making in social dilemmas. In B. Brehmer, H. Jungermann, P. Lourens, & G. Sevon (Eds.), *New directions in research on decision making* (pp. 219–228). Amsterdam: North Holland.

Messick, D. M. (1987). Egocentric biases and the golden section. *Journal of Social and Biological Structures, 10,* 241–247.

Messick, D. M. (1988a). Coda. In M. Bond (Ed.), *The cross-cultural challenge to social psychology* (pp. 286–289). Newbury Park, CA: Sage.

Messick, D. M. (1988b). On the limitations of cross-cultural research in social psychology. In M. Bond (Ed.), *The cross-cultural challenge to social psychology* (pp. 41–47). Newbury Park, CA: Sage.

Messick, D. M. (1988c). Soviet collectives and small group research [Book review]. *Contemporary Psychology, 33,* 802.

Messick, D. M. (1989). [Review of the book *Decision analysis and behavioral research*]. *Psychometrika, 54,* 363–364.

Messick, D. M. (1991a). On the evolution of group-based altruism. In R. Selten (Eds.), *Game equilibrium models* (Vol. 1, pp. 304–328). Berlin: Springer Verlag.

Messick, D. M. (1991b). Social dilemmas, shared resources, and social justice. In H. Steensma & R. Vermunt (Eds.), *Social justice in human relations* (Vol. 2, pp. 49–69). New York: Plenum.

Messick, D. M. (1993). Equality as a decision heuristic. In B. A. Mellers & J. Baron (Eds.), *Psychological perspectives on justice* (pp. 11–31). New York: Cambridge University Press.

Messick, D. M. (1994). [Review of the book *Choosing justice*]. *Social Justice Research, 7,* 415–418.

Messick, D. M. (1995). Equality, fairness, and social conflict. *Social Justice Research, 8,* 153–173.

Messick, D. M. (1996). Why ethics is not the only thing that matters. *Business Ethics Quarterly, 6,* 223–226.

Messick, D. M. (1997). Philosophy and the resolution of equality conflicts. *Social Justice Research, 10,* 35–37.

Messick, D. M. (1998). Social categories and business ethics. *Business Ethics Quarterly, 8*(1), 149–172.

Messick, D. M. (1999a). Alternative logics for decision making in social settings. *Journal of Economic Behavior and Organization, 39,* 11–28.

Messick, D. M. (1999b). Dirty secrets: Strategic uses of ignorance and uncertainty. In L. Thompson, J. Levine, & D. M. Messick (Eds.), *Shared cognition in organizations.* (pp. 71–90). Mahwah, NJ: Lawrence Erlbaum.

Messick, D. M. (1999c). Models of decision making in social dilemmas. In M. Foddy, M. Smithson, S. Schneider, & M. Hogg (Eds.), *Resolving social dilemmas: Dynamic, structural, and intergroup aspects.* Philadelphia: Psychology Press.

Messick, D. M. (2000). Context, norms, and cooperation in modern society: A postscript. In M. van Vugt, M. Snyder, T. Tyler, & A. Biel (Eds.), *Cooperation in modern society.* London: Routledge.

Messick, D. M. (2004a). Human nature and business ethics. In R. E. Freeman & P. H. Werhane (Eds.), *The Ruffin Series: Vol. 4. Business, science, and ethics.* Charlottesville, VA: Society for Business Ethics.

Messick, D. M. (2004b). On the psychological exchange between leaders and followers. In D. M. Messick & R. Kramer (Eds.), *The psychology of leadership: New perspectives and research* (pp. 81–96). Mahwah, NJ: Lawrence Erlbaum.

Messick, D. M. (2005). Commentary: Conflict of interest as a threat to consequentialist reasoning. In D. A. Moore, D. M. Cain, G. Loewenstein, & M. H. Bazerman (Eds.), *Conflicts of interest* (pp. 284–287). New York: Cambridge University Press.

Messick, D. M. (2006). Ethical judgment and moral leadership: Three barriers. In D. L. Rhode (Ed.) *Moral leadership* (pp. 17–30). San Francisco: Jossey-Bass.

Messick, D. M., & Allison, S. T. (1987). Accepting unfairness: Outcomes and attributions. *Representative Research in Social Psychology, 17*, 39–51.

Messick, D. M., Allison, S. T., & Samuelson, C. D. (1988). Framing and communication effects on group members' responses to environmental and social uncertainty. In S. Maital (Ed.), *Applied behavioral economics* (Vol. 2, pp. 677–700). Brighton, UK: Wheatsheaf.

Messick, D. M., & Asuncion, A. (1993). The Will Rogers illusion in judgments about social groups. *Psychological Science, 4*, 46–48.

Messick, D. M., & Bazerman, M. (1996). Ethical leadership and the psychology of decision making. *Sloan Management Review, 37*, 9–22.

Messick, D. M., Bloom, S., Boldizar, J. P., & Samuelson, C. D. (1985). Why we are fairer than others. *Journal of Experimental Social Psychology, 21*, 480–500.

Messick, D. M., & Brewer, M. B. (1983). Solving social dilemmas: A review. In L. Wheeler & P. Shaver (Eds.), *Review of personality and social psychology* (Vol. 4, pp. 11–44). Beverly Hills, CA: Sage.

Messick, D. M., & Campos, F. T. (1972). Training and conservatism in subjective probability revision. *Journal of Experimental Psychology, 94*, 335–337.

Messick, D. M., & Cook, K. S. (Eds.). (1983). *Equity theory: Psychological and sociological perspectives*. New York: Praeger.

Messick, D. M., Fiske, S. T., & Gruder, C. L. (1988). Editorial. *Journal of Experimental Social Psychology, 24*, 467–468.

Messick, D. M., & Kramer, R. M. (1996). Ethical cognition and the framing of organizational dilemmas: Decision makers as intuitive lawyers. In D. M. Messick & A. E. Tenbrunsel (Eds.), *Codes of conduct* (pp. 59–85). New York: Russell Sage.

Messick, D. M., & Kramer, R. M. (2001). Trust as a form of shallow morality. In K. Cook (Ed.), *Trust in society*. (pp. 89–117). New York: Russell Sage Foundation.

Messick, D. M., & Kramer, R. (Eds.). (2004). *The psychology of leadership: New perspectives and research*. Mahwah, NJ: Lawrence Erlbaum.

Messick, D. M., & Liebrand, W. B. G. (1993). Computer simulations of the relation between individual heuristics and global cooperation in prisoner's dilemmas. *Social Science Computer Review, 11*(3), 301–312.

Messick, D. M., & Liebrand, W. B. G. (1995). Individual heuristics and the dynamics of cooperation in large groups. *Psychological Review, 102*, 131–145.

Messick, D. M., & Liebrand, W. B. G. (1997a). Levels of analysis and the explanation of the costs and benefits of cooperation. *Personality and Social Psychology Review, 1*(2), 129–139.

Messick, D. M., & Liebrand, W. B. G. (1997b). The new dynamical social psychology. *Psychological Inquiry, 8*(2), 135–137.

Messick, D. M., & Mackie, D. M. (1989). Intergroup relations. *Annual Review of Psychology, 40*, 45–81.

Messick, D. M., & McClelland, C. L. (1983). Social traps and temporal traps. *Personality and Social Psychology Bulletin, 9*, 105–110.

Messick, D. M., & McClintock, C. G. (1967). Measures of homogeneity in two-person, two-choice games. *Behavioral Science, 12*, 474–479.

Messick, D. M., & McClintock, C. G. (1968). Motivational bases of choice in experimental games. *Journal of Experimental Social Psychology, 4*, 1–25.

Messick, D. M., Moore, D. A., & Bazerman, M. H. (1997). Ultimatum bargaining with a group: Underestimating the importance of the decision rule. *Organizational Behavior and Human Decision Processes, 69*, 87–101.

Messick, D. M., & Ohme, R. K. (1998). Some ethical aspects of the social psychology of social influence. In R. M. Kramer & M. A. Neale (Eds.), *Power and influence in organizations* (pp. 181–202). Thousand Oaks, CA: Sage.

Messick, D. M., & Rapoport, A. (1963). *The effect of payoff functions on multiple-choice decision behavior* (Rep. No. 34). Chapel Hill: University of North Carolina, Psychometric Laboratory.

Messick, D. M., & Rapoport, A. (1964a). Computer controlled experiments in psychology. *Behavioral Science, 9,* 378–382.

Messick, D. M., & Rapoport, A. (1964b). *Expected value and response uncertainty in multiple-choice decision behavior* (Rep. No. 40). Chapel Hill: University of North Carolina, Psychometric Laboratory.

Messick, D. M., & Rapoport, A. (1965a). A comparison of two payoff functions on multiple-choice decision behavior. *Journal of Experimental Psychology, 69,* 75–83.

Messick, D. M., & Rapoport, A. (1965b). Expected value and response uncertainty in multiple-choice decision behavior. *Journal of Experimental Psychology, 70,* 224–230.

Messick, D. M., & Rapoport, A. (1966). A supplementary study of response uncertainty and relative expected value in multiple-choice decision behavior. *Psychonomic Science, 4,* 143–144.

Messick, D. M., & Reeder, G. (1972). Perceived motivation, role variations, and attribution of personal characteristics. *Journal of Experimental Social Psychology, 8,* 482–491.

Messick, D. M., & Reeder, G. D. (1973). Roles, occupations, behaviors, and attributions. *Journal of Experimental Social Psychology, 9,* 126–132.

Messick, D. M., & Rutte, C. G. (1992). The provision of public goods by experts: The Groningen study. In W. B. G. Liebrand, D. M. Messick, & H. A. M. Wilke (Eds.), *Social dilemmas: Theoretical issues and research findings* (pp. 101–109). London: Pergamon.

Messick, D. M., & Schell, T. (1992). Evidence for an equality heuristic in social decision making. *Acta Psychologica, 80,* 311–323.

Messick, D. M., & Sentis, K. P. (1979). Fairness and preference. *Journal of Experimental Social Psychology, 15,* 418–434.

Messick, D. M., & Sentis, K. (1983). Fairness, preference, and fairness biases. In D. M. Messick & K. S. Cook (Eds.), *Equity theory: Psychological and sociological perspectives* (pp. 61–94). New York: Praeger.

Messick, D. M., & Sentis, K. P. (1985). Estimating social and nonsocial utility functions from ordinal data. *European Journal of Social Psychology, 15,* 389–399.

Messick, D. M., & Tenbrunsel, A. E. (1996a). Behavioral research into business ethics. In D. M. Messick & A. E. Tenbrunsel (Eds.), *Codes of conduct* (pp. 1–10). New York: Russell Sage.

Messick, D. M., & Tenbrunsel, A. E. (Eds.). (1996b). *Codes of conduct.* New York: Russell Sage Foundation.

Messick, D. M., & Thorngate, W. B. (1967). Relative gain maximization in experimental games. *Journal of Experimental Social Psychology, 3,* 85–101.

Messick, D. M., & van de Geer, J. P. (1981). A reversal paradox. *Psychological Bulletin, 90,* 582–593.

Messick, D. M., Wilke, H. A. M., Brewer, M. B., Kramer, R., Zemke, P. E., & Lui, L. (1983). Individual adaptations and structural changes as solutions to social dilemmas. *Journal of Personality and Social Psychology, 44,* 294–309.

Parker, R., Lui, L., Messick, C., Messick, D. M., Brewer, M., Kramer, R., et al. (1983). A computer laboratory for studying social dilemmas. *Behavioral Science, 28,* 298–304.

Petrison, L. A., Wang, P., & Messick, D. M. (1994). Consumer privacy. In J. I. Reitman (Ed.), *Beyond 2000: The future of direct marketing* (pp. 45–56). Lincolnwood, IL: NTC Business Books.

Reeder, G. D., Messick, D. M., & van Avermaet, E. (1977). Dimensional asymmetry in attributional inference. *Journal of Experimental Social Psychology, 13*, 46–57.

Rutte, C., & Messick, D. M. (1995). An integrated model of unfairness in organizations. *Social Justice Research, 8*, 239–261.

Rutte, C., Wilke, H. A. M., & Messick, D. M. (1987a). Scarcity and abundance caused by people or the environment as determinants of behavior in the resource dilemma. *Journal of Experimental Social Psychology, 23*, 208–216.

Rutte, C., Wilke, H. A. M., & Messick, D. M. (1987b). The effects of framing social dilemmas as give-some or take-some games. *British Journal of Social Psychology, 26*, 103–108.

Rutte, C. G., Diekmann, K. A., Polzer, J. T., Crosby, F. J., & Messick, D. M. (1994). Organization of information and the detection of gender discrimination. *Psychological Science, 5*, 226–231.

Rutte, C. G., & Messick, D. M. (1996). Detecting salary discrimination against male and female managers. *European Journal of Social Psychology, 26*, 727–740.

Samuelson, C. D., & Messick, D. M. (1986a). Alternative structural solutions to social dilemmas. *Organizational Behavior and Human Decision Processes, 37*, 139–155.

Samuelson, C. D., & Messick, D. M. (1986b). Inequities in access to and use of shared resources. *Journal of Personality and Social Psychology, 51*, 960–967.

Samuelson, C. D., & Messick, D. M. (1995). When do people want to change the rules for allocating shared resources? In D. A. Schroeder (Ed.), *Social dilemmas* (pp. 143–162). Westport, CT: Praeger.

Samuelson, C. D., Messick, D. M., Allison, S. T., & Beggan, J. (1986). Utopia or myopia: A reply to Fox. *American Psychologist, 40*, 227–229.

Samuelson, C., Messick, D. M., Rutte, C., & Wilke, H. A. M. (1984). Individual and structural solutions to resource dilemmas in two cultures. *Journal of Personality and Social Psychology, 47*, 94–104.

Samuelson, C. D., Messick, D. M., Rutte, C. G., & Wilke, H. A. M. (1986). Individual restraint and structural change as solutions to social dilemmas. In H. A. M. Wilke, D. M. Messick, & C. G. Rutte (Eds.), *Experimental social dilemmas* (pp. 29–54). Frankfurt: Peter Lang.

Suleiman, R., Budescu, D. V., Fischer, I., & Messick, D. M. (Eds.). (2004). *Contemporary psychological research on social dilemmas*. Cambridge, UK: Cambridge University Press.

Takigawa, T., & Messick, D. M. (1993). Group size uncertainty in shared resource use. *Japanese Psychological Research, 35*(4), 193–203.

Taormina, R., & Messick, D. M. (1983). Deservingness for foreign aid: Effects of need, similarity and estimated effectiveness. *Journal of Applied Social Psychology, 13*, 371–391.

Taormina, R. J., Messick, D. M., Iwawaki, S., & Wilke, H. A. M. (1988). Cross-cultural perspectives on foreign aid deservingness decisions. *Journal of Cross-Cultural Psychology, 19*, 387–412.

Taylor, R. D., Messick, D. M., Leyman, G. A., & Hirsch, J. K. (1982). Sex, dependency, and helping revisited. *Journal of Social Psychology, 118*, 59–65.

Tenbrunsel, A. E., & Messick, D. M. (1996a). Behavioral research, business ethics, and social justice. *Social Justice Research, 9*(1), 1–6.

Tenbrunsel, A. E., & Messick, D. M. (Eds.). (1996b). Psychological contributions to business ethics [Special issue]. *Social Justice Research, 9*(1).

Tenbrunsel, A. E., & Messick, D. M. (1999). Sanctioning systems, decision frames, and cooperation. *Administrative Science Quarterly, 44*, 684–707.

Tenbrunsel, A. E., & Messick, D. M. (2001). Power asymmetries and the ethical atmosphere in negotiations. In J. M. Darley, D. M. Messick, & T. R. Tyler (Eds.), *Social influences on ethical behavior in organizations* (pp. 201–216). Mahwah, NJ: Lawrence Erlbaum.

Tenbrunsel, A. E. & Messick, D. M. (2004). Ethical fading: The role of self-deception in unethical behaviour. *Social Justice Research, 17*, 223–236.

Tenbrunsel, A. E., Wade-Benzoni, K. A., Messick, D. M., & Bazerman, M. H. (1997a). Introduction. In M. H. Bazerman, D. M. Messick, A. E. Tenbrunsel, & K. A. Wade-Benzoni (Eds.), *Environment, ethics, and behavior: The psychology of environmental valuation and degradation* (pp. 1–9). San Francisco: The New Lexington Press.

Tenbrunsel, A. E., Wade-Benzoni, K. A., Messick, D. M., & Bazerman, M. H. (1997b). The dysfunctional aspects of environmental standards. In M. H. Bazerman, D. M. Messick, A. E. Tenbrunsel, & K. A. Wade-Benzoni (Eds.), *Environment, ethics, and behavior: The psychology of environmental valuation and degradation* (pp. 105–121). San Francisco: The New Lexington Press.

Tenbrunsel, A. E., Wade-Benzoni, K. A., Messick, D. M., & Bazerman, M. H. (2000). Understanding the influence of environmental standards on judgement and choice. *Academy of Management Journal, 43*, 854–866.

Thompson, L., Levine, J., & Messick, D. M. (Eds.). (1999). *Shared cognition in organizations*. Mahwah, NJ: Lawrence Erlbaum.

Van Lange, P. A. M., & Messick, D. M. (1996). Psychological processes underlying cooperation in social dilemmas. In W. Gasparski, M. Mlicki, & B. Banathy (Eds.), *Social agency: Dilemmas and educational praxiology* (Vol. 4, pp. 93–112). New Brunswick, NJ: Transaction.

Weber, J. M., Kopelman, S., & Messick, D. (2004). A conceptual review of decision making in social dilemmas: Applying a logic of appropriateness. *Personality and Social Psychology Review, 8*(3), 281–307.

Weber, J. M., & Messick, D. (2004). Conflicting interests in social life: Understanding social dilemma dynamics. In M. J. Gelfand & J. M. Brett (Eds.), *The handbook of negotiation and culture* (pp. 187–205). Stanford, CA: Stanford University Press.

Wilke, H. A. M., Liebrand, W. B. G., & Messick, D. M. (1983). Sociale dilemmas: Een overzicht [Social dilemmas: An overview]. *Nederlands Tijdschrift voor de Psychologie*, 463–480.

Wilke, H. A. M., Messick, D. M., & Rutte, C. G. (Eds.). (1986). *Experimental social dilemmas*. Frankfurt: Peter Lang.

Wilke, H. A. M., Rutte, C. G., Wit, A. P., Messick, D. M., & Samuelson, C. D. (1986). Leadership in social dilemmas: Efficiency and equity. In H. A. M. Wilke, D. M. Messick, & C. G. Rutte (Eds.), *Experimental social dilemmas* (pp. 55–76). Frankfurt: Peter Lang.

Worringham, C., & Messick, D. M. (1983). Social facilitation of running: An unobtrusive study. *Journal of Social Psychology, 121*, 23–29.

Worth, L. T., Allison, S. T., & Messick, D. M. (1987). Impact of a group decision on perception of one's own and others' attitude. *Journal of Personality and Social Psychology, 53*, 673–682.

Subject Index

Author Index

A

Ackerman, F., 317
Adams, J. S., 292
Adler, A., 208
Adriansen, L., 20
Agarwal, R., 24
Aggarwal, R. K., 317
Agnew, C. R., 86
Ahmad, N., 78
Aldeguer, C. M. R., 83
Alicke, M. D., 242
Allen, J., 176
Allison, S. T., 4, 5, 14, 48, 50, 52, 79, 101,
    137, 140, 150, 167, 171, 291–314,
    353, 355, 357–359
Ames, C., 106
Anderson, C., 19, 321
Anderson, J., 82, 87
Anderson, S., 318, 327
Ang, S., 198
Apted, M., 106
Arendt, H., 362
Ariely, D., 347
Arkin, R. M., 302
Arriaga, S. B., 140
Arrow, H., 19, 26
Asuncion, A., 5, 357
Au, W. T., 78
Avila, R. A., 176
Axelrod, R., 85, 123–124, 127–128, 130,
    138, 167, 346

B

Babcock, L., 52, 246
Baker, G. A., 23, 25, 37
Balliet, D., 82
Baltes, B. B., 20, 22, 25, 32, 37
Banaji, M. R., 242–243, 274, 323
Bargh, J. A., 321
Barkema, H. G., 319

Baron, J., 253, 255–256
Barrens, R., 277
Barsade, S. G., 172–177, 180
Bartky, S. L., 321
Bastianutti, L. M., 20
Batson, C. D., 78–79, 83, 292, 305
Batson, J. G., 83
Bauer, C. C., 20, 22, 25, 32, 37
Baum, B. H., 319
Baumhart, R., 242
Bazerman, M. H., 1–12, 52–53, 107, 110,
    112, 172, 197, 199, 241–264, 274,
    280, 316, 353, 356, 361–362
Beach, L. R., 100
Bebchuk, L. A., 318, 326
Bednar, L. L., 305
Beggan, J. K., 299, 300, 307, 353
Behn, R. D., 104
Bekkers, R., 91n4
Bem, D. J., 150, 167
Bembeneck, A. F., 59
Bendor, J., 124
Bentham, J., 270, 282
Berardino, J. F., 257
Berenson, A., 250
Berglas, S., 302
Bettman, J. R., 100
Bhaskar, R., 242
Bicchieri, C., 14, 16–18, 20, 35, 37–38
Biel, A., 48, 58
Blascovich, J., 111
Bloom, S., 241, 311, 359
Bochet, O., 17, 20, 23
Bodur, M., 197
Boldizar, J. P., 241, 311, 359
Boles, T. L., 5, 6, 100–101, 171–204
Bond, M. H., 198
Boninger, D. S., 73, 81, 82, 87
Boone, C., 172, 180, 197
Borden, R. J., 294
Bordia, P., 20
Bornstein, G., 13, 83, 88
Bos, N., 20

For Product Safety Concerns and Information please contact our EU
representative GPSR@taylorandfrancis.com
Taylor & Francis Verlag GmbH, Kaufingerstraße 24, 80331 München, Germany